Alexis Ulysses Floridi, S. J.

MOSCOW
AND THE
VATICAN

Ardis, Ann Arbor

Alexis Ulysses Floridi, *Moscow and the Vatican.*
Copyright © 1986 by Ardis Publishers
All rights reserved under International and Pan-American Copyright Conventions.
Printed in the United States of America

Ardis Publishers
2901 Heatherway
Ann Arbor, Michigan 48104

Library of Congress Cataloging-in Publication Data

Floridi, Alexis Ulysses.
  Moscow and the Vatican.

  Bibliography: p.
  1. Catholic Church—Relations (diplomatic)—Soviet
Union. 2. Soviet Union—Foreign relations—Catholic
Church. I. Title.
BX1558.F56 1986   261.7'0947   85-30719
ISBN 0-88233-647-9 (alk. paper)

Contents

Introduction   7

Part I   From Monologue to Dialogue

1   How to Cheat the "Devil"   11
2   New Priorities in the Vatican's Ostpolitik   35
3   The Aims of Détente   79

Part II   The Unexpected Obstacle

4   The Rise of Dissent   97
5   The Church in Lithuania   133
6   Ukrainian Catholics and Vatican Diplomacy   167

Part III   From Paul VI to John Paul II

7   Normalization or Evangelization?   207

Epilogue: The Vatican's Ostpolitik under John Paul II   229

Notes   251
Bibliography   275

Introduction

Many bitter and justifiable words about the Vatican's "Eastern policy" have been heard from Christians who live in totalitarian countries. At the same time as the unelected regimes in those countries are persecuting any expression of religion—even those that are officially recognized—the Roman curia is helping them to cover up their militant atheism with the deceptive mask of religious tolerance. While widely proclaiming a so-called dialogue with the East, the Vatican does not notice or pretends it does not notice that its proposed partner not only is not reciprocating but is even intensifying the persecution of Faith in its territories which are completely closed to the influence of world public opinion.

For this reason the sensible and solidly documented testimony of such an authoritative representative of Catholicism as Father Floridi deserves the greatest attention. A consistent Catholic, the author with pain and incomprehension analyzes different aspects of the Vatican's "Eastern policy": he examines facts, verifies reliable sources and, finally, comes to the conclusion that this policy is the consequence of a complete failure to comprehend the goals and nature of the system that governs the totalitarian world—a system directed above all against Man as a being and likeness of God.

In recent times when even the initiators and active practitioners of détente such as Mr. Kissinger have for all practical purposes admitted the groundlessness of their previous policy, the Vatican continues to talk about "cooperation with countries in which the position of the Church is highly unsatisfactory," about "a political line for which there is at the same time both much 'for' and 'against'," about "honest and deep rapprochement between East and West." And it is often hard to understand what is greater in this rhetoric—narrow-mindedness or cynicism.

A paradoxical situation has emerged: convinced atheists such as A. Sakharov, B. Bukovsky, A. Amalrik and many others are constantly defending their Christian compatriots, including Catholics, while the Holy See abandons them to their fate or restricts itself to dropping demagogical, ambiguous remarks. In Catholicism, as in contemporary Orthodoxy, however, a dynamic process of renewal from below is beginning—a process which sooner or later will restore the radiance of the Church's sublime ideals.

Vl. M., 1978

The election of the Polish Cardinal Wojtyla to the Papal throne is a striking symbol of the union of two traditions—Eastern and Western—in the universal religious renaissance of our time. The Christian church has undergone two mortal temptations of the spirit—the sufferings of persecution and satiety—and is beginning an era of a new and already irreversible transformation. In many of its theses the book by Father Floridi has anticipated the inevitable course of these events which we are now witnessing and which have ultimately led to the appearance on the historical stage of such a remarkable figure as John-Paul II. Herein, I believe, lies the true value and importance of *Moscow and the Vatican.*

Vl. Maximov
1985

Part I

From Monologue to Dialogue

1

How to Cheat the "Devil"

The history of the USSR demonstrates that Stalin's dictatorship, one of the most terrible and bloody of all times, took place and flourished during the period of the greatest friendship with the USA, under Roosevelt's presidency, before and during World War II.

During that time, blind Western politicians and members of the intelligentsia did not want to hear about the real situation in the Soviet Union, to such an extent that Orwell couldn't be published in England: all were afraid to harm or even only to offend a friendly power. On the other hand there are several examples of how world public opinion positively influenced the internal policies of the USSR. It suffices to mention the campaign of protest against the frightful antireligious terror started toward the end of 1929, during which hundreds of thousands of human lives and innumerable cultural values were destroyed. As is well known, in answer to the antireligious terror, the Pope of Rome called for a day of prayer for the believers in Russia to be held on March 19, 1930, in which Protestants, Orthodox and Jews took part. From Moscow many kinds of threats against the West were heard. The chief of the Union of Militant Godless, E. Yaroslavsky, threatened to destroy the best churches of the country, but Stalin, confronted with the firmness and cohesion of Western believers, had to pull back. Only a few days before the day of prayer sponsored by the Pope, on March 15, the Central Committee approved a resolution in which it recognized the excesses of Soviet religious policy....[1]

These words were written not by a Western anticommunist, enemy of détente, but by a Soviet cyberneticist and essayist, Mikhail S. Agursky, on November 1973, in support of Sakharov's and Solzhenitsyn's call for outside pressures that certain conditions for détente be required from the Soviet government. Agursky's article was directed against the opinion of two other well-known dissenters, the twin brothers Zhores and Roy Medvedev, that "the source of our difficulties is not the socialist system," but the anti-democratic traditions and norms of public life which appeared during Stalin's period and have not been completely liquidated to the present time.[2] The two brothers believe that détente will help their country to go back to Leninist democracy and legality, while conditions and pressures from outside, especially from non-leftist groups, can hamper the development of this democratic process. Nevertheless Zhores, a biologist who experienced Soviet psychiatric repression, was deprived of his Soviet citizenship and is living now in England.[3] Roy, the author of a book on the origins and consequences of Stalinism,[4] was called to the Moscow public prosecutor's office and warned to drop his new journal, *The Twentieth Century,* intended to voice "loyal criticism" of the Soviet regime.[5]

Academician Andrei D. Sakharov thinks that the Western powers should ask the Soviet government for some guarantees before committing themselves to détente, because "a rapprochement without democratization... would not really solve the world's problems... it would be highly perilous for all mankind, for international confidence and détente."[6] In an autobiographical essay devoted to his evolution from one of the key and most trusted participants in the development of the Soviet Union's hydrogen bomb in the 1950s to its best-known advocate of human rights, Sakharov writes: "I have appealed, and again appeal to all international organizations concerned with this problem—and especially to the international Red Cross—to abandon their policy of nonintervention in the internal affairs of the socialist countries as regards defending human rights and to manifest the utmost persistence... I am not an opponent of détente, trade or disarmament. To the contrary, in several writings I have called for just these things." Sakharov agrees with the Medvedevs that the era of Stalinist terror has passed, "but," he adds, "we are still living in the spiritual atmosphere created by that era." On the other hand, a return to Leninist socialism doesn't make sense to him:

> I began by thinking that I understood it and that it was good. Then gradually I ceased to understand a great deal—I didn't even understand its economic [basis]; I couldn't make out whether there was anything to it but mere words and propaganda for internal and international consumption. Actually, what hits you in the eye is the state's extreme concentration—economic, political, and ideological—that is, its extreme monopolization of these fields. One may say, exactly as Lenin did at the beginning of our revolution, that it is simple state capitalism, that the state has simply assumed a monopoly role over all the economy. But in that case this socialism contains nothing new. It is only an extreme form of that capitalist path of development found in the United States and other Western countries but in an extremely monopolized form. Thus, we should not be surprised that we have the same kinds of problems—that is, crime and personal alienation—that are to be found in the capitalist world. But our society represents an extreme case with maximum restraint, maximum ideological restrictions, and so forth.... Moreover, and very characteristically, we are also the most pretentious—that is, although we are not the best society we pretend that we are much more...[7]

It is important to stress the fact that Andrei Sakharov, a non-believer himself, in a declaration of November 20, 1973, accepted the defense of his position expressed by two Christian intellectuals, Agursky and the writer Vladimir Maximov:

> I do not agree with many declarations and, in general, with the kind of morality which inspired the recent interventions of Roy and Zhores Medvedev. On the contrary I support the views expressed in the letters of M. Agursky and V. Maximov. The Medvedevs, with their pragmatism, put themselves against those who today conduct a moral fight for man's right to live and think freely. The liberation of political prisoners, the freedom of emigration and thought are all highly moral demands. On   their

implementation depends the spiritual health of society... I think that we have to speak openly and loudly about our tragic problems, addressing ourselves to all honest men, independently of their political ideas. This is our duty toward our country and the world. The position of the Medvedevs, who ostensibly address themselves only to the so-called leftist forces, seems to me erroneous.[8]

Agursky and Maximov belong to a group of dissenters led by Alexander Solzhenitsyn who are fighting not only for human rights but also for the religious rebirth of their country. They want help from the West, but they do not wish to live as many Western people do. As Solzhenitsyn said in his *Nobel Lecture:*

Our twentieth century has turned out to be more cruel than those preceeding it, and all that is terrible in it did not come to an end with the first half. The same old caveman feelings—greed, envy, violence, and mutual hate, which along the way assumed respectable pseudonyms like class struggle, racial struggle, mass struggle, labor-union struggle—are tearing our world to pieces.... Young people... take as a splendid example the Chinese Red Guard's degradation of people into nonentities. A superficial lack of understanding of the timeless essence of humanity, a naive smugness on the part of their inexperienced hearts—We'll kick out those fierce, greedy oppressors, those governors, and the rest (we!), we'll then lay down our grenades and machine guns, and become just and compassionate. Oh, of course! Of those who have lived their lives and have come to understand, who could refute the young, many do not dare argue against them; on the contrary, they flatter them in order not to seem "conservative," again a Russian phenomenon of the nineteenth century, something which Dostoevsky called slavery to half-cocked progressive ideas."[9]

With the Power of the Spirit

It was not accidental that Agursky, discussing with his fellow dissenters what kind of support they needed from the West, thought of Pope Pius XI's appeal in 1930. Armed only with the strength of the spirit, he fearlessly confronted giants of the political scene of his time such as Lenin, Hitler, Mussolini, Stalin and Franklin Delano Roosevelt. In handling international problems, this great Pope went as far as possible in order to save peace, but his moral integrity abhorred those "demoniac games" about which Vladimir Maximov wrote in his courageous letter to Heinrich Boell when the latter decided to change his Nobel lecture with the intent of keeping certain "contacts."[10] Ultimately the perplexities of the dissenters toward détente stem from the duplicity and self-interest of the West, something that was completely alien to Pope Pius XI. "If we speak of the West," said Sakharov, "then it is difficult each time to tell whether they want to help us or whether, on the contrary, there is some kind of capitulation, a game involving the internal interests of the people of the West in which we merely play the role of small change."[11]

Indeed, when Pope Pius XI, on February 2, 1930, addressed himself to the world, through his Vicar in Rome, Cardinal Basilio Pompili, he had in mind not so much the interests of the peoples of the West, but rather the "innumerable populations of Russia, all dear to our heart."[12] He was speaking not only for Catholics, but also for Orthodox and believers of every denomination, against those who "trying to strike religion and God himself, are seeking to ruin the intellect and human nature itself." A year before, on April 8, 1929, the Soviet government had promulgated a comprehensive law on religious associations which, with few amendments, is still in force today.[13] It was an attempt to give some legality to the pitiless offensive against the churches which was launched together with the First Five-Year Plan. The Pope pointed out the arbitrary atrocities and vulgarities employed by the Union of Militant Godless which "are going beyond and in contrast to the text of the already antireligious revolutionary Constitution." Pius XI also recalled the "efforts" he and his predecessor made at the diplomatic level to "halt the terrible persecution," and he blamed the Western powers which failed to support him "for the sake of temporal interests." That the action of the Pope was not just an outburst of the moment can be gathered from his announcement of the establishment of a "Special Committee for Russia" presided over by a Cardinal, and his mandate to "Our Institute for Eastern Studies" to organize lectures, on the documentary and scientific levels, on the situation in Russia. A year before, this great friend of the Russian people founded a Pontifical Russian College (Russicum) in Rome in order to prepare priests for Russia and help the religious revival of Russian people at home and abroad.[14] The alumni of Russicum are still doing a wonderful job, especially in Belgium, France, Germany, and Italy.[15] Their publications are known and read by Soviet dissenters. Among the admirers of Pius XI should be mentioned the great Russian poet Vyacheslav Ivanov, who died in Rome in 1969.[16]

Comments on Pius XI's letter pointed out the "silence" and "sluggishness" of the "civilized world"[17] as well as the "cowardice" of politicians, masked by different pretexts:

> The Pope's letter of February 2, 1930, is not an unwarranted interference in the internal affairs of the Russian people, nor an incitement to political action. It is a defense of one of the most fundamental, universal, and inalienable human rights against an unjust aggressor. Within its own sphere, which is the spiritual and the supernatural, it in no wise differs from his previous acts of protest. The Soviet government, by its deliberate choice, has transferred its belligerency to every hearth and home, and enlarged a domestic policy into an international menace which strikes at the very foundations of Christian civilization. It is intellectual suicide for a man, whether he be a prime minister, a senator, or a paid propagandist, to avert his eyes from the evidence now so abundant and keep repeating stale platitudes about "keeping hands off a purely internal question." In the face of the established facts it becomes moral cowardice to remain dumb.[18]

An English historian recently recognized the impact of Pius XI's appeal. The expiatory Liturgy he celebrated in St. Peter's basilica was attended by 50,000 people, including many non-Catholics. But it was significant that, although the diplomats of all the countries represented at the Vatican were invited, "those who had already recognized the Soviet government did not attend. Von Bergen, for instance, was instructed by his government to absent himself, so that 'German-Soviet trade relations might not be endangered'...."[19] Nevertheless, as Agursky recalls it, the efforts made, among others, by the English Labor government and by liberal circles to boycott the Pope's campaign failed: "the protest of world public opinion succeeded in halting the antireligious terror for a year and a half, until Stalin, who was waiting for a relaxation of the vigilance of the West, furiously renewed it, without finding any more obstacles."

Referring to that same action of Pius XI, the Soviet "expert" on Vatican affairs, Mikhail M. Sheinman, called it an "anti-Soviet crusade" which was embraced by "the most reactionary elements, and made easier the imperialists' plot to provoke a war against the Soviet Union."[20] Although history proves this accusation to be false, it was repeated by the Soviets and their allies also against Pope Pius XII, to such an extent that even some Catholics uncritically accepted this slogan of Soviet propaganda.[21] Today some Catholics, such as those belonging to the Movement of Christians for Socialism, to the Polish organization Pax, etc., insist that the Vatican should not only recognize the reality of Communist regimes, but also permit Catholics "loyally" to collaborate with them, accept their conditions and interference in the life of the Church and become an ally of the Communist countries. They forget that since the beginning of the Bolshevik revolution, the Popes have tried to establish some kind of dialogue with the new regime. For this reason they were blamed both by the Reds[22] and the Whites.[23] But for many years the Vatican didn't give up its attempts at negotiating with the Soviets, even though Soviet intentions to destroy every Church and religion were evident not only in the official ideology but especially in the brutal treatment reserved for the clergy and the faithful. It should also be stressed that the diplomatic activity of the Vatican was directed not only in favor of Catholics, but also for the Orthodox and the persecuted and the suffering of every belief.

Among others, there were three major occasions on which the Vatican negotiated with the Bolsheviks: when it interceded for the Russian Orthodox; when a Papal Relief Mission to Russia for the victims of the famine was established; and when the Conference of Genoa was convened to consider the situation of the defeated nations.

1. The "separation" of Church and State promulgated by the Soviets on January 23, 1918, "was so construed," writes Solzhenitsyn, "that the churches themselves and everything that hung in them... belonged to the state, and the only church remaining was that church which, in accordance

with the Scriptures, lay *within the heart*. And in 1918, when political victory seemed to have been attained faster and more easily than had been expected, they had pressed the right to confiscate church property. However, this leap had aroused too fierce a wave of popular indignation. In the heat of the Civil War, it was not very intelligent to create, in addition, an internal front against the believers. And it proved necessary to postpone for the time being the dialogue between Communists and the Christians."[24]

The Catholic Archbishop of Mohilev, Edward de Ropp, was one of the earliest victims of the 1918 decree on "separation of Church and State." Toward the end of August 1918 he protested against the decree and later organized parochial and central "commissions" in defense of the Church. For this reason on April 19, 1919, he was put under house arrest. Only in November, due to negotiations between nuncio Ratti and foreign commissar Chicherin, was he released and exiled to Poland. At the same time millions of Orthodox were persecuted and the life of Patriarch Tikhon was in danger. On March 12, 1919, Cardinal Gasparri, secretary of State for Benedict XV, sent a telegram of protest to Lenin. But "his reward was a long reply in which the Soviet foreign minister noted with irony the Pope's 'special concern' for 'a religion regarded by Rome as schismatic and heretical.' According to Chicherin, the Pope would do better to exercise his concern for humanity on behalf of the friends of the Bolsheviks who were fighting for humanity and were enduring harsh treatment at the hands of the 'Whites.' This gesture of the Pope was acknowledged with thanks by Patriarch Tikhon in a letter to Archbishop de Ropp dated July 22, 1919."[25]

2. "At the end of the Civil War, and as its natural consequence, an unprecedented famine developed in the Volga area... to the point of cannibalism... A brilliant idea was born:... let the priests feed the Volga region... If they refuse, we will blame the whole famine on them and destroy the Church. If they agree, we will clean out the churches. In either case, we will replenish our stocks of foreign exchange and precious metals."[26] Solzhenitsyn meticulously continues his account of how the Patriarch agreed to give up church valuables except those obtained by forced requisition, but referring to some writings of Lenin, concludes that "what was important (for the Communists) was not to feed the starving but to make use of a convenient opportunity to break the back of the Church."[27] In another secret letter to Molotov about a brutal attack against the faithful of the city of Shuya, Lenin gave precise orders to apply terrorism against the Church.[28] This letter confirms beyond any doubt Solzhenitsyn's conclusion.

At this time the Vatican again interceded for Tikhon in a letter of May 14, 1922, signed by Monsignor Pizzardo. The Vatican declared the Pope's readiness to pay a ransom for objects of worship confiscated by the government. "On May 17 Chicherin acknowledged receipt of this communication and said it would be forwarded to Moscow. No answer was forthcoming to this proposal; nor was an answer given to another telegram sent directly by Gasparri to Lenin on June 7."[29]

Solzhenitsyn recalls also how "the Patriarch had appealed to the Pope in Rome and to the Archbishop of Canterbury for assistance [to the starving]—but he was rebuked for this, too, on the grounds that only the Soviet authorities had the right to enter into discussions with foreigners."[30] A few days later, on August 5, 1921, Benedict XV wrote to Cardinal Gasparri: "We are in the presence of one of the most fearful disasters in history. From the Volga basin to the Black Sea, tens of thousands of human beings destined to the cruelest death cry out for help."[31] Immediately he offered to send a Papal Relief Mission with food and clothing. When the Pope died near the end of January 1922, the negotiations for the Mission between Cardinal Gasparri and Soviet representative Vorovsky were still going on. On September 29, the Mission finally landed at Odessa; however, it was prohibited against engaging in "apostolic activity."

The generous help of the Pope didn't prevent the Catholic Church from undergoing the same treatment reserved for all religious groups. As Solzhenitsyn wrote, "the so-called Eastern Catholics, followers of Vladimir Solovyev, were arrested and destroyed in passing, as was the group of A. I. Abrikosova. And, of course, ordinary Roman Catholics, Polish Catholic priests, etc., were arrested, too, as part of the normal course of events."[32] In March-April 1923, fifteen Catholic clergymen were tried in Moscow.[33] Archbishop John Cieplak and Msgr. Constantin Budkiewicz were sentenced to death, Exarch Leonid Feodorov[34] and the others to prison terms from three to ten years. Msgr. Budkiewicz was executed immediately. Archbishop Cieplak was allowed to leave Russia in April 1924 and died in February 1926 in Passaic, N.J.[35]

By orders from Rome the Papal Mission was not withdrawn and remained in Russia until September 1924. Pius XI wanted the continuation of the Mission not only because the victims of the famine needed it, but also in order to affirm and defend the religious and civil rights of the people: "the inviolability of these rights," said the Pope, "will always be for us a line over which it is not possible to pass, desirous as we ever are to be in peace with all and to cooperate in the universal pacification; willing as we are, where it is permissible, to make all concessions which may be necessary to attain less troubled conditions of life for the Church, and pacification of minds everywhere."[36] That is why the negotiations for the nomination of an Apostolic Delegate to Moscow, Father Giulio Roi, S.J., a member of the Papal Mission, were interrupted and the Mission withdrawn.

3. Pius XI's will to give top priority to religious rights in dealing with dictatorships was evident at the Genoa Conference and, later, in the

concordats with Mussolini and Hitler. The Genoa Conference (1922) was the first international meeting to which the Bolshevist regime was admitted. Because it was still not recognized *de jure* by most of the participants, the government of Moscow took that opportunity to seek recognition. Thus, during an official supper held on April 22 on board the Italian battleship *Dante Alighieri* for the opening of the Conference, the Soviet Foreign Minister Chicherin was very kind to the Archbishop of Genoa, Signori, who by pure coincidence found himself facing him at the same table. But Chicherin's attitude changed a few days later, when an official envoy of the Vatican, Msgr. Giuseppe Pizzardo, brought a memorandum to the members of the Conference with the suggestion that "the readmission of Russia to the community of civilized nations" should be done on the condition that "religious interests ... should be safeguarded" and the following clauses should be included as "an essential element":

1. Full freedom of conscience for all Russian citizens or foreigners is guaranteed in Russia;
2. The public and private practice of religion and worship is also guaranteed;
3. The real property which belonged or still belongs to any religious denomination whatever will be restored to it and respected.[37]

Father Robert Graham writes that the memorandum "bore the marks of a sudden decision, if not of a reversal of policy."[38] Others believe that the "unexpected intervention" of Msgr. Pizzardo, "even though it did not constitute an explicit declaration of rupture, had to have, in fact, the effect of blowing away many seeds sown" by Archbishop Signori "or at least had to appear to the eyes of Moscow as a sign that the conduct of the Vatican in respect to the Bolsheviks was not univocal,"[39] i.e., not straightforward. But, in fact, the Pope had approved an earlier appeal of the Archbishop of Genoa asking his people to pray for the success of the conference and later had established the conditions for that success with the memorandum. On the other hand, Chicherin only expected recognition of Soviet Russia from the Vatican, and it is absurd to believe that the reciprocal smiles and toasts between Archbishop Signori and the Soviet Minister could have been satisfactory for both sides. Far from interrupting his relationship with Chicherin, Msgr. Pizzardo, while still in Rapallo, had the already mentioned exchange of letters with him regarding the release of Patriarch Tikhon and the readiness of the Pope to pay for the confiscated objects of cult. It was only much later that Chicherin told the German ambassador in Moscow that "Pius XI flirted with us at Genoa, in the hope that we would break the monopoly of the Orthodox Church in Russia, and open the way for him."[40] The memorandum proves that this hope was not in the mind of the Pope, but history demonstrates that the Soviets, in order to achieve their aims, were ready to support anti-Tikhon groups. In their contacts with Western countries the Bolsheviks were so clearly looking for recognition that they allowed foreign relief agencies into Russia mainly for that purpose, not for "mercy,"[41] because, as Solzhenitsyn put it, "what was there to be alarmed about? The newspapers wrote that the government itself had all the necessary means to cope with the famine."[42]

The United States was one of the last countries to recognize the Soviet Union. When President Roosevelt made this decision in 1933, Father Edmund A. Walsh, S.J., former head of the Papal Relief Mission in Russia, was invited to the White House "not to discuss the recognition of Russia, but rather to reveal his reaction to the announcement that recognition had already been decided upon, though not as yet granted."[43] During the interview Fr. Walsh had the impression that the President was not willing to receive too much advice, because at a certain point "with that disarming assurance so characteristic of his technique in dealing with visitors," he told the priest: "Leave it to me, Father; I am a good horse dealer." Nevertheless the President was kind enough to ask Fr. Walsh to prepare two reports for him, one relative to religious liberties in Russia and another regarding the background and the personality of Maxim Litvinov, the Soviet negotiator then preparing to leave Moscow for Washington. Fr. Walsh concluded his first report with this remark: "Unless concrete results are achieved before recognition, it is the mature judgment of the undersigned, based on long experience with Bolshevik negotiators, that the liberties now being assailed in Russia will never be restored . . . They are masters in all forms of evasion and concealment, and in diverting attention away from damaging facts."[44]

After more than forty years Sakharov and the Soviet dissenters are telling the Western powers exactly the same thing.[45] But what is even more striking is that Fr. Walsh had already given the same warning to the Vatican ten years before and now, after more than fifty years, that warning is still astonishingly pertinent. In 1923, immediately after the trial of the Catholic clergymen, four major problems had to be solved: the continuation of relief work, requested by the Soviet government after the departure of the American Relief Administration; the release of the imprisoned clergy; the opening of the churches; and the recovery of the relics of Blessed Andrew Bobola. Father Walsh

realized that a longer sojourn of the Papal Mission offered little or no hope of strengthening the tenuous hold of the Catholic Church in Russia, but he realized also that there were advantages to be gained by a delayed departure. He was well aware of the fact that the ultimate purpose of the Soviet Government in asking the Mission to stay on, and to continue its work, was to obtain from the Vatican a de facto recognition of its existence, something he had determined never to encourage or to countenance. They knew this and, hence, never missed an opportunity to embarrass him in his official capacity in Moscow. Their idea was to settle on him the full blame for all difficulties arising between Rome and Moscow and thus to have him recalled. Their method was to present a promising outlook to the Vatican by means of verbal and written agreements, made by their representative in Rome, and then to have some minor official in Moscow defer, delay or repudiate the agreements.[46]

In a message from Rome the head of the Papal Mission was informed that Mr. Yordansky, the Soviet representative in Rome, had entered

> a complaint that your manner of dealing with the Soviet authorities was somewhat rude, that you did not have sufficient consideration for the mentality of the new Russian regime and for the difficulties it was encountering, and finally that you give no evidence of a full understanding of the Slav mentality. He finally concluded by formally demanding that the Holy See replace you with an agent who had a better understanding of the overall situation. The Holy See is fully aware that there is no foundation whatsoever for these complaints. However, we might ask if it would not be more convenient, and perhaps productive of better results, if you were to moderate to some extent your manner of dealing with the Russian authorities.[47]

In his answer to the Vatican Fr. Walsh wrote:

> It is not strange that they find my insistence on justice and the rights of religion irksome. I beg to point out to the Holy See that such a result is practically inevitable. It is not necessarily the person who becomes thus 'non grata' but the facts, the injustice and savagery which are in themselves a continual reproach. . . . I regret to be obliged to communicate to Your Eminence information of a disturbing nature. In my last two reports I outlined the increasing difficulties we were meeting in the reorganization of the work of relief. I now find that the Soviet officials are not willing to make an agreement or contract of such a character as to guarantee the success of our work. In general they require that we begin to work again without any protecting agreement such as was concluded at the Vatican with Mr. Vorovsky in 1922. They say the time for all that is past and relief organizations must be content with the ordinary conditions of work in Russia. In particular they refuse the following points which I submitted and without which our work is impossible. In the selection of individuals and institutions to be helped the final decision shall rest with the Papal Mission. If the experience of the past fifteen months in Russia has proved anything, it is that unless the Papal Mission has the liberty to give its food, clothing and other help to those whom it finds to be really in need, then our work is impossible. . . .

We take the liberty of interrupting the report to cite a few reasons for the demand for liberty of internal administration. During the whole time that the Papal Mission was working in Russia, the director was aware of the fact that the house servants at all the Mission centers, and especially in Moscow, were periodically summoned by the police to give a detailed report of what was going on in the mission houses. At one outlying station the two men in charge later found out that the local police were kept informed of where they went, with whom they talked, when they retired and when they got up, when and what they ate and drank, and what they were reading. Fortunately, the two priests, dressed as laymen, were exempted from reading the breviary and spoke a language which none of the servants understood. The newly suggested system of police inspection which was now being proposed would continue this surveillance plus give the added advantage of entrance without notice and search without warrant.

To return to the text of the report.

> They require, in general, that we begin to work, assume heavy expenses and get as much material onto Russian Territory as possible. Then when the inevitable difficulties begin, as they began in the past, and will continue as long as the present group of Bolsheviks rule this country, we will have no guarantee of protection beyond what the ordinary Russian citizen now has. Those of us who know the executions, imprisonments, exiling, confiscations and other savage manifestations of class hatred and revenge that have been going on in Russia, know and beg to inform you that our work is impossible under such conditions. If, consequently, I can not obtain a definite written agreement of a tolerable nature, I see no alternative but immediate and dignified withdrawal of the Relief Mission.[48]

The guarantees asked by Fr. Walsh were never given to him nor the Archbishop Eugenio Pacelli, Papal Nuncio in Berlin, who in 1925-28 made the last attempts with the Soviets to negotiate conditions for Catholics in the USSR. He had even agreed that all correspondence between Rome and Catholic bishops in Russia should be censored. "But it soon became clear that the more the Vatican conceded, the more Moscow demanded. After interminable discussions... the crisis came to a head, when the Soviets suddenly announced that there could be no question of a concordat; they intended henceforth to deal with all Catholic problems, Church property, religious education, priests' stipends, etc., by unilateral legislation. The Vatican would not even be consulted."[49]

In this situation the Pope had no other alternative than to publicly denounce the Bolsheviks (1930, 1937) and secretly provide religious assistance for the persecuted Catholics. In 1926 Pius XI had already sent a Jesuit bishop, Michel D'Herbigny, to Russia to reorganize the Catholic hierarchy and ordain several bishops in secret. Due to circumstances not yet well clarified, these bishops were all discovered and arrested and one of them, Alexander Frison, was shot (August 2, 1937). From the failure of D'Herbigny's "mission," however, it cannot be concluded that the only valid Ostpolitik for the Vatican is to compromise with Communist governments and allow Catholic clergymen to be "loyal" to Communist regimes.[50] Today there are still secret bishops in the Soviet Union who successfully work in the illegality of the "catacombs." It is well known that the Soviets have succeeded in placing their spies in Catholic institutions not only at the time of Bishop D'Herbigny, but even today. Father Walter Ciszek, S.J., in his book "With God in Russia," attributes to the work of these spies his arrest, long imprisonment and exile in the Soviet Union. This writer had the opportunity to know one of these spies, Fr. Dorofei Bezchasnov, who was a protégé of a Cardinal and a Jesuit. Once discovered, he returned to the USSR to work as an atheist activist. By allowing Catholic clergymen to be "loyal" to the regime, the Vatican could only increase and make easier these unfortunate activities.

Pope Pius XI was not against a dialogue with Soviet and other dictatorships. Speaking to the students of the Jesuit-run Collegio Mondragone, on May 14, 1929, he said: "When there is a question of saving souls or preventing greater harm to souls, we feel the courage to deal with the devil in person."[51] But the pontiff placed such tough conditions on the "devil" that he preferred to stay away. On June 29, 1931, in his encyclical "Non abbiame bisogne," the Pope protested against "acts of brutality and violence, blows and shedding of blood" promoted by the Fascists against young people and university students affiliated with Catholic Action.[52] In the encyclical "Mit brennender Sorge" of March 14, 1937, he condemned the neopaganism and racism of the Nazis, and a few days later, on March 19, he issued the encyclical "Divini Redemptoris" condemning atheistic Communism.[53] He was about to denounce Mussolini, but died on the eve of his speech.

Soviet propaganda and supporters of "dialogue" saw Pope Pius' encyclical on "Atheistic Communism" as nothing more than a political document and a recognition of defeat. In reality it was just the opposite. It was a strong appeal for the renewal of faith and for the struggle against evil. Having exhausted all the possibilities of a diplomatic rapprochement, the Pope did not hesitate to call for a world-wide battle of the spirit. It was not a retreat into the sphere of unreality, but a resumption of the fight on a higher level where victory is inevitable:

> When the Apostles asked the Savior why they had been unable to drive the evil spirit from a demoniac, Our Lord answered: "This kind is not cast out but by prayer and fasting." So, too, the evil which today torments humanity can be conquered only by a world-wide holy crusade of prayer and penance ... Since belief in God is the unshakable foundation of all social order and of all responsibility on earth, it follows that all those who do not want anarchy and terrorism ought to take energetic steps to prevent the enemies of religion from attaining the goal they have so brazenly proclaimed to the world.[54]

The admiration of Soviet dissenters for Pius XI can be explained only by their similarity in the faith and in the strength of the spirit. "The conception that a higher Whole has to exist is the only one which can put an end to our irresponsibility. ... In our heart and soul, we have to realize that it's almost a joke now to speak of good and evil. But they are real concepts, good and evil. They come from a higher source" (Solzhenitsyn).[55] Our struggle "is waged more or less consciously, on the firm awareness and evidence that man is spiritual and that this spirituality is the source of his freedom and dignity. In fact the Spirit 'touching the mud, creates the man out of it,' only the spirit makes men" (D. Nelidov).[56] "The theosophs fear the words 'devil' and 'God'. They always are afraid of being suspected of ignorance and want to reason scientifically. This precaution does not inspire trust" (A. Sinyavsky).[57] "A fighter for freedom is worth more than one million conformists" because the chances of society's renewal depend not on the number of people, but on "the power of the spirit" (Volny).[58]

Mikhail Bulgakov, a brilliant Russian writer who died in obscurity in 1940, wrote a powerful novel on the devil, *The Master and Margarita,* published posthumously in 1967. This is a fantastic story where persons of ancient times appear and are used to stress the struggle between evil and good. The novel opens with a prologue of sorts by one of the devils, who denies the existence of God. Two writers, Mikhail Alexandrovich Berlioz, editor of a literary magazine, and the young poet Ivan Nikolaich Ponyryov, who writes under the pseudonym of Bezdomny, are sitting on a bench at the Patriarch's Pond in Moscow. They are talking about Jesus Christ. In fact the editor had commissioned the poet to write a long antireligious poem for one of the regular issues of his magazine. Ivan Nikolaich has written his poem in record time, but unfortunately the editor does not care for it at all. Bezdomny drew the chief figure in his poem, Jesus, in very somber colors, and in the editor's opinion the whole poem had to be written again. "It was hard to say what had made Bezdomny write as he had—whether it was his great talent for graphic descriptions or complete ignorance of his subject, but his Jesus had come out . . . well, completely alive, a Jesus who had really existed, although admittedly a Jesus who had every possible fault." Berlioz, however, wants to prove to the poet that the main problem is not who Jesus was, whether he was bad or good, but that as a person Jesus has never existed at all and that all the stories about him are mere inventions, pure myth. At this moment a man, who had stood for a while near the bench occupied by the editor and the poet, turns to them and starts a tempting conversation about God's existence. After refusing St. Thomas' five proofs of the existence of God, the learned editor also rejects the sixth proof formulated by Kant. "Kant ought to be arrested and given three years in Solovky for that proof of his," Ivan Nikolaich burst out unexpectedly. But then "if there is no God, who rules the life of man and keeps the world in order?" Berlioz dies in an accident that very night and Bezdomny ends up in a mental hospital because nobody will believe his account, nobody will forgive him for having "tried to drag into print an apologia for Jesus Christ." About Satan, a mysterious visitor tells him: "here you are, shut up in a psychiatric clinic, and you still say he doesn't exist. How strange!"[59]

Two other well-known dissenters, the Orthodox priest Gleb Yakunin and the physicist Lev Regelson, in a letter addressed to the Fifth Assembly of the World Council of Churches gathered in Nairoby (November 23-December 10, 1975), praised Pope Pius XI with these words: "a great step forward in genuine ecumenism was the world day of prayers for the persecuted Russian Church organized in 1930. . . . Russian Christians will keep in their thankful memory the leading role of Pope Pius XI in organizing that day, his strong denunciations of the persecutors, the great sorrow expressed by him for the sufferings of the Russian people" (*Religiia i Ateizm v SSSR,* December 1975, pp. 3-9).

By Avoiding the Snares of Politicians

The Molotov-Ribbentrop pact and World War II put extremely difficult decisions before the new Pope, Pius XII. As father of all, he could not take the side of one nation against another, but spoke courageously to the heads of the nations: "It is with the force of reason and not the force of arms that justice advances. Empires not founded on justice are not blessed by God. Dangers are imminent, but there is still time; nothing is lost through peace, everything may be lost through war. Let them again understand each other, let them resume negotiations.... We have with us the heart of mothers which beat with ours; fathers who would have to abandon their families; the humble who work and know not; the innocent on whom weighs the tremendous menace; the young generous knights of the pure and most noble ideals. . . ."[60] Fifteen days later the Nazis and the Soviets invaded Poland, killing, terrorizing and deporting the people.

On October 26, 1939, the Pope published his first encyclical.

> The document was meant as guidance for the clergy and Catholics all over the world concerning the attitude they should take in regard to the war. It placed the Church squarely against the totalitarian form of government, racism, and the forces that were attempting to abolish religion. It was a direct reply to those who had criticized the Vatican for not having taken a firmer stand against Germany and Russia, and showed that there could be no compromise between the doctrinal principles of the Church and those of Nazism and Bolshevism. It sharply criticized Hitler's policies, both domestic and foreign, and openly supported the restoration of the Polish state.... Stripped of its religious references, the encyclical was tantamount to a declaration of war on Germany and Russia. By condemning their policies and theories, the pontiff substantially served notice that he would continue to fight, as Pius XI had done, those manifestations of the totalitarian regimes that injured religion and the carrying out of the Church's spiritual mission.[61]

As soon as other nations, Finland, Belgium, the Netherlands, etc. experienced the brutality of the invaders, the Pope raised his voice both in public and through diplomatic channels. At the Vatican he organized an Information Bureau under the direction of Russian Archbishop Alexander Evreinov to meet inquiries of relatives as to the fate of POWs and refugees. For these reasons he had to keep a strict neutrality, a circumstance that was often misunderstood by ethnic groups and nationalities and even by members of the Catholic clergy.

In the United States some Catholic clergymen, like Archbishop Joseph Hurley of St. Augustine, supported American aid to the USSR, while others, like Archbishop Francis Beckman of Dubuque, were against it. The latter shared former President Hoover's opinion that "if we go further and join the war and we win, then we have won for Stalin the grip of Communism on Russia and more opportunity for it to extend over the world."[62] But Father John La Farge, S.J., explained that "if such help is to be extended" that would be "no endorsement of the revolution which Soviet Russia represents. It is promised to Soviet Russia simply as a nation: to help Russia which is fighting Nazi Germany, not to help Communism or Bolshevism as combatants." He added that some guarantees should be asked from the Soviets regarding freedom of religion and that the Red Army should not undertake, after conquering Hitler, "to do a little footwork in Western Europe."[63]

The main source of Catholic refusal to support American aid to the USSR was Pius XI's statement in the encyclical "Divini Redemptoris": "Communism is intrinsically evil and no one who would save Christian civilization may collaborate with it in any field whatsoever."[64] For this reason an editorial published in the Jesuit magazine *America* concluded that "Catholics can have no part in any plan to aid Communism."[65] But Father La Farge opposed the idea that "for our government to extend aid to Soviet Russia is clearly, as Father Gillis has pointed out, to make a covenant with Hell." Writing in the same magazine, he asked: "Why has no reminder to that effect so far come from our present Holy Father? . . . We may suspect that he relies upon us to use our own wisdom and prudence. . . . The strength that the Russian people have displayed up to the present. . . . is derived from the spirit of traditional Russian national-ism. . . . An undiscriminating identification of the Russian people and all that concerns them with the very soul of Communism plays into the corresponding error of identifying the German people with Nazism." And again he warned that "no stone should be left unturned by our Department of State to keep insisting that whatever aid is granted carries with it an understanding that full religious freedom shall be given by the Soviets."[66]

Archbishop Amleto Cicognani, Apostolic Delegate in Washington, after gathering all the pros and cons, on September 1, 1941, sent a report to the Vatican together with a memorandum of a visit paid by Archbishop Edward Mooney of Detroit to the Undersecretary of State, Sumner Welles.[67] President Roosevelt, in a message to Pius XII of September 3, assured the Pope that "the churches in Russia are open. I believe there is a real possibility that Russia may, as a result of the present conflict, recognize freedom of religion in Russia, although, of course, without recognition of any official intervention on the part of any Church in education or political matters within Russia . . . I believe that this Russian dictatorship is less dangerous to the safety of other nations than is the German form of dictatorship."[68] Nevertheless the Vatican, true to its principle of not condemning nations by name in war time, didn't accept the suggestion of Roosevelt's representative, Mr. Taylor, to publicly associate itself with the signatories of the Atlantic Charter. But it instructed Archbishop Cicognani to find among the American bishops a prelate who would give the right interpretation to Pius XI's encyclical.

On the other hand, the Vatican resisted the pressures from the Axis Powers to support the war against the Soviet Union as a "religious crusade." Monsignor Domenico Tardini, Undersecretary of State, told Mr. Attolico, Italian Ambassador to the Vatican:

> I see the crusade, but I don't see the crusaders.... To speak now it would easily take a political character, while the Holy See had spoken clearly *tempore non suspecto*.... For my part I should be only too pleased to see Communism disappear from the face of the earth. It is the Church's worst enemy. But it is not the only one. Nazism has conducted, and still conducts, a violent persecution of the Church. As a result, the Church can hardly regard the Hakenkreuz as... the symbol of a crusade.... For this very reason today, instead of talking about a crusade, it would be better to quote the old proverb, "It is a case of one devil chasing out the other."[69]

Later, in the Apostolic letter "Sacro Vergente Anno" of July 7, 1952, addressed to the peoples of the Soviet Union, Pope Pius XII recalled:

> When the last long and terrible conflict broke out, We did all that was within Our power, with words, with exhortations and with action, that discords might be healed with an equitable and just peace, and that all peoples, without difference of origin, might unite in friendly and fraternal concord and work together for the attaining of a great prosperity. Never, even at that time, did there come from Our lips a word that could have seemed to any of the belligerents to be unjust or harsh. We certainy reproached, as was our duty, every iniquity and every violation of rights, but We did this in such a way as to avoid with all diligence whatever might become, even unjustly, an occasion for the greater affliction of oppressed peoples. And when pressure was brought to bear upon us to give Our approval in some way, either verbally or in writing, to the war undertaken against Russia in 1941, We never consented to do so, as We stated clearly on February 25, 1946, in Our allocution to the Sacred College of Cardinals and all diplomatic representatives accredited to the Holy See.[70]

Soviet and leftist writers maintain that after World War II, Pius XII favored the cold war, blessed NATO and obstructed the "normalization" of church-state relations with the Communist countries.[71] According to them, the Pope manifested his "antidemocratic" position especially

1. with his approval of the July 1, 1949 decree of the Holy Office excommunicating Catholics who supported atheistic Communism;[72]
2. with his warnings to those Catholics who, on their own personal authority, wanted to engage in a "dialogue" with Communists. "Out of respect for the name of Christian," said the Pope," "compliance with such tactics should cease, for, as the Apostle warns, it is inconsistent to sit both at the table of God and at that of His enemies";[73]
3. with his strong protest against Khrushchev's bloody repression of the Hungarian revolution: "We, as head of the Church, have up to now avoided, just as we did in previous cases, calling Christendom to a crusade. We can, however, call for full understanding for the fact that, where religion is a vital living heritage, men look upon the struggle unjustly forced upon them by their enemy as a crusade... No one can accuse us of favoring the stiffening of opposing blocs, and still less of having in

some fashion abandoned that mission of peace which flows from our apostolic office. Rather, if we kept silence we would have to fear the judgment of God. We remain closely allied to the cause of peace...."[74]

Certainly Pope Pius XII, while he did not oppose negotiations with Socialist countries, such as Yugoslavia, thought it his duty to reject the "errors" and the "lies" of Communist regimes and appealed, as did his predecessor, to the spiritual values of Christianity. In the already quoted letter to the Soviet peoples he expressed many views that are familiar today in the writings of Soviet dissenters:

We have, it is true, condemned and rejected, as the duty of Our office demands, the errors that the upholders of atheistic Communism teach and try to spread, to the great detriment of nations; but, far from rejecting the erring, We want them to return to truth and to be led back on the right road. We have also unmasked and condemned those lies that were often presented in the false guise of truth, precisely because We cherish paternal affection for you and seek your welfare. For We are firmly convinced that nothing but great harm will come to you from these errors, and that they not only deprive your souls of that supernatural light and those supreme comforts that piety and worship of God bestow, but also strip you of human dignity and of that just freedom which is every citizen's birthright.

We are aware that many of you cling to the Christian faith in the sanctuary of your conscience, that in no way do you allow yourselves to be induced to favor the enemies of religion, but that, on the contrary, it is your ardent desire to profess the precepts of Christianity, the only sure foundation of civil life, not only in private but, if it were possible, as it should be for all free people, also openly. And We know, too—and this gives Us hope and great comfort—that you love and honor with eager affection the Virgin Mary, Mother of God, and that you venerate Her sacred images. We know that in the Kremlin itself a temple was built—today, unfortunately, no longer used for divine worship—dedicated to the Most Holy Mary Assumed into Heaven; and this is evident proof of the love your ancestors and you bear the Great Mother of God.

Now, We know that where people turn with sincere and ardent piety toward the Most Holy Mother of God, there is always hope of salvation even when powerful and impious men are seeking to uproot holy religion and Christian virtue from the hearts of the citizens, though even Satan himself strives to foster with every means this sacrilegious struggle, in accordance with the saying of the Apostle of the peoples: "For our wrestling is not against flesh and blood, but against the principalities and the powers, against the world rulers of this darkness, against the spiritual forces of wickedness on high...," yet, if Mary intervenes with her support, the gates of Hell will not prevail. For She is the benign and powerful Mother of God and of all of us, and never has it happened in the world that anyone has turned to Her in supplication without experiencing Her all-powerful intercession. Go on, then, as is your wont, venerating Her with fervent piety, loving Her ardently, and invoking Her with these words, which are familiar to you: "To thee alone it has been granted, most holy and pure Mother of God, never to be refused."

We, too, together with you raise to Her Our supplicant invocations, that the Christian truth, the adornment and support of human society, may flourish and gain vigor among the peoples of Russia, and that all the deceptions of the enemies of religion, all their errors and deceitful tricks, may be rejected by you....[75]

This letter would find support from Alexander Solzhenitsyn, who wrote the famous appeal "Don't live with the lie!",[76] who praised the "infinitely eloquent" liturgical hymn "Acathist to the Mother of God,"[77] and who said in his Nobel Lecture that "Dostoevsky's demons, a provincial nightmare of the last century, one would have thought, are, before our very eyes, crawling over the whole world into countries where they were unimaginable."[78] Nor would Vladimir Maximov find the words of the Pope hyperbolical because Maximov described so strongly the frightful consequences of the fact that "the demons of earthly passions overcame men's souls" to such an extent that "the brother robs his brother, the son sends his father to death, the neighbor denounces his neighbor...."[79] Many Soviet Christians will be comforted by Pius XII's invocation of the "Merciful Mother," whom Alexander Galich, in his poem "Ave Maria," calls "the concentration of all the sufferings of the earth."[80]

With Courtesy and Negotiations

When, on October 28, 1958, Cardinal Angelo Giuseppe Roncalli became Pope John XXIII at the age of 76, he was considered an "interim" Pope. In his first encyclical "Ad Petri Cathedram" he recalled "the many venerable brethren in the episcopate and the beloved priests and faithful who have either been driven into exile or are held under restraint or in prisons, simply because they have refused to abandon the office of Bishop or priest committed to them" and affirmed that "those who support truth, justice and the advantage of each individual and each state do not refuse liberty, do not put it in bonds, do not suppress it."[81] The Soviets understood and wrote that the Catholic Church had a "new" Pope, but that his "course" was "old."[82]

Nevertheless, John XXIII was a different Pope. What distinguished him from his predecessors was his innate friendliness, his gift to communicate and fraternize with people of every political and religious faith, his sincere belief in the fundamental goodness of every man. Before being a priest, a bishop and a Pope, he wanted to be a man interested, first of all, in simple and common questions, in what unites men rather than in what divides them. Smoking a good cigar or sipping a glass of wine, he liked to chat with everyone, be he a Turk in Constantinople or a Socialist leader in Paris. As a Cardinal and Patriarch of Venice, he sent a message to the Congress of the Italian Socialist Party held in his city (February 1, 1957).[83] To the officials of the Roman Curia who blamed him for that step, he answered that it was intended as an act of "courtesy,"[84] a word that he always used to explain his overtures to the left.

The Soviets heard about the kindness of Pope John from Italian Communist leaders who were aware of the popularity of the new Pope. He visited the wretchedly poor slum districts, which were strongholds of Communism.

In June 1959, Pope John raised the pay of employees of the Holy See from 25 percent to 40 percent. It was a long-needed reform: they had been getting starvation wages even for Italy. This fact was reportedly drawn to his attention when he went in to talk to an electrician who was working to get the telephones installed. "How are things going?" asked the Pope. "Badly, badly, Your Holiness," said the man. He looked so tired and thin that John took time to ask him about his family and his work; the electrician poured out his tale of struggle against poverty. . . . The Vatican employees who were being paid the least received the biggest advances in wages, and extra allowances were made realistically according to the number of children in a man's family. Shopping in the tax-free shops of Vatican City and accommodations in low-rent flats that were provided for many of them by the Holy See also helped."[85]

Giorgio La Pira, a Christian-Democrat professor of law, mayor of Florence and fervent Catholic dedicated to the poor, wrote several letters to Khrushchev, which I had the opportunity to see in their Russian translation. During a trip to Moscow, on August 15, 1959, feast of the Assumption, La Pira sent a telegram to John XXIII, which was very much criticized by the press, but it was received with joy by the Pope.[86]

John XXIII was already known as a different Pope at the Kremlin when the American editor Norman Cousins, during the Cuban crisis, suggested that the Pope be an intermediary between Khrushchev and Kennedy. The suggestion was promptly accepted by Moscow.[87] But when Cousins went to Moscow on behalf of the Vatican to explore the possibilities of an amelioration of the religious situation inside the Soviet Union, Khrushchev was less enthusiastic. While closing thousands of churches, Khrushchev reluctantly agreed to free the head of the Ukrainian Catholics, Metropolitan Joseph Slipyj, but told Mr. Cousins several lies, among them that he "would be glad to look into the matter" regarding "publication of Bibles or other religious literature" in the USSR.[88]

In his desire to attain peace and normalize the prolonged painful situation of Christians in Communist countries, Pope John gave credibility to Khrushchev and allowed Catholics more freedom to associate with Communists and Socialists. In the encyclical "Mater et Magistra" (1961) he wrote that Catholics "should weigh the opinions of others with fitting courtesy and not measure everything in the light of their own interests. They should be prepared to join sincerely in doing whatever is naturally good or conductive to good."[89] More explicitly in the encyclical "Pacem in Terris" (1963) he elaborated:

It is, therefore, especially to the point to make a clear distinction between false philosophical teachings regarding the nature, origin, and destiny of the universe and of man, and movements which have a direct bearing either on economic and social questions, or cultural matters or on the organization of the state, even if these movements owe their origin and inspiration to these false tenets. While the teaching once it has been clearly set forth is no longer subject to change, the movements, precisely because they take place in the midst of changing conditions, are readily susceptible of change. Besides, who can deny that those movements, in so far as they conform to the dictates of right reason and are interpreters of the lawful aspirations of the human person, contain elements that are positive and deserving of approval?

For these reasons it can at times happen that meetings for the attainment of some practical results which previously seemed completely useless now are either actually useful or may be looked upon as profitable for the future.[90]

The "pastoral" policy of John XXIII to win over the enemy through dialogue and cooperation in many cases achieved the opposite effect: Catholics were converted to Communism. The Colombian guerrilla priest Camilo Torres, who joined the Communists and died while fighting against the regular army (February 15,1966), stated: "I don't care if the big press continues to call me a Communist. I prefer to follow my conscience rather than bend before pressures of the oligarchy. I would rather follow the rules of the pontiffs of the Church than those of our ruling class. John XXIII authorizes me to march along with the Communists."[91] It is true, however, that the Pope, in "Pacem in Terris," had quoted the following words of Pius XII: "Salvation and justice are not to be found in revolution, but in evolution through concord. Violence has always achieved only destruction and not construction." But, once collaboration was permitted, even though only in principle, certain consequences were to be expected.

With John XXIII and Paul VI Catholic "social doctrine" became less rigid and more cautious. During the Vatican Council II some of the bishops even questioned the wisdom of using such an expression: "social doctrine" which appeared to them to be a contradiction in terms.[92] Doctrine indicates the content and the substance of a theoretical teaching, a group of abstract principles, which are the results of elaboration and reflection and are universally valid and immutable, while the adjective "social" adds to the generic concept of doctrine the further characterization of intrinsic and conscious intention to act by the members of the community for the achievement of a common interest, which cannot be but concrete and changing, being, as it is, conditioned by extrinsic elements of cultural, local, political and economic nature. For these reasons those bishops preferred to speak rather of a social "teaching" of the Church. This question is less academic than it appears, because it poses a serious dilemma for the Church and it uncovers an even more serious crisis in the way the faithful and the clergy itself accept the Church's teachings.

We cannot deny that in the official teaching of the Catholic Church on social matters the interest in the philosophical, moral and religious aspects of problems has always prevailed. However, in more recent times there has been more attention given to both the historical and political aspects. There has been a ripening of the conflict between an essentially deductive, static conception of the social doctrine and the new needs of the modern conscience for a more continuous comparison between the principles and the historical situation, and for the recognition of a measure of autonomy of the historical-political steps with respect to the doctrinal speculation. With the development of positive sciences, such as economics, social psychology, labor laws etc., it is more and more evident that it is impossible to elaborate a program of social reform only on the basis of ethico-philosophical principles. The Church is aware of the fact that it does not have specific competence in the field of politico-technical choices. It is significant, in this respect, to observe the insistence with which the Church in its most recent documents requests the assistance and the technical collaboration of the experts in the various social disciplines. In his encyclical "Populorum Progressio" (March 26, 1967) Paul VI states: "In countries undergoing development, no less than in others, the laymen should take up as their own proper task the renewal of the temporal order."[93]

This new position, in which the Church calls the laymen to greater action, without assuming responsibility for their choices, was stressed again by Pope Paul in the "Octogesima Adveniens," the apostolic letter he sent on May 14, 1971, to Cardinal Maurice Roy on the eightieth anniversary of "Rerum Novarum." One of the most important points in this document is a new definition of the attitude one might assume with regard to present-day ideologies, in particular socialism:

> Some Christians are today attracted by socialist currents and their various developments. They try to recognize therein a certain number of aspirations which they carry within themselves in the name of their faith. They feel that they are a part of that historical current and wish to play a part within it. Now this historical current takes on, under the same name, different forms according to different continents and cultures, even if it drew its inspiration, and still does in many cases, from ideologies incompatible with faith. Careful judgement is called for. Too often Christians attracted by socialism tend to idealize it in terms which, apart from anything else, are very general: a will for justice, solidarity and equality. They refuse to recognize the limitations of the historical socialist movements, which remain conditioned by the ideologies from which they originated. Distinctions must be made to guide concrete choices between the various levels of expression of socialism: a generous aspiration and a seeking for a more just society, historical movements with a political organization and aim, and an ideology which claims to give a complete and self-sufficient picture of man. Nevertheless, these distinctions must not lead one to consider such levels as completely separate and independent. The concrete link which, according to circumstances, exists between them must be clearly marked out. This insight will enable Christians to see the degree of commitment possible along these lines, while safeguarding the values, especially those of liberty, responsibility and openness to the spiritual, which guarantee the integral development of man.
>
> Other Christians even ask whether the historical development of Marxism might not authorize certain concrete rapprochements. They note, in fact, a certain splintering of Marxism, which until recently presented itself as a unified ideology that explained the totality of man and the world in the process of their development and in atheistic terms. Apart from the ideological difference in officially separating the various champions of

Marxism-Leninism in their individual interpretations of the thought of its founders, and apart from the open opposition between the political systems which make use of its name today, some people have established distinctions among the various levels at which Marxism can be expressed.

For some, Marxism remains essentially the active practice of class struggle. Experiencing the ever present and continually renewed force of the relationships of domination and exploitation among men, they reduce Marxism to no more than a struggle—at times with no other purpose—to be pursued and even stirred up in permanent fashion. For others, it is first and foremost the collective exercise of political and economic power under the direction of a single party, which would be the sole expression and guarantee of the welfare of all, and would deprive individuals and other groups of any possibility of initiative and choice. At a third level, Marxism, whether in power or not, is viewed as a sócialist ideology based on historical materialism and the denial of everything transcendent. At other times, finally, it presents itself in a more attenuated form, one also more attractive to the modern mind; as a scientific activity, as a rigorous method of examining social and political reality, and as the rational link, tested by history, between theoretical knowledge and the practice of revolutionary transformation. Although this type of analysis gives a privileged position to certain aspects of reality to the detriment of the rest, and interprets them in the light of its ideology, it nevertheless furnishes some people not only with a working tool but also a certitude preliminary to action: the claim to decipher in a scientific manner the mainsprings of the evolution of society.

While, through the concrete existing form of Marxism, one can distinguish these various aspects and the questions they pose for the reflection and activity of Christians, it would be illusory and dangerous to reach a point of forgetting the intimate link which radically binds them together, to accept the elements of Marxist analysis without recognizing their relationships with ideology, and to enter into the practice of class struggle and its Marxist interpretations, while failing to note the kind of totalitarian and violent society to which this process leads.[94]

The many distinctions made by the Pope in his analysis of the different forms of socialism did not convince those Catholic priests and laymen who decided, with their organizations, to join the socialist camp. Among these groups should be mentioned particularly the ACLI (Christian Associations of Italian Workers) because of the personal interest and involvement shown by Msgr. Montini, now Paul VI, in this movement since its foundation in 1946. When in 1969-70 the ACLI declared themselves against private ownership of the means of production and in favor of socialism, the Pope deplored their choice saying: "We have witnessed with regret the recent drama of the ACLI, and we have deplored (without interfering with their freedom) the fact that the leaders of ACLI have decided to change the bylaws of the movement and to qualify it politically, particularly toward the left, with all the questionable and dangerous implications on the doctrinal and social level . . . ."[95]

In such matters the writings of Soviet dissenters could give the Popes the assistance they have requested from the laymen. The dissenters are in a unique position to speak about "concrete choices" among the various levels of expression of Socialism.[96] But, on the other hand, for the sake of peace and détente, the Vatican is willing to continue its dialogue with the leaders of the Communist countries. Today the Vatican has full diplomatic relations with Cuba and Yugoslavia, and channels are open not only with Poland, Hungaria, Czechoslovakia, Rumania, North Vietnam and the Viet Cong, but also with the Kremlin. Therefore one can question whether Soviet dissenters can expect Rome to give them the same support given by Pius XI to the victims of Stalin's terror in 1930. While John XXIII acted in a personal and charismatic way in dealing with Communists, Paul VI prefers to employ all the skill of Vatican diplomacy in which he was brought up since the early days of his priesthood. While John XXIII believed in Utopia, Paul VI believes in diplomatic negotiations.

Now the Soviets are ready to pass from monologue to dialogue. To orthodox Communists who were afraid that dialogue and détente could ideologically "disarm" Soviet citizens, Vladimir N. Yagodin, Moscow party secretary for ideology and propaganda, answered that "there is nothing wrong about signing a pact with the devil if you are certain that you can cheat the devil."[97]

2

New Priorities in the Vatican's Ostpolitik

In the light of the Second Vatican Council more and more Catholics consider contemporary Vatican diplomacy inconsistent with the teaching of the Council Fathers and harmful to the life of the Church. Increasingly Vatican diplomats are seen as symbols of collusion with the "mighty of this world" and of insensitivity to the humble and oppressed—symbols which obfuscate the true face and the real nature of the Pilgrim Church on earth. The Belgian Cardinal Leo J. Suenens, who drafted the conciliar Constitution on the Church in the modern world, pictured the nuncios as "Vatican spies" and asked for a total reordering of papal diplomacy.[1] Father Peter Hebblethwaite, former editor of the British Jesuit magazine *Month*, called Archbishop Giovanni Benelli, the Vatican's Deputy Secretary of State, "repressive, secretive, mysterious...at odds with the best thinking of the Church."[2] An anonymous official, who described himself as "someone who has the misfortune to work in the Vatican diplomatic service, without approving of the system," leaked an important document regarding a German bishop, and wrote in his covering note: "see how the nuncio is trying to disrupt your institutions by methods that are worse than Soviet methods."[3] Father Raymond Leopold Brukberger, a French Dominican priest, accused the Pope of keeping silent over the persecution of Christians on the other side of the Iron Curtain: "Believing more in diplomacy than in charity," wrote the Dominican, "the Pope renders useless the efforts of the faithful."[4]

Paul VI took several steps to improve the Roman Curia, but defended the validity of the Vatican's diplomatic efforts. On the tenth anniversary of his election, answering to the greetings of the cardinals, he declared that, despite many disappointments, the Vatican intended to continue efforts for world peace, and announced that it would participate in the forthcoming European Security Conference in Helsinki. He also noted that in the ten years of his pontificate, the number of countries with which the Vatican maintained diplomatic relations had almost doubled, stressing the fact that many of these nations were of non-Christian culture and that the Holy See in its diplomatic activity was not moved by "a desire of human affirmation nor by the temptation to interfere in a field alien to the mission of the Church."[5]

On the other hand, as Father Robert A. Graham, S.J., a specialist on Vatican diplomacy, pointed out, "today no one is worried about the Church interfering in politics. In fact the general public seems to be insisting that the 'institutional' Church take a stand of its own and by that fact impose its views on all members of the laity. It is breathtaking and refreshing to see how the non-Catholic and the secular worlds now welcome the kind of 'institutional' concern with global problems that a few years ago would have been castigated as medieval."[6]

The Vatican as an "Ally and Collaborator" of all Nations, including the Communist Ones

The accessibility of Vatican diplomatic representatives to various governments and their presence at the most important international institutions is aimed especially at the elimination of the danger of war and the achievement of peace. Archbishop Giovanni Benelli declared that "the laborious and long effort to promote and consolidate peace absorbs 90 percent of the diplomatic activity of the pontifical representatives."[7] This aspect of Vatican diplomacy was emphasized by Pope Paul in his annual address to diplomats accredited to the Vatican who gathered on January 12, 1974, to present their formal New Year's greetings. The Pope observed that the traditional definition of diplomacy as the art of making peace is sometimes criticized as oversimplified on the grounds that diplomacy embraces many other activities, "yet it cannot be denied that the search for peace is the pivotal point of the diplomatic mission in international life. And in this task, the diplomacy of states had the Holy See as ally and collaborator."[8] The following year, on January 11, the Pope again told the diplomats that the Holy See gives the states not only its "moral support," but its "concrete help."

One thing that the Pope apparently concedes in his speeches is that diplomacy, as part of politics, is also the art of compromising. Especially regarding the Soviet Union, it is this aspect of Vatican diplomacy which worries both Catholics and non-Catholics as well as Soviet dissenters.

When Archbishop Agostino Casaroli, Secretary of the Council for Public Affairs of the Roman Catholic Church, went to Moscow some years ago (February 24—March 1, 1971) to deposit the Holy See's declaration of adherence to the Nuclear Non-Proliferation Treaty with the Soviet government, there was great speculation about this visit, the first ever made by a member of the Vatican diplomatic corps since the establishment of the Soviet regime in Russia. That tiny Vatican City should so ratify a treaty seemed somewhat strange to many observers. No one could take seriously the idea that the Vatican might have a few nuclear weapons nestled among the halberds in the Swiss Guard armory. Understandably, therefore, the trip touched off rumors that the Pope's envoy would be meeting Soviet Foreign Minister Andrei Gromyko to plead religious freedom for the twelve million Catholics living in the Soviet republics (this figure is taken from N. Struve, *Christians in Contemporary Russia*, p. 258), and that he would consider terms for establishing diplomatic relations between the Vatican and the USSR or sound out the Soviets on a Papal visit. Some other people drew the conclusion that they were right when they were charging that Rome was becoming "soft on Communism."

Anticipating or answering these speculations, Vatican spokesmen explained that in papal diplomacy such contacts do not presuppose approval of those with whom the conversations are undertaken, nor, for that matter, does even the exchange of diplomats on a formal basis suggest that the state involved is "friendly" with the Holy See.

The purpose of the Vatican's adherence to the treaty was expressed in an "additional declaration," signed by Cardinal Jean Villot, Vatican Secretary of State, which started with these words:

> This accession by the Holy See is inspired by its constant desire, illuminated by the teachings of universal brotherhood and of justice and peace between men and nations contained in the Gospel message, to make its contribution to undertakings, which, through disarmament as well as by other means, promote security, mutual trust and peaceful cooperation in relations between peoples.[9]

Nevertheless, for the following reasons it seems that some of the rumors mentioned above had some basis:

—It was not technically necessary for the Vatican to send anyone to the Soviet Union with a declaration of adherence. Without giving such a tremendous credibility to a regime so many times unfaithful to pacts and solemn declarations, the deposit of that diplomatic instrument with any one of the other two depository governments, the United States or Britain, would have sufficed.

—Once it had been decided for whatever reason to deposit the declaration with the Soviet government, it was not necessary to send a three-man mission headed by such a high official as Archbishop Casaroli, equal in rank to a Foreign Minister.[10] Another papal diplomat could have served that simple purpose.

—Archbishop Casaroli's political views are quite controversial. He is an open advocate of maintaining or establishing communications with Communist governments, however tenuous or two-edged such communications might be. In 1964 he told newsmen that he bases his policy on the hope or expectation that one day the professional anti-religious bias of Communist regimes will weaken or wither away. "When and if that day dawns," he said, "the Holy See will at least have channels of communications open and ready for use,"[11] something which is very doubtful, because when and if that day will come, the people in power will be very different and the established channels of communication will be of no use and even might discredit the Holy See.

This writer had the privilege to know Archbishop Agostino Casaroli many years ago, soon after the Second World War, when many boys left alone in the streets of Rome became victims of crime and immorality, ending up in the San Michele prison and reformatory for minors. The Jesuit students who were in charge of the religious instruction at the institution frequently saw the then simple monsignore coming with huge packages of food for the hungry mouths, smiling or listening patiently to the most fantastic stories of the little liars. They couldn't deceive the monsignore, but he appeared to be convinced and spent a lot of time and money for them. In order to save them from falling again into the hands of unscrupulous men after leaving the institution, Casaroli opened a home for them at Villa Agnese. He is still going there every day to do what he calls "the work of his heart." For the boys he remains simply Don Agostí.

Named by Pope John XXIII to his higher position, Archbishop Casaroli kept his gentle manners in his frequent dealings with Communist diplomats. Later, in 1963, he began to take frequent flights to East European capitals, and he needed a bigger staff of specialists on Communist affairs. His former right-hand man with special responsibility for Eastern Europe, Msgr. Giovanni Cheli, is now the Vatican observer to the United Nations, where Communist representatives, including the Chinese, can be easily reached and consulted. Meanwhile, a new post of "roving nuncio" has been devised for Archbishop Luigi Poggi who keeps the contacts with UNESCO and is setting the dialogue with Communist governments and the Churches.[12] The acceptance, if not the success, of Archbishop Casaroli among Communist diplomatic circles led the press to name him "the Kissinger of the Vatican."[13] But unlike the American Secretary of State, the papal diplomat prefers to remain hidden behind the anonymity of the Holy See. Thus, approval or criticism of his negotiations become approval or criticism of the Pope, who personally lays the guidelines of Vatican policies.

Upon his return from Moscow, Archbishop Casaroli emphasized that the purpose of his six-day trip was to deposit the Holy See's declaration of adherence to the Nuclear Non-Proliferation Treaty with the Soviet government, as one of the so-called depository governments: "This purpose explained my trip and defined its real character."[14] From this point of view it was an undeniable success. He made however, no effort to conceal his attempt to profit by his presence in Moscow to have contacts at three levels: Soviet foreign ministry, Council for Religious Affairs, and the Russian Orthodox Church.

With the officials of the Soviet Foreign Ministry the Vatican envoy said that he discussed those international questions "that at this moment are drawing the attention of all governments." He characterized the talks as "substantial and interesting," and stressed the fact that they were held "in an atmosphere of great openness and, above all, of great respect and

consideration for the activity of the Holy Father in favor of peace."
Unfortunately, from what is published in the Soviet press and affirmed in
public by Soviet officials, we do not have any knowledge of this "great
respect" for the Catholic Church and its head, the Pope.This must be part
of the secrecy of the talks, although the Vatican diplomat did mention,
along with "concrete coincidences," some unspecified "divergences."

Nevertheless Archbishop Casaroli didn't pay too much attention to
this fact because, as he explains, his contacts at the Foreign Ministry
"allowed us to continue usefully a dialogue already started, directed to the
establishment of the possibility for cooperation and a parallel or con-
vergent action in favor of peace in the world . . . What I have in mind, for
instance, is the progress in favor of disarmament, or activities relative to the
plan for a conference on European security. In these fields, cooperation is
already in progress with the USSR as well as with many other governments, from East to West—and can develop with good and solid
prospects." Regarding those areas of action in which the Holy See and the
Soviet Union can work on a parallel basis, or those areas in which either the
Vatican or the USSR can more successfully appeal to one side or the other,
Archbishop Casaroli said that "the results of these separate actions serve a
common aim, which is peace. There is no lack of cases in which the Holy
See as well as the USSR has the possibility of exercising influence on only
one of the parties—on that with which one or the other has a better
relationship—and not with the other."

In the meeting with the President and Vice President of the Council for
Religious Affairs of the USSR's Council of Ministers, Vladimir A.
Kuroedov and Pyotr V. Makartsev, Archbishop Casaroli said that the
discussion on the situation of the Catholics in the Soviet Union "did not go
into details," but he felt that a thaw was starting as in other Communist
countries, such as Poland and Hungary, which "do not question Vatican
influence over their Catholics." Therefore, in general, he judged the
discussion "positive," taking into consideration the fact that for the first
time, after more than 50 years, the idea of "passing from the phase, so to
speak, of monologue to dialogue was accepted." More cautiously he added
that "due to the cordial atmosphere in which the meeting was held, there is
hope, if I am not mistaken, that the continuation of the dialogue will be
possible."

A notable sidelight of Archbishop Casaroli's trip was the meeting with
high officials of the Russian Orthodox Church, including Metropolitan
Pimen of Krutitsa and Kolomna, "locum tenens" of the Patriarchate since
the death of Alexis (April 1970), who was elected Patriarch of Moscow a
few months later. A sign of their friendly relations was an exhange of gifts
for Pope Paul and an ecumenical service. But, as the Vatican envoy pointed
out:

these contacts did not have an official character, because ecumenical activity is entrusted by the Holy See to a special body, the Secretariat for Promoting Christian Unity, presided over by Cardinal Jan Willebrands, who has travelled to Moscow and the Soviet Union several times. I can say, however, that the atmosphere of these contacts could not have been better. Of course, that is not enough to solve the problems, but I had an even more vivid impression of what the possibilities are of bringing forth, in a climate of fraternity and reciprocal and truly sincere respect, the examination of the problems that still divide the two Churches.

Summarizing the impressions of Archbishop Casaroli's "mission" to Moscow we can say, using his own words, that it did not go beyond "a reciprocal gesture" and the "feeling" that "there was a spark and that 'they' accepted the idea of a dialogue."

As the Vatican's diplomat pointed out, attempts to engage in a dialogue with the Soviets had already been going on for several years. On March 7, 1963, Alexei Adzhubei, Khrushchev's son-in-law and editor of *Izvestiia,* visited Pope John XXIII. Paul VI first met Soviet foreign minister Andrei Gromyko at the United Nations (October 4, 1965), when the Pope flew to New York for a one-day visit to plead the cause of peace before the UN General Assembly. They met a second time when Gromyko accompanied Soviet President Nikolai Podgorny on a visit to the Vatican in February 1967, and again in November 1970, February 1974 and June 1975.

After the meetings no official communiqué was issued, but a Vatican press officer told newsmen that among the topics discussed were disarmament, world peace, the Middle East, Jerusalem and the Conference on European Security. He also indicated that on religious matters "Soviet diplomats had limited their participation to listening to the Vatican position,"[15] confirming the general impression that with regard to the religious needs of Soviet citizens a monologue, rather than a dialogue, is still going on. The paucity of information on official contacts as well as the secrecy of other, at times, most unthinkable channels make it difficult to figure exactly the range and the results of Vatican diplomatic efforts. As Pope Paul VI told journalists not long ago, the Vatican has no intention of revealing everything about the Church's affairs or of depending on public opinion:

There remain limits demanded by discretion and the common good, in the Church more than in other societies.

The reason is simple. If the Church must have a good knowledge of the world she must care for, and if she must arouse broad cooperation from her children, her decisions are based upon the Gospel and her own living Tradition, not on the world's spirit or on public opinion, which often fails to grasp the complexity of the theological or pastoral problems at stake.[16]

Evidently the Pope was alluding here to theological matters in which he enjoys the particular gift of infallibility. But the Vatican is very reluctant to comment publicly even on its political and diplomatic policies, in which mistakes are possible and, in fact, occurred in the past. The Pope never gives interviews or holds news conferences and his small team of international advisers are bound by the strictest secrecy, recently tightened by new regulations. For these reasons Rome can always escape criticism by saying that journalists and authors do not have the complete picture of the facts.[17]

Nevertheless, regarding Soviet-Vatican relations, it is quite clear that Moscow seeks support from Rome because of its importance in the international arena. Gone is the old attitude of Stalin, who once asked ironically how many divisions the Vatican had. On its part, as Archbishop Casaroli said, Rome is ready now to give "its support and moral encouragement" to the Soviets because "the aims of disarmament and easing of international tensions correspond with its own mission of peace."[18] Of course, the Vatican diplomat knows that the Soviets are looking for peace and détente because they are experiencing troubles at home and with their big brother Mao. But he gives the impression of believing that a fundamental "sincerity" and "convergence" of aims is taking place between the Vatican and the Soviet leaders. That is why both of them are disappointed at the doubts expressed by their critics. "When Pope Paul VI and USSR Foreign Minister Andrei Gromyko met for a private conversation in the Vatican," asks the editor of the Jesuit magazine *America* (July 19, 1975):

> did they lament together over criticisms leveled against their respective efforts to work out grounds for more peaceful coexistence between religion and Communist political rule? The late Cardinal Józef Mindszenty was not the only, or the last, outspoken critic of the present Pope's Ostpolitik.... If the Holy Father voiced a concern about his critics, Mr. Gromyko could have assured him that the Soviet Union had critics of its own to confront. Lately, for example, the Albanian national radio charged that the "poisonous roots of religion are being ever more deeply extended" inside the USSR.... Pope Paul and Mr. Gromyko might well have consoled one another with the thought that at times you can't win with some people....

Since the armed clashes on the Chinese-Soviet frontier in the winter of 1969, Chinese denunciations have increased, especially after the Communist victories in Indochina. The Chinese press accused the Soviet Union of trying to "swallow Southeast Asia at a gulp," compared L. Brezhnev to Hitler and declared that "Soviet Social Imperialists have honey on their lips and murder in their hearts." Mao Tse-tung warned Kissinger that by appeasing the Soviets the US is gaining nothing, but risking another World War.[19]

The Soviet dissenter Andrei Amalrik doubted that "the situation will improve in the next ten years," and that the USSR would survive until 1984:

"all signs point to a war (between the USSR and China) that will be protracted and exhausting, with no quick victory for either side." Analyzing the problem of a US rapprochement with either the Soviet Union or China, Amalrik wrote:

> I believe that a rapprochement between the United States and the Soviet Union would make sense only after serious steps toward democracy were taken in the U.S.S.R. Until such time, any agreements on the part of the Soviet Union will be motivated either by fear of China or by an attempt to preserve the regime with the aid of American economic assistance (similar to the loans given by France to the Czarist regime, which prolonged its existence by several years), or by the desire to use American friendship to install or maintain Soviet influence in other countries. In addition, of course, there is the interest of both countries in preserving their commanding roles in the world by mutual cooperation. This last objective is apparent, for example, in Soviet-American cooperation to prevent the proliferation of nuclear weapons.
>
> Apart from a few benefits, such a "friendship," based as it would be on hypocrisy and fear, would bring the United States nothing but the same sort of troubles that arose from the cooperation between Roosevelt and Stalin. Cooperation presupposes mutual reliance, but how can one rely on a country that has been capable of no other aim over the centuries than distending itself and sprawling in all directions like sour dough? A genuine rapprochement must be based on similarity of interests, culture and traditions, and on mutual understanding. Nothing like this exists.[20]

Regarding the future of the USSR, Amalrik was convinced that even without a war, "this great Eastern Slav empire, created by Germans, Byzantines and Mongols, has entered the last decades of its existence. Just as the adoption of Christianity postponed the fall of the Roman Empire but did not prevent its inevitable end, so Marxist doctrine has delayed the break-up of the Russian Empire—the third Rome—but it does not possess the power to prevent it."[21]

If these predictions are not completely fantastic, it would be wiser for the Vatican to support those peoples who will emerge from the disintegration of the Soviet empire. By trying to collaborate with the oppressors the Vatican risks alienating the freedom fighters without obtaining substantial concessions from atheistic regimes. The dissenters, who have a lot of values in common with the Vatican, are told: be patient, "Rome thinks in centuries," a saying which is not applied to Soviet and Chinese tyrants. The Vatican is worried about the strength of the two Communist powers and fears their further expansion in the world. Therefore it takes every opportunity to show its readiness for a dialogue. Pope Paul VI, during his historical visit to the United Nations on October 4, 1965, in a direct allusion to the possible admission of Peking into the international organization, exhorted the Assembly to "act so that those still outside will desire and merit the confidence of all and then be generous in granting such confidence."[22] In 1970, he made a dramatic stopover in Hong Kong at the end of his Asian journey. By carefully avoiding Taipei, the Pope reached out to the people on the mainland by saying: "Christ is a teacher, shepherd and a loving redeemer for China, too."[23]

Archbishop Edward Cassidy, Apostolic Pro-Nuncio to Taiwan, was called to Rome in the fall of 1971, shortly before the United Nations voted the admission (November 15, 1971) of the People's Republic of China. While on an extended home leave in his native Australia, the absent diplomat emphasized in an interview that he was the successor of the previous Apostolic Internuncio to China, Archbishop Antonio Riberi, who was expelled because of his foreign citizenship rather than his diplomatic status. That Archbishop Cassidy thereafter resided in Dacca, Bangladesh, as the Vatican representative to that country as well as to China, instead of maintaining a high profile from the nunciature in Taipei, demonstrates how far the Vatican has gone in reaching out towards Peking.[24]

But perhaps the most significant development in the current attitude of the Vatican with respect to China was an article on the common ground between Christianity and Maoism published in "Fides," the bulletin of the Vatican's central mission offices, the Congregation for the Evangelization of Peoples.[25] The article asserted that Maoist doctrine "finds authentic and complete expression in modern social Christian teaching" and that, while socialism in the Soviet Union has become pragmatic and economic, in China the Maoist brand of socialism is "a moral socialism of thought and conduct, independent of the accidental conditions of the country's wealth or poverty." Present-day China, according to "Fides," is devoted to a mystique of disinterested work for others, to inspiration by justice, to exaltation of a simple and frugal life, to the rehabilitation of the rural masses and to a mixing of social classes." These aspirations, concludes the bulletin, are pressed in the encyclicals of Popes John XXIII and Paul VI and in other recent documents of the Catholic hierarchy which have received a world-wide appreciation "and must have come to the notice of the Peking leaders, who may find in them the best evidence that religion, and Christianity in particular, is not a leech-like superstition, but a genuine servant of man, and therefore also of Chinese man."[26]

Officials of the Congregation for the Evangelization of Peoples declared that they were surprised, even alarmed, to hear that the views of "Fides" had been interpreted by some of the press as opportunistic or "as a trial balloon either from the Secretariat of State, or from us."[27] Archbishop Giovanni Benelli, the Vatican's Deputy Secretary of State, felt it necessary to apologize for "the serious mistakes" of the article to Taiwan's Ambassador, Chen Chih-mai.[28] Nevertheless, Rome should not disregard Solzhenitsyn's impression that "the spirit of Munich is dominant in the twentieth century. The intimidated civilized world has found nothing to oppose the onslaught of a suddenly resurgent fang-bearing barbarism, except concessions and smiles. . . . The reckoning for cowardice will only be more cruel. Courage and the power to overcome will be ours only when we dare to make sacrifices. . . . One word of truth outweighs the world."[29]

Whether or not the article in "Fides" was inspired by leftist clergymen working in the highest levels of Vatican bureaucracy or is to be considered simply as a form of *captatio benevolentiae,* the Vatican's disrespect toward Free China became evident on the occasion of Chiang Kai-shek's death. It was only on the day of his funeral that a telegram arrived from the Vatican naming the nunciature's charge d'affaires as papal representative. Because of the delay the press failed to mention the appointment and as a result considerable resentment was felt by Catholics.[30]

What First: God, Man or Peace?

One of the turnpoints in this reversal of the Vatican's politics regarding Communist states goes back to 1969. In March of that year the members of the Warsaw pact issued the so-called "Budapest Appeal" and sent a copy to the Vatican through the Hungarian embassy in Rome. The Holy See accepted the appeal and the invitation to participate together with the other West European countries in the Helsinki Conference on European security and cooperation. It sent its representatives to the preparation (December 1972) and to the working sessions of the same conference (July 1973).[31]

What the Vatican cannot obtain directly, it hopes to achieve indirectly in the frame of a new kind of dialogue on global and general issues. But this signifies that strictly religious matters as well as the defense of human rights do not have the priority that many expected from the Vatican, while the hopes of the oppressed become more and more frustrated.

This new strategy of the Vatican was clearly unveiled by Archbishop Casaroli a year after his trip to Moscow in a speech, "The Holy See and Europe," given on January 20, 1972, in Milan.[32] The following are the major points of the new policy adopted by the Vatican in its dealings with Communist countries:

1. The objectives of dialogue are, for the Holy See, first of all the establishment or preservation of conditions—at least minimal—for the unfolding of Christian life, the existence and activity of the Church. This is not a selfish purpose once the meaning of Church teachings and guidance both for Christians and non-Christians is considered.

2. The Holy See as well as the Church is deeply interested also in the legitimate human values of social progress, culture and peace.

3. Although service to the Church is its primary duty, today the Holy See does not believe that service to humanity and peace are secondary, nor does it think that the latter should be subordinated to the former. This explains why the Holy See does not refuse to collaborate in the field of international peace with countries where the condition of the Church is still far from satisfactory.

4. Even if it is necessary to act cautiously with those who still have not disavowed the ideological bases at the root of the old dissension, "this is not a sufficient reason to abandon a way not known to be safe (along which arrests and repressions can still occur and which does not promise general results in the short run), but which has in its favor pros no less valid than cons and does answer to great necessities and to what appears to a Christian to be, the providential course of History."

5. The Holy See supports the efforts for a "fair and meaningful reconciliation between East and West and for the economic and political unity of Europe. It stresses the "necessity of sacrificing national egotism or even national rights and of cooperation" in a climate of sufficient trust, notwithstanding the present ideological divergences.

Points 3, 4 and 5 are less convincing, especially since they imply "sacrifices" which, in many cases, would lead to self-destruction, and suppose intentions and changes in Communist leaders which not only are still not in sight, but are in contradiction with their confessed aims. As Andrei Sakharov affirms in *My Country and the World*, "we must not call upon our people, our youth, to make sacrifices. As for victims, we have already had more than enough of them." Furthermore, can the Church cooperate with Communists to the point of losing credibility among the people? Is this the "course of history" hinted by Archbishop Casaroli? If not, this is certainly what Communists mean with their "historic materialism." For this reason points 3 and 4 practically annul points 1 and 2 or, at least, confirm the impression that points 1 and 2 no longer have that top priority they had during the pontificates of Pius XI and Pius XII when the Communists and their collaborators were solemnly condemned.

The imperative necessity of avoiding a nuclear war is something that only a fool could deny. But is that imperative so absolute to have priority over the rights of God or to be used as an argument against resistance while entire nations are being enslaved? On the other hand, very few free men will agree with the Vatican Foreign Minister that there are "signs" that Soviet détente should be trusted and no longer regarded as a tactic. Even pacifist delegates to the World Congress of Peace Forces in Moscow (November 1973) were unable to see those signs. An American ex-Benedictine wrote an unscheduled and unexpected statement attacking the Soviet government for its efforts to silence dissenters. The statement was signed by a number of American anti-war activists, including Jesuit Fr. Daniel Berrigan, and by Professor Noam Chomsky, the world-famous linguist who teaches at the Massachusetts Institute of Technology. The man who read the statement, Mr. Paul Mayer, teaches at New York Theological Seminary and was co-chairman of the US delegation to the Congress, which was convoked by the Communist-led World Peace Council. The statement pointed out that many of those who had signed it had been tried or imprisoned for criticism of US policies and had "earned the right to speak on the question of Soviet dissenters." Describing themselves as "outspoken critics of the foreign policy of the US," the signatories condemned the Soviet government for "a campaign to silence not only your intellectuals, but any Soviet citizens who seek to exercise their rights—rights already defined by and contained in the Soviet constitution.... It is absolutely intolerable for anyone to set the limits of free speech or of the freedom to write and openly distribute and discuss what has been written ... We support the Soviet dissenters in their demands for free speech and assembly."[33]

Points 4 and 5 do not seem to take into consideration the will of the peoples oppressed by antihuman ideologies and regimes. To ask these peoples for more "sacrifices," "cooperation" with and "loyalty" to governments they never elected and to Church officials who are cooperating with atheists against religious freedom, "might signify," as Archbishop Casaroli admitted in his Milan speech, "abandoning and disavowing those who fought and suffered for the Church" and for the freedom of their countries. Nevertheless, he assures them, this is the only way they can "survive" and make possible a "dialogue" between Rome and their Communist dictators.

A few examples will show how the new priorities of Vatican Ostpolitik work in Communist states where diplomatic relations are established or the "dialogue" is more advanced.

Yugoslavia. Glas Koncila, a weekly newspaper for Croatian Catholics considered one of the most interesting Catholic publications in Europe, was confiscated several times and in October 1972 and May 1975 threatened with suppression because it reported arrests of Catholic students, searches of church buildings and administrative measures restricting Catholic publications, indicating that in the matter of freedom it is becoming increasingly difficult to distinguish between Yugoslavian Titoism and Soviet Stalinism. Since 1972, in consecutive waves of purges, hundreds of university professors and students as well as believers lost their jobs. On February 28, 1975, the famous Yugoslav writer Mihailo Mihajlov, a son of Russian immigrants and a man of deep religious convictions, was for the second time condemned to seven years of prison in a country which once seemed seriously bent on proving that Marxist economics did not necessitate the repression of the right to express opinions openly.[34] When Archbishop Franjo Kuharic of Zagreb declared that no man should be considered of less worth because of his world view or of his religion, he became a target of bitter personal attack by *Vjesnik,* the largest daily in Zagreb. His action was called "an intemperate deviation" from the norms set by the 1966 protocol between Yugoslavia and the Holy See.[35] The *Vjesnik* article maintained that the Archbishop was meddling in politics, by affirming that political programs and social systems go beyond their proper limits when they are presented as the only possible approaches to problems. The article accused Kuharic of "false rhetoric" and said that he was endangering all that had been achieved in relations between Yugoslavia and the Vatican. The fact that these criticisms against the Archbishop were reprinted by the central Communist organs "Borba," "Kommunist" and "NIN," suggests that the Yugoslavian government was indirectly reminding the Vatican that with the agreement of 1966 bishops were permitted to occupy their sees as long as they stood clear of political involvement and loyally collaborated with the state. In fact, the protocol of 1966 recognizes the Socialist nature of the Yugoslav state and concedes to the Vatican jurisdiction in matters of spiritual, ecclesiastical and religious character. This concession, however, is limited by the clause "in so far as they are not opposed to the internal order of the Socialistic Federative Republic of Yugoslavia." Furthermore the Church promised to lend a hand in dealing with "political terrorism or similar forms of violence."

Capuchin Father Tomislav Sagi-Bunic, a Zagreb theology professor and a member of the Vatican's International Theological Commission, writing in *Glas Koncila,* had already pointed out the weaknesses of the 1966 protocols. In a series of articles which examined the state of Christian-Communist relations in Yugoslavia he described them as unsatisfactory and expressed concern that relations might become worse as the regime gradually reimposes ideological controls. The Yugoslavian bishop Skvorc was even more categorical. Speaking at the World Synod of Catholic Bishops in Rome in October 1974, he said that "a true and fruitful dialogue with atheists is impossible."[36] The following month a Federal Conference of the Socialist Alliance attacked those "prelates who appeal to the public opinion and act as if in our country there didn't exist a Constitution and a law.... Under the appearance of good intentions toward our social system, they develop a thesis long ago refuted, according to which the Church is not bound to any particular human culture nor to any particular political and economic system. Logically, this is nothing else than an attempt to ridicule the doctrine on the separation of church and state."[37]

Cuba. Archbishop Casaroli's visit to Cuba in the spring of 1974 was considered in Vatican circles as a breakthrough in an impasse between church and state that had existed since Castro took power fifteen years before. Catholic newspapers saw a "sign of the times" in the fact that Castro himself sought out the Vatican diplomat. In their meeting on April 4, which lasted for an hour and forty minutes, three major subjects were discussed: the lack of priests on the island (500 Spanish priests and other missionaries were expelled from Cuba in 1961-68); "the greater participation of Roman Catholics as such, professedly within the framework of public life in Cuba"; and the religious instruction of Cuban children. The Archbishop said that Castro was "very courteous" and that they were quickly able to begin discussing "basic questions" from an agreed point of departure, which was: "let us not look at the past, but to the present and the future, with a spirit of good will." Paying tribute to what he called the "huge efforts" made by the Cuban government in the field of education, the Vatican representative admitted that problems still exist and further negotiations are necessary, but fundamentally he considered the visit constructive.[38]

It was the first time that a Vatican diplomat revealed publicly that he was offering to the head of a Communist government the "loyal collaboration" of Catholics as such in return for a little more religious freedom. The Marxist and dictatorial nature of Castro's regime, which was never endorsed by a popular vote, did not disturb him very much. It was accepted as an unavoidable reality which every Cuban Catholic should respect and support. There is no doubt that the Archbishop's proposal was perfectly in accord with Vatican policy toward Communist states which requests that for the sake of peace, Catholics "sacrifice" national and religious "rights." But the question is how legitimately can the Church and even more the Vatican decide on the political choices of the faithful? Surely Casaroli consulted with the Cuban bishops before his meeting with Castro, something that often is not even done by Vatican diplomats. Nevertheless, at the level of political decisions, such consultations cannot be a substitute for the individual choices of the citizens.

There is another reason why Archbishop Casaroli's offer of Cuban Catholics' loyalty to Castro was rather surprising. This is in fact the main point of the program of the Movement of Christians for Socialism, founded by Fr. Gonzalo Arroyo, S. J. in Chile (April 14-16, 1971) and now spread in other Latin American countries and even in Spain, Italy and Germany. Meeting with Fidel Castro in Santiago, Chile (November 1971), 140 priests led by Fr. Arroyo agreed that "Christians are not merely tactical allies, but strategical allies in a revolutionary process.... Christians can accept Marxist method without compromising their faith."[39] Despite the condemnation of the Chilean bishops, the Movement held several encounters in Santiago (April 1972), Avila, Spain (January 1973), and Bologna, Italy (September 1973), in which the "loyalty" or "strategic alliance" with Communists was more particularly expressed. Here are some of the declarations made during those meetings by several delegates, among them by Fr. Giulio Girardi, an Italian priest who was one of the "periti" (experts) on Communism at the Second Vatican Council:

1. The presence of Christians in the construction of Socialism cannot be understood as a "dialogue" between two different groups.

2. Ours is not merely the position of collaborators, of fellow-travelers, but a position of simple and true militants in Marxist-class organizations.

3. Christians do not add something different or superior or new to the process of liberation.

4. There are no essential Christian values.... The fundamental Christian values are not specifically Christian, but simply human.

5. We adopt the Marxist scientific method of analysis of capitalistic

society, the position of historical materialism, as the foundation of our class struggle.

6. Our option is not against our Christian faith because it presupposes a change in the traditional understanding of Church and theology through a new reading of the Bible.

7. Religious truth has to be judged in the light of human truth. If in the religious message there is something which contradicts the conclusions of an authentic human research, that certainly does not come from God, but reflects the culture of another epoch, of another class.

8. If there is something in the religious message which contradicts human liberation or is an obstacle to the class struggle, it does not come from God.

9. We oppose a faith based on the primacy of the spirit.

10. Faith does not precede or surpass human culture and history, but is immanent in them.[40]

Evidently the "loyalty" offered to Castro by Archbishop Casaroli cannot be understood in the terms expressed by the priests of the Movement of Christians for Socialism. But this is the only "loyalty" acceptable to Castro. Judging by a letter sent by "certain Cubans" to the World Synod of Bishops in Rome (October 1974), it seems that some Cuban Catholic lay leaders, after Casaroli's visit, are now more inclined to switch to the kind of loyalty sponsored by the Movement of Christians for Socialism.[41]

Despite the appeal of Bishop E. Boza Masvidal, the exiled auxiliary bishop of Havana and last rector of the Catholic University of Villanova in Cuba, the fate of many Cuban political and religious prisoners did not figure among the "basic questions" discussed at the Havana meeting. In regard to Communist countries both the Vatican and the National Conferences of Catholic Bishops take a more restrained attitude than toward other nations.[42] Andrei Sakharov calls this kind of policy "a false détente" or "a capitulation détente."[43]

Czechoslovakia. After many efforts, in 1973 Archbishop Casaroli succeeded in consecrating personally four new Czechoslovakian bishops. One of them, Bishop Joseph Vrana of Olomouc, was the president of the government-sponsored "Peace priests" movement. During Dubchek's experiment of "Socialism with a human face," the president of this movement, Msgr. J. Plojhar, for many years Minister of Health, published a message to the party, which called for adapting to the new course. He was quickly answered by his fellow priests who sent the following letter to the editor of *Literarni Listy:*

In this period when we are reappraising our views and seeking a more sincere approach to the work in various areas of public life, a report was published that the Catholic clergy expressed their gratitude to the representatives of the state and Party for having solved the Church-State relations twenty years ago. Over all those years the signators, Messrs. Plojhar and Benes, have represented just one faction which today has proved to be totally incapable of any critical approach and which plays a very tragic role in this country. First of all, they do not speak for all Catholic clergymen—not to mention the believers. It is most embarrassing that a Catholic priest maintains that the problem of the church and state was solved many years ago. The representatives of the state have already had several consultations with the true representatives of the Church and these consultations are still not completed.

In this situation the fossilised and bureaucratic attitude expressed by the aforenamed "representatives" harms the church on the one hand and the state on the other hand, and strives to support the most conservative views which have appeared in our press in recent days. In these moments when a real turnover and a search for an enlightened activity are taking place, the proclamations of a few clergymen contradict these generally accepted tendencies.

The point of view of those people who are assuming the right to speak on behalf of the Catholics may be shown by their relation toward those clergymen and believers who in recent time have in some way suffered for their faith. These are not few, and if they [Plojhar and Benes] still recognize them, this is their [Plojhar's and Benes'] opportunity to prove their words about peace by deeds right here and now.[44]

The Catholic Church has a new bishop in Olomouc, but he will take orders from Communist officials, not from Rome. His duty will be to check on the "loyalty" of his priests, not to encourage them toward apostolic activity. As Jaroslav Hajek, Slovak Minister of Culture said: "it is not possible to grant 'freedom of action,' to Catholicism in Socialist countries because that would mean going along with its anti-socialist, anti-communist, anti-state and anti-national attitudes. Therefore, it is indispensable that it be placed under the control of the socialist state so that political activity and the exploitation of the religious feelings of believers may be halted."[45]

Shortly after the consecration of the new bishops the plight of Catholic institutions started to worsen. Many priests had their licenses taken away with the tacit consent of the bishops. But one refused to become an accomplice of the persecutors, Cardinal Stepan Trochta, bishop of Litomerice, who paid with his life for his disobedience to Communist authorities. A member of the Salesian Society, he had already shown his extraordinary strength on different occasions. In 1942 he was arrested by the Nazis and sent to Dachau. In 1951 he was imprisoned by the Communists and sentenced to 25 years. Under Dubchek he was rehabilitated and, although seriously ill, again took up his pastoral duties. In 1969, after the death of the heroic Cardinal Beran, Paul VI named him a Cardinal "in pectore" and proclaimed his nomination on March 5, 1973. As a consequence of an unsuccessful operation to his eyes he was almost blind when on April 5, 1974, Dlabal, a representative of the state agency for ecclesiastical affairs, went to his house in order to convince him to expel the Salesian Fathers from his diocese and transfer or suspend some of his best priests. The "conversation" lasted from 11 a.m. until 5 p.m. among threats and rude invectives. That night he went to bed exhausted. On the following morning he was found unconscious. As soon as he recovered consciousness, he asked for the last rites and died that same day.[46] Cardinal Trochta did not benefit from détente; he was one of its illustrious victims.

After another useless official visit of Archbishop Casaroli to Czechoslovakia (February 24—26, 1975), the bishops and clergymen of the movement "Pacem in Terris" made such shameful declarations of "loyalty" to the regime that, as the review *Russia Cristiana* writes in its issue of July—August 1975, "it is difficult to find something similar in the mouths of the most fanatic apparatchiki" or among the "lies" of their "colleagues" of the Russian Orthodox Church.

Poland. When in 1972 Pope Paul VI created new dioceses in Poland, a number of Vatican officials quietly drew deep sighs of relief. The world press signaled the event with such headlines as "Vatican recognizes Oder-Neisse border." The decision of the Holy See settled a controversy of 27 years' duration. As Fr. Robert Graham explained:

> The political and legal aspects of the question are complicated, but the Vatican's "golden rule" is elementary. Ever since the First World War the Holy See has followed the policy of refraining from changing diocesan boundaries in disputed territories until a secular settlement is agreed on and in force.... When in virtue of military conquest the Nazis demanded the right of overseeing church nominations in annexed Poland, the Holy See let it be known that it could not concede such a prerogative until the war was over.... In 1945 the shoe was on the other foot. At the Potsdam conference, the "Big Three" awarded to Poland large areas of eastern Germany which the Poles themselves regarded simply as a \restitution to the rightful owners. But Potsdam spoke only of what it called "the provisional administration by the Polish government," pending the ultimate peace settlement.... This was accomplished when the Warsaw treaty, initiated by West German Chancellor Willy Brandt recognizing the Oder-Neisse demarcation line as official, finally was ratified by the Bundestag.[47]

Now the Vatican could rightly act hoping to improve the situation of Polish Catholicism. The Polish Bishops could not be accused any more of being anti-patriotic and agents of a foreign state (the Vatican).

However the recognition of the Oder-Neisse border by the Vatican did not bring peace to Polish Catholics. The Communist government attacked the Church in two new ways. First, it declared politics strictly off-limits to the Church, and at the same time defined politics so broadly and all-inclusively that nothing was left for religious life and youth education.[48] With the exception of the magazine *Tygodnik Powszechny* and the diocesan bulletins, there is no access by Catholics (save those openly favorable to "socialism") to the mass media. There are no widespread Catholic cultural, social or relief organizations and no Catholic activities except pastoral care. An exception is made for so-called Catholic organizations fostered by the regime but disavowed by the bishops. The second way was to limit the number of churches on the principle that people without churches become people without religion.[49]

While the Vatican resumed talks on détente with the Polish government, the bishops continued their fight. On November 1973 Polish minister of Foreign Affairs Olszowski was received at the Vatican. On December 16 Father Piotr Zabielski was arrested for having celebrated Mass in his own home and sent to a psychiatric hospital. At the beginning of February 1974 Archbishop Casaroli met in Warsaw with Poland's President Henryk Jablonski and again with Foreign Minister Stefan Olszowski. A joint communiqué described the talks as "open and cordial" and declared that the two parties discussed general problems of world peace and had a useful exchange of their respective points of view on the Conference for European Security and Cooperation. "The Polish government," the communiqué stated, "expressed to the Holy See its esteem for its efforts and proofs of goodwill, seeking to consolidate the peaceful coexistence of peoples and justice in international relations."[50]

Meanwhile the Polish bishops took the opportunity to remind Rome that administrative decisions "cannot by themselves lead to normalization" of relations between State and Church in Poland, repeatedly warned the Vatican to "consult local church leaders at every step of negotiations with the Warsaw government" and strongly deplored Fr. Zabielski's arrest as "an abuse of power, a dangerous action which contradicts the rights of civil liberties."[51]

Until then the Polish Catholic Church, under the guidance of Cardinal Wyszyński managed remarkably well without official Vatican representation in Warsaw.

> Catechetical instruction of children and youth, which, since 1960, has been conducted outside of schools, often under difficult material and moral circumstances, [shows that] the percentage of participants is quite strong (70%-75%) with the highest proportion (95%) before the First Communion and the lowest among high-school seniors (45%-50%). ... After tremendous war losses (close to 30%), the size of the clergy now reaches a new height of almost 18,000, thus restoring pre-war proportions of one priest for every 2,300 of the faithful. The number of new ordinations is satisfactory (30 for each 100,000 Catholics), and the number of vocations is even better than before the Communist takeover (one for every 9,400 of the faithful in 1962 as compared to one for every 10,828 in 1939). While in 1937, diocesan seminaries had an enrollment of 2,078 clerics, in 1967 there were about 4,000 seminarians. The work of diocesan priests is assisted by monks and nuns, who not only greatly enlarged their numbers after World War II (from about 22,000 to 36,500 in 1960), but also show remarkable vitality in organizational development (there were 2,022 monasteries and convents in 1937; 2,512 in 1950, and 2,977 in 1958), and in pastoral work. ... The whole of Church activities is directed by an episcopate, doubly numerous in comparison to its pre-war size ...[52]

It is thus understandable why the Polish clergy fears that a direct Rome-Warsaw accord, instead of improving the situation, could make it worse.

On July 6, 1974, the Vatican and Poland agreed to establish "permanent working contacts," a further step toward formal diplomatic ties.[53] But months passed and nothing happened. On the following October, at the World Synod of Bishops in Rome, something very unusual took place. Cardinal Wyszyński's speech remained secret and was not delivered to the press even in summary. The Information Committee of the Synod instead published the following short declaration: "After a brief announcement from the Secretary General, Cardinal Stefan Wyszyński, Archbishop of Gniezno and Warsaw, took the floor. At the express request of the presiding cardinals, Cardinal Wyszyński addressed the Holy Father and the whole Assembly and completed the reports presented at the beginning of the work by explaining the situation of the so-called Second World, compared with the situation of the First and Third Worlds with regard to the conditions of evangelization."[54]

Nevertheless a few days later Cardinal Wyszyński again managed to take the floor and *L'Osservatore Romano* published this brief summary of his speech:

> The Archbishop of Gniezno and Warsaw notes that among the forms of atheistic propaganda should be mentioned the monopoly that some governments have on the instruments of social communication; the bishops ought to be vigilant. It is also necessary and dutiful to speak and defend the exercise of the rights of the human person, indispensable for the normal progress of evangelization. It must be repeated that it is not the right of the State to take away faith from citizens, employing for this end the means at its disposal for the common good; it cannot use the public money of all citizens, even believers, for atheistic propaganda; it cannot resort to violence and coercion to instill mistrust toward the Church. The Synod has the duty to undertake the defense of oppressed and persecuted men; many Christian communities living in atheistic countries are waiting for this.[55]

Soviet dissenters hold Cardinal Wyszyński in high esteem. Alexander Solzhenitsyn, in his letter to Patriarch Pimen, pointed out the "independence" and strength of the Polish Church.[56] There is no doubt that at the Vatican the Cardinal is considered both the stronghold of the faith and the most troublesome impediment to détente and "normalization" of relations with the state. The delay in the establishment of full diplomatic representations between Rome and Warsaw is due to the Cardinal's intransigence. After further talks in November 1974 between Archbishop Casaroli and Poland's Undersecretary of State, Józef Czyrek, an agreement seemed to be close. But on December 1, in a statement read in churches throughout Warsaw, the Cardinal blasted the government for demolishing a church near the Soviet Embassy. He called the act "unprecedented since the war... I am asking you for expiation prayers... May God enlighten the minds of those who curtail the rights of believers who go to church for religious reasons."[57]

Hungary. The principle of the Vatican's Ostpolitik that it is better for the Church to exist under constraint than in the catacombs was tried unsuccessfully several times in Hungary after the 1956 revolution. At the request of the government, on August 29, 1957, the bishops declared that "mutual trust, the prerequisite for peaceful cooperation between Church and State, has been restored in recent months" and deplored a report of the UN on Hungarian affairs as one-sided and "calculated to increase international tension and imperil the true interests of our country." In return for this "loyal" attitude the bishops expected to "preserve imperiled religious instruction in the schools and avert the even greater peril that would result if the peace priests returned to their posts."[58] But the declaration did not save religious instruction and did not prevent the appointment of "democratic priests" to directive positions in the Church.

In 1964 Archbishop Casaroli worked out a "partial agreement" with the Hungarian regime. But again the bishops appointed by the Vatican were hedged in between Vicar Generals and Chancellors put there by the Communist party. The Vatican diplomat, writes Cardinal Mindszenty, "scarcely heard the demands of Hungarian Catholicism, and it was for that reason that diplomatic agencies of the Vatican entered into negotiations without a precise knowledge of the situation—negotiations that could bring only advantages to the Communists and grave disadvantages to Hungarian Catholicism."[59]

Finally the Vatican itself discovered where the obstacle was located. It was in the American embassy in Budapest. It was Cardinal Mindszenty who had taken refuge there in 1956 and had not spoken a single word since that time. Peace and détente demanded the removal of that obstacle. In June 1971, two monsignors from Rome visited him and informed him of the wish of the Holy Father that he leave the country. A tentative agreement was drafted, but the Cardinal refused to sign it. The departure for Rome was finally fixed for September 29, 1971. The Pope received him with great honor and assured him: "You are and remain Archbishop of Esztergom and primate of Hungary. Continue working, and if you have difficulties, always turn trustfully to us."

After settling in Vienna, the Cardinal asked the Holy See to make it possible for him to care for Hungarian Catholics in foreign countries and to appoint suffragan bishops for them. His requests were not granted. Lacking a suffragan bishop, he set out in person to conduct pastoral tours of Hungarians in exile. One of his speeches was censored by the nuncio's office in Lisbon when it was already in the printshop. When he was informed by the papal nuncio in Vienna that the Holy See in the summer of 1971 had given the Hungarian government a pledge that while he was abroad he would not do or say anything that would possibly displease that government, he replied that in the negotiations conducted ... between the Holy Father's personal emissary and himself there had been no mention of any such pledge. "Had I known about any guarantee of this sort, I would have been so shocked that I would have asked the Holy Father to rescind all the arrangements that had been made in conjunction with my departure from Hungary.... I asked the nuncio to inform the appropriate Vatican authorities that a sinister silence already prevailed within Hungary and that I shrank from the thought of having to keep silent in the free world as well."[60]

Under the "bombardment of the Budapest regime, which demanded the fulfillment of the Vatican guarantee, the Pope could no longer resist," writes the Cardinal. Asked to resign his archiepiscopal office, Mindszenty again refused. When on February 5, 1974, the announcement of his removal from the See of Esztergom was published his office declared:

A number of news agencies have transmitted the Vatican decision in such a way as to imply that József Cardinal Mindszenty has voluntarily retired. The news agencies furthermore stressed that before the papal decision there was an intense exchange of letters between the Vatican and the cardinal-archbishop, who is living in Vienna. Some persons have therefore drawn the conclusion that an agreement concerning this decision had been reached between the Vatican and the Hungarian primate. In the interests of truth Cardinal Mindszenty has authorized his office to issue the following statement:

Cardinal Mindszenty has not abdicated his office as archbishop nor his dignity as primate of Hungary. The decision was taken by the Holy See alone.

After long and conscientious consideration the cardinal justified his attitude on this question as follows:

1. Hungary and the Catholic Church of Hungary are not free.

2. The leadership of the Hungarian dioceses is in the hands of a church administration built and controlled by the communist regime.

3. Not a single archbishop or apostolic administrator is in a position to alter the composition or the functioning of the above-mentioned church administration.

4. The regime decides who is to occupy ecclesiastical positions and for how long. Furthermore, the regime also decides what persons the bishops will be allowed to consecrate as priests.

5. The freedom of conscience and religion guaranteed by the Constitution is in practice suppressed. "Optional" religious instruction has been banned from the schools in the cities and the larger towns. At present the struggle for optional religious instruction in the schools is continuing in the smaller communities. Young people, contrary to the will of their parents, are being educated exclusively in an atheistic spirit. Believers are discriminated against in many areas of daily life. Religious teachers have recently been confronted with the alternative of choosing between their professions and their religion.

6. The appointment of bishops or apostolic administrators without the elimination of the above-mentioned abuses does not solve the problems of the Hungarian Church. The installation of "peace priests" in important ecclesiastical posts has shaken the confidence of loyal priests and lay Catholics in the highest administration of the Church. In these grave circumstances Cardinal Mindszenty cannot abdicate.[61]

At the beginning of 1975 Pope Paul VI named five new bishops in Hungary and transferred four others in a major move that placed residential bishops in all but two of the eleven Hungarian dioceses. The two sees remaining under Apostolic administrators are the primatial Archdiocese of

Esztergom and the Gyor diocese. A Vatican official declared that "the former dearth of residential bishops had caused tension and uneasiness among both the hierarchy and the body of priests in Hungary. Now that is all over. A new sense of tranquillity will be attained."[62] But he admitted that there are still important problems to be discussed with the Budapest government, such as religious instruction, the Catholic press, Catholic associations, seminaries, regular contacts between the Hungarian Church and Rome including major seminary study at pontifical universities, the religious orders, and the freedom of diocesan bishops to make parish and other priestly nominations without prior approval by the state.

The filling of empty episcopal sees without redressing the Hungarian religious situation can hardly be interpreted as an "important consolidation of the Church's position in Hungary."[63] This is the reason why the old and ailing Cardinal Mindszenty did not consider going into retirement. During 1974 he spent two months in the US and published his memoirs. He agreed to join in the efforts of Soviet dissenters who, together with other intellectuals from Eastern Europe, started the publication of a new magazine, *Kontinent.* Its editorial board, which at first included V. Maximov (chief editor), A. Galich, M. Djilas, E. Ionesco, A. Sakharov, and A. Sinyavsky, declared the following aims or priorities: (1) unconditional religious idealism, (2) unconditional antitotalitarianism, (3) unconditional democratism, (4) unconditional non-partisanship, "that is, categorical refusal to express the interests of any of the existing political groups."[64] Significantly on the cover of its first issue *Kontinent* printed three pictures with three quotations. The pictures are those of Alexander Solzhenitsyn, Milovan Djilas, and Cardinal Mindszenty. The following quotation accompanies the Cardinal's picture: "The Church does not ask to be defended by secular powers because its refuge is under the wings of God. The picture over the altar in the church of Papa represents the stoning of St. Stephen. I pointed to this picture and appealed to the Hungarians not to stone each other, but imitate the virtue of this protomartyr of the Holy Church."

Cardinal Mindszenty died in Vienna on May 6, 1975. In his eulogy, Fr. Werenfried van Straaten, the founder of an organization to aid priests in Eastern Europe and a friend of the Cardinal, accused both the Communists and the Vatican of subjecting the former primate of Hungary to needless suffering.

Justice or Peace: The Unsolved Dilemma

The overwhelming majority of the dissenters are not against "peace" and "reconciliation," the key themes in Pope Paul's proclamation of the 1975 Holy Year. But they cannot agree with the Vatican's policy of sacrificing their religious and human rights for the sake of peace. They believe that peace will be achieved better through non-violent resistance and, if necessary, through martyrdom.

In his Lenten Letter to Patriarch Pimen, Alexander Solzhenitsyn wrote:

> Let us not deceive the people, and more importantly, let us not deceive ourselves while praying, by thinking that external fetters are stronger than our spirit. It was not any easier at the time of Christianity's birth, but it has survived and flourished and has shown us the way: that of sacrifice. He who is deprived of all material power is always victorious through sacrifice. The same martyrdom worthy of the first centuries was accepted by our priests and fellow believers in our living memory. But at that time they were thrown to the lions, today one can only lose well-being.[65]

The Evangelical Baptists of the Soviet Union are arrested, imprisoned and separated from their families because, as they write in their letters and underground publications, they believe in the word of God: "Happy those who are persecuted in the cause of right: theirs is the kingdom of heaven" (Mt. 5: 10). "You happily accepted being stripped of your belongings, knowing that you owned something that was better and lasting" (Heb. 10: 34). "Everyone who has left houses, brothers, sisters, father, mother, children or land for the sake of my name will be repaid a hundred times over and also inherit eternal life" (Mt. 19: 29). "It would be a sign from God that he has given you the privilege not only of believing in Christ, but of suffering for him as well" (Phil. 1: 29).[66]

Three Lithuanian Catholic priests, Fathers A. Seskevicius, J. Zdebskis and P. Bubnys, were tried and condemned for having imparted religious instruction to children. In their answers to the judges and their "loyal" bishops they quoted the following sentences from the Holy Scriptures: "You must judge whether in God's eyes it is right to listen to you and not to God. We cannot promise to stop proclaiming what we have seen and heard" (Acts 4: 19—20). "Go, make disciples of all the nations" (I Cor. 9: 16). "Give thanks to God for the things which now make them denounce you as criminals" (I Pet. 2: 12).[67]

At the Vatican the "crimes" of the dissenters against domestic peace and international détente are not unknown. They were again reviewed and answered by Archbishop Casaroli in two important speeches on October 31 and December 10, 1974.[68] Going right to the heart of the matter, the Papal Foreign Minister first recalled the good intentions of the Holy See and secondly explained why, by giving priority to peace, religious and human rights are not left behind in second or third place:

> The problem of the relationship between the aspiration to peace and the demand of justice is certainly among the most difficult and tormenting, especially for those who—as the Pope—have the very special duty to defend the victims of every oppression, and

particularly when this [oppression] touches the Church, the religious life of the peoples, the rights of conscience. It can be serenely affirmed that never did the desire to act for peace make the Pope forgetful of this duty of his, nor did the attention to problems of peace ever diminish in him the consideration of doctrinal questions regarding the internal life of the Church.

In case of conflict between the demands of justice and peace do the Church and the Pope give preference to one of the two? Even though concrete situations might sometimes put the problem in a form which imposes difficult practical solutions, we should say that "in principle" the Church does not see an objective opposition between the two terms of the dilemma, but rather that they integrate and condition each other. Not only because of their ethical character, nor because a "peace" without justice (which hardly would deserve this name) would be unstable and unsafe, bearing in itself the germs of its own destruction, but also because the implementation of a true and complete justice among nations becomes really possible only in a situation of peace.... In this prospective the Holy See gave and gives its support to those forms of international association which, on a world or regional scale, might substitute armed confrontation with that of law.[69]

In this rather evasive explanation one thing is clear: the Church's concept of peace is such that it implies justice, religious and human rights. By collaborating for peace, even with Communist states, ultimately the Church collaborates in order to establish justice and the betterment of religious and human conditions in those nations. Now, however, the question to be asked is whether or not the Communist concepts of peace and justice coincide with those of the Church. Furthermore, the solution of the dilemma depends on the clarification of these abstract terms and also on the concrete attitudes taken both by the Church and by the Communist states.

3

The Aims of Détente

The peaceful coexistence of states with differing social systems was always considered by Lenin and the Soviet Communists as a temporary measure determined by the need to adapt to the international situation, on the understanding that it could, at any time, be replaced by military confrontation to extend the revolution. Cooperation with bourgeois states, therefore, is possible only to a limited extent. First of all, it should not interfere in the international political and ideological affairs of socialist countries. Secondly, it can be adopted only for the purposes of strengthening the international position of socialism, expanding the social base of the world revolutionary process, and enhancing the impact of Communism on history. Cooperation is a form of class struggle on the international scene that provides favorable conditions for resolving the key class objectives of Communism: higher productivity and the ever fuller satisfaction of the growing requirements of all the people at home and the defeat of the idea of a "Communist menace" abroad.

The threat of a universal thermonuclear war forced the Soviets to see détente, or peaceful coexistence, as an agreement by the nuclear powers to follow certain rules of the game in order to avert mutual destruction. In this view the peoples of the Communist countries are assured of their status quo, while the people dominated by "imperialism" are helped toward their "liberation." These aims are publicly acknowledged by the Communists:

International détente—the initial stage of which we are now witnessing—does not moderate the class confrontation within a capitalist country or on the world scene generally. But it does offer new opportunities for the anti-imperialist struggle, and this calls for further theoretical elaboration of its strategy and tactics. In gauging the international situation, the fraternal parties, as evidenced by their policy statements, congress and CC plenum resolutions, and by the communiques of international meetings and conferences, have come to the conclusion that a point has been reached when it is becoming possible, by countering the serious resistance of the imperialist and reactionary elements and uniting all the peace-loving forces of mankind, to consolidate détente, make it a stable and irreversible phenomenon and, building on what has been achieved, substantially activize the people's struggle against their main foe—imperialism....

Peaceful coexistence does not extend to the sphere of ideology, which includes policy principles. The history of class struggle confirms that ideological compromise means, in practice, political surrender to the enemy. Yielding on ideological principles expressive of class goals and interests inevitably means, in effect, changing ideology, i.e., accepting another class position.[1]

Peace: "A New Democratic and Human Approach?"

Only recently the Western countries took the idea of coexistence or détente seriously. The first move in this direction was made by Molotov in February 1954 with the proposal of a "general treaty for collective European security." But the proposal was disregarded, because only a few months before, Krushchev had suppressed the uprising in East Berlin (June-July, 1953). Then came the brutal repression of the Hungarian revolution (1956), the end of the "spirit of Camp David" (1960), the Cuban confrontation (1962) and the rift with China (1964), which was preceded by a long dispute on how to interpret Lenin's theories on war and coexistence. Krushchev conceded that in the atomic era it is impossible to repeat "mechanically" what Lenin said decades before on imperialism and the inevitability of the war,[2] but he strongly reaffirmed that "there can be no such thing as ideological peaceful coexistence."[3] Also the Chinese still did not trust détente. Addressing the National People's Congress of China on January 13, 1975, premier Chou En-Lai repeated that a US-Soviet Union war is inevitable:

> The present international situation is still characterized by great disorder under heaven, a disorder which is growing greater and greater. The capitalist world is facing the most serious economic crisis since the war, and all the basic contradictions in the world are sharpening.
>
> On the one hand the trend of revolution by the people of the world is actively developing; countries want independence, nations want liberation and the people want revolution—this has become an irresistible historical current. On the other hand the contention for world hegemony between the two superpowers, the United States and the Soviet Union, is becoming more and more intense. Their contention has extended to every corner of the world, the focus of their contention being Europe.
>
> Soviet social-imperialism "makes a feint to the East while attacking the West." The two superpowers are the biggest international oppressors and exploiters today, and they are the source of a new world war. Their fierce contention is bound to lead to world war some day. The people of all countries must be prepared. Détente and peace are being talked about everywhere in the world; precisely this shows that there is no détente, let alone lasting peace, in this world.
>
> At present factors for both revolution and war are increasing. Whether war gives rise to revolution or revolution prevents war, in either case the international situation will develop in a direction favorable to the people and the future of the world will be bright.
>
> The third world is the main force in combating colonialism, imperialism and hegemonism. China is a developing socialist country belonging to the third world. We should enhance our unity with the countries and people of Asia, Africa and Latin America and resolutely support them in their struggle to win or safeguard national independence, defend their state sovereignty, protect their national resources and develop their national economy.[4]

Peaceful coexistence and European security were often examined by Pius XII in his speeches. To the ideal of merely co-existing he preferred that of "living together." For him peaceful coexistence was not a means to reach true peace. On the contrary it represented an "error... which again joins together the two parts in which today's world is divided."[5] He clearly pointed out that "the close union of all peoples who are masters of their own destiny and who are united by sentiments of reciprocal trust and mutual assistance is the sole means for the defense of peace and the best guarantee of its re-establishment." But alarmed by the even deeper "cleavage which divides the international community into opposite camps," Pius XII exclaimed: "Away with the barriers! Break down the barbed-wire fences! Let each people be free to know the life of other peoples; let the segregation of some countries from the rest of the civilized world, so dangerous to the cause of peace, be abolished!...."[6]

Anticipating what Soviet dissenters are saying today, the Pope asked that "solid guarantees," based primarily on "values of spiritual order," should be sought by those who want peace and cooperation in Europe:

> Our grave apprehensions with regard to Europe are motivated by the incessant disillusionment which for many years has wrecked the sincere desire for peace... largely because of a materialistic approach to the problem of peace. We are thinking especially of those who consider the question of peace as being of a technical nature and view the life of individuals and nations under a combined technical-economic aspect... They believe that the secret of the solution would be to give material prosperity to all peoples through constant increase in the productivity of labor and the standard of living, just as, a hundred years ago, another similar formula won the absolute confidence of statesmen: Free trade means eternal peace. But no sort of materialism has ever been a satisfactory means for the establishment of peace, since peace is above all an attitude of the spirit and only on a secondary level is it a harmonious equilibrium of external forces....[7]

The campaign for a European security conference was resumed by the Warsaw Pact countries in a meeting held in Bucharest in July 1966 and, in the following year, by the representatives of 24 European Communist parties gathered at Karlovy Vary in Czechoslovakia. The August 1968 occupation of this country temporarily halted Moscow's plans, but the campaign was soon resumed. On March 17, 1969, a meeting in Budapest of the Warsaw Pact states published an appeal to all the European countries calling for a security conference, and in May the Finnish government, very likely at Moscow's suggestion, sent a memorandum to the governments of all European countries proposing Helsinki as the venue. The World Communist summit meeting in June 1969 in Moscow also declared its support for a European security conference, as did a meeting of Warsaw Pact foreign ministers in Prague in October 1969 and a Moscow gathering of leading representatives of socialist countries on December 3 and 4, 1969.

In all these meetings the Communists emphasized that their insistent call for détente represented not only an alternative to global thermonuclear disaster, but a new democratic and human approach in international relations which creates the political basis for the development of mutually advantageous economic, scientific, technical and cultural contacts. The desire to break the economic and scientific isolation played a big role in Soviet rapprochement with the United States and West Europe. In 1969 *Pravda* wrote: "Along with the path of development of all-European economic cooperation there are still many artificial barriers set up by awkward cold-war recidivists. This applies particularly to the continuing existence of export-import restrictions for NATO countries and the discriminating policy of the Common Market."[8] Because of intensifying domestic economic difficulties the Soviets received the U.S. President notwithstanding the bombing of Haiphong and insisted upon the presence of the U. S. at the European conference, whereas before they had always opposed it. In its agreement with the American leaders in Moscow (1972) and in Washington (1973) the Soviet Union accepted a mutual quantitative restraint on further buildup in nuclear weaponry, obtained credits at low interest rates with the promise of most-favored-nation treatment, and pledged mutual cooperation in scientific endeavors.

For different reasons many doubted the wisdom of such agreements which, as Dr. Kissinger repeatedly stressed, were aimed at overcoming the narrow limits of the old Soviet conception of coexistence. As Professor Brzezinski wrote, "more disturbing has been the deterioration in the administration's performance on the two critically important fronts of foreign policy, namely, in its handling of the emerging U.S.-Soviet détente and its conduct of relations with America's closest and most important friends, Western Europe and Japan." After having noted the weakness of the negotiations to counterbalance the Soviet Union's aggressive modernization program, Brzezinski wrote:

> While the Soviet side has continued to proclaim domestically that the ideological conflict must go unabated and that therefore severe restrictions of basic human rights are justified, the US side has been relatively inactive at the West-East European Conference now in progress, where the West Europeans have been assertively demanding freer East-West contacts, and it has been quietly reducing the effectiveness of both Radio Free Europe and Radio Liberty, which for less than 15 cents per head per year have become the most significant US lever for freer communications—and thus for social change—in Eastern Europe and the Soviet Union.... The modernization and rationalization of the Soviet economy will be undertaken with de facto US aid, thus reducing domestic pressures in the Soviet Union for needed reforms, which reforms eventually would have also had a political impact. Thus we are also buttressing the Soviet political system.[9]

According to Soviet dissenters, Moscow's eagerness for détente, far from reflecting a positive trend of going beyond peaceful coexistence toward a democratic and more human structure of society, shows exactly the opposite. It is aimed at the resolution to obtain credibility for a regime "antidemocratic in its essence" (Sakharov), strengthen the hegemony of the "obsolete, decrepit, dead-ended, angry" Communist ideology over the peoples of the USSR and Eastern Europe (Solzhenitsyn), export revolution (Sakharov) and, not least, crackdown on dissent at home.[10]

In June 1968 Andrei Sakharov wrote his famous essay on "Progress, Coexistence and Intellectual Freedom," in which he expressed his view that peaceful coexistence will lead to a "convergence" of socialist and capitalist systems if from both sides police dictatorships and extremisms were abandoned in favor of a real freedom. "Intellectual freedom is essential to human society," wrote the Soviet scientist: "freedom to obtain and distribute information, freedom for open minded and unfearing debate and freedom from pressure by officialdom and prejudices." Among the proposals addressed to the leadership of his country, he mentioned (1) the drafting of a law on press and information "adopted with the aim not only of ending irresponsible and irrational censorship, but of encouraging self-study in our society, fearless discussion, and the search for truth," (2) the abrogation of "all unconstitutional laws and decrees violating human rights," (3) amnesty for political prisoners and revision of their political trials, (4) the necessity that "the exposure of Stalin be carried through to the end, to the complete truth, and not just to the carefully weighed half-truth dictated by caste considerations. The influence of neo-Stalinists in our political life must be restricted in every way."[11]

The invasion of Czechoslovakia on August 21, 1968 was the immediate answer of the Soviet leadership to Sakharov's proposals which, of course, were never printed in the USSR. Those who spoke and demonstrated against the brutal repression of Czechoslovakia's "socialism with a human face" were arrested and condemned.

On July 22, 1968 Anatoly Marchenko, a worker who had already spent six years in a labor camp (an experience that he described in *My Testimony*, a book published in the West), sent a letter to Czechoslovakian, French, Italian and British Communist newspapers disapproving the decision of five Warsaw Pact countries to use *all means available* to combat "antisocialist" forces in Czechoslovakia. "It is too bad," wrote Marchenko, "that the fraternal parties were not more specific, that they did not say concretely what kind of means: Kolyma? Norilsk? Khunviiny? 'Open' courts? Political concentration camps and prisons? Or merely conventional censorship and non-judicial reprisals such as discharging people from their jobs?"[12] It is interesting that Marchenko did not think of the worst that was going to happen: the shedding of the blood and the military occupation of the country. On July 29 Marchenko was arrested and sent to a camp for one year. While serving this term, Marchenko was sentenced to two more years for "slandering" the Soviet Union in his book, which he begins with these words:

Today's Soviet camps for political prisoners are just as horrific as in Stalin's time. A few things are better, a few things are worse. But everybody must know about it.

I would like my testimony on Soviet camps and prisons for political prisoners to come to the attention of humanists and progressive people in other countries, those who stick up for political prisoners in Greece and Portugal and Spain and South Africa.

Let them ask their Soviet colleagues in the struggle against humanity: And what have you done in your country to prevent political prisoners from being re-educated by starvation?[13]

Marchenko was released on July 28, 1971, one day short of the expiration of his term. In September 1973, during the Geneva session of the European Conference, he again appealed to the West to insist on a genuinely free movement of people and ideas.[14]

After the invasion of Czechoslovakia the "convergence theory," which arose during the 1950s as a forerunner of détente, was finally rejected. The theory of convergence, wrote *Pravda,* "serves as a kind of pseudo-scientific basis for making tactical advances towards individual socialist countries in order to 'build bridges' and 'dig trenches' and, with the aid of a 'silent counterrevolution', to wrench these countries from the socialist common-wealth, restore capitalism in them and undermine the power of world socialism."[15] These words, written by such prominent figures as Rumyantsev and Mitin, were a warning to those Soviet scientists who were giving too much attention to this foreign bourgeois theory. A few days earlier, a leading Soviet physicist, Peter Kapitsa, had visited the United States. In a lecture to the National Academy of Science in Washington on October 8, 1969, he expressed his belief in the concept of convergence and also praised Sakharov's essay. His speech was printed the following day in the *New York Times*. The newspaper reported also that Kapitsa had stated that only through convergence along the lines advocated by Sakharov "can the two great powers avoid a fatal clash."[16]

Soviet critics of the theory of convergence believe that mankind is predetermined to turn to Communism and to acknowledge that theory would be an admission that the Soviet system is imperfect, that modern capitalism is capable of reforming itself and not doomed to extinction as Marxism-Leninism teaches. They also point to an unbridgeable gulf between private property in the West and socialized or state property in the USSR, and claim that there is increasing exploitation of the workers in the West and a total absence of this exploitation in the USSR. Leaving apart all these useless disputes, Sakharov concentrated in the struggle for the rights of his countrymen as a prerequisite for world peace and détente. On November 4, 1970, together with two other physicists, Andrei Tverdokhlebov and Valery Chalidze, he established a non-political, non-governmental Human Rights Committee. Two more scientists were elected experts of the Committee, Alexander Volpin, son of the poet Sergei Esenin, and Boris Zuckermann. Alexander Galich, playwright and poet, and Alexander Solzhenitsyn were elected honorary corresponding members. A fourth member Igor Shafarevich, a specialist in algebra, was elected on

May 20, 1971. The Moscow Human Rights Committee formally affiliated with the International League for the Rights of Man on June 23, 1971. The League announced that it considered this affiliation as "an important event which could improve not only East-West relations and cultural exchange but also prospects for peace and security in the world."[17]

On March 5, 1971, Sakharov's Committee sent to Brezhnev, the Secretary of the CPSU, a memorandum concerning some urgent problems: political persecution; publicity, and the freedom to exchange information, freedom of beliefs; nationalities problems, the freedom to leave the country, international problems. The memorandum received no answer. In June Sakharov wrote a "postscript to the memorandum" and published the two documents. Continuing in his spiritual growth, Sakharov stated that

> the only true guarantee for the safeguarding of human values in the chaos of uncontrollable changes and tragic upheavals is man's freedom of conscience and his moral yearning for the good.... The country's spiritual regeneration demands the elimination of those conditions that drive people into becoming hypocritical and opportunistic, and that lead to feelings of impotence, discontent, and disillusionment. Everybody must be assured, in deed and not just in word, of equal opportunities... Full intellectual freedom must be assured and all forms of persecution for beliefs must cease.... The most essential condition for the cure of our society is the abandonment of political persecution, in its juridical and psychiatric form, of which our bureaucratic and bigoted system is capable, with its totalitarian interference by the state in the lives of citizens, such as dismissal from work, expulsion from college, refusal of residence permits, limitation of promotion at work...[18]

The above demands were also formulated by other dissident groups of the USSR. In 1969, a "Program for the Democratic Movement of the Soviet Union" was put out by "democrats of Russia, Ukraine and the Baltic countries." The authors of this Program as well as the members of Sakharov's Human Rights Committee call for a non-violent struggle for a better future for the USSR and the whole world: "We, the democrats of the country, announce that we are filled with the firm resolution to struggle unswervingly for the proclaimed values: the freedom and welfare of the people, regardless of any difficulties and sacrifices! We, the democrats of the country, appeal to all honest, thinking and courageous citizens of our society... to take an active part in the peaceful, non-violent struggle for lofty democratic ideals!"[19]

The program stressed two means for overcoming the limits of détente and achieving domestic and international peace: self-determination for the nationalities under the United Nation's control and an end to the ideological and political struggle against capitalism. "The Soviet Union (which) is the greatest colonialist power detaining the greatest number of people around the Russian national nucleus... must give political independence and cultural autonomy to all the peoples who want this or assure a real brotherly union and fatherly protection to those who do not reject it.

This will be an authentic act of humanism and democracy, corresponding to the spirit of the epoch in which we live." Among the peoples striving to obtain "cultural and economic self-determination" the Program mentions Ukrainians, Jews, Tatars, and the peoples of the Baltic nations, the Caucasus, and Middle Asia.[20]

As for capitalism, the Program listed eight of its most important defects, but maintained that the Soviet Union lags behind all advanced countries in production and per capita consumption, and occupies "one of the last positions" as far as human liberties are concerned. "We consider that capitalism embodies positive social values and is constantly cultivating them...and that the struggle against capitalism in any of its forms is criminal and purposeless."[21] Logically then the Program asked for the "abandonment of the doctrine of militant communism" and for "reconciliation and rapprochement with the capitalist countries (convergence) aiming at friendship and collaboration with them, first of all with the USA and Western Europe."[22]

In several interviews to foreign correspondents Sakharov further explained his thought. To those who favor socialism he said that he was now convinced that Communist ideology is "antidemocratic in its essence" and that the Soviet regime perpetuates criminality and privilege:

> The Soviet Union has the same sort of problems as the capitalist world: criminality and estrangement. The difference is that our society is an extreme case, with maximum unfreedom, maximum ideological rigidity, and —and this is most typical—a society with maximum pretensions about being best, although it certainly isn't that.... Realistically speaking, the Russian state represents an unprecedented concentration of economic and political power.... It is state capitalism, in which the state completely dominates economic life.... The visa system secures divisions within our society. Territorial differences and injustices exist between different parts of the country.

The single-party system gives advantages to party functionaries at the expense of the working class; "they have huge material privileges ... People from the West often say: your society has many drawbacks, but at least you have free hospital care. But it is obvious that it is not any more free than in Western countries and is often more expensive." The antidemocratic nature of Soviet Marxism has had as a consequence "isolation from the outside world, the absence of the right to travel beyond the borders and return."[23]

Commenting on détente as a "rapprochement without democratization, in which the West in effect accepts the Soviet Union's rules of the game," Sakharov declared that "such a rapprochement would be dangerous...and would mean simply capitulating in the face of...Soviet power," with the result that "the world would become more helpless before this uncontrollable bureaucratic machine." It would mean "cultivating a country where anything that happens may be shielded from outside eyes—

a masked country that hides its real face.... No one should ever be expected to live next to such a neighbor, especially one who is armed to the teeth."[24]

Sakharov's declarations prompted a storm of "spontaneous" protests in the USSR and also among Western Communists and advocates of economic cooperation between East and West at any cost, who pictured him as a promoter of wars and "ultimatums between states."[25] It was not difficult for Sakharov to remind them of his long-held views in favor of East-West conciliation and his efforts to stop the testing of the hydrogen bomb, which he had developed for the Soviet Union. A confirmation of this ignored aspect of Sakharov's biography came in 1974 with the publication of Khrushchev's memoirs. Here is how the former dictator recalls the facts:

> I would like to compare Kapitsa with another of our most brilliant nuclear physicists, Academician [Andrei] Sakharov. He, too, had misgivings about military research. I used to meet frequently with Sakharov, and I considered him an extremely talented man.
>
> Literally a day or two before the resumption of our [hydrogen] bomb testing program, I got a telephone call from Sakharov. He addressed me in my capacity as the Chairman of the Council of Ministers and said he had a petition to present. The petition called on our government to cancel the scheduled explosion and not to engage in any further testing, at least not of the hydrogen bomb. "As a scientist and as the designer of the hydrogen bomb, I know what harm these explosions can bring down on the head of mankind."
>
> "Comrade Sakharov," I said, "you must understand my position. My responsibilities do not allow me to cancel the tests. Our party and government have already made abudantly clear that we would like nothing better than to suspend nuclear testing forever. Our leadership has already unilaterally discontinued nuclear testing and called on the United States and other countries to follow our example for the good of all mankind. The Americans wouldn't listen to our proposals. As a scientist, surely you know that they have gone right on conducting their tests. If we don't test our own bombs, how will we know whether they work or not?"
>
> He wasn't satisfied. He still insisted that we not resume our own testing.
>
> I wanted to be absolutely frank with him: "Comrade Sakharov, believe me, I deeply sympathize with your point of view. But as the man responsible for the security of our country, I have no right to do what you're asking. For me to cancel the tests would be a crime against our state. Can't you understand that?"
>
> My arguments didn't change his mind, and his didn't change mine; but that was to be expected. The scientist in him saw his patriotic duty and performed it well, while the pacifist in him made him hesitate. I have nothing against pacifists—or at least I won't have anything against them if and when we create conditions which make war impossible. But as long as we live in a world in which we have to keep both eyes open lest the imperialists gobble us up, then pacifism is a dangerous sentiment.
>
> This conflict between Sakharov and me left a lasting imprint on us both. I took it as evidence that he didn't fully understand what was in the best interests of the state, and therefore from that moment on I was somewhat on my guard with him. I hope that the time will come when Comrade Sakharov will see the correctness of my position—if not now, then some time in the future.[26]

More than ten years later, the successors to Khrushchev were repeating the same accusation against Sakharov: his pacifism was a "dangerous sentiment." While more and more Soviet intellectuals were jumping on the anti-Sakharov band-wagon, Alexander Solzhenitsyn and three prominent Soviet dissenters, academician Igor Shafarevich and the writers Galich and Maximov proposed that the 1973 Nobel Peace Prize be awarded to Andrei Sakharov. Two years later the Oslo Nobel Prize committee selected the Soviet nuclear physicist for the 1975 Peace Prize because he "has fought not only against the abuse of power and violations of human dignity in all its forms, but he has with equal vigor fought for the ideal of a state founded on a principle of justice for all."[27] It is important to stress that in its decision the Oslo committee ignored the ambiguities of the policy of détente followed by various powers at the Helsinki conference, including the Vatican, and agreed with the dissenters. In a philosophical treatise dealing with the basic issues of "peace and violence," Solzhenitsyn had already written that peace in the world is today threatened not so much by international conflict as by concealed and open acts of violence perpetrated by the state within its own national territory. It was in this context, he suggested, that Sakharov deserved the Nobel Peace Prize. Precisely because he was seeking to combat this international type of violence Solzhenitsyn commended him, describing him as an "indefatigable fighter who, at great sacrifice and often personal danger to himself, has been opposing continuing violence by the state against individuals and groups."[28] Igor Shafarevich declared that "the downtrodden and the humiliated are looking to Sakharov for hope and strength. Though not a dogmatic believer, he represents an example of truly Christian behavior on earth... He is an outstanding fighter for real democracy, for the rights and dignity of man, and for a genuine, not an illusory, peace."[29]

In a "Letter to the Leaders of the Soviet Union" A. Solzhenitsyn saw the salvation of the world from nuclear war, especially with China, in the abandonment of Communist ideology, freedom for the nationalities, retrenchment of Russians within their boundaries and development of the empty spaces of the North-East.[30] As a deeply religious person Solzhenitsyn, like Pius XII, sees errors in the East and in the West "which are both in a blind alley."[31] Therefore he does not trust "convergence" or the myth of continual industrial progress and giganticism.[32] As he later explained, peace can be achieved only through self-limitation.[33] But above all peace requires the end of religious persecution and the rejection of the "ideological lie." "This ideology, which has led to sharp conflicts in the international situation, ceased long ago to help us in our internal affairs." "What have you to fear?... Allow freedom in the arts, in literature," freedom of thought, freedom of religion, freedom of "parochial activity," of religious education and organization of the youth... "All this will yield a rich harvest, it will bear fruit for Russia. Such a free growth of thought will soon save you the trouble of belatedly translating every new idea from Western languages, as has happened throughout this half-century, as you know."

Commenting on this letter, Sakharov particularly objected to what he called:

> the impulse to fence our country off from the allegedly pernicious influence of the West, from trade and from what is termed "the exchange of people and ideas." The only reasonable form of isolation for us is to refrain from socialist messianism in other countries, to stop covert and overt support of sedition on other continents, to stop the export of deadly weapons . . . our country cannot exist in economic and scientific-technical isolation, without world trade, including trade in the country's natural resources, or divorced from the world's scientific-technical progress—a condition that holds not only danger but at the same time the only real chance of saving mankind.[34]

On several occasions Solzhenitsyn clarified his apparent discrepancies with Sakharov. His criticism of the West and his love for Russian traditions cannot be confused with isolationism or chauvinism. Unfortunately, the West, including the Christians and the Churches, does not have the moral strength and consistency necessary to assist the peoples of the USSR in reaching their goals. Speaking in Washington about the terrible price of détente, Solzhenitsyn said:

> Something which is almost incomprehensible to the human mind is the West's fantastic greed for profit and gain, which goes beyond all reason, all limitations, all conscience. I have to admit that Lenin foretold this whole process. Lenin, who spent most of his life in the West and knew it better than Russia, always said that the Western capitalists would do anything to supply the Soviet economy . . . Nikita Khruschev came here and said: "We're going to bury you." People didn't believe that—they took it as a joke. Now, of course, the Communists have become more clever in my country. They do not say, "We're going to bury you" any more. Now they say, "Détente." Nothing has changed in Communist ideology. The goals are the same as they were. . . . So what are we to conclude from that? Is détente needed or not? Not only is it needed, it is like air . . . we must have détente, but a true détente. I would say that there are very definite characteristic marks of what a genuine détente would be . . . That there be disarmament—not limited only to the goal of no more war, but also to no more violence. . . . It has to be based not on smiles, not on verbal concessions, but on a firm foundation. You know the passage from the Bible, "Not on sand, but on rock" . . . Not on "ideological war," but on real friendship. Not on "political calculations," but on "what is noble, what is honest and honorable, not only on what is useful. . . . On our small planet, there are no longer internal affairs. The Communist leaders say: "Don't interfere in our internal affairs. Let us strangle our citizens in quiet and peace." But I tell you: interfere more and more, interfere as much as you can. We beg you to come and interfere.[35]

One can say of Solzhenitsyn and Sakharov what the great Russian thinker and democrat Alexander Herzen said about the Westerners and Slavophiles: "We had the same love, but we did not love in the same

manner; we were like the two-headed eagle, or Janus, facing simultaneously in opposite directions, but beneath, in the body, the heart beats as one."[36]
Both Solzhenitsyn and Sakharov as well as the other dissenters are fighting for the same aims: the rejection of Stalinism and the end of any form of violence. In a new book, *My Country and the World,* Sakharov maintains views strikingly similar to those expressed by Solzhenitsyn in his Washington speech. In sending the typescript to the West, the Soviet physicist asked that excerpts be published on the eve of the Helsinki summit meeting. Like Solzhenitsyn, Sakharov calls for the United States and the West to be more resolute and consistent in dealing with the Soviet Union. Updating his 1968 manifesto, "Progress, Coexistence and Intellectual Freedom," in which he urged East-West convergence, he describes the earlier statement as a "dream," as "optimistic futurology," and adds: "today I feel called upon to lay chief emphasis on the dangers, illusions and dramas of the present, on all the things that stand between dream and reality." For Sakharov, too, the foremost threats are Soviet totalitarianism and the "amazing miscalculations and failures of Western foreign policy, which is yielding bit by bit without a struggle to its partner in détente."[37]

It is hard to believe that the Helsinki summit represents a new step toward a "democratic and humane" establishment of peace in Europe and in the world. The conference's recognition of the territorial and political "realities" of Europe and the approval of the principle of "non-intervention" in the internal affairs of states amounts, in Solzhenitsyn's words, to the "betrayal of Eastern Europe, to an acknowledgment of its eternal enslavement."[38]

Western politicians believe that the human rights section of the European declaration will put some pressure on Communist regimes to relax travel restrictions, give easier access to Western information and make room for maneuver between the Soviet and East European brands of Communism. They point out that the declaration not only states that "the participating states all regard each other's frontiers as inviolable . . . and will refrain now and in the future from assaulting these frontiers," but also that: "they consider that their frontiers can be changed, in accordance with the law, by peaceful means and by agreement."

However, far from renouncing the so-called "Brezhnev-doctrine," the General Secretary of the Soviet Communist Party at Helsinki made it clear that "no one should try to dictate to other peoples, on the basis of foreign policy considerations of one kind or another, the manner in which they ought to manage their internal affairs. It is only the people of each given state, and no one else, that has the sovereign right to resolve its internal affairs and establish its internal laws. A different approach is a flimsy and perilous ground for the cause of international cooperation."[39]

The respect of these "internal laws" provided by the Helsinki declaration and by other international documents nullifies the hopes of the oppressed and is a clear reflection of the current state of détente. By this "legal realism," as Solzhenitsyn calls it, the Western powers "push aside any moral evaluation of affairs." For them, "law is higher than morality." But, as Sakharov wrote in his message to the "Sakharov-hearings" organized in Denmark by Soviet exiles, guarantees of the rights of man in the USSR are for every person in the West "not only a matter of conscience, but also the safeguard of his own and his children's future" (*The New York Times*, October 18, 1975).

International Conventions and Human Rights

From a legal point of view, the Soviet regime cannot claim to be immune from international concern about human rights in the USSR because it has ratified the various international conventions protecting basic rights and freedoms. Veniamin Levich, the highest ranking Soviet scientist who has managed to leave the Soviet Union, has correctly pointed out that:

> By the Soviet act of ratification, the problem of free emigration [and, one might add, other basic rights-ed.] is no longer a domestic problem of this country. The request that it implement an international obligation should not be considered intervention in the domestic affairs of this country. It is curious logic to uphold the impossibility of persecuting and executing anyone for Communist ideas while allowing this possibility for other ideas. When Communists are concerned, intervention in their fate is said to be humanitarian. But when concern about the fate of other citizens is expressed, no matter how tragic, this is interpreted as intervention in internal affairs.[40]

Therefore it is an international duty to expose the violations of human rights anywhere. But the Soviet government does not agree. Its representative at the United Nations declared that the emigration of Soviet citizens is strictly an "internal affair" of the Soviet government.[41] In a letter to the Congress of the United States Andrei Sakharov wrote:

> If every nation is entitled to choose the political system under which it wishes to live, this is true all the more of every individual person. A country whose citizens are deprived of this minimal right is not free even if there is not a single citizen who would want to exercise that right.
> But, as you know, there are tens of thousands of citizens in the Soviet Union—Jews, Germans, Russians, Ukrainians, Lithuanians, Armenians, Estonians, Latvians, Turks, and members of other ethnic groups—who want to leave the country and who have been seeking to exercise that right for years and for decades at the cost of endless difficulty and humiliation.
> You know that prisons, labor camps, and mental hospitals are full of people who have sought to exercise this legitimate right.
> You surely know the name of the Lithuanian Simas A. Kudirka, who was handed over to the Soviet authorities by an American vessel, as well as the names of the defendants in

the tragic 1970 hijacking trial in Leningrad. You know about the victims of the Berlin wall.

There are many more lesser-known victims. Remember them, too.

For decades the Soviet Union has been developing under conditions of intolerable isolation, bringing with it the ugliest consequences. Even a partial preservation of those conditions would be highly perilous for all mankind, for international confidence and détente.[42]

In 1973 the Soviet Union took several steps at the UN level which were interpreted by American and Vatican observers as an effort of good will by the Soviets to improve the situation of their citizens in the spirit of détente. Some words pronounced by Leonid Brezhnev in a speech delivered in Sophia, Bulgaria, on September 19, 1973, gave the impression that "peaceful coexistence" was in fact now understood by the Soviets in a different way:

We and our allies firmly believe that there are opportunities for a radical, stable improvement in the international climate. We believe that a new system of international relations can and must be built by honestly and consistently observing the principles of sovereignity, non-interference in internal affairs, by unswervingly implementing treaties and agreements signed, without any doubledealing and ambiguous maneuvers. But, of course, this requires an absolutely different approach, different methods and, perhaps, a different psychology from that which existed before....

One occasionally hears in the West that since the Soviet Union and other socialist countries show great interest in solving the questions of European security, in developing political and economic cooperation, why then not pressure them and bargain for some concessions?

What can one say to this? This is a naive and at the same time unseemly, I should say, merchants' approach to the question. Relaxation of tension in Europe is the common achievement of all the peoples, peace is needed by all the peoples of the continent and, therefore, its preservation and consolidation ought to be the common concern of all the participants in the conference. We believe that this should not be a matter of some diplomatic "trade exchange," but of joint, multilateral efforts towards eventually working out an effective system that would ensure the security of all European countries and peoples and mutually advantageous cooperation among them.

We are against narrow, selfish designs, against artificially giving prominence to particular questions to the detriment of the principal aims of the conference. We want questions pertaining both to European security, and to cooperation in the fields of economy, science, technology, culture and in the humanitarian field to occupy an appropriate place in the work of the conference. But we always remember, and believe others should remember this too, that broad and fruitful development of economic and cultural relations, the effective solution of humanitarian problems are possible only given the removal of the threat of war. The paramount importance of strengthening peace for all peoples, for their progress, for their future—is the only historical yardstick that in our time is valid for assessment of world politics. And this fully applies to the forthcoming discussions at the conference in Geneva.[43]

Brezhnev's speech reiterated the Soviets' stand that human rights can be discussed only after the achievement of peace. Unfortunately, Brezhnev's call for "honesty" in international relations cannot be taken seriously.

Moscow's acceptance of world copyright law and its ratification of two covenants on human rights, as well as the handling of the question of religious liberties at the UN in 1973, show that the Soviet Union is not ready to sign treaties and implement them "without doubledealing and ambiguous maneuvers."

On February 27, 1973, the Soviet government formally notified UNESCO of its intention to adhere to the 1952 Geneva Copyright Convention beginning May 27. Subsequently, the government published an amendment to Soviet copyright laws tightening control of foreign publication of Soviet writings by requiring that foreign copyrights be granted only through an official Soviet agency. With this move Moscow was trying to shut off the flow of dissident writings published in the West. Thus, a month later, on March 27, six Soviet intellectuals warned that "it would be impermissible that censorship should now acquire the possibility of operating on an international scale supported by the Geneva Convention. The international concept of copyrights implies that this right is purely a personal one that the author may transfer to any publishing house, theater, movie studio and so on. Governments may and must protect copyrights of their citizens but not appropriate them. In the special conditions of our country the law on the monopoly of foreign trade would be transferred into a power that limits and even suppresses international copyrights of Soviet citizens."[44]

The warning addressed to UNESCO was signed by Andrei Sakharov; Igor Shafarevich; Grigory Podyapolsky, a geophysicist; Alexander Voronel, a mathematician; and two writers, Alexander Galich and Vladimir Maximov. The paradox of the Moscow move is that the Soviet Constitution does not forbid the sending of manuscripts abroad. The dissenters were not punished for this, but for allegedly "slandering" the regime in their works. Now they can be punished simply for exercising their constitutional rights.[45]

A revision of Soviet income-tax legislation now authorizes the Soviet government to collect as much as 75 percent of all foreign royalties earned by Soviet authors. This new legislation also established the principle that the Soviet tax rates may apply to foreign authors who derive royalties from works published in the Soviet Union. The income-tax decree, revising a basic 1943 tax law, was adopted on September 4, 1973 by the Presidium of the Supreme Soviet. Among other provisions, the decree increases the term of copyright from the author's lifetime plus 15 years to the author's lifetime plus 25, the minimum term under the convention.

Western copyright experts have interpreted the new decree as an attempt to prevent the publication of Soviet dissident authors abroad, thus conceding that Sakharov's warning was right. To prevent such a contingency, the Authors' League of America urged enactment of legislation that would prohibit foreign governments from using United States copyright law in order to prevent publication in the United States of works that do not meet with their approval. Senator John I. McClellan and Congressman Jonathan B. Bingham, respectively, introduced such a bill in the Senate and the House of Representatives.[46]

Soon after the announcement of the establishment of the new Soviet copyright agency, Alexander Solzhenitsyn challenged the government to "protect" his works from unauthorized publication in foreign countries. In an interview to foreign newsmen he declared: "Now, according to what the Soviet authorities say, the rights of Soviet writers are solidly protected . . . Works can be submitted without fear, and our readers can get to know works that have not appeared in public print."[47] It is known that the Nobel Prize winning novelist always took pride in the underground readership of his works and criticized foreign publishers for having printed unauthorized versions of his books. Very likely, in fact, *The First Circle* and *The Cancer Ward* were seized by Soviet security agents and sold abroad for publication with the aim of embarrassing the author. Far from expecting "protection" from the government, Solzhenitsyn revealed in the same interview that the police had arrested a Leningrad woman, Elizaveta Voronyanskaya, to whom he had given one copy of the *The Gulag Archipelago* for safekeeping. At the end of nearly 120 hours of continuous questioning, without sleep, worn down and terrorized, the woman broke down and revealed the whereabouts of Solzhenitsyn's manuscript. Released by the police, she returned home and committed suicide. For this reason Solzhenitsyn announced that he had no alternative but to make sure of the publication of his work abroad. In discussing threats on his life which he had received in the mail, he warned: "My death will not make happy those people who count on my death to stop my literary activities. Immediately after my death or immediately after I have disappeared or have been deprived of my liberty, my literary last will and testament will irrevocably come into effect. The main part of my works will start being published—works I have refrained from publishing all these years."[48]

When the *The Gulag Archipelago, 1918-1956* was issued in Paris at the end of 1973, the author took full responsibility for its publication and for the translations already contracted. Although many experts in Soviet copyright matters thought it was unlikely that the Soviet government would take legal action against the publication of Solzhenitsyn's book, Robert L. Bernstein, chairman of a committee on Soviet-American publishing relations, said: "I would hope that the Russians would try to sue in our courts because I think that would highlight and clarify international publishing involving countries that try to use government pressure—and still have the protection of the Universal Copyright Convention."[49]

Despite the feeling that the Soviets, in their own interest, will not resort to foreign courts to prevent publication of dissident writers' works, the risk of those writers who attempt to bypass official censorship is very high. Boris D. Pankin, the head of the new All-Union Copyright Agency, a former editor of the Young Communist League newspaper *Komsomolskaya Pravda*, has repeatedly affirmed that works can be submitted for publication abroad only through his agency. To do otherwise opens a writer to prosecution under Soviet law.[50] On these conditions Pankin's declarations that Soviet adherence to the copyright convention was aimed at the broadening of cultural ties and international exchanges in science, literature and the arts, is only a lie and cannot be viewed as an improvement in the international climate.

Another demonstration of how the Soviet Union is using international pacts as weapons against its own citizens while providing a democratic façade can be seen in a carefully studied and timely adopted move. On September 18, 1973, Moscow suddenly ratified two covenants on human rights adopted by the UN General Assembly in 1966. The disclosure of the ratification[51] came at a moment when the right of emigration for Soviet Jews was a major point of contention in American policies. Dissenter A. Volpin already suggested that the Supreme Soviet should ratify the covenants in the hope of getting legal protection for Soviet citizens.[52] But this was not the case. The covenants, in fact, are utterly unsatisfactory and the Soviet Union had nothing to fear in approving them.

On December 10, 1948, a Universal Declaration of Human Rights was adopted by the United Nations. This fundamental charter of principles was never ratified by the Soviet Union. The efforts to put the lofty principles of the Declaration into some kind of legally binding pact did not succeed until December 16, 1966, when the UN's General Assembly unanimously approved two documents: the International Covenant on Civil and Political Rights and the International Covenant on Economic, Social and Cultural Rights. For different reasons, however, the majority of the UN's member nations did not ratify these two covenants, which include worthy pacts such as those against slavery and forced labor, but which are worded in such a poor way as to practically destroy the rights they purport to protect in as much as they can be easily manipulated by a government. Ratification by 35 member nations is required for the covenants to go into effect, but by the end of 1973 only 21 nations had officially ratified the two covenants.

Articles 12 and 18 of the International Covenant on Civil and Political Rights state: "Everyone ... has the right to liberty of movement and freedom to choose his residence. Everyone shall be free to leave any country, including his own.... Everyone shall have the right to freedom of thought, conscience and religion ... to manifest his religion or belief in worship, observance, practice and teaching...." And these same two articles also stipulate that "the above mentioned rights should not be subject to any restrictions, except those which are approved by law, are necessary to protect national security, public order, public health or morals or the rights and freedoms of others."[53]

As can be gathered from the comments on the Soviet press, the USSR decided to ratify the two documents in order to strengthen its legal argument against the emigration and freedom of thought of its citizens. *Pravda*, for instance, underscored the inclusion of the "important principle" that exercise of individual liberties could not "impinge upon the interests of public order and national security."[54] Secretary General Brezhnev in his speech of December 21, 1973, marking the 50th anniversary of the USSR, took a hard line in respect to the nationality policy and implied that in the proposed new Constitution the role of the individual republics might be minimized even further:

> It should not be forgotten that nationalistic prejudices and exaggerated or distorted manifestations of national feelings are extremely tenacious phenomena that are deeply embedded in the psychology of people with insufficient political maturity. These prejudices continue to exist even in conditions in which objective preconditions for any antagonism in relations between nations have long since ceased to exist. We should also bear in mind the fact that manifestations of nationalistic tendencies are frequently intertwined with parochialism, which appears to be akin to nationalism.
>
> We also have no right to forget that nationalistic survivals are being fanned in every way from outside by politicians and propagandists in the bourgeois world. Our class adversaries seize upon every manifestation of this kind with great zeal, inflating and encouraging these phenomena in the hope of at least to some degree weakening the unity of our country's peoples.
>
> Finally, Comrades, there are also objective problems in our federal state—such as finding the best paths for the development of the individual nations and nationalities and the most correct combination of the interests of each of them with the common interests of the Soviet people as a whole. In solving these problems, our party is completely guided by Lenin's behest concerning the need to show maximum concern for the development of each nation and for its interests.
>
> The further drawing together of the nations and nationalities of our country is an objective process. The Party is against the forcing of this process—there is no need for this, since the process is dictated by the entire course of our Soviet life. At the same time, the Party regards as impermissible any attempt whatsoever to hold back the process of the drawing together of nations, to obstruct it on any pretext or artificially to reinforce national isolation, because this would be at variance with the general direction of the development of our society, the Communists' internationalist ideals and ideology and the interests of Communist construction.[55]

Another reason why Western countries refrained to ratify the covenants is that the machinery provided for dealing with violations is completely inadequate. Under the treaty on civil and political rights no complaint can be brought against a state unless this state is willing to have it raised. Only then would it go to an 18-member human rights committee, which would be set up once 35 countries have ratified the covenant and brought it into operation.

Moreover, the Soviet Union has not yet signed an optional protocol under which individuals as well as governments can bring complaints to the United Nations. Thus, the doors of the United Nations are practically closed to protests and petitions from Soviet dissidents.

In his Nobel Lecture Solzhenitsyn affirmed:

A quarter of a century ago, with the great hopes of mankind, the United Nations was born. Alas, in the immoral world it, too, became immoral. It is not a United Nations but a United Governments, in which those freely elected, and those imposed by force, and those which seized power by arms are all on a par. Through the mercenary bias of the majority, the UN jealously worries about the freedom of some peoples and pays no attention to the freedom of others. By an officious vote it rejected the review of private complaints—the groans, shouts, and pleadings of individual, common plain people—insects too small for such a great organization. The UN has never tried to make governments honor the Declaration of Human Rights—a condition of their membership and the outstanding document of its 25 years. Thus the UN has betrayed the common people to the will of governments they have not chosen.[56]

There is no doubt that the UN Human Rights Commission very often fails to defend the oppressed because of the narrow nationalism of the Commission's members who fear to condemn another's atrocity lest their own be revealed. But the basic problem rests with the inadequacy of the instruments of the Commission, with the contradictory wording of the covenants, which renders their enforcement impossible. Nevertheless the Pontifical Commission Justitia et Pax as well as other National Catholic Commissions are pressing the governments to ratify the two covenants instead of asking for a new draft.[57] Vatican diplomacy is thrilled by the fact that the covenants include many "positive principles" dear to the teachings of the Roman Pontiffs. But what's the use if the covenants permit the governments to limit the freedoms they proclaim?

The performance of the Vatican's representatives at the UN gives the impression that they are striving to win religious freedom without insisting enough on true human rights. It would be wiser for them to change the order of priorities because religious liberty is only a part, even if the most important, of man's rights.

As one of 26 states responding to a draft declaration on the elimination of all forms of religious intolerance, the Holy See contributed to the discussion by submitting a list of observations largely based on Pope John XXIII's encyclical "Pacem in Terris." At the same time it stated that it would also prefer that the document be a covenant or a binding convention rather than a declaration. Nevertheless, Rev. Carlos Vela, an observer of the Holy See, assured them that the Vatican felt that even a declaration, although it would not have any effect in law, could be a step toward effective measures.[58]

According to the Vatican, the preliminary draft has been drawn up in accordance with "too individual a conception of religious freedom" and needs to be clarified "by laying greater stress on freedom to express inner convictions in public observances or professions of faith.... It is clear, and history bears ample witness, that without this possibility of outward and public expression and without freedom of worship, religious freedom is gravely diminished, sometimes to the point of being nothing more than a mere affirmation of principle." Therefore, religious bodies should be permitted to freely exist in order that they may govern themselves according to their own norms, assist their members in their religious life and promote institutions and activities among themselves in accordance with their beliefs.

Regarding the right of individuals to adhere or not to any religion, to profess it, in public or in private, to change it in accordance with the dictates of their conscience, the Vatican suggested that this freedom should be granted "without being subjected to any legal administrative, political, economic, or other coercion likely to impair freedom of choice, decision, and exercise in the matter." On the other hand, the religious bodies should not be prohibited from "undertaking freely to show the special value of their doctrine in what concerns the organization of society and the inspiration of the whole human activity."

Concerning religious education in particular, the Vatican proposed that the existing draft article be expanded, adding that "the rights of the parents are also violated if their children are forced to attend lessons or instructions which are not in agreement with the religious beliefs of the parents, or if a single system of education, from which all religious beliefs of the parents, or if a single system of education, from which all religious formation is excluded, is imposed upon all."

An article dealing with funds of churches and religious groups was also proposed by the Vatican so that all persons should have the right to give expression to their religion by "performing acts of charity, by making donations or bequests, by founding or maintaining charitable institutions (hospitals, leprosaria, orphanages, homes for aged, etc.) as well as educational establishments, and by expressing the precepts of religion or belief in the social, economic and political fields, on both the national and international level."

Regarding international ties, the Vatican suggested that religions of a universal character should have the right to maintain "organic relations" with their adherents and, likewise, believers should be free to entertain such relations with the seats of their religion.

The fact that the UN General Assembly since 1962 has been engaged in periodic deliberations on religious freedom without concluding even a declaration on the subject is rather frustrating. It is not surprising that the stronger opposition came from the communist countries led by the USSR. The Soviet republic of Byelorussia saw in the Vatican's suggestions proof that the proposed declaration demonstrated "the bias of the draft towards the Roman Catholic Church, which has always been a gigantic reactionary force and which has destroyed some of the world's greatest thinkers."

The angry attack of the Byelorussian delegates shows that, after so many years of dialogue, the old Soviet anti-Catholic position is still the same, despite the asserted "respect" for papal efforts toward world peace. The Soviet representative informed the other delegations, particularly those from Africa, on the relationship between the Catholic Church and "colonialism" and insisted on the warning that religion cannot be used or abused for political purposes. About his country he said that the Soviet state does not "interfere in churches or allow churches to interfere in state matters." According to the Soviet representative, despite the incompatibility between Communism and religion in the Soviet Union "all are united in full agreement with respect to the common struggle of humanity for an enlightened future."

We believe that the Vatican at the UN could have obtained more support for religious freedom by concentrating on the correction of the Covenants on Human Rights instead of calling on "those nations which may not as yet have done this.... to follow without pause the example of the others."

The participation of the Vatican in the signing of the Helsinki declaration, so eagerly supported by the European Communist states, did not bring the expected clarification in the present policies of détente. The Holy See, in the words of the Pope, was particularly happy to see in the conference document that "in a specific way, among rights mentioned, religious liberty was stressed." But the 100-page document is nothing more than a declaration of good intentions, which will not be legally binding on anyone. On his return from Helsinki, the chief of the Vatican delegation, Archbishop Casaroli, defended the conference against "pessimistic opinions." He told newsmen that, in his judgment, the efforts of the conference for peace were "undoubtedly positive," not merely "empty words." "I don't believe," he added, "that pessimistic opinions have foundation inasmuch as they saw and perhaps still see in a conference of this sort a peril to peace, through the creation of an unjustified sense of security ... At Helsinki the representatives of all participating countries have taken on a commitment so solemn that one has to think that they will try to hold themselves to it." According to him, President Ford's speech was "truly interesting, well thought out, and concrete," while the speech of Leonid Brezhnev was "reassuring." Taking a final swipe at critics, the archbishop stated that the conference did not "consecrate the existing status quo in regard to certain situations which some consider to be unjust ... I do not believe that the effort to guarantee the security and peace should imply the sacrifice of rights which can be considered just."[59]

Ecumenism: A Political Fiction or a Christian Witness?

The "ecumenical dialogue" between the Moscow Patriarchate and the Roman Catholic Church was a consequence of the political rapprochement between the Vatican and the Kremlin and it still depends upon it. The spiritual needs of the faithful as well as the brotherly love and unity among Christians not only do not interest the Communist atheistic regime, but are opposed by it ever since the Bolshevik revolution. Patriarch Tikhon was persecuted also because he dared to establish contacts with the heads of Christian Churches abroad without the permission of the atheist government. What the Soviets expect from the Church is its "loyal" collaboration in the strengthening of Communism at home and abroad.

This collaboration was finally achieved on July 29, 1927, when Metropolitan Sergei, the locum tenens or keeper of the patriarchal throne, understanding, as he wrote, the "signs of the times," issued a pro-Soviet declaration, condemned the "enemies" of the Soviet state at home and abroad as "mad, insensate instruments of intrigues," and expressed his "gratitude to the Soviet government for the interest which it has manifested to all the spiritual needs of the Orthodox population."[60] As a reward the Soviets granted legal status to Sergei's administration and withdrew their support from other Orthodox pro-Communist splinter groups. But this unity built upon a lie immediately produced other more serious divisions. In fact a great number of clergymen and faithful, led by hundreds of bishops imprisoned in the Solovki islands and Siberia,[61] repudiated Sergei's compromise and started a "catacomb Church," which inspired the activity of modern Orthodox dissenters.[62]

Another turning point in the collaboration of the Russian Orthodox Church with Soviet authorities came during World War II. Realizing that religion was still relevant to many citizens and that an open support of the Red Army by Church leaders would help very much in defeating the enemy and strengthening Communism at home and abroad, Stalin on September 4, 1943, received Metropolitans Sergei, Alexei and Nikolai. They were allowed to elect a patriarch in the person of Sergei (enthroned September 12) and granted other privileges in exchange for their "patriotism."[63] After the death of Sergei, Alexei became patriarch (February 27, 1945). In his inaugural address and in an "Appeal to Christians of the Whole World" he expressed his program of support of Soviet interests in domestic and foreign affairs and, implying the Vatican, attacked "those who presume to call themselves Christians . . . and recommend forgiveness for child-murderers and traitors."[64] In the same year of his election Alexei visited the Middle East, in 1946 Bulgaria and in 1947 Rumania. All these trips, for which the Soviet government provided airplanes specially chartered, helped to consolidate the prestige of both the Moscow Patriarchate and the Soviet regime. But the visits and contacts with other Orthodox Churches were less successful. In many cases "success" was achieved only with the help of the secular arm of Communist governments. The isolation of the Church of Moscow increased with Tito's breach with Stalin. In order to continue its services in Soviet foreign policies the Russian Orthodox

Church joined the Moscow-sponsored World Peace Council.

In February 1949, Patriarch Alexei called for the defense of peace in response to the International Committee of Cultural Workers, who had proposed a World Peace Congress. On October 2, of the same year, International Peace Day in the USSR, Russian Orthodox believers gathered in churches to pray for peace and to hear a new message from their Patriarch. Five months later on March 3, 1950, Alexei sent an open letter to the heads of the Orthodox Churches charging them that they have, as a prime duty, the responsibility of pursuing and creating peace on earth. At the same time he stated that the non-Soviets are wrong in their assessment of the problems of the world and gave no room for the Orthodox prelates to choose since, according to him, to refuse the Soviet position would be tantamount to being hypocritical.[65] Although he requested a reply, only the Bulgarian, Rumanian and Albanian Churches, and the Patriarch of Antioch, gave a positive response to his appeal.

Patriarch Alexei was ably assisted in the peace movement by Metropolitan Nikolai, Chairman of the Department of Foreign Relations of the Russian Orthodox Church and permanent member of the Central Committee of the World Peace Council. While he travelled everywhere in order to "proclaim the virtues of the pax Sovietica" he was applauded and decorated by his government. But when he dared to oppose Khrushchev's new restrictions on religion, he was dismissed from all his official posts and "died as a martyr."[66]

While tightening the control of the Russian Orthodox Church at home, the Soviet government, in view of political advantages, encouraged the expansion of its external relations with the Protestant and Catholic Churches. Now that the nations of the Third World were just emerging in the international arena, it was important to help the Soviet Union to win them to the Socialist camp.[67] But to switch from the previous anti-Roman and anti-World Council of Churches attitude to a larger "ecumenical dialogue" was not an easy task for the Moscow Patriarchate. Here we will summarize the steps of this unprecedented "ecumenical dialogue" directed by a powerful atheist state. We do not exclude any good intention on the part of the protagonists of the dialogue, but only stress their essential dependence upon Communist authorities.

In 1948 during a so-called pan-Orthodox Conference in Moscow (July 9-17), three different documents the Vatican and the Ecumenical Movement were harshly condemned.[68] Regarding the latter the Conference declared that "the attempt being made by the Ecumenical Movement to organize political and social life and to create an Ecumenical Church as an international power is, in fact, yielding to the temptation which Christ withstood in the wilderness" and it accused Protestantism of fostering a "fictitious form of unity" which would "reduce Christian doctrine to a belief which even demons would find acceptable."[69]

Ten years later in August 1958, representatives of the Moscow Patriarchate and the World Council of Churches met for the first time. Metropolitan Nikolai talked about two topics: "The Russian Orthodox Church and the ecumenical movement" and "The problem of Christian unity in the defence and strengthening of peace."[70] It was clear that the Moscow Patriarchate was reconsidering its attitude toward the World Council of Churches in order to contribute more effectively to Soviet peace propaganda.[71] On April 11, 1961 Patriarch Alexei sent to Geneva his formal request for membership in the World Council of Churches, and the General Assembly at New Delhi (December 1961) admitted almost unanimously the Russian Orthodox Church as a member. One of the first acts of the Russian delegation was taken in the Commission for Refugees, when bishop John Wendland, then the Exarch of Central Europe "emphatically insisted that it was a matter of urgency for the refugees to be repatriated. At the meeting of the Executive Committee in Paris (August 1962), he took the opportunity to put forward his government's views on the problems of Berlin."[72]

It is not the purpose of this study to analyze the developments of the relations between the World Council of Churches and the Russian Orthodox Church but, speaking on ecumenism, it is interesting to note how the Patriarchs of Moscow responded to the concerns of the WCC about the invasion of Czechoslovakia and the trampling upon human rights in the USSR.

Replying to a cable from general secretary Eugene Carson Blake (August 22, 1968) requesting an assessment of the Czech situation, leaders of the churches in Poland and Russia advised the WCC officers to make no statement. When, in the days following the entry of Warsaw Pact troops, enquiries were made as to the position of the WCC and requests for a statement came from within several member churches, the officers of the WCC did make a statement on August 28 in which they deplored the military intervention.[73] At this point Patriarch Alexei sent a letter to the chairman of the WCC in which he regretted the publication of the statement because he doubted that sufficient reasons existed for the use of such "categorical" terms as "military intervention":

> As everyone knows, Czechoslovakia is a constituent part of the socialist fellowship. Czechoslovakia, the USSR, Bulgaria, Hungary, the German Democratic Republic and Poland are bound together by bilateral pacts of friendship, mutual assistance and cooperation both in ideological and practical issues, and they are all members of the organization of the Warsaw Pact, whose responsibility (as stated in the text of the agreements) is mutual defence of socialism and of the independence of these countries. It suffices to refer to the communique on the Soviet-Czechoslovak negotiations in Moscow published on August 27, which was prior to your own statement.
>
> This communique said: "The troops of the allied countries, being temporarily introduced into Czechoslovakia, will not interfere in the inner affairs of the Czechoslovak Socialist Republic."

This statement—as we heard—is confirmed by the daily life in Czechoslovakia, which is governed by its constitutional organs headed by its legitimately elected leaders respected by the people.[74]

Joseph Hromadka, the founder of the Prague-based Christian Peace Conference (CPC), who for many years defended Moscow's peaceful coexistence and won the Lenin Peace Prize, immediately after the invasion of Czechoslovakia changed his mind. After receiving a letter full of lies from Patriarch Alexei and after a fruitless "long talk" with Metropolitan Nikodim, during which—as he later wrote—he had the clear impression of Nikodim's bad faith, he resigned from the presidency of the CPC and shortly afterwards died.[75] Under the presidency of Metropolitan Nikodim, the CPC became a strong supporter of détente.[76]

In September 1973 Patriarch Pimen of Moscow visited, for the first time since his election, the headquarters of the WCC in Geneva. At that time the world was shocked by the protests of the most qualified dissenters in the Soviet Union. The patriarch was asked why he had failed to denounce such enormous injustices in his own country. His answer was that the critics of the USSR were influenced by Western propaganda that blinded them to the "unquestionable merits of a socialist mode of life. The social evils so typical for the life of many people today cannot occur within our socialist structure." In the Soviet Union there are "no rich, no poor" and "no priviliged and no oppressed"; each citizen has "wide and equal rights." In contrast with the situation in the West, the "defects" that exist in Soviet society do not require the clergy to speak out in condemnation.[77]

If the conversion of the Russian Orthodox Church to Ecumenism came as a surprise to the WCC, the change in Moscow-Rome relations was even more unexpected and politically motivated. Since World War II the Church of Moscow has taken a violent anti-Catholic attitude. Declarations on Catholicism and the Vatican by Russian Orthodox leaders as well as articles on the same subject in the journal of the Moscow Patriarchate were in no way different from the speeches and the writings of the militant atheists of the country. The bishops gathered in Moscow in 1945 for the election of Patriarch Alexei raised "their voices against the efforts of those, particularly the Vatican," who were said to advocate Fascism and "recommend forgiveness for child-murderers and traitors."[78] At the inter-Orthodox conference in Moscow in 1948 the popes and the Vatican were condemned in those terms:

The popes have always been on the side of the powerful of "this world" and against the weak and exploited. So today, Vatican activity is directed against the interests of the workers. The Vatican is the centre of international intrigues against the interests of the peoples, especially the Slav people, and is the centre of international Fascism. The essence of Christian morality is our Saviour's call to charity, whereas the Vatican has been one of the instigators of two imperialist wars and is at present taking an active part in promoting another war and, in general, in the political attack against world democracy.... Men everywhere must be made to see the abyss into which the papacy is leading them.[79]

The election of Pope John XXIII and the announcement of the Vatican Council II (1959) brought no change in these stormy relations. The assumption of atheist writers was that the pope was new, but the "course" remained "old" and that the Council was summoned in an attempt to halt the flight of the faithful from the Church, to reaffirm papal absolutism and combat communism.[80] On these same assumptions the leaders of the Moscow Patriarchate based their early criticism of Pope John and their rejection of the Council. This writer was drawn into a bitter exchange with the editor-in-chief of the journal of the Moscow Patriarchate, the late Professor Alexander Shishkin. He furiously attacked my article published in *La Civiltà Cattolica*.[81] In it I charged, as I have consistently, that the Church of Moscow was borrowing its anti-Roman arguments from Soviet atheisitic propaganda and bore the responsibility for the destruction of the Ukrainian Catholic Church. In his five-page reply, Professor Shishkin accused me of "anti-Communist blindness" and of "being incapable of thinking realistically." He went on to question the "humility" and good intentions of Pope John in summoning the Council.[82] Patriarch Alexei declared that the Council was an internal affair of the Roman Catholic Church and to the last moment declined the invitation to send observers to the Council with a definite "non possumus."[83]

At the first All-Christian Peace Assembly in Prague (June 13-18, 1961) Metropolitan Nikodim presented a lengthy paper in which he blamed the worldliness of the papal system, predicted the collapse of the Catholic Church and praised the proposals of Nikita Khrushchev as the only alternative to a real Christian peace in the world:

... The theory of the Pope is the clearest and most concentrated expression of the spirit of external legalism and worldliness which has considerably penetrated into the teaching and life of the Catholic Church...

It is not just by accident that the abyss between the Vatican and progressive mankind is getting wider every day. It seems to us that a conflict between the masses of Catholic believers on the one hand and the leaders of the Vatican on the other is inevitable. This conflict has already started by the liquidation of unions such as that of Brest, so important for the Vatican as a bridgehead for penetration into the East...

It is well known to all that N. S. Khrushchev, head of the Soviet delegation to the sixth session of the General Assembly of the UN, submitted for the discussion in the UN basic proposals for an agreement on universal and total disarmament. Do these humane acts of the Government of our country go counter to the demands of Christian conscience? By no means!... Is it not the main task of modern Christian conscience to conform as closely as possible to that aim?...[84]

Suddenly, three months later, Nikita Khrushchev contradicted Metropolitan Nikodim. In an interview to the correspondents of *Pravda* and

Izvestiia the Soviet leader had commented favourably on a message of Pope John in support of the proposals of the neutral nations. The concern of the Pope for peace, said Khrushchev, was proof that he was taking into consideration "the feelings of millions of Catholics all over the world... His appeal is a good omen... As a Communist and atheist, I don't believe in Divine Providence. But because we always were and are for a peaceful solution of the conflicts, we can't but approve an appeal to negotiate in the interests of peace from wherever it comes. And now I am asking myself if fervent Catholics such as John Kennedy, Konrad Adenauer and others are going to understand the warning of the Pope."[85]

It took a few days for Metropolitan Nikodim to understand the warning of Khrushchev, because during the pan-orthodox Conference of Rhodes (Sept. 24-Oct. 1) he was still attacking the Vatican.[86] But, especially after Khrushchev had sent a greetings telegram to the Pope on November 23 for his 80th birthday, it was clear that the Moscow Patriarchate had to drop its political and ecclesiastical objection to the Council. Now its role was not to oppose, but to influence the Council through the presence of its observers in Rome. The only question to be solved was a tactical one: how to retract the categorical "non possumus" and obey the orders of an atheist boss without losing face.

The Vatican had decided to invite the observers of the Orthodox Churches through the Ecumenical Patriarch of Constantinople, Athenagoras, who personally was willing to accept the invitation, but preferred to act in solidarity with the other sister Churches. This way the Patriarch of Constantinople, who is "primus inter pares," could avoid the accusation of taking unilateral decisions and the Vatican could be spared the embarrassment of direct refusals. The Moscow Patriarchate took advantage of this situation to play its diplomatic game. In international gatherings officials of the Russian Orthodox Church started to spread the rumor that if directly invited, they could reconsider their attitude. Archbishop Nikodim, in New Delhi, asked whether or not Moscow would send observers to Rome, replied: "We are almost ashamed at being unable to answer. But how can we reply, when we have not yet been invited?"[87] Later, in August 1962, he met in Paris Msgr. Jan Willebrands, then secretary of the Roman Secretariat for Christian Unity, and let him understand that if he would make a personal visit to Moscow, the question of the observers could be settled. The Roman official spent five days from September 27 to October 2 in Moscow. On the evening of the inauguration of the Council (October 11) two Russian observers arrived in Rome. Meanwhile, on the night before, Patriarch Athenagoras had telegraphed to Rome that the heads of the Orthodox Churches, including the Patriarch of Moscow, had decided not to send observers.

The diplomatic maneuvers had worked successfully. The Russian representatives were the only Orthodox observers present in Rome at the opening of the Second Vatican Council. The prestige of Rome and the face of Moscow were saved.[88] Archbishop Yakovos of New York indignantly commented that the Moscow-Vatican dealing had been "apparently aimed at disrupting Orthodox unity and undermining the authority of the Ecumenical Patriarchate."[89] The Moscow-Constantinople rivalry as well as the dependence of the Russian Church upon the Soviet government were facts well known to the Vatican, but interests of diplomacy, even of Vatican diplomacy, cannot be stopped by considerations of human decency. In the pre-Vatican Council II days the question of Vatican prestige was of singular importance to the organizers of the Council. In the context of the ecumenical feelers being extended by Vatican officials to the Orthodox world, it would be embarrassing were the Council to open with no Orthodox observers. The readiness of the Moscow Patriarchate to send observers could not be disregarded, even if this Church lacked two important qualities (freedom of speech and action and solidarity with the other Orthodox Churches) and was about to demand a high price for its "ecumenical" services.

No one knows precisely the terms of the accord by which the Moscow Patriarchate agreed to send observers to Vatican II. On Moscow's part there was profound concern to scuttle any attempt to issue a condemnation of Communism by the Council. Msgr. Willebrands was in a position to give assurances that the Council "would not undertake anti-Communist polemics"[90] because, as Pope John had already declared, the Council was expected to be a pastoral one. On the other hand the presence of the Russian observers in Rome would be the best guarantee that the bishops would refrain from taking any harsh attitude. When the Ukrainian Catholic bishops protested against the presence of the observers from Moscow, the Secretariat for Christian Unity immediately reprimanded them and defended its "guests."[91] Nevertheless, as can be gathered from the reading of the accounts and articles on the Council published by the journal of the Moscow Patriarchate, the representatives of the Russian Orthodox Church abstained from any favorable declaration almost until the end, fearing that the question of Communism would spoil everything. On several occasions the Russian prelates had made it clear that silence on the question of Communism was a *conditio sino qua non* for their continued presence in Rome. As Fr. Georges Dejaifve, S.J. , wrote about the stand taken by the representatives of the Moscow Patriarchate at the Third Pan-Orthodox Conference inRhodes (Nov. 1-15, 1964): "The Russian Church showed that it was impossible to speak of a dialogue with the Church of Rome before the closing of the Council... because in the eyes of public opinion a condemnation of atheism would be equal to a condemnation of Communism and consequently of the Soviet regime."[92]

That Fr. Dejaifve was not reporting mere rumors appears also from what the well-known anti-religious writer N. Sheinman wrote during the

Vatican Council: "In the same Roman Curia and in the Council the bitter fight on whether to go along the line of John XXIII or to go back to Pius XII's course is not yet concluded. This was shown also during the second session of the Vatican Council. On the eve of the closing of the session, on December 3, 1963, more than 200 bishops from 46 countries, sent to the Vatican Secretariat of State the proposal of a declaration 'on Communism' to be discussed the following session. Thus, these bishops and their supporters are pushing the Council toward an anti-Communist 'crusade.'"[93]

The "reserves" of the Russian Orthodox Church regarding the Vatican Council II were finally lifted toward the end of the same when the request of more than 300 bishops to discuss Communism was inexplicably blocked and dropped.[94] Now the "dialogue" was possible, but it became mostly a useless exercise in rhetorical speeches, a diplomatic exchange of official delegations without the necessary contacts with the base. Since 1967 four major "theological conversations" took place among representatives of the Russian and Roman Churches.

The first dialogue, "On Catholic Social Thought," was held from December 9 to 13, 1967, at the Leningrad Theological Academy.[95] It was an offshoot of a proposal made by Bishop Willebrands to Nikodim during the Geneva World Conference on Church and Society a year before. On that occasion Nikodim said that the Catholic Church now accepts also "a public form of property like the Soviet type of Socialism."[96] Another Russian delegate, Archpriest Vitaly Borovoy, was wildly applauded when he analyzed the "theology of revolution," strongly criticizing the early attitude of the Russian Orthodox Church.[97] Among many historical lies, lately unveiled by Solzhenitsyn in *Gulag Archipelago*, Borovoy affirmed:

> All Christians should keep in mind the experiences of our Church in their relationships with the social revolutions of our time. Our Church, in the person of its hierarchy and of part of its clergy, has gone through all the stages of rejection, from opposition to direct action against the revolution and against the changes brought by it on the life of the Church. It was not just theoretical opposition and passive resistance. It was a cruel and open fight. . . . This has helped our clergy and the hierarchy to join the fate of the people and to accept what had happened. Our Western Christian brothers should take these facts as a lesson for them. The Christians should join courageously, actively and honorably the new life, based on social justice; they should bring a christian social fervor to the social revolutions of our time.[98]

Bishop Willebrand's proposal to continue the Geneva conversations could have resulted in some very interesting developments if the Russians and the Catholics had had the courage to freely express themselves. But at Leningrad not only the word "revolution" was no longer mentioned, but even the allusion to any form of "dissent" was carefully avoided from both sides.

While Western dissent is characterized by secularism and violence, Soviet dissent consists in a search for authentic human and religious values and is aimed at the spiritual rebirth of an atheistic society through the power of the spirit. Those were the years in which Boris Pasternak and Anna Akhmatova were attracting the attention of young intellectuals. At their funerals, in 1960 and 1966, conducted in the Orthodox rite, the best representatives of the intelligentsia were present. The students, inspired by the works of Berdyaev and Solovyov, two giants of spiritual and ecumenical thought, were publishing the first underground literary magazines.[99] Andrei Voznesensky was searching for soul among the world of machines and technology when he wrote:

> Technologies, like states, are mortal;
> They fade away and die.
> There's only one steady thing on earth.
> Something like the light of a star that has vanished
> But keeps on shining.
> We used to call it the soul.[100]

Some young Leningraders were asking "not just 'What is it for an individual to be religious?' or 'What is it for an individual to be a Christian?' but what does it mean for a culture to be religious or to be Christian? Is West European culture Christian? Is Soviet Russian culture non-Christian, post-Christian, or in some sense Christian?"[101] For asking such questions some people were brutally punished. The trials and imprisonment of Joseph Brodsky (1964), Andrei Sinyavsky and Yuly Daniel (1966), the suspension of two Moscow priests, Nikolai Eshliman and Gleb Yakunin, for entreating in an Open Letter to the Patriarch to "atone for his grievous sin before the Russian Church" (1965),[102] shake the conscience of many in the USSR and abroad, but did not touch the hearts of those Soviet prelates who, in December 1967, were giving lessons on revolutionary fervor to Catholic theologians.

The second dialogue took place in Bari, Italy, on December 6-10, 1970. The main topic was "the role of the Christian in a developing society." Father Jerome Hammer, O.P., stressed the necessity of combatting evil at the individual as well as the social level, and the leadership the Church should provide toward peace and social justice in a changing world. Again these important questions remained unanswered from the other side.[103]

Soviet clergymen from the department of foreign relations of the Russian Orthodox Church had extensively travelled in the Third World. Bilateral relationships had been developed with churchmen in Madagascar, Ethiopia, Kenya, and Uganda. Students from Ethiopia had been invited to pursue theological studies in the USSR, and medical supplies had been donated to the National Christian Council of Kenya by the

Moscow Patriarchate, Soviet churchmen had on occasion visited Cuba and other Latin American countries. The Moscow Patriarchate has been able to develop relations in India with the Malancar Church in Kerala, a province with a strong Communist party. Relations with Vietnamese and Japanese religious groups were steadily increasing. Surveying the contribution of the Russian Orthodox Church to Soviet foreign policy in the West and in the developing nations, William Fletcher writes:

> Such international religious activities represent no small allocation of resources: the cost in man-hours is high, for a large number of individuals have been engaged, full-time or part-time, in these activities over the past quarter of a century; the financial investments required for these endeavors is considerable; and the logistics of planning, administration and control, and direct and indirect support services are complex. Even though matters of the spiritual and intellectual world are scarcely open to quantitative analysis, such aspects of the role of religion in Soviet foreign policy as might be qualifiable indicate that the Churches represent a serious and important aspect of the USSR's international operations.[104]

Solzhenitsyn's Lenten Letter to Patriarch Pimen opens with this remark: "Perhaps for the first time in half a century, you finally spoke about children... But what is the purpose of all this? Why is your earnest appeal directed only to Russian émigrés?..."[105] This is also the question about Moscow ecumenism: why?

The third discussion between representatives of the Catholic Church and the Moscow Patriarchate was held at the Trinity-St. Sergei Monastery in Zagorsk from June 4 to 7, 1973. The theme of the study was a very interesting one: "The Church in a world in transformation."[106] From the joint communique, signed by the heads of the two delegations (Metropolitan Yuvenali of Tula and Belev, Chairman of the Department of External Church Relations of the Patriarchate, and Archbishop Angelo Innocent Fernandes of Delhi) it appears that the Moscow representatives gained some ground in convincing their partners to agree on "the fact that there is a strong tendency towards a certain pattern of socialism in many parts of the world. The nature of these tendencies and the degree of their importance were not made a subject of discussion. The participants nevertheless agreed that there were positive aspects in these tendencies which Christians should recognize and try to understand."[107]

Other interesting points discussed at Zagorsk, such as the possibility and necessity of the cooperation of Christians with non-Christians and non-believers, were clearly aimed at justifying the "loyalty" of the Moscow Patriarchate toward the Communist regime. Metropolitan Nikodim, Chairman of the Commission of the Holy Synod of the Russian Orthodox Church on Problems of Christian Unity and Inter-Church Relations, observed that in the course of everyday life a Christian is constantly faced with the question of how he should behave in order to follow Christ faithfully. On answering this question Metropolitan Nikodim emphasized: "Being Christ-centered basically and in their very core, Christian reflection and action demand the self-perfection of a Christian. This is to be achieved, however, not in isolation from the surrounding world and one's neighbor, but by unfailingly taking part in it in order to serve in the Spirit of Christ."[108]

While Metropolitan Yuvenali reinforced, for internal purposes, Nikodim's position, saying that "one cannot think of the Church apart from the world," the other members of the Russian delegation interpreted the cooperation of Christians with non-believers according to the principles of Soviet foreign policy. Professor Dmitri Ogitsky, indicating that the process of change in the world began from the first day of creation, said that "Christians welcome the process of democratization of life in national communities, the socialization of production, the success of peaceful coexistence, the strengthening of cooperation among peoples of differing convictions for the good of the world." Archpriest Vladimir Sorokin stressed the importance of the above mentioned cooperation "for achieving success in strengthening social justice and international peace." Alexei Buyevsky, secretary of the Department of External Church Relations, said that "the members of the Church . . . faced with modern spiritual degradation in many parts of the world (moral decline, cult of violence, personal gain, egoism), must work actively for the consolidation of genuine moral values in their societies . . . He pointed out the importance of the World Congress of Peace Forces to be held in Moscow next October."[109]

In Soviet terminology to be "isolated" from the world, from the people or from reality means to hold a different view from the party's line. That's why the Russian Church does not support the believers who fight against the closing of the churches or defend the human rights of their fellow citizens. These dissenters, clergymen or laymen, are excluded from the ecumenical dialogue as "isolated" people. But this is also the reason why the "dialogue" becomes more and more one-sided and misleading.

When the Russian Orthodox clergymen speak about socialism they mean Soviet socialism, of course purged from the aberrations of Stalinism. But even this kind of socialism, which respects the so-called "democratic" Leninist ideas of legality, nationality and religion, is not in sight in the USSR. That's why even those dissenters who call themselves Leninists are against today's Soviet socialism. In one of the best analyses of the present Soviet situation, "The Ideocratic Conscience and the Person," Dmitri Nelidov (a pen name) wrote that the real trouble in today's Soviet society is represented by its "ideocracy," the tyranny of an ideology completely alienated from any personal and individual conscience. One of the consequences of this ideocracy is the double meaning of the words and even of the thinking (dvoemyslie.) The content of the Chronicle of Current

Events could be published by *Pravda*. In fact the *Chronicle* is mostly filled with dry lists of names of people imprisoned. In that case those names would only bear witness to the justice of the Soviet courts. But when those names are published by the *Chronicle* they become "dirty slanders" of the USSR.[110] The representatives of the Moscow Patriarchate, too, are dominated by the ideocracy, their conscience is alienated. That's why it is so difficult to have a personal dialogue with them.

Continuing Nelidov's analysis, another dissenter, Yevgeny Baraba-nov, writing on the "schism" or isolation of the Church from the world, stresses that this fact is only a consequence of the adaptation to or acceptance on the part of the Church of the ideocratic principle that religion is doomed to die. "In the framework of this ecclesiology there is no place for the problem of a christianization of Russia... The absence of external freedom paralyzes the life [of the Church] and affects her internal freedom; it establishes itself in her conscience and becomes identi-fied with ecclesiastical tradition."[111] In order to achieve a "Christian rebirth" of Russia "one must make a Christian initiative" to put an end to "passive-ness" and develop a strong "religious will" to transform the world.[112] Barabanov had already expressed himself about this "initiative" and the support it can receive from the ecumenical movement. Commenting on the "silence of the Churches," he wrote:

> Is it possible that Christianity lost the initiative also regarding the spiritual life. Today, in its moral reaction, the a-religious world, in the majority of cases, puts itself at the avant-garde of the Churches. Through its "a-religious" committees and leagues, it speaks of the sufferings and helps the oppressed. Not the World Council of Churches, but Amnesty International answered the calls of the imprisoned Baptists. Meanwhile the Churches are preoccupied in finding their unity. Their representatives continue to gather as before. They are reading reports to each other, are engaged in diplomatic trips and pilgrimages. As before, they live in the artificial world of general theories and theological discussions. They seriously hope that when these discussions are ended, the long-waited Christian unity will be achieved. But even if one day this diplomatic unity will be obtained, this will be nothing else than a political fiction likewise fruitless as the "friendship of the peoples" whose governments only yesterday reconciled themselves and stipulated profitable commercial contracts. But this is not the unity which Christians need. Once they lose the moral readiness to witness about the evil and suffering, will they really still remain with Christ and constitute His Body? Is this not the evangelical moral basis, that elementary premise without which an authentic Christian unity is impossible?[113]

Barabanov and other religious dissenters, especially Mikhail Meer-son-Aksyonov, considered the importance of ecclesiastical and liturgical reforms in order to modernize the missionary action of the Church especially among the youth. But this is not enough. As Aksyonov pointed out, "what makes the Baptists the sole missionary active force in Russia is that they conceive the profession of their faith as their number one religious activity."[114] Armed with the simple words of the Gospel they witness to the truth and resist evil. Alexander Solzhenitsyn, who loves them so much, must have had them in mind when he wrote in his appeal "Live Not according to Lie": from now on no honest man "should write, sign, print any declaration, not even a single sentence which might deform, according to him, the truth...."[115] The Moscow-Vatican ecumenical dialogue would very much benefit from giving careful consideration to this long list of lies which every Christian should avoid.

Regarding the cooperation of Christians with non-believers, Anatoly Levitin-Krasnov made the following surprising declaration:

> The establishment of full, as opposed to imaginary, freedom of religion in our country would destroy the artificial barriers between atheists and believers and would leave room for that atmosphere of friendship and collaboration in which they could search for the truth together.
>
> The struggle for freedom of religion, for freedom of atheism, and for full freedom of conscience is the olive branch that I stretch out to my friends—believers and atheists.
>
> I intended to finish here, but after some consideration, I feel that my appeal to fight for freedom of atheism may astonish many people, while others may consider it demagoguery.
>
> Yet, no—this is not demagoguery, it is the truth of life. For, in our society, atheism is not free, any more than religion is free. The situation of atheism at present strongly recalls the situation of the Orthodox Church in prerevolutionary Russia.
>
> Orthodoxy, as is well known, was, at the time, the official ideology. Any disputes over that ideology were categorically prohibited. "In our society, a priest is an unfortunate person; one must not argue with him," wrote V.S. Soloviev. The church was under compulsion and, therefore, not free.
>
> Atheism is not free in the Soviet Union, because it, too, is under compulsion; it is obligatory and not open to discussion. (One can conclude this even from the above discussion, since all the participants were convinced that a believer could not possibly be a teacher.)
>
> Therefore, the struggle for religious freedom is also a struggle for the freedom of atheism—because methods of compulsion (direct or indirect) compromise atheism, depriving it of all ideological meaning and all spiritual fascination.
>
> And therefore: Long live free religion and free atheism![116]

The fourth meeting, held at the end of June 1975 at Trento (Italy) did not touch any of the questions suggested by the struggling Christians of the Soviet Union. Chairmen for the meeting were Metropolitan Nikodim and Archbishop Roger Etchegaray of Marseilles, whose statement at the World Synod in Rome, in November 1974, that the Church does not condemn Marxism brought a sharp contradiction from other bishops. The final declaration stated that "The Church, realizing that salvation in a changing world means liberation from evil both personal and collective, is striving to bring this about by cooperating with all people of good will, believers and nonbelievers." The condition suggested by Anatoly Levitin that believers and nonbelievers should be "free" was not included in the declaration. In what was called "a remarkable ecumenical gesture," Pope Paul authorized the celebration of a Russian liturgy at the tomb of St. Peter. The liturgy was conducted by Metropolitan Nikodim, assisted by Bishop Mikhail of Astrakhan and four Russian Orthodox priests.[117]

On several occasions the Secretariat for Christian Unity stressed the "positive" results of Rome-Moscow dialogue. The decision of the Moscow Holy Synod to recognize the legality of mixed marriages between Catholic and Orthodox (April 4, 1967)[118] and to admit Catholics to Holy Communion (December 16, 1969)[119] are recorded as the most important achievements along with a number of personal exchanges of messages between the Pope and the Patriarch. The increasingly cordial relations were proved by frequent visits of representatives from both sides, accompanied by communal prayers, lectures, presentation of gifts and receptions. Since 1968 some Russian Orthodox priests and laymen from the Moscow and Leningrad Theological Academies have been guests of the Pontifical College Russicum in Rome in order to get acquainted with Catholic theology.

But despite or because of the intensification of these official relations, the contact with the Russian Orthodox faithful has been lost. Considering that the *sobornost* (conciliarity) or the participation of laity is required by Orthodox tradition in important ecclesiastical decisions, this loss cannot be underestimated by Roman ecumenists. The silence kept by Cardinal Willebrand and his aids on several occasions, especially regarding the suppression of the Ukrainian Catholic Church[120] and the dissenters, is a grave omission in Moscow-Vatican ecumenical dialogue. In the church of Russicum in Rome the prayer "for the long suffering Russian land" has been dropped from the Divine Liturgy since the beginning of the dialogue. At a meeting of the alumni of Russicum (October 1970) the suggestion of expressing in the final draft of the minutes the concern of many alumni for the oppression of Catholic and Orthodox faithful in the USSR was not accepted. Definitely in Rome, the city of the catacombs and the martyrs, détente is prevailing over dissent. Why? For the sake of peace or because "silence is gold?" Alexander Galich wrote on that "silence":

> How easy it is to become rich!
> How easy it is to become famous!
> How easy it is to become a hangman!
> Keep quiet! Keep quiet! Keep quiet![121]

What the dissenters are trying to do is to break this wall of silence. In the already quoted letter to the Fifth Assembly of the World Council of Churches (Nairobi, Nov. 23-Dec. 10, 1975) the Orthodox priest Gleb Yakunin and the layman Lev Regelson asked the Churches to return to the "spirit of veneration of the confessors of the faith" which inspired the first Christians and which "must become today's main ecumenical concern." Instead of keeping quiet, they should get acquainted with the facts, the closing of thousands of churches, the imprisonment of hundreds of believers, their appeals and courageous stand in front of the persecutors, know the names of the new martyrs, possibly get in touch with them by mail or on tourist trips, and publicize these facts and names in the press and radio broadcasts. Instead of ceasing to mention the confessors and the martyrs in their public services and prayers, the Churches should organize, as Pope Pius did in 1930, gatherings and lectures in support of those who have no voice and are under such great pressure and violence to be "forced to smile and protest against the help" from outside.

"We hope," wrote the two dissenters, "that many delegates to the Assembly . . . are convinced, as we are, that only at the foot of the Cross on Golgotha can be born that impetus of love which has the power to really overcome confessional fanaticism and isolationism and prepare the hearts of Christians to genuine unity."

Yakunin and Regelson were right. Many delegates shared their views. At first, the Assembly approved a resolution in which it expressed its concern for "the limitation of religious freedom in the USSR." But when the representatives of the Moscow Patriarchate protested, the leadership of the Assembly annulled the resolution "for technical reasons." Metropolitan Nikodim of Leningrad, one of the six newly elected Presidents of the Council, declared that the Assembly didn't have "enough facts" to approve the resolution which, according to him, was "based only on emotional factors."[122]

The political maneuvering of world "ecumenists" won again over Christian witness at Nairobi. Ironically or sadly enough, WCC General Secretary Philip Potter built his farewell speech around the theme: "He came into the world to free and unite."

Part II

The Unexpected Obstacle

4

The Rise of Dissent

One of the objectives—without doubt the primary one—Rome sought in initiating a "dialogue" was to help Catholics under Communist control. Until recently Rome took for granted that they would accept any initiative promoted by the Vatican for the "betterment" of East-West relations. No criticism could be expected from those who were described as the "Church of silence." Even if, for diplomatic reasons, their sufferings are now less mentioned, they shouldn't be so unjust as to suppose that Rome has forgotten them. They should be patient, because their miserable fate cannot be improved unless the general world relations are first changed. As Archbishop Casaroli said, a dialogue on peace should now have top priority in Moscow-Vatican meetings: this dialogue, which seems to be "hardly reversible," in the long run, will be beneficial not only to Catholics under direct or indirect Soviet rule, but for all mankind. That's why "sacrifices" should be continued and détente trusted, for the only alternative realistically valid in the present situation... remains the progressive reduction and elimination of the points of contrast and the search for those of contact."[1]

The patient work done by Vatican diplomats over an entire decade to build up the Vatican's long-range strategy was spoiled by precisely those least expected to interfere. Many of them are imprisoned or confined to insane asylums. Many are intellectuals, others workers or peasants. Some are believers and Catholics. They are known as "dissenters," fighters for democracy and human rights or simply *podpisanty,* "persons who sign innumerous petitions in defence of persecuted men."[2] Lately their voice has grown so strong that the ambitious US-USSR plan for détente is being threatened and the slight hopes of a Moscow-Vatican dialogue are in real trouble. Their views, though perfectly right, are very disturbing to Western and Vatican diplomats in these formative stages of dialogue. But, as Andrei Sakharov said, precisely because "the world is just entering on a new course of détente it is essential that the proper direction be followed from the outset."[3]

Just before and after Archbishop Casaroli's trip to Moscow in 1971 hundreds of priests and thousands of Lithuanian Catholics sent letters of protest to their civil and ecclesiastical authorities. During President Nixon's visit to the Soviet Union in May 1972, 15 Evangelical Baptists invaded the US embassy seeking America's help in getting the Kremlin to relax its antireligious policy (May 9). On May 14, in the Lithuanian city of Kaunas a Catholic young man, Romas Kalanta, burned himself to death in protest against Soviet oppression of his country. Kalanta's funeral became a mass demonstration demanding national and religious freedom. On May 21, in Moscow and several other cities police arrested nine Jews who had planned to present a petition to the American president stating their case for religious and cultural freedom and the right of unrestricted emigration to Israel.

The existence of civil and religious opponents in the Soviet Union is nothing new. But the 1970s dissent movement is something different from past counter-revolutionary movements. It is against the evils impersoned by Stalin and denounced by Khrushchev, for respect of legality and individual rights proclaimed in the Soviet Constitution, in the UN Declaration of Human Rights and promised by the Party. It would be a mistake to think, as some Western politicians and churchmen do, that this movement is unrealistic in its requests and will soon disappear. The fact that it doesn't come from outside, but from within the Soviet system and embraces a large range of Soviet citizens, representatives of intellectual, national and religious groups, suggests that it constitutes the most serious moral and ideological threat to the Soviet regime. Its voice should be listened to very carefully by those engaged in a dialogue with Moscow and who are about to make historical decisions which could result in harm for the peoples of the USSR and for the peoples of the world.

Freedom of Thought and Expression

For those who like to establish an approximate date of birth of dissent, December 5, 1965, can be selected.[4] On that day, the "Day of the Soviet Constitution," about one hundred people, mostly students, held a demonstration in Pushkin Square in Moscow, demanding "respect for the Constitution" and an "open trial for Sinyavsky and Daniel," two writers whose works, under the respective pen names of Abram Tertz and Nikolai Arzhak, had been smuggled and published abroad. They had been under arrest since September and held incommunicado. The foreign press took great interest in the fate of these two writers, especially Sinyavsky-Tertz, considered one of the best literary critics of the Soviet Union, contributor to the literary magazine *Novy Mir*, whose editor, Alexander Tvardovsky, had published Solzhenitsyn's first novel and was under attack for his liberal orientation. Andrei Sinyavsky was a personal friend of Boris Pasternak. He wrote a remarkable essay on Pasternak's poetry which was highly praised by the Nobel prize winner.[5] A widely publicized photo shows Sinyavsky and Yuli Daniel as pallbearers at Pasternak's funeral.

The demonstration in Pushkin Square was sponsored by friends and admirers of the two writers, representatives of SMOG,[6] a club of young intellectuals, and underground literary magazines such as *Sintaksis* (1958-

1960), *Feniks* (1961 and 1966) and *Sfinsky* (1965).[7] Several demonstrators were arrested and shortly afterwards released. But one of them, Vladimir Bukovsky (age 24), was put in a mental asylum for six months. He had already been committed to psychiatric clinics from 1963 until the spring of 1965 for his contributions to *Feniks* and the organization of unauthorized poetry readings in Mayakovsky Square.[8]

As a consequence of the protests of many intellectuals, both in and outside of the Soviet Union, the trial of Sinyavsky and Daniel (February 10-14, 1966) though not completely public, was held before a hand-picked audience of about 70 people so that the young dissenter Alexander Ginzburg was able to compile a White Book on the case containing the transcript of the proceedings and many Soviet and foreign reactions. He sent copies of his typewritten book to Kosygin and abroad. Sinyavsky and Daniel were sentenced, respectively, to 7 and 5 years hard labor for "slandering" the Soviet Union.

After the so-called de-Stalinization the Soviet leaders succeeded in presenting to the world a "different" image of their country. President Kennedy thought that "one of the principal hopes for world peace was that the leaders of the Soviet Union would continue their break away from Stalinist habits, suspicions, goals."[9] John XXIII was very much pleased when he received a Christmas message from Khrushchev written in his own hand, in which the First Secretary of the Communist Party "used religious terminology" and "made a specific reference to the Holy Days."[10] Now the leaders could not tolerate, as we read in the indictment against Sinyavsky and Daniel, that "anti-Soviet slanderous works of underground writers are being passed off by hostile propaganda as truthful accounts about the Soviet Union."[11]

Sinyavsky and Daniel are both believers. But their faith is not limited to "religious terminology." During the trial Sinyavsky was blamed for having called Communism "a new religion" and for having treated Lenin in a calumnious way. He answered: "I use the word 'religious' in various senses—with reference to the moral imperative and ironically, with reference, for example, to the mystique of *The Short Course,* the History of the Communist Party of the Soviet Union ascribed to Stalin and which was regarded as holy writ from the time of its publication in 1938 until after Stalin's death.[12] I spoke of these things in my article on Socialist Realism, because literature is nourished by a certain sap. The literature of Stalin's period was a literature of a religious character... As far as Lenin is concerned, I said that it was impossible to create a cult about him. For me Lenin is only a man; there is nothing negative in that."[13] But the judges were particularly furious at the "lyrical digressions" expressed by Sinyavsky in his *Thought Unaware*, a booklet of poetic prose and philosophic reflections that cannot be read, but only meditated on. There we find the simple faith of the great souls, a realistic concept of the Church and a courageous understanding of Christianity:

The theosophs fear the word "devil" and "God." They are always afraid of being suspected of ignorance and want to reason scientifically. This precaution does not inspire trust....

It is necessary to believe not just because of a tradition, not for fear of death, not for "in any case," not for humanistic principles, not in order to be saved and not to be original. It is necessary to believe for the simple reason that God exists....

The Church cannot but be conservative if she wants to remain faithful to tradition. She doesn't have the right to say one thing today and tomorrow something else according to the interests of progress... This natural (in principle) slowness to react to contemporaneity threatens the Church with immobilism and atrophy. But even so she is the incorrupt mummy waiting for the hour when it will be said (to her): Get up and walk! If only she would listen....

Present Christianity is sinning by its good manners. It thinks only of how not to get dirty, not to appear indelicate... They have exchanged the Church of Christ for an institution for noble girls. In the final analysis everything that is living and brilliant has passed into the hands of vice... The Church has forgotten the inflamed cursing of the Bible. But Christianity must be courageous and call things by their names. It is time to renounce the little angels with little halos so that the angels may become stronger and more evident than the airplanes. "Airplanes"—not in order to ape the style of the contemporary world, but to overcome it. Along this way one may fall into heresy. But now heresy is not so dangerous as the drying of the root. O Lord, better I err in your name than to forget you. Better I lose my soul than that you disappear from (my) sight.

Along with other religions Christianity fulfills the role of an assault battalion, launched into the most dangerous and heated part of the front... Look at the heroes of Christianity. Here the wise are not too many, but numerous are the militant who acquire glory by (their) constancy and death. The lives of the saints are an enumeration of tortures and executions suffered by an army of followers in the footsteps of an executed God. They are soldiers who show to the world scars and wounds as signs of valor. And of whom is this army composed? Of men of all nations, of the rabble, even of criminals who decided to carry over their shoulders the cross. Everyone, even the least, the most ignorant and sinful, provided he be ready to throw himself into the fire... Christianity is the religion of the greatest hopes born from desperation; the religion of chastity, affirmed in the most acute consciousness of one's own sinfulness; the religion of the resurrection of the flesh from stench and corruption. Nowhere, as in Christianity, is there such a near contact with death. The fear of death is not eliminated in it, but it is developed to the point of becoming capable of opening a breach in the sepulchre and springing to the other side. Christianity is not the contemplation of eternity, but the conquering of it in the battle, in the struggle with only one weapon—the readiness to die.[14]

During his trial Yuly Daniel was asked to explain how he got the idea for the story "Atonement," "in which he depicts Soviet society as being in a state of moral and political decay. The story suggests that the entire Soviet people is to blame for the cult of personality, that 'our prisons are within us,' that 'the government is unable to give us freedom,' that 'we sent ourselves to prison'...." Daniel replied:

In recent years we have often heard about people being exposed as slanderers whose denunciations landed innocent people in jail. I wanted to show a rather different situation—how a man must feel if he has been falsely accused of doing something as terrible as this. This was something that actually happened to somebody I knew well. That's how the idea of the story came to me. The indictment says that the underlying notion of the story is that everybody is to blame for the cult of personality and the mass persecutions. I agree with this interpretation, but not with the word "slanderous" used to describe the story. I feel that every member of society is responsible for what happens in society. And I make no exception for myself. I wrote that "everybody is to blame" because there has been no reply to the question of who is to blame. Nobody has ever publicly stated who was to blame for these crimes, and I will never believe that three men—Stalin, Beria and Ryumin—could alone do such terrible things to the whole country. But nobody has yet replied to the question as to who is guilty.[15]

With the exception of the young poet Joseph Brodsky (born in 1940), sentenced in 1964 to 5 years' hard labor as a "parasite," for the first time Stalinist terror was resumed against members of the intelligentsia, provoking a chain of strong reactions at home and abroad. An anonymous author wrote:

> The sentence in the Siniavsky-Daniel case plunges Soviet society once more into an atmosphere of terror and persecution.
> The Soviet government has done little enough for the rapprochement of East and West. An action such as the Siniavsky-Daniel trial can only destroy what bond there is.[16]

On September 16, 1966, three new paragraphs were added to article 190 of the Criminal Code in order to "legally" stop public protests, written and verbal statements "derogatory to the Soviet state and social system." In a letter to Soviet authorities prominent Soviet writers and scientists, among them Sakharov and Shostakovich, wrote that "the addition to the Criminal Code of Articles 190/1 and 190/3 opens the way to the subjective and arbitrary interpretation of any statement as deliberately false and derogatory to the Soviet State and social system . . . and will form a potential obstacle to the exercise of liberties guaranteed by the Constitution of the USSR."[17]

Here is the text of articles 70, 190/1 and 190/3 most frequently mentioned in the dissenters' trials:

Article 70
Agitation or propaganda carried on for the purpose of subverting or weakening Soviet power or of committing particular especially dangerous crimes against the state, or the [verbal] spreading for the same purpose of slanderous fabrications which defame the Soviet political and social system, or the circulation or preparation or keeping, for the same purpose, of literature of such content, shall be punished by deprivation of freedom for a term of six months to seven years, with or without additional exile for a term of two to five years, or by exile for a term of two to five years.

Article 190/1
The systematic dissemination by word of mouth of deliberately false statements derogatory to the Soviet state and social system, as well as the preparation or dissemination of such statements in written, printed, or any other form, is punishable by three years of detention, or one year of corrective labor, or a fine up to one hundred rubles.

Article 190/3

The organization of, or active participation in, group activities involving a grave breach of public order, or clear disobedience to the legitimate demands of representatives of authority, or interference with the work of transport, state, or public institutions or services, is punishable by three years of detention, or one year of corrective labor, or a fine up to one hundred rubles.[18]

The editor of the White Book on the trial of Daniel and Sinyavsky, A. Ginzburg, and his associates Yury Galanskov, Alexei Dobrovolsky and Vera Lashkova were arrested (January 1967) and tried under the new law (February 1968). Ginzburg got 5 years hard labor, Galanskov 7 years and died in prison on November 2, 1972 at the age of 33.

On January 22, 1967 another demonstration was held in Pushkin Square to protest the arrest of the above-mentioned dissenters and the introduction of the new paragraphs into article 190 of the Criminal Code. The organizer of the demonstration, Vladimir Bukovsky, and some of the participants were arrested and tried separately. Viktor Khaustov and Ilya Gabay were tried on February 16; Bukovsky, Vadim Delone and Evgeny Kushev on August 30-September 1, 1967. Pavel Litvinov, grandson of former Soviet Foreign Minister Maxim Litvinov, disregarding the warnings of the KGB, gathered the documents of the trials and sent them abroad.[19] Bukovsky got the maximum sentence under article 190/3: three years in a corrective labor camp, notwithstanding the fact that the lawyers who defended him and his friends had asked for their acquital.

The speeches for the defense were essentially good. "The demonstration in question was illegal. But illegality and criminal liability are two different things, and the demonstrators are not criminally liable," said Melamed defending Delone.[20] Kaminskaya, counsel for Bukovsky, was even more explicit, affirming that:

Demonstrations are allowed in our country—in accordance with the Constitution this freedom is guaranteed by law. It is not my view that Article 190/3 abrogates the citizen's right to hold demonstrations: criminal liability for taking part in a demonstration is accompanied by a breach of the peace as defined by some article in our Criminal Code ...

We can't make our own laws and find people guilty without legal grounds—and criticism of existing laws or of the KGB is not a crime under Article 190/3.[21]

The best defense came from Bukovsky himself, who aroused the indignation of the judge when he compared the policies of the Soviet government with those of the Fascist regimes:

The Prosecutor regards our demonstration as impudent. Yet here I have before me the text of our Constitution: "In the interests of the workers and in order to strengthen the Socialist System, the citizens of the USSR are guaranteed by law ... freedom to march and to demonstrate in the streets." Why was this article put in? To legalize the demonstrations of October and May Day? But that wasn't necessary—everybody knows that if the Government has organized a demonstration, nobody is going to break it up.

What is the use of freedom to demonstrate "for" if we can't demonstrate "against"? We know that protest demonstrations are a powerful weapon in the hands of the workers and that the right to hold them exists in every democracy. And where is this right denied? Here is *Pravda* of the 19th of August—a news item from Paris says that May Day demonstrators are being tried in Madrid. They were tried under a new law: it had recently been passed in Spain and it imposes terms of eighteen months to three years in prison for taking part in a demonstration. Note the touching unanimity of Fascist and Soviet law.[22]

These initial trials already showed how wide were the interests of the dissenters. They were defending not only their personal rights, but the legal and constitutional rights of the writers and the workers, of the national and religious groups. Delone, referring to the Jewish and Ukrainian ferment, told the judges: "I knew that similar meetings and demonstrations were taking place in other cities—the one in Kiev, for instance, held late last year at Babi Yar."[23] Kushev, according to the indictment, "fell under the influence of the religious fanatic A. Levitin (Krasnov), became imbued with the ideas of Christian Democracy, and adopted its viewpoint in regard to Soviet life." During the trial Kushev admitted that he believed in God and had been baptized. Levitin, called to the stand, praised the young man as "very unselfish, always thinking of others, never of himself, a gifted poet, deeply interested in art, history, philosophy" and defended the right of the nineteen-year-old boy to be baptized. "What I simply can't understand," declared Kushev, "is what religion has got to do with it. Why was there such a lot of talk about it? All it did was to create a tense atmosphere—after all, religion is a purely private matter . . . What we both (he and Levitin) think is simply that Christianity and Socialism go together."[24] Evidently the judges thought differently. These young dissenters in Pushkin Square displayed three banners, two of them with the slogan "Freedom for Dobrovolsky, Galanskov, Lashkova and Radzievsky" and another saying "We demand the revision of the anti-constitutional Decree and of Article 70 of the Criminal Code." According to the judges they were asking for too many freedoms.

The validity of the underground literature as well as the courage of the young demonstrators was acknowledged by several Soviet writers and intellectuals. In 1967 Alexander Solzhenitsyn proposed to the Fourth Congress of Soviet Writers "that the Congress adopt a resolution that would demand and ensure the abolition of all censorship, open or hidden, of all fictional writings and that would release publishing houses from the obligation to obtain authorization for the publication of every printed page."[25] But, as Arkady Belinkov pointed out, Glavlit (Main Board for the protection of Military and State Secrets in the Press) is "merely one" of the institutions in the total Soviet system of censorship and thought control. During a conversation on usual literary subjects an old and very famous author remarked to him: "What I'm going to say will not be published in my memoirs, although I might write it down. But perhaps in ten or fifteen years you will write about it or tell someone." Some fifteen years have passed and I am telling you. The author related the following incident:

> In 1954 we were all sitting in my dacha in a state of confusion, unable to grasp what was happening. Things were being written that we ourselves were writing thirty years before; everything was strange and unfamiliar. How should one write? Everything was incomprehensible. And then Kostya, Viktor and Sasha said to me, "Listen, go to *him* and explain. Let *him* tell you." I went to *him* and said, "Look, some write this, others write that. We are at a loss to know what to do. Guide us, as we have always been guided." And he replied, "No, that's your business. You are master in your own literary house. Do what you think is necessary. The time of the personality cult is over and will never return."
>
> The "business" referred to was Soviet literature, Kostya was Fedin, Viktor was Shklovsky and Sasha was Bek. The person who told me this story was Ilya Ehrenburg, and *him* was Khrushchev.
>
> I quote this incident to show that the writers themselves share the blame. The tragedy of Soviet Russian literature exists, it is not just a consequence of the censorship, and the latter's misdeeds should not be exaggerated. Most of the blame lies with the Soviet dictatorship which created the censorship along with the rest of the system, and which is mainly responsible for the vices of Soviet literature.[26]

The situation of Soviet journalism is even worse. There is a department "D" in the Central Administration of the KGB, where "D" probably stands for *dezinformatsiya* (misinformation), because the employees of this department specialize in spreading rumors and suppressing true information. TASS and Novosti, the Soviet news agencies, *Pravda, Izvestiia* and the other newspapers are directly controlled by the party at the Central Committee level. Not only world news, but what is happening in the next town remains unknown to the Soviet citizen. Lidiya Chukovskaya, a prominent critic expelled from the Moscow Writers Union, compared the Soviet press to a "soundproof wall" built up between "the thoughtful and the carefree."[27]

In order to knock down that "wall," Soviet dissenters rely on two means: *samizdat* and *glasnost*. *Samizdat*, a word invented in 1966 means "we-publish-ourselves." The literary works and documents rejected by the Gosizdat (State Publishing Houses) are reproduced uncensured on typewriters and printed in the *tamizdat*, that is "overthere, abroad." Since April 30, 1968, *samizdat* has published a *Chronicle of Current Events*, which provides regular, accurate and concrete information about the situation in the Soviet Union.[28] The *samizdat* is aimed at *glasnost*, that is, publicity at home and abroad. One of the best expressions of *glasnost* was the appeal to World Public Opinion by Pavel Litvinov and Larisa Bogoraz (wife of Yuly Daniel) to protest against the sentences of Galanskov and Ginzburg:

> We appeal to world public opinion, and in the first place to Soviet public opinion. We appeal to all in whom conscience is not dead and who are sufficiently courageous.
>
> Demand a public condemnation of this shameful trial and the punishment of those responsible.

Demand the release of the accused from custody.

Demand a fresh investigation, to be carried out in accordance with all legal standards and in the presence of international observers.

Citizens of our country! This trial is a blot on the honour of our state and on the conscience of each one of us. You elected this court, these judges—demand their dismissal from the offices which they have abused. In danger today are not only the destinies of the three accused—their trial is not a jot better than the notorious trials of the 1930s, which brought upon us all so much shame and so much blood that to this day we have not been able to recover from them.

We are giving this appeal to the Western progressive press and asking that it be published and broadcast as soon as possible. We are not appealing to the Soviet press, since this is hopeless.

11 January 1968[29]

The protest of Bogoraz and Litvinov was not the only one; 15 letters of protest, signed by about 700 people, reached Western journalists in Moscow in those days. That explains the panic of Soviet authorities and the new waves of persecutions and trials "Stalin style" resumed by the Brezhnev administration. Since December 1971, the secret police have been trying intensively to stop *samizdat* and thus demoralize the dissidents. In June 1972 Pyotr Yakir, a historian and son of a Red Army general liquidated under Stalin, and Viktor Krasin, an economist, were arrested and charged with illegal activities, clandestine meetings with foreigners, and preparation and distribution of the *Chronicle of Current Events*. Yakir's daughter, Irina, wife of Yuly Kim, an underground singer, was also harassed and interrogated almost daily over several weeks. After a six-day trial Yakir and Krasin confessed and on September 1, 1973 were sentenced to three years' confinement to be followed by three years' enforced residence in a remote part of the country. The prosecution said it had asked for a milder sentence because of their willingness to cooperate with the authorities. In fact a few days later the two dissidents were presented at a news conference to recant once more in public.[30] Soviet officials took the occasion to warn that "no Soviet citizen" is immune to prosecution for unlawful activities. The warning was clearly directed against the physicist Andrei Sakharov and the novelist Alexander Solzhenitsyn, who were currently targets of a growing press campaign for having criticized Soviet policies in meetings with Western newsmen.[31]

The *Chronicle of Current Events*, which usually appeared bimonthly and was regularly translated into English by Amnesty International Publications, was suspended with the No. 27 of October 15, 1972. In its place *A Chronicle of Human Rights in the USSR* was published in New York by Khronika Press. The efforts of Western free individuals and institutions to support Soviet dissenters' appeal for *glasnost* was not in vain. In May 1974 the *samizdat* was able to resume the publication of the *Chronicle of Current Events* after a hiatus of eighteen months. Nos. 28, 29, and 30 were published first. Somewhat later, on May 17, they were followed by No. 31, devoted to the movement for the return of the Crimean Tatars to the Crimea.[32]

Freedom for the Nationalities

The case of the Crimean Tatars is only one illustration of the oppression of national minorities in the USSR. In his secret speech at the 20th Congress of the Communist Party in 1956 Khrushchev recalled Stalin's "deportation of all the Karachai from the lands on which they lived. In the same period, at the end of December 1943, the same lot befell the whole population of the Autonomous Kalmyk Republic. In March 1944 all the Chechen and Ingush peoples were deported and the Chechen-Ingush Autonomous Republic was liquidated. In April 1944, all Balkars were deported to faraway places from the territory of the Kabardino-Balkar Autonomous Republic and the republic itself was renamed the Autonomous Kabardin Republic. The Ukrainians avoided meeting this fate only because there were too many of them and there was no place to which to deport them. Otherwise, Stalin would have deported them also."[33] It is significant that the Crimean Tatars, the Germans of the Volga Valley, the Jews, the Lithuanians, the Latvians and the Estonians, who also were deported, were not even mentioned by Khrushchev.[34]

In capitalist and former colonial countries, the USSR has always been quick to support and encourage nationalistic movements against the center if this served its political ends of world domination. The question of the nationalities was discussed among the Bolsheviks at the beginning of this century. In 1904, when asked whether "national independence" was good or dangerous for the proletariat, Stalin answered that "to require a definitive answer to this question is an evident stupidity."[35] Playing on the ambiguity of their position, the Bolsheviks won the support of the nationalities, but when they took power, the rights of the nationalities were denied. Stalin didn't see a contradiction in this policy of the Soviet Union because, as he explained, the Soviet Union favored the separation of India, Egypt, etc. from imperialist oppression, but it opposed the separation of the peripheric regions from Russia because "in this case separation means imperialist oppression, the weakening of Russia's revolutionary strength, the strengthening of the imperialists' positions."[36] Later, in his articles on Soviet linguistics, Stalin maintained against the theories of Nikolai Marr that the Russian language will prevail over the national ones, but prudently explained that this will happen gradually, because the law of transition from one quality to another by way of leaps (or explosions or revolutions) continues to hold in the sphere of social development only for the society divided into mutually hostile classes, not for the socialist classless society.[37]

It is difficult to prove, as many Marxist-Leninists (including dissenters) try to do, that Stalin deviated from Lenin's principles in his nationality policies. Soviet efforts of russification are often justified with Lenin's declaration that "every inhabitant of Russia ought to have the opportunity to learn the great Russian language."[38] At any rate, both Lenin and Stalin approved the slogan of "self-determination to the point of secession" for national minorities. This principle was even incorporated into the Soviet Constitution, but along with other constitutional declarations of freedom, it remains void and strictly subordinated to the interests of the Communist state and of so-called "proletarian internationalism." Although for different reasons, Soviet communists and Russian nationalists hold the old tsarist tenet that "Rossiya—yedinaya i mnogonarodnaya" (Russia is one, formed by many peoples).But now the dissenters think differently. Former Major-General Pyotr Grigorenko, who considers himself a Leninist, speaking at a gathering of Crimean Tatars on March 17, 1968, blamed with inflamed words the Soviet leadership:

> You did not commit the crimes for which you were driven from the Crimea; yet you are not permitted to return there ... We think that the main reason for this lies in the fact that you underestimate your enemy. You think that you are dealing only with honest people. This is not so. What happened to your nation was not the work of Stalin alone. And his accomplices not only are still alive but hold responsible positions. They are afraid that, if you are given back what was unlawfully taken from you, they may, in time, be called upon to answer for their participation in such arbitrary rule ....
>
> In your fight, don't lock yourselves into a narrow nationalist shell. Form contacts with all progressive persons of other nationalities in the Soviet Union, first of all those nationalities among whom you live—Russians, Ukrainians, the nationalities that have been and continue to be subjected to the same indignities as your people.
>
> Don't consider your case to be inner-governmental. Seek help from the whole of progressive society and from international organizations. There is a specific name for what was done to your people in 1944. It is *genocide*, pure and simple—"one of the gravest crimes against humanity" (B.S.E., Vol. 10, p.441).
>
> The convention adopted by the U.N. General Assembly on December 9, 1948, included in the category of genocide "acts committed with intent to destroy, in whole or part, a national, ethnic, racial, or religious group as such" by any of various methods and specifically, "by deliberately inflicting on the group conditions of life calculated to bring about its physical destruction in whole or in part...." Such acts—*i.e.*, "genocide"—are, from the viewpoint of international law, crimes condemned by the civilized world, for which the chief culprits and their accomplices are liable to punishment under law. So you see, international law is also on your side. [*Wild applause.*] If you cannot obtain a solution of the problem within the country, you have a right to appeal to the U.N. and the international tribunal.
>
> Stop begging! Take back that which was taken from you unlawfully! [*Wild applause; in a single outburst of emotion, those in the audience jump up from their seats shouting* "Crimean A.S.S.R.!"] And remember, in this just and noble struggle, you must not allow your opponents to snatch with impunity the fighters who are in the foremost ranks of your movement.

There have already been a series of trials in Central Asia in which fighters for equal rights for the Crimean Tatars have been sentenced unlawfully and on false grounds. Right now in Tashkent, a trial of a similar nature is being prepared for Mamed Enver, Yuri and Savri Osmanov, and others.

Do not permit judicial reprisals to be carried out against these people. Demand and obtain for them an open trial, come to it in great numbers, and do not permit the court to be filled with specially selected spectators....

I raise my glass in honor of all brave and inflexible fighters for national equality, to one of the most outstanding warriors on this front, the writer and Bolshevik-internationalist Aleksei Yevgrafovich Kosterin, and to the health of the Crimean people! To our future meeting in Crimea, dear friends, on the territory of a re-established and reborn Crimean Autonomous Soviet Socialist Republic!!! [*Wild applause; toasts ...*][39]

The idea of a union among the nationalities in order to achieve self-determination was expressed in 1969 in a "Program of the Democratic Movement of the Soviet Union" signed by "democrats of Russia, Ukraine and the Baltic countries." The impartial help of the UN is highly welcomed in this Program, which allots to the United Nations the role of the "supreme arbiter."[40] Despite Andrei Amalrik's prediction that "the unavoidable 'deimperialization' [of the USSR] will take place in an extremely painful way, power will pass into the hands of extremist elements and groups, and the country will begin to disintegrate into anarchy, violence and intense national hatred,"[41] at the present moment the dissenters are strongly supporting the rights of the nationalities.

Sergei Kovalyov, a Russian dissident biologist active in Sakharov's Human Rights Movement, was arrested on December 27, 1974, by Soviet authorities investigating an underground Lithuanian Roman Catholic journal, the *Chronicle of the Catholic Church in Lithuania,* which is fighting for Lithuanian religious and national freedom.[42]

"Let us think logically," writes Ivan Dzyuba, a Ukrainian literary critic and writer. "Was tsarist Russia a despotic empire, or not? If it was, how can a Marxist-Leninist admit even the possibility of a genuine (and not merely formal) voluntary annexation or reunion as a part of that process which went down in history as a classical example of a colonial offensive?"[43] Recognizing the mistakes of his own people, Dzyuba wrote: "We Ukrainians must fight against all manifestations in our midst of anti-Semitism or disrespect toward the Jews ... You Jews must fight against those who do not respect the Ukrainian people, the Ukrainian culture, the Ukrainian language... We must outgrow all forms of human hatred, overcome all misunderstandings, and by our own efforts win true brotherhood."[44]

Many of the Soviet dissenters are Jews or of Jewish extraction. This fact, while representing a great honor for them, plays a significant role in their repression. On August 25, 1968, for instance, when a number of young people mounted a demonstration in Moscow's Red Square calling for the immediate withdrawal of Soviet troops from Czechoslovakia, the demonstration was broken up by the militia shouting, according to one of the demonstrators, Natalya Gorbanevskaya: "These are all dirty Jews! Beat the anti-Soviets."[45]

The Soviet Union is one of the few countries in the world where anti-Semitism is practiced at state level. The Jews are accused of being either Zionists or "Fatherlandless or Rootless Cosmopolitans." Stalin tried to "exile" them to Birobidzhan, suppressed their culture, imprisoned and shot to death some of their best intellectuals.[46] Soviet literature, both Russian and Yiddish, evidences the various stages of the exile endured by the Jewish people on Soviet soil. Among the positive and negative characters created by Soviet literature, some Jews are portrayed, but the "real" Jew is always a despicable person. In order to have the right to live in a socialist society, he must shed his traditions, renounce his nationality, and stop being what it is to be a Jew.[47]

In a Yiddish anecdote on Birobidzhan, a young man traveling toward the new land turns to one of his friends and asks, "Well, now, Comrade Mot'l Shklovr, what was it you said we are going to build?" The friend replies, "Something very simple. Is it really so hard to remember? We are going to build socialism."[48] Jewish culture would have had to become more socialist according to Stalin's formula: in Soviet society culture is "national in form and socialist in content," in order to "consolidate" the dictatorship of the proletariat. But it turned out that the Jews as well as the other nationalities are permitted in the USSR only as a socialist "anational" culture.

"Elie Yehudin" is a short story by S. Gordon (1944) recounting the evacuation of a Jewish district in the Ukraine before the Nazi advance. Elie, the young organizer, sees some old Jews in a railroad carriage dressed in their very best. "They were tenderly clutching long bundles in their hands. 'What do you have there,' he asked. 'The sacred books,' they replied. 'Perhaps you think we should have left them behind for the Hamans, imach shemom (may the name be erased)? Elie Yehudin, do you know the significance of Lech-lecho maertsecha umimoladetecha (Get thee out of thy country, and from thy father's house)?' 'I know it.' And the old people, referring to their sad fate, conclude, 'This is what it means!'"[49] Elie Yehudin, though a Communist, not only knew the sacred writings, but knew them in Hebrew, which since 1926 has been prohibited in the USSR as a Biblical and Zionist language.

The Jewish identity of religion and nationality was one of the main reasons why a Jewish socialist culture proved to be impossible in the USSR.

Jewish nationhood has been religiously impregnated from the days of its inception. In their earliest days the Israelites, surrounded as they were by stronger neighbours, had to base their national unity and strength on something non-physical, something the material power of their enemies could not touch. This religious form of Jewish nationality evolved still further in the dispersion, after the territorial framework of Jewish peoplehood was destroyed. Jews now had to make the Torah their "portable

Fatherland," and had to preserve their national existence by an elaborate and religiously sanctioned code of belief and conduct, which guides not only man's relation to his Creator and to his fellow men on the basis of high moral principles, but also regulates aspects of his daily life that would appear extraneous material in any other religion. Indeed it was entirely through the medium of religion that Jewry preserved its national heritage, evolved a specific Jewish way of life, and maintained the body of the nation.[50]

The attempts conducted by the Jews themselves through the Yevsektsiya, the Jewish section of the Communist Party, to build up a Jewish socialist culture were doomed to failure. Isaac Babel was reprimanded for having placed Lenin beside Maimonides in his Red Cavalry, for the two "cannot live in peace... Maimonides is incompatible with Lenin."[51] The Yiddish writers paid with their lives for their effort to create a Jewish culture on purely Marxist-Leninist principles. That's why when Golda Meir went to Moscow as Israel's first envoy in September 1948 and raised the question of Jewish immigration from the Soviet Union to Israel, she was so enthusiastically welcomed by thousands of Russian Jews.[52]

On September 21, with an article by Ilya Ehrenburg published in *Pravda,* the Soviet government let the Israelis and the Soviet Jews know that Soviet Jews were not to have any contact with Jews outside the Soviet Union. There would be no immigration to Israel from Communist countries. Nevertheless, even Ehrenburg, described by his compatriots as an "Honorary Aryan" because of the privileged position he won in Soviet culture betraying his people, had to take a stand against anti-Semitism. During the festivities for his sixtieth birthday, the writer spoke of the great Russian national and literary traditions to which he felt bound. "On my passport the blank for nationality is filled in with Jew... However, in culture, tradition and formation I feel myself a Russian writer. But as long as there is a single anti-Semite in the world, whoever asks me my nationality will hear me reply with pride that I am a Jew."[53] A great applause interrupted him when he mentioned his Jewish nationality, but Ehrenburg turned on his public with annoyance and said: "Why are you applauding? I write Jew on the passport because I am a Jew. If I were Russian, I would write Russian. There is nothing to applaud for."[54]

Ehrenburg's timid blow against anti-Semitism and his protest against the applause when he mentioned his Jewish nationality are extremely eloquent. While Khrushchev and his successors denied the existence of a "Jewish question" in the USSR, anti-Jewish repression continued. In the years 1961-1963, during the campaign against economic speculators, Jews were heavily overrepresented in these "crimes", which allegedly took place in the shadow of the synagogue.[55] More recently, in December 1974, Mikhail Leviyev, a Jewish former manager of a popular store in Moscow, and Mikhail Shtern, a Jewish doctor from Vinnitsa, were tried and sentenced to death and nine years at hard labor, respectively, on charges of bribery.[56]

This anti-Jewish campaign is not theological or scientific. Its vicious and vulgar character is evident in Soviet anti-Semitic publications such as Trofim Kichko's "Judaism without Embellishment" (Kiev, 1963) and "Judaism and Zionism" (Kiev, 1968) and Yuri Ivanov's "Beware: Zionism!" (Moscow, 1969). Here Judaism is described as an immoral, corrupt, anti-human, racist creed, as a bond of allegiance to a foreign country and to reactionary pro-imperialist Zionism. Rightly S. Ettinger wrote that in the USSR Jewish nationality could be described as a purely "negative nationality," a nationality which exists only for purposes of restrictions, discrimination and abusive definition.[57]

Due to these unbearable conditions a strong exodus movement developed among the Soviet Jews. At first it was limited to those who were seeking reunification with members of their families. The Soviet press attacked Israeli tourists who, during their stay in the Soviet Union, were contacting Soviet Jews. The same accusations were repeated against Ambassador Tekoah.[58] But then, strengthened by the official anti-Israeli propaganda conducted before, during and after the Six-Day war, the movement assumed unprecedented proportions. The Soviet Jews sent hundreds of letters and appeals to Soviet leaders and abroad, openly renounced their Soviet citizenship, returned Soviet decorations, organized demonstrations and sit-in strikes in public and ministerial offices. An underground journal called *Iskhod (Exodus)* was started in 1970 with the purpose of making known the numerous cases of Jews being subjected to coercion, threats and physical violence after stating their desire to emigrate to Israel.

Soviet interest in détente and trade with the United States brought some relief to Soviet Jews after Congressional insistence that more favorable trade terms be linked to an easing of restrictions on emigration. The exorbitant tax for the education received, imposed on Jews willing to emigrate, was dropped, but still each applicant must pay 500 rubles for an exit visa plus another 400 for surrendering their citizenship, a considerable outlay in a country where the average monthly salary is 135 rubles. Furthermore the applicants must check in with the local police before proceeding to the OVIR (Department of Visas and Registration), which intimidates some applicants even from the beginning. Among the documents required are a letter of invitation from a relative, permission of parents if they are not going, and a reference from the employer. Out of fear, the employers often give poor references. As a consequence, some Jews were quitting their jobs with a good reference before applying to emigrate. But this practice has been frustrated by a new regulation that the reference must date back six months. On the other hand anyone unemployed for more than four months faces prosecution for "parasitism." For instance, 433 Georgian Jews from Tbilisi, Kutaisi, Poti and Kulashi Settlement, in an appeal to the Organizing Committee of the 24th Party

Congress in 1971, declared: "Several years ago we submitted applications to emigrate from the USSR. In expectation of our departure many of us have sold our belongings and homes and given up our jobs, and now we live in corners of other people's homes... For two fruitless years we have haunted government organizations. Nothing makes any difference."[59]

Despite all these difficulties, 110,000 Soviet Jews have been able to emigrate to Israel since 1971, but the decrease from 1973 to 1975 has been disastrous. The high of 33,500 emigres in 1973 fell to 19,700 in 1974 and to 4,290 in the first six months of 1975. The decline of almost 40 per cent in 1974 was interpreted as a Soviet pressure move to show that the rate of emigration could be reduced if the 1972 agreed trade concessions were not granted.[60] But when in December 1974 the American Senate and Congress, under Kissinger's "assurances", ratified the trade bill, the Soviets categorically denied the existence of any pact on emigration, saying that Foreign Minister Andrei Gromyko had made the Soviet position clear in a letter to Secretary of State Kissinger on October 26.[61]

Literaturnaya Gazeta charged that the "assurances" of Soviet concessions on emigration were fabricated to give the members of Congress a face-saving explanation for not voting against the trade reform bill because such a negative vote might have cost them the support of American businessmen who favored the measure.[62] On the other hand Western diplomats were wrong assuming that a less formal understanding was reached and that Moscow's denial was made for domestic consumption.[63] In July 1975 the Soviets restated to a delegation of 14 US Senators their refusal to relax emigration restrictions in return for American trade benefits.[64] This is why A. Sakharov rightly told foreign newsmen that "Moscow's disavowal of concessions should have been taken more seriously by the United States Congress."[65]

Whatever the developments of Jewish emigration and emigration in general from the Soviet Union may be, Communism continues to drive the people away from the "earthly paradise" it claims to create. Among the "emigrants" who recently left or were deported from the USSR are the writers Alexander Solzhenitsyn, Andrei Sinyavsky, Vladimir Maximov, Viktor Nekrasov and Anatoly Levitin-Krasnov; the scientists Valery Chalidze, Alexander Yesenin-Volpin and Alexander Voronel; the singer-satirist Alexander Galich, the dancer Valery Panov, the cellist Mstislav Rostropovich, the poets Joseph Brodsky and Naum Korzhavin; and the scholars Yefim Etkind and Pavel Litvinov, and the Lithuanian seaman Simas Kudirka.

"We are living on a moonscape," said a literary critic who remains. "There is no one left. We are all alone on the moon." Quoting these words and the verses of Soviet poets like Andrei Voznesensky and Yevgeny Yevtushenko, Hedrick Smith, former chief of the Moscow bureau of the *New York Times,* sees a sense of despair pervading Soviet society and a general disappointment with regard to détente which "has not borne the fruit of liberalization and greater access to the outside world."[66]

The great merit of the Jewish dissenters and their brethren abroad is to have set an example on how to react against despair. As the Jewish poet Naum Korzhavin puts it in his poem "The Trumpeters," "after all, except for us, there are no trumpeters on earth."[67]

The responsibility of each individual for the oppression of the regime was stressed by another Jew, Anatoly Kuznetsov, a Soviet writer who defected in 1969 while in London. He blames himself and all the Soviet writers for having accepted not only the official censorship from above, but also a self-censorship from within. In 1970 Anatoly republished his novel *Babyi Yar*, which had been previously printed in the Soviet Union with drastic changes and cuts so that there was nothing left of the broader humanistic idea and was reduced to just one more indictment of German Fascism. "In my novel," writes Anatoly in an introductory note, "there are three chapters called 'They Burned Books.' First the books are burnt in 1937 during the Stalin purges, then in 1942 under the Germans, and finally in 1946 after Zhdanov's interventions. Only the middle chapter on the burning of the books under the Germans survived censorship."[68] In order to have his book published, Anatoly had to add to the text even "some anti-Semitic nuances." Yevgeny Yevtushenko, who wrote his famous poem "Babyi Yar" after they visited together the remains of the death camp, was more fortunate because of his "connections." Anatoly concludes his remarks with a kind of confession-accusation, which explains why life in the Soviet Union became so unbearable for the creativity of the writers and the sincerity of the citizens:

> Alexander Solzhenitsyn and Joseph Brodsky do not cultivate friendships with the high and mighty. Yevtushenko does, as a matter of tactics, and it enabled him to publish a poem branding the heirs of Stalin with the help of these very heirs. But there are dangers involved in prostituting yourself, of bartering away your conscience in that strange world of perpetual intrigues and constant self-censorship. It is the road to destruction, because the official, external, censorship, by engendering self-censorship and compromise, destroys the artist and destroys the human being. I, personally, have gone down the road of surrender to the very brink of destruction, where I felt like either committing suicide or going out of my mind. I fled from the Soviet Union like an animal saving itself from a natural calamity: anywhere, but only away, away; otherwise—destruction.
>
> A truly great Soviet literature cannot exist, because although there are many gifted artists, true genius is squandered. Genius is uncompromising, genius and villainy are incompatible, and that crystal purity, without which there is no genius, is absolutely impossible in the Soviet Union....
>
> I regard my own past silence as a crime. My own self-censorship was motivated by cowardice and the instinct of self-preservation. It is nothing to be proud of; I would even go further and say that no writer in the Soviet Union has anything very much to be proud of, not one writer! Even the great—Pasternak, Tsvetayeva and Akhmatova—practised at least the self-censorship of silence. And the contemporary poetess Bella Akhmadulina, who is near to greatness, writes only about eternal values and does not reveal her attitude

to the Orwellian horrors surrounding her: the invasion of Czechoslovakia, the imprisonment of Sinyavsky, Daniel, Ginzburg and Marchenko, and much else.

Perhaps the greatest living Soviet writer, Alexander Solzhenitsyn, has every right to be proud of his work, but can we say this entirely without reservation? He speaks as an anti-Soviet, revealing shocking details about the Soviet regime, but about the nature of the regime itself—the naked king himself—he says nothing. He allows us to draw our own conclusions from the complex pattern of images and allusions which he weaves, but by not stating his own conclusions he exercises self-censorship. At one time the Party allowed some of Solzhenitsyn's works to be published because they fitted in with the official policy of discrediting Stalin. When he began to take too many liberties they muzzled him, and he became a martyr for exposing the evils of Stalinism. But what about Lenin and Leninism, and communism in general? Solzhenitsyn employs rigid self-censorship when dealing with these questions....[69]

When Kuznetsov wrote these remarks Solzhenitsyn's *Gulag Arch-ipelago* had not yet been published as well as his literary memoirs *(Bodalsya telenok s dubom)* and his appeal to fight uncompromisingly against the "lie" of Marxism-Leninism. In these works Solzhenitsyn agrees with Kuznetsov that true human life will be possible in the Soviet Union only after a future de-Leninization. To put all the blame on Stalin and say that Lenin was a friend of the Jews and wanted real freedom for the peoples is a lie, it's merely another kind of self-censorship in dealing with the Soviets which many supporters of détente are knowingly imposing on themselves. That's why Solzhenitsyn and Sakharov do not like what they call Western "leftist-liberal faddishness." The example of the Jews is not followed by those Christians, including Vatican officials who, in the spirit of détente, are trying to find a common ground with the Soviets and keep silent even on religious persecutions. Father Robert Drinan, S.J., a member of the US House of Representatives, in August 1975 went to the Soviet Union with a group of nine Church-related Americans "to express our solidarity with Soviet Jews." Andrei Sakharov, whom he visited in Moscow, "expressed with remarkable vigor his conviction that the 'role of Christians' in helping Soviet Jews 'can be immense.' He urged that Christian spokesmen from America avoid the official religious leaders in the USSR who are 'collaborators' and establish contacts with Russia's religious dissidents, at least 300 of whom are in prison.... Sakharov suggested that Russia's prisoners of Zion received some moral support and help but that Christians imprisoned in Russia for their religion received almost no domestic or international encouragement...."[70]

Freedom for the Religious Groups

The great ambition of Nikita Khrushchev was to lead the country more speedily toward the goal of a Communist society, something that many Western observers didn't realize. All his economic, bureaucratic and educational reforms, including the so-called de-Stalinization, as well as his dynamic foreign policy were aimed at the establishment of the "technico-material basis" of Communism by 1980. That's why he didn't allow any liberalization in regard to freedom of thought and freedom of religion. The first step taken by Khrushchev in order to correct Stalin's relaxation on religious matters goes back to July 7, 1954, when he was first secretary of the Party and not yet prime minister. On that date the Central Committee issued a decree, remaining unpublished until 1963,[71] which reintroduced the vulgarities and rudeness of the old militant atheism, arousing the protests of the believers and the clergymen, who during the "patriotic war" stood up and fought for the country. For this reason the Central Committee on November 10 of the same 1954 issued another decree signed by Khrushchev himself, lamenting the mistakes in atheistic propaganda and calling for a more "scientific" approach in antireligious matters.[72]

After 1954, a period of relative peace for the Church can be observed, but it didn't last long. The decision to change the religious policy was discussed as early as August 1957, but the attack started in 1959. *Pravda* denounced any attempt to reconcile religion with Communism[73] and in September the antireligious review *Nauka i Religiya* began its publications. The Ilichev report[74] made official the persecution already in progress. Thousands of churches were closed (1959-61), antireligious laws were tightened up (1961-62)[75], the influence on the youth by the clergy and the families strongly reduced (1963-64). Contrary to previous persecutions, the leaders of the Churches were not touched, but persuaded to accept "voluntarily" the new restrictions, enforce them, and punish the transgressors.

Groups of religious dissenters start to appear in 1961 as a reaction to the inability of the leadership of the Churches to oppose illegal interference of the state in ecclesiastical affairs. In May 1961, an "Action Group" *(initsiativnaya gruppa)* was formed among the Evangelical Christians and Baptists of the Soviet Union in order to elect a new All-Union Council of the Evangelical Christians and Baptists (AUCECB), the official body which presides over this federation of Protestant denominations. The leaders of the initsiativniki, G. K. Kryuchkov, A. A. Shalashov and A. F. Prokofiev in a letter to Khrushchev (August 13) and in declaration to the faithful affirmed:

> The AUCECB was not elected by the Church but was formed by state organs, mainly from churchmen who gave their consent both to deviate from Evangelical doctrine and to collaborate illegally with various state organs, for which purpose some of them were released from detention before their terms were up....
>
> The direction and control over the church has come through two main channels: one more overt, through the representatives of the Council for the Affairs of Religious Cults, the other more disguised, through the thousands of threads of a dense net of official and unofficial agents of the KGB....
>
> Today Satan is dictating through the servants of the AUCECB while the church

accepts all sorts of decrees which openly contradict the commandments of God . . . .
Because of the subservience of the AUCECB leadership to human directives, the church
has deviated from the Lord's teaching and is riddled with unworthy people; this is the
reason for the schism in our communities.[76]

In 1962 the Action Group was transformed into an Organizing
Committee and Prokofiev was arrested and sentenced to ten years (five in
prison and 5 in exile). Hundreds of Baptists were sent to camps and mental
asylums, separated from their children, tortured and even murdered. On
February 23, 1964, the initsiativniki held the first Congress of the prisoners'
relatives, which led to the establishment of the Council of Relatives of
Prisoners belonging to the ECB and, on the following year, to the
schismatic organization of a Council of Churches of the ECB (CCECB)
independent from the AUCECB. Meanwhile, in order to answer to the lies
and accusations of the *Bratsky Vestnik (Fraternal Herald)*, the organ of the
pro-government AUCECB, the initsiativniki circulated their own samizdat
with underground periodicals such as *Bratsky Listok (Fraternal Leaflet,*
from 1964), *Vestnik Spaseniya (Messenger of Salvation)* and the *Bulletin
of the Council of Prisoners' Relatives of ECB in the USSR* (from April
1971).

Since 1964 a steady flow of documents has been reaching the West
through the ECB's samizdat, presenting circumstantial details about the
oppression of the believers, a good knowledge of the laws and, above all, a
great courage and endurance of Christian joy under duress. In 1972, Ivan
Moiseyev, a young Soviet soldier, was killed after he had resisted all
attempts to stop him bearing witness to Christ. The account of his murder
published in the *Bulletin of the Council of Prisoners' Relatives* together
with Ivan's letters and transcripts of tapes which he made on his last home
leave shows that we are in the presence of a true martyr of Christ.[77]

The faith and fortitude of Evangelical leaders like Georgy Vins, so
many times arrested and imprisoned, impressed all the churches of the
world.[78] The best praise of the Baptists was written by Alexander
Solzhenitsyn in his first novel *One Day in the Life of Ivan Denisovich*:
"They were an unlucky group too. What harm did they do anyone by
praying to God? Every damn one of them had been given twenty-five
years." Shukhov (Ivan Denisovich) ridicules Alyosha, a young Baptist who
prays and suffers in silence:

Prayers are like those appeals of ours. Either they don't get through or they're returned
with "rejected" scrawled across 'em . . . However much you pray it doesn't shorten your
stretch. You'll sit it out from beginning to end anyhow." Alyosha answers: "We didn't
pray for that . . . You shouldn't pray to get parcels or for extra stew, not for that. Things
that man puts a high price on are vile in the eyes of Our Lord. We must pray about things
of the spirit—that the Lord Jesus should remove the scum of anger from our hearts."
When Shukhov, in order to support his unbelief, brings up the case of his parish priest, a
greedy and immoral man, Alyosha replys: "Why are you talking to me about priests? The

Orthodox Church has departed from Scripture. It's because their faith is unstable that they're not in prison.[79]

Solzhenitsyn's criticism of the Russian Orthodox Church to which he belongs and has no intention of abandoning, came in a more open and articulate form later, in 1972, in his famous "Lenten letter" to Patriarch Pimen. The main points of the letter are (1) that the Church is ruled by atheists, (2) something that cannot be accepted by the Patriarch as a lesser evil, (3) but should be rejected at the cost of suffering the Cross and the sacrifices as Jesus and the modern and early Christians did.

... The whole administration of the Church is conducted secretly by the *council for religious affairs*, including the appointment of pastors and bishops (even those who commit outrages, so as to make it easier to ridicule and destroy the Church).

The Church is ruled dictatorially by atheists—a sight never before seen in two millennia! The whole of the Church's property and the use of Church funds—the mites contributed by pious fingers—is under their control. Five million roubles at a time are donated to outside funds with grandiloquent gestures, while beggars are thrown off the church porch on their necks and there is nothing with which to repair a leaking roof in a poor parish.

Priests have no rights in their own parishes; only the act of worship is still entrusted to them for the time being, so long as they do not go outside the church for it, and they have to ask permission of the the town council if they want to visit a sick person or enter the churchyard.

By what reasoning is it possible to convince oneself that the planned *destruction* of the spirit and body of the Church under the guidance of atheists is the best way of *preserving* it? Preserving it for *whom*? By *falsehood*? But after the falsehood by whose hands are the holy mysteries to be celebrated?

Most Holy Father, Do not ignore altogether my unworthy cry. Perhaps such a cry will not reach your ears every seven years. Do not let it be supposed, do not make people think, that for the bishops of the Russian Church earthly power is more important than heavenly power or that their temporal responsibilities are more awesome to them than their responsibility before God.

Let us not deceive ourselves before men—and even less in prayer—that external chains have power over our souls. Things were no easier at the birth of the Christian faith; nevertheless it held out and prospered. And it showed us the way: *sacrifice*. Though deprived of all material strength, it is always victorious in *sacrifice*.

Within our own living memory many of our priests and fellow-believers have accepted such a martyrdom, worthy of the early Christians. But in those days they were thrown to the *lions*, whereas today you can lose only your material well-being.

In these days, as you go down on your knees before the Cross brought out into the middle of the church, ask the Lord what other purpose but sacrifice can there be in your service to your people, who have almost lost their Christian countenance and even the spirit of the faith?[80]

Father Sergei Zheludkov, a well-known dissident priest, active in the defense of civil rights for Soviet citizens, thought that Solzhenitsyn's letter was one-sided, containing only "half-truths," and wrote to him that:

the full truth is that the legal church organization cannot be an island of freedom in our strictly unified society, directed from a single centre... We are not permitted to work at the religious education of children or of adults, just as we are not permitted to do many other things necessary for the existence of real church life. We are permitted only one thing—to conduct divine worship in our churches...Should we say: all or nothing? Should we try to go underground, which in the present system is unthinkable? Or should we try somehow to accept the system and for the present make use of those opportunities that are permitted? The Russian hierarchy took the latter decision.[81]

This contradiction seen in Zheludkov's concept of dissent was not new. Even when he protested in favor of Marchenko[82] and Litvinov[83] he tried to excuse his Church. In a brief answer Solzhenitsyn wrote to Fr. Zheludkov: "You surprise me too. 'If there is a future, then there will also inevitably be a renaissance of Russian Christianity,' you say. Are we not going to do anything about it? It is precisely the inward defence of the faith that has gone... Of course it would be wrong to incite people to martyrdom. But may we not call them to the way of sacrifice? Why should you forbid this?"[84]

A more extensive and concrete answer to Fr. Zheludkov was given by Felix Karelin, a Russian Orthodox layman living in Moscow. Solzhenitsyn, says Karelin, is not calling for a revolution, but for the respect of the rights of the faithful and reminding the Patriarch of his duty to demand from the government to honor the Constitution and the laws which recognize those rights:

What you call the whole truth is in fact a mixture of two basic untruths paralysing the Russian Church today: one pertaining to the Church in itself (the ecclesia), the other pertaining to the Church in society. The essence of the first untruth is unbelief in the Church's spiritual power... the heart of the second untruth is the idea that believers have no civil rights—an idea that has eaten into the thinking of almost the entire Russian clergy... Do you think that among the reproaches addressed to the Russian hierarchy by Solzhenitsyn... there is a single one contradicting the laws of the state?... It is also clear that there are no Soviet laws demanding the registration of church sacraments... or hindering the conduct of funeral services in cemeteries and in homes, or limiting the participation of children and young people in the sacraments and church services; there are no laws stopping the bishops—who are full citizens of the Soviet State—from appealing for reopening of monasteries... churches... forbidding the priests to preside over their church councils.... [85]

Here Karelin is speaking about the difficulties which had arisen at parish level as a result of changes in the administration of the parishes. Following government pressures, in April 1961, the Patriarchal Synod adopted an amendment to the Church's 1945 statute,[86] which was ratified, but not unanimously, by the Sobor (Council) of the bishops in the following month of August.[87] The main consequence of the amendment was that the clergy was deprived of membership in the parish assemblies and treated as hired personnel of the local religious associations. The adoption of this amendment and the acceptance of the above-mentioned "measures" prompted the reaction of the dissenters.[88]

On November 21, 1965, two priests of the Moscow diocese, Nikolai Eshliman and Gleb Yakunin, addressed an open letter to the Patriarch with a note for the Russian bishops and a declaration to the President of the USSR, N. V. Podgorny.[89] To the Patriarch they said that "the Church is grieviously and seriously ill" not only and not so much by reason of persecution by the state as through its own cowardice and acquiescence: the church administration "has embarked on a course of subservience to unofficial, verbal directives" from the authorities. The open letter lists several cases in which the church has accepted orders in violation of its pastoral duties and canon laws and beyond Soviet legislation itself: (1) the unlawful registration of baptisms ordered by secular authorities was given approval by the Patriarch's Circular of December 12, 1964, which, in effect, transformed the priest into an informer against his own flock; (2) the bishops, by their silence and passivity, must be held responsible for the wholesale closing of churches (the figure of 10,000 is given), monasteries and seminaries. By way of contrast the priests cite the example of Archbishop Yermogen, who has actively resisted the closure of churches; (3) the hierarchy failed to protest against the illegal ban on ceremonies in private homes and requiems at cemeteries; (4) there was a similar failure to protest against the compulsory exclusion of children from churches, and (5) against the interference of secular authorities in the appointment of the clergy.

In the last part of their letter the Moscow priests insisted on the necessity of a spiritual renewal for the Russian Church. They mentioned the activity of the Second Vatican Council, the examples of Metropolitan Filipp of Moscow, who sacrificed his life instead of bending to the wishes of secular authority, the teachings of the great Russian clergymen and thinkers of the past. But the Patriarch and his aids disregarded everything. Without discussing any of the matters presented by the priests, they suspended them from their priestly duties.[90] Archbishop Yermogen, who in the summer of 1965 together with seven other bishops demanded that a Local Council be convened to consider the whole Church situation and seek a solution, was forced to retire to the monastery of Zhirovitsy near Minsk and was never restored to his see, notwithstanding his request for reinstatement.[91]

The pastor of Nikolo-Kuznetsky parish in Moscow, Fr. Vsevolod Shpiller, who partially supported the two priests,[92] was rebuked and put under the surveillance of his churchwarden *(starosta)* even in such delicate matters as the administration of the sacraments. He kept his parish only because his successor died a few days after his appointment. Having decided to accept the official line, Father Shpiller twice attacked Solzhenitsyn: in 1972 on the occasion of his open letter to Patriarch Pimen,[93] and in 1974 when the writer was expelled from the USSR.[94] According to samizdat sources, Archpriest Shpiller, abusing the secret of confession, instigated

Natalya Reshetovskaya, former wife of Solzhenitsyn, to publicly uncover the writer's moral behavior while she was in an extremely depressed condition.[95] Metropolitan Serafim (Nikitin) of Krutitsa, with the approval of Patriarch Pimen, published in *Pravda* of February 16, 1974, a disgusting attack on Solzhenitsyn.[96] The Patriarch, while Metropolitan of Krutitsa, did the same thing against Stalin's daughter, Svetlana Alliluyeva, with an article in *Izvestiia,* on September 7, 1967.

Two more priests had also voiced their disapproval of the Russian Orthodox hierarchy. Father Nikolai Gainov, of the Holy Trinity Church in Moscow, writing in the underground neo-slavophile magazine *Veche*, warned the Russian bishops who were about to elect the new Patriarch to distrust Metropolitan Nikodim.[97] Father Dmitri Dudko, pastor of the little church of St. Nicholas on Preobrazhenskaya Street in northeast Moscow, on May 1974, was forced to resign because "he had used his pulpit not for religious purposes." A very popular priest, who still as a seminarian had spent more than eight years in prison camps under Stalin, Father Dudko had started a series of talks after the services, answering questions about the meaning of religion in an officially atheist state. Throngs of young people came to swell the small congregation. Once he recounted the story of a school teacher who was trying to prove to her class that God did not exist by telling them that Soviet astronauts in orbit had not seen him. "They fly too low," replied a seven-year-old boy. When he was asked about the present situation in Russia his answer was that "Russia is at Calvary and Christ is crucified in Russia." To a questioner, who said that he was ashamed of attending church because the hierarchy only expressed views that coincided with the views of the state, the priest observed: "You see faults in the modern clergy and point to the Patriarch himself, but do you know that you are looking too superficially? Who else is in such an arbitrary position as the Patriarch? They say he is surrounded by thousands of informers. He sighs and it is heard by all the organs" ("organs" means the secret police). At this point the Patriarchate stopped the priest and decided to transfer him out of Moscow. Fr. Dudko refused to comply with the order because of "the interference by the godless in the internal affairs of the Church ... I can only say with sadness: have priests stopped doing God's work?"[98] On May 17, 1974, the parishioners asked the Patriarch "to return him to us. Rule by the right, the word of truth. Do not close the mouth of a preacher. Everyone is answerable before God."[99] But the effort was useless.

After a period of uncertainty Fr. Dudko accepted a transfer to the village of Kabanovo where he continued his religious "conversations" with believers and non-believers. In his first and last sermon-dialogue at Kabanovo, reported in his volume *O nashem upovanii* printed in Paris, he answered to questions on the meaning of human life and immortality brought up by young people struggling for their future. "When you know that Christ is risen," he said, "all threats are ridiculous . . . Go and announce to all: Christ is risen!" In the spring of 1975 he had both legs broken in a car accident, which appears to be an attempt of assassination.

Among the laymen who supported the rights of the believers against the abuses of the civil authorities and the subservience of the hierarchy there are simple people and members of the intelligentsia. On January 31, 1971, a lady, T.G. Drozdovaya, who perfectly knew what was going on in the Holy Trinity Church in Leningrad, wrote a letter to the future Patriarch Pimen proving that her church was ruled by thieves and anticlericals.[100] Two members of Sakharov's Committee for Human Rights, Valery Chalidze and Igor Shafarevich, gave judicial assistance to the faithful.[101] Chalidze spent a lot of time and energy supporting the request of the Orthodox of Narofominsk for a church.[102] On February 26, 1971, he addressed himself to Pimen, quoting the incredible answer of his secretary, Fr. Viktor, to the faithful: "if the authority doesn't agree to open the church, this signifies that God doesn't want it and we should not bless your request."[103] In order to expose the violation of the rights of the believers, Igor Shafarevich wrote an accurate essay on religious legislation in the USSR.[104]

Particularly important in the defense of the Orthodox faith was the activity of Anatoly Levitin-Krasnov and Vladimir Talantov. As men of deep spirituality, ready to sacrifice their lives for their religious convictions, they greatly suffered looking at the indifference of their pastors. "With Love and Anger"[105] and "The Ailing Church" are the titles of two moving articles written by Levitin. In the last one he sadly affirmed that "many bishops of the Russian Orthodox Church are branches of a dead, sterile and useless fig tree."[106] Father Vladimir Rodzyanko, a commentator on the Russian-language broadcasts of the London BBC, found these criticisms too strong and invited Levitin to more understanding and moderation. In another article, "Listening to the Radio," Levitin responded to Rodzyanko with an avalanche of proofs that the majority of the Russian bishops are just executors of the orders of the Soviet (Council) for Religious Affairs,[107] who did nothing to save glorious monasteries while all over world public opinion was protesting.[108] The case of the Pochaev Lavra in Volhynia became internationally known due to statements and appeals by believers and monks. From 1961 the Soviet authorities had tried to prevent pilgrimages to Pochaev, and by persuasion and threats to cause the monks to leave the monastery. The police measures against the monastery several times took on the nature of a pogrom. Believers and monks were searched, beaten and robbed, and women were raped. The names of two women killed by the militia are known.[109] Yuri Galanskov in *Feniks 66* wrote an introductory note to "Description of Events in the Pochaevsky Monastery" by an anonymous author.[110] Samizdat and Western protests, not the Patriarch, saved the Pochaev Lavra. That's why Levitin rightly answered to Fr. Rodzyanko that not only the Patriarch suffered during the persecutions of 1937, but millions of faithful. Later the Patriarch became a collaborator, "another Petain"; if he did something good in the past, "this does not give to all (or to some of us) the right to act wrongly now."[111]

Talantov's "Open Letter of the Kirov Believers to Patriarch Alexei" signed by 11 persons (August 1966) who "fully and completely" support Fathers Eshliman and Yakunin, deals extensively with the destruction of historical churches and monasteries, accusing the hierarchy of having become "an obedient tool in the hands of the atheists in power."[112] When Metropolitan Nikodim, in London on February 15, 1967, declared the open letter to be "another anonymous communication and therefore quite untrustworthy," Talantov unmasked the liar and revealed that one of the signers, N. Kamenskikh, was dismissed from the Odessa Theological Seminary because he refused to repudiate his signature.

The idea that Khrushchev and his successors adopted a kind of tolerance toward the private life of the citizens, including their religious beliefs, is still widely accepted outside the Soviet Union. Unfortunately this idea finds support in many statements of the Russian Orthodox hierarchy. The value of Talantov's writings is in proving with concrete details how different the reality is. For instance, the methods for closing churches are usually these: the regional official of the Council for Church Affairs would arbitrarily cancel the registration of the priest of the church due to be closed, or he would be transferred elsewhere. Then over a period of six to eleven months he would refuse to register any of the suggested candidates as priest for this church. When representatives from the church congregation *(dvadtsatka)* ask him why he refuses, he gives no answer. Meanwhile the local authorities would try, through intimidation, to force various members out of the "dvadtsatka," afterwards declaring the congregation disintegrated and closing the church. If the "dvadtsatka" approaches the bishop, he would send it back to the regional official or would tell the believers: "I have no more candidates and if the official won't register them, then I can do nothing more." When the astonished believers address themselves to the Patriarchate for help, they get this short answer: "On the question of appointing a priest, apply to the bishop." Sometimes the bishop (Talantov gives his name, Bishop Ioann, "a protégé" of Metropolitans Nikodim and Pimen, now Patriarch of Russia) would replace strong Christian priests by drunkards or dismiss the faithful: "I'll send you off to the NKVD."[113] Then come the official declarations: "In the spring of 1964 Metropolitans Nikodim and Pimen made official statements when abroad . . . confirming that the churches were being shut because of the number of people who were voluntarily abandoning their faith."[114]

The end of Khrushchev's era didn't bring any change. "The believers of Korshik," writes Talantov, "greeted the news of Khrushchev's removal from power with joy, and in great hope they submitted to A.N. Kosygin a request for the re-establishment of the congregation's rights. It was signed by 111 believers and was received in Moscow on December 4, 1964 ... The Korshik believers ... sent a new complaint to Kosygin signed by 477 of their number. It was received in Moscow on March 21, 1965. In May S.S. Ponomaryov gave a verbal answer to Ye. I. Shchennikova, a member of the *dvadtsatka*: 'If you sign any more petitions for the opening of the church, you'll be given according to your deserts—either a couple of years in prison or exile for good ....'"[115]

Unlike other dissenters, Talantov mentioned that under Marxism-Leninism, "the widely propagated teaching in our country about the rise and decay of religion is erroneous. Our belief derives from actually living in a socialist society and is not based on bourgeois propaganda from the West." This persuasion was not derived from books, but from his personal experience. In a complaint to the Procurator-General of the USSR, protesting the libellous assertions, coarse threats and baseless insults directed against him by O. Lyubovikov in an article printed in *Kirovskaya Pravda* (May 31, 1967), he thus recalled his long sufferings:

> I and my close relatives suffered greatly from the lawless and arbitrary actions of the state security in Stalin's time. In 1937 my father, at the age of 62, was sentenced by a tribunal. Despite his age and ill health, he was sent to the Temnikov camps, where the writer Yu. Daniel now is. On 5 February 1940 I petitioned the Procurator's office of the RSFSR for his early release from prison because of his illness. After a great deal of red tape, it was not until 19 December 1940 that the ministry informed me that my father had died in the camps on 12 March that year. The only reason for his arrest and imprisonment had been that he was a priest. My brother, Serafim Vladimirovich Talantov, who was working as a hydraulic engineer at Vologda, was arrested in 1930 at the age of 22. He was sentenced for no reason at all and died in the concentration camps on the Baltic-White Sea Canal. Thanks to my origins, I was myself under constant threats from the security organs from 1930 until 1941. In 1954 I was dismissed from the staff of my teachers' training college because of my religious convictions, although ill health was given as the formal reason for my dismissal ....
>
> My wife, Nina Agafangelova Talantova, a sufferer from high blood pressure, was unable to endure the threats and libellous accusations in Lyubovikov's article, couched as they were in the tone of the abusive attacks written against imaginary enemies of the people in Yezhov's time. On 7 September 1967, as a consequence of the grievous experience endured, she had a seizure and died on 16 September.
>
> The day she died I wanted, at her request, to have the last rites administered by the church, but the priest of the only church in Kirov told me that the local authorities forbade such rites being administered in a private home. This lamentable fact shows that Christian believers in Kirov are nowadays deprived even of those rights which were provided for them by Stalin. This is irrefutable evidence of the way believers continue to be persecuted. What kind of freedom of conscience is it if a dying person is not entitled to be granted his last request of receiving the last rites at home...?[116]

Although Talantov's main concern was religion, he protested against "the tyranny and lawlessness of the state security and judicial agencies in the cases of Sinyavsky, Daniel, Galanskov, Ginzburg, Dobrovolsky, Laskova and Litvinov. When in 1969 he was arrested and sentenced to two years in a prison camp, Lashkova and six other believing dissenters (Vishnevskaya, Dubovenko, Kokorev, Rakityansky, Stroeva and Titov) appealed to the World Council of Churches and Pope Paul for his release.[117] But he died in prison as a martyr on January 4, 1971 at the age of 68. Bearing in mind that Talantov sealed with his death a long life of courageous witness to Christ, his strong condemnation of the leaders of his Church cannot be considered exaggerated:

> The activity of the Patriarchate is directed towards using lies and false presentation of evidence to set the Christian movement in the whole world on a false course and thereby undermine it.
>
> Such, for example, was the suggestion of the Moscow Patriarchate, at the Rhodes consultation of Orthodox Churches, that Christian apologetics and the ideological struggle with modern atheism should be renounced. The activity of the Moscow Patriarchate abroad is a conscious betrayal of the Russian Orthodox Church and the Christian faith. The Patriarchate appears on the world platform as a secret agent combating world Christianity.
>
> Metropolitan Nikodim is betraying the church not out of fear, but out of conscience; a full unmasking of what he and the Patriarchate are doing would mean the end of his undercover enterprise. The time has come to unmask the betrayal by the Moscow Patriarchate abroad; Metropolitan Nikodim's hour has struck....
>
> A universal unmasking of the betrayal by the princes of the church will inevitably lead to a crisis in church leadership, but not to a schism (as is maintained by some ill-wishers of the church and others who unconsciously follow them).
>
> The faithful must cleanse the church from false brothers and false pastors (according to the command of St. Paul: "Drive out the wicked person from among you"). Only after such a cleansing will a true rebirth of the church be possible.[118]

The Vatican's Reaction

The Vatican's response to the plea of Soviet dissenters was surprisingly weak. Although our picture of Soviet dissent is still far from complete, the main aspirations of both civil and religious dissent have been tentatively sketched here. The situation of Catholicism, in its Latin and Slavonic expressions, is still to be examined. But there is a feeling, shared among the dissenters who left the Soviet Union and those who are still living in the "Gulag Archipelago," that the Vatican didn't help them. The sudden emergence of dissent caught the Vatican unprepared. While all its efforts were directed toward contacts and negotiations with the Soviet state and toward a dialogue with the Church of Moscow, the dissenters began to call for "glasnost"; they wanted to be heard too. The Vatican concentrates on détente as something beneficial for the rights of the citizens and on ecumenism as something useful for the believers

Rome is trying to obtain two things: (1) to have some bishops, even bad ones, officially recognized by the Soviets, because "a Catholic Church without a hierarchy is unthinkable," and (2) to "salvage what is salvageable" of Catholicism in the USSR. But it has turned out that the Communists are infiltrating the Churches and continue their persecution. The best citizens and believers, on the other hand, have been excluded from détente and ecumenism, two problems that cannot be solved above or without them. At the Vatican the "periti", or experts in politics and ecumenism, were disturbed by the interference of the dissenters, whom they simply thought to be anti-Soviet and anti-Church. Their call was rejected as unrealistic and even dangerous.

Anatoly Levitin-Krasnov understood the trouble and addressed to Pope Paul VI his famous letter on "The Situation of the Russian Orthodox Church." In the West, he wrote, "they very poorly grasp the psychology of the modern Russian person and the position of the Russian Church. This is evident in the daily broadcasts of the Vatican radio in the Russian language." The author then takes a deep look at the Russian tradition, the openness of the youth, the true ecumenical experience born through common sufferings in prison camps, the "adaptation" of the Patriarchal Church to the system, the consequent crisis of Church authority and the need for an inner revival of Russian Orthodoxy. Levitin, who characterizes himself as a person "not used to compromise," answers those churchmen in the West, including Fr. Christophe Dumont, O.P., a member of the Secretariat for promoting Christian Unity, who criticized his language for being too harsh toward the hierarchy:

> ...What can one say about this? Only that all these worthy persons are completely ignorant of Russian conditions. Here in Russia we never had the modus of parliamentary debate. Our discussions were always heated and sharp. This is to be explained not by any sort of crude habits... but by love for truth and by being passionately caught up in ideas. The Russian person, using the words of Dostoevsky, "does not eat an idea, the idea eats him up," and consequently the parliamentary structure of speeches, easy flowing formulations, purposely minimizing and politely emphasizing—are alien to him... And this manner of expressing harsh truths to the great ones of this world, without modification or equivocation, so characteristic of Russian people, seems to me to accord with the Gospels... Easy flowing formulations are not suited to the followers of Him who said, "let your words be yea, yea, nay, nay; for whatsoever is more than these cometh of evil" (Matt. 5: 37). Thus we say "yea, yea" when we see how bishops, such as the late Pope John XXIII fulfilled his arch-episcopal duties and in everything followed the example of our Beloved Teacher and Lord Jesus Christ; and we say "nay, nay" when they do not do their duty and depart from the path of Christ....[19]

Levitin's letter never got a reply from Rome. Notwithstanding the fact that many other appeals were addressed by the dissenters to the Pope or to the cardinals, the Vatican remained silent or, if it did something, this is still a secret of its "quiet diplomacy". But later, as reported by the Catholic press (see for instance the *Pilot*, October 10, 1975), Levitin "told the Vatican's top negotiator with Eastern Europe that Vatican policies toward Communist regimes have produced nothing...are unrealistic. The Church ought to take a vigorous public stand against Soviet policies which actually deny freedom of worship even though it is nominally guaranteed by the Soviet constitution."

In December 1970 sentences of death were pronounced in Leningrad and Burgos, Spain. After a quick trial (December 15-24) the Leningrad City Court sentenced Eduard S. Kuznetsov and Mark Yu. Dymshits to death and eight other persons, mostly Jews, to many years in prison for having hijacked an airplane in order to get to Israel. The Pope was among the world personalities who asked General Franco and President Podgorny to suspend and review the sentences. On December 30 General Franco set aside the death sentences imposed at Burgos. On the following day the Soviet Supreme Court "considering that the criminal activity of Dymshits and Kuznetsov was interrupted before it had reached the stage of execution," changed the death penalties to 15 years in prison and reduced the sentences of three members of the group.[120] Kuznetsov's diary about his ordeal in Soviet prisons was published in the West. One of the most moving pages is that dedicated to his request to be deprived of Soviet citizenship, because "according to my conscience . . . nationality and philosophy, I am de facto a citizen of Israel."[121]

With unprecedented courage Pope Paul VI publicly condemned the execution by Franco's regime of five terrorists on September 27, 1975, recalling to Rome his nuncio to Madrid. But with the Soviet regime his attitude was always more controlled and moderate. Once, in a public speech, he alluded to Alexander Solzhenitsyn. Without mentioning his name or the Soviet Union, the Pope told a general audience: "A well-known French review informs us recently of the ban imposed in a certain country, which even has great religious traditions, upon writing the name of God with a capital letter. We've arrived even at this today."[122] Later the Vatican press office said the periodical Pope Paul referred to was the January (1973) issue of *Revue des Deux Mondes*. Evidently the French review was writing about Solzhenitsyn's novel *August 1914*. In an "afterword" to this work the author declared: "This book cannot at the present time be published in our native land because of censorship, an objection unintelligible to normal human reason and which, in addition, demands that the word of God be unfailingly written without a capital letter. To this indignity I cannot stoop. The directive to write God in small letters is the cheapest kind of atheistic pettiness. Both believers and unbelievers must agree that when the Region Procurement Administration is written with capital letters or KGB (the secret police) or ZAGS (the city registration bureau) are written in all caps, then we might at least employ one capital letter to designate the highest Creative Force in the Universe." Instead of praising the courageous witness of Solzhenitsyn and publicly encouraging millions of Soviet believers, the Pope carefully generalized, saying that the absence of God "seems to characterize current history and civilization," something that "afflicts us deeply, and gives us the desolate impression of an anachronistic solitude."

On the occasion of Gromyko's visit in 1970, Pope Paul VI was quoted as having said from the window of his quarters overlooking St. Peter's Square, that the state of religion appears to be calm and respected but that the reality is quite different since "in many countries an oppressive legalism, in others a secular anti-clericalism, a peaceful atheism, if you wish, though radical in thought and custom, attempts, to some extent everywhere, to smother Christian thought and the institutions inspired by it." Vatican spokesmen later offered the explanation that the Pope alluded to curbs on religious liberties in socialist countries and to anti-Church trends in the urban societies of the West.[123]

This sybilline way of protesting, traditional in papal speeches, doesn't meet the needs of the oppressed or the wishes of the dissenters. A Dominican priest, O. Brukberger, concluded a strong emotional open-letter to the Pope on this matter with these words: "You have to be very deaf if you do not hear."[124] As Fr. R. Graham wrote about the "silences" of Pius XII, the only explanation of this apparent deafness is that:

> Even Catholic countries had to be treated with delicate phrases for the simple reason that harsher words only would be self-defeating. The Vatican had almost nothing on which to base any appeal, except the broad moral law.
>
> This explains the vagueness of the papal formulas in public utterances. And this vagueness—or at least treading softly—emerges also in the correspondence. One deplores, one expresses regrets, one asks for reconsideration, one appeals, but one does not threaten.
>
> Nowadays this "rhetoric" seems lamentably insufficient for the kind of issues then in question—the treatment of the Poles, the bombardment of cities, the blockade of hungry populations, the deportation of Jews, the shooting of hostages and a host of other crimes. But it was the only kind of language form possible for the head of a world religious organization in time of war.
>
> Extensive documentation shows the Holy See calmly and tenaciously holding to its own norms of conduct. It admonished when men were willing to listen; it put itself on the record by attempting to clear the moral and political hurdles. When it was rejected, it bided its time for another try. It also deftly sidestepped the various traps that were laid for it by the governments with which it dealt, including the United States.[125]

What Fr. Graham is trying to say is that the Vatican should be realistic and speak or keep silent according to the real probability of the effectiveness of its actions. Unfortunately this is also the rule of the politicians, who put the so-called realpolitik above any principle of morality. The dissenters appeal to moral ideals, compassion and sacrifice, something that the realpolitik rejects. The dissenters appeal to the Vatican precisely because they trust in its only strength: the moral law. The religious dissenters ask for a spiritual rebirth of their country, for the end of the political compromise of their Churches, for a new society and a new man, for what a man should be, not for what he may be allowed to be by a particular regime. If the Vatican fails to respond to the dissenters' cry, its good intentions will not justify it before God's and history's judgment.

Gromyko's visit to Pope Paul on February 21, 1974, coincided with the bitter campaign against Alexander Solzhenitsyn, who was arrested and deported from the USSR a few days before (February 12). There was no indication in official reports that, during the long meeting at the Vatican, Solzhenitsyn's "case" was discussed. What is even more revealing is the silence of the Vatican and Catholic hierarchies during the preceeding months when Soviet Jews, Sakharov and Solzhenitsyn were asking for public support. Stressing the necessity of speaking up "publicly", Solzhenitsyn recognized that this kind of action "is priceless, has always been effective and always helps. We (both he and Sakharov) are alive and well only thanks to this."[126] As William Buckley put it, "though Solzhenitsyn is only one man, his elimination would amount to an act of genocide. Would the West, in such circumstances, do anything about it? Or would that interrupt the rhythm of détente?" And appealing to Dr. Kissinger, he concluded that "we cannot willingly play the role of Pontius Pilate."[127]

At the last moment a Vatican Radio editorial rushed to the defense of a "grand writer of international fame, who was arrested for having informed the world of the repressive measures of a regime and who...has been expelled from his country." The Vatican Radio editorial was aired February 13, the day after the Nobel prizewinner was arrested in Moscow and the same day he arrived in West Germany. The editorial did not comment on his expulsion but said in his defense that "he has done nothing more than report in his book the crimes already known and denounced by the regime itself...According to Article 19 of the Universal Declaration on Human Rights every individual has the right to freedom of opinion and expression, including the right of not being molested for his opinion."[128]

The US Catholic Conference, which is usually very eloquent on matters of civil rights in foreign countries, also kept silent on Sakharov and Solzhenitsyn. When criticized by this writer the answer was that a statement by the US Catholic Conferences' Division for Justice and Peace was "possible."[129] The statement came but only on February 20, signed by Bishop James S. Rausch, the General Secretary of the Conference.[130] Several months later, in a document sent to members of the US Senate, Bishop Rausch praised attempts at détente, but argued that granting most-favored nation status to the USSR "would be most inappropriate" in the light of continuing Soviet restrictions on human rights and freedom.

The Vatican's failure to support the Soviet dissenters' call for "glasnost" cannot be explained away with the fear of harming the dissenters.[131] The conclusion of Solzhenitsyn's case proves that public protests didn't harm him. On the other hand he repeatedly said that he was ready to die. As another dissenter, Vladimir Bukovsky, pointed out, the number one problem for millions of Soviet citizens now is to overcome "the fear which has gripped the people since the time of Stalin":

> I am often asked about the prospects for change in this country, what we hope to get from our activity, how many supporters we have, and these are understandable, legitimate questions. But they are very difficult to answer. You have to understand first of all what's the essence of our struggle. The essence of it is, in my view, the struggle against fear, the fear which has gripped the people since the time of Stalin, which has still not left the people, and thanks to which this system continues to exist, the system of dictatorship of pressure, of oppression. It's into the struggle against fear that we put our greatest efforts, and in that struggle great importance attaches to personal example, the example which we give people. I personally did what I considered right, spoke out on those occasions when I wanted to, and I'm alive, I am now sitting here and not in prison. I'm alive, I can get about, I can live. For me and for many people that's very important—it shows that it's possible to fight, and that it is necessary to fight.[132]

Vladimir Bukovsky, born in 1942, pronounced these noble words in 1970 during a short period of freedom. With his life he set an example of how to struggle against fear. He was expelled twice from Soviet schools: in 1960 for publishing the underground student magazine *Martyr* and in 1961 for his contributions to *Feniks*. From 1963-65 and again for six months in 1966 he was locked up in several mental asylums. From January 1967 to January 1970 he was in a labor camp. As soon as he was released he joined the struggle for human rights, gave an interview on the situation of political prisoners in psychiatric hospitals[133] and assembled a collection of documents about the methods used in those institutions. The materials include copies of the diagnostic reports of forensic-psychiatric experts and letters written in confinement by persons judged to be of unsound mind. These materials were destined for Western psychiatrists, to whom Bukovsky appealed in a letter of January 28, 1971.[134] For this reason he was arrested on March 29, 1971 and on January 5, 1972 sentenced to a total of 12 years imprisonment and exile.[135] His mother declared that, although seriously ill, her son has been repeatedly punished and confined for demanding better treatment.[136] She appealed to Pope Paul. Another appeal to the Pope was written by Levitin (July 2, 1974).[137]

"The fools for Christ's sake" constitute a particular order of canonized saints in the Eastern Orthodox Church.[138] In Russian history these *yurodivye* (holy fools) or *blazhennye* (innocents or blessed) played quite a role. In Pushkin's *Boris Godunov,* the idiot Nick tells the Tsar: "Boris, Boris, the boys are hunting Nick . . . they killed little children . . . as you killed the tsarevich." Boyars: "Go away fool! Seize the fool!" Tsar: "Leave him alone. Pray for me, poor Nick." Idiot: "No, no. It's impossible to pray for tsar Herod; the Mother of God forbids it." Another *yurodivy* offered Ivan the Terrible to eat raw meat despite its being Lent. "I am a Christian and do not eat meat in Lent," said the tsar. To which the idiot replied: "But you drink Christian blood."[139]

Under the Soviets the role of the *yurodivye* is continued by the dissenters. With the difference that the new "fools" are locked up in insane asylums. The practice of putting absolutely sane dissident intellectuals into madhouses recalls the case of Pyotr Chaadaev[140] and "Ward Number Six," a story by Anton Chekhov, which was recalled by the Medvedev brothers,[141] and inspired Tarsis' "Ward Number Seven." In a survival guide for detention in a mental hospital for their non-conformist attitudes, Vladimir Bukovsky and Semyon Gluzman wrote: "There are no grounds for hope in the conscience of doctors; even the pressure of world public opinion has little effect as regards the criminal use of psychiatry in the USSR."[142]

Bukovsky and Gluzman are perfectly right. World public opinion, including that of the Vatican, while sincerely condemning the use of drugs as a means of re-education and punishment against the dissenters, is still divided regarding the psychic balance and realism of victims of Communist repressions. Cardinals Mindszenty and Slipyj in Rome are thought to be, at least, unrealistic. In private conversations, as happened with me, you can hear high Vatican officials say that they are fools. Two Jesuit friends of mine, Fathers Peter Alagiagian and Peter Leoni, were considered psychically unbalanced when, upon their return from Soviet captivity, they wrote about atheistic infiltration into the Russian Orthodox Church.[143] Despite their painful personal experiences and first-hand documentation they were thought to suffer from a prisoner's complex or mentality. When later their declarations were confirmed by Soviet dissenters, their opponents still remained doubtful. In Rome as well as Moscow the old attitude of Metropolitan Cyril, so well described by Solzhenitsyn, still prevails: "Our Church lasted because, after the invasion, Metropolitan Cyril, before any other Russian, went and bowed down before the Khan and requested protection for the clergy. It was with the Tatar sword that the Russian clergy protected its lands, its serfs, and its religious services! And, in fact, Metropolitan Cyril was right, he was a realist in politics. That's just what he should have done. That's the only way to win."[144]

According to samizdat's sources, in 1974 Bukovsky was brought to Moscow and promised freedom and permission to leave the country if, for a while, he would keep quiet. Bukovsky declared that he will never accept freedom unless the same will be given to those kept in insane asylums, whose names he publicly revealed.[145] It seems that this courageous solitary man is practicing more than any clergyman St. Paul's advice: "if any one of you thinks of himself as wise, in the ordinary sense of the word, then he must learn to be a fool before he really can be wise. Because the wisdom of this world is foolishness to God."[146]

As we will see, the Catholics of the Soviet Union are expecting from the Church, especially from Rome, no more delicate phrases, but a clear and firm policy: that God is first and man only second. According to them, the order of priorities cannot be reversed. It is a serious question which implies the very future of papal credibility in a land where patriarchal authority is already worn out and discredited. As Soviet dissenter G. Lauter wrote, "the Pope of Rome and the Protestant Churches are more responsible...than Patriarch Pimen" because "Pimen is in captivity, but they are free."[147]

5

The Church in Lithuania

The Vatican's efforts to establish a dialogue on peace and a policy of détente with the Soviet government are regarded by Lithuanian Catholic dissenters as "utter capitulation, complete betrayal of the Church's cause." Knowing what Rome means to the Lithuanians, a nation 80 per cent Roman Catholic, this statement may appear incredible and even false. But its authenticity is unquestionable: it is written in the fourth issue of *The Chronicle of the Catholic Church in Lithuania,* an underground magazine which began to circulate on March 19, 1972.[1]

John XXIII, the Pope who started the dialogue with Moscow, undoubtedly wanted to save the Catholic Church in the USSR. He tried to obtain from Khrushchev permission for Lithuanian clergymen to take part in Vatican Council II and to fill the Lithuanian episcopal sees (two archdioceses, four dioceses and a Prelatura nullius) deprived of their pastors. All these intentions and facts are well acknowledged by the dissenters who, nevertheless, "are disturbed that the Holy See, while defending victims of discrimination all over the world, barely recalls the 'Church of Silence and Suffering', does not bring up and does not condemn covert or overt persecution of the faithful in the Soviet Union." According to the dissenters, the Church cannot be saved by appointing or supporting "loyal" bishops and clergymen ready to tell lies and to punish those who are fighting for religious and national freedom. In this way the Church will be destroyed by the loss of credibility among the people, something more dangerous than any other form of persecution:

> In Lithuania no one believes dialogue with the Soviet government possible. It is needed by the atheistic government only so that, having gained our confidence, they might more easily wreck the Church from within. In Lithuania, it is plain to all that the Church will not be destroyed if priests are imprisoned, if school children are forced to speak and to act against their own convictions, if there is no press, no officially published prayer book or catechism. However, the Catholic Church in Lithuania will lose the people if it loses credibility by boot-licking the Soviet regime. This is what happened to the Orthodox Church in Russia ...
>
> When the Vatican conferred the title of monsignor on certain priests "loyal" to the Soviet system, thus to all appearances approving their behavior; when it nominated as bishops the hand-picked candidates of the government, remaining silent about the painful situation of the faithful in Lithuania, voices were heard to say, "The Vatican is deceived! The Chekists have infiltrated the Roman Curia! We are betrayed!"
>
> In such difficult times, the only recourse left to Catholics in Lithuania is to trust in Divine Providence and to seek ways by which the true message might reach the Vatican

and the rest of the world, that the most deadly thing for the Catholic Church in Lithuania is not persecution, but the noose being tied by some of our people...[2]

The Lithuanians' disbelief in a dialogue with the Soviet Union stems from the fact that, since June 15, 1940, their country has been under Soviet occupation, with the parenthesis of Nazi rule from 1941 to 1944. During mass deportations in 1941 and 1944-1950 more than 300,000 were swallowed up in Siberian slave labor camps. Some 30,000 Lithuanian freedom fighters were killed between 1944 and 1950 in guerilla warfare resisting Soviet oppression.[3] The efforts to eliminate a nation of 3,2000,000 inhabitants (in 1940 they were 3,238,000) are still continued today by a policy of spiritual genocide through intense russification, denationalization and religious persecution.[4]

Religious détente as a limited and controlled religious freedom in exchange for "loyalty" to the regime was previously offered to the Lithuanian Church in 1945-47 under two conditions: 1) to persuade the freedom fighters to surrender, 2) denounce the Vatican as "Fascist and enemy of the Lithuanian people" and start an independent National Church. The offer was rejected and the few "independent" priests quickly unmasked.[5] Today the second condition has been dropped with the result that the religious and civil dissenters have to fight not only against the oppressors, but also against the "loyal" clergy supported by the Vatican.

Commenting on the visits of Archbishop Casaroli to Moscow and of Andrei Gromyko to Pope Paul (March 1974), the *Chronicle LCC* writes that the Lithuanian Catholics think "dialogue is needed, but one should not abandon oneself to illusions. Dialogue can be useful if the two parties are fully led by good will. Concerning the Communists' "good will" witness the trials against priests for teaching religion to children, the prison terms imposed on the faithful P. Pliuira, P. Petronis, and I. Stasaitis for typing prayerbooks and religious literature... It seems to us that a dialogue with the Church is needed by the Soviet authority only so that the Vatican will keep silent about the persecution of the Catholics in the USSR in the hope of a betterment of the faithful's situation. The dialogue is being used to deceive world public opinion that in the USSR freedom of religion is preserved."[6]

Regarding the "respect" shown by Soviet officials toward the Holy Father, about which Archbishop Casaroli spoke upon his return from Moscow, the *Chronicle LCC* quotes the article by Prof. A. Augus, "Here They are—The Friends of the People in Cassock," published on March 1, 1974, in the *Kauno Tiesa* (the *Pravda* of Kaunas). The author writes that "at the beginning of 1945 (Lithuanian) Bishop Piatras Bucys, at the instigation of Vatican Secretary of State Cardinal Montini, asked Fr. P. Raciunas, a priest from Panevezys, to spy on the Red Army. Raciunas was supposed to give the information to the Vatican's secret agent Laberger in

Moscow, who would transmit to the Vatican and the Vatican to the American intelligence service." Father Raciunas, answering Prof. Augus in the *Chronicle LCC,* tells the real reason why he went to Moscow. By that time three Lithuanian bishops were already arrested. Bishop Paltarokas of Panevezys needed the permission of Rome to ordain new bishops. Therefore Raciunas was sent to Moscow to see Fr. Laberger, chaplain of the American Embassy. Fr. Raciunas was sentenced to 25 years without a trial. But when in 1965 his sentence was revised, the Military Court decided that it was "not proved that Laberger was a foreign agent." It was not difficult for Fr. Raciunas to prove that Pope Paul (Montini) at that time was a simple monsignor and that bishop Bucys was living in Rome and since 1941 had no relations with him. But Fr. Raciunas wonders why the story of the chief spy "Cardinal Montini" was published while Gromyko was visiting the Pope at the Vatican.[7]

Can the "Unity" of the Church Be Built on "Lies, Subservience and Terrorism?"

During 1945 and 1946 nearly every priest in Lithuania was required to present himself for interrogation at one of the 480 "centers of terror" set up throughout the land. At these centers the Soviets demanded that each priest sign a "loyalty" oath—a promise to spy on his own people and to make reports to the police. He was also required to help organize "The Living Church," which was to be independent of Rome and loyal to the occupational government of Soviet Russia. As a result of these terror tactics, several bishops and 100 priests were imprisoned and another 180 deported.

The occupational government of Soviet Russia sought to control the Catholic Church by forbidding the appointment of new bishops to dioceses that had lost their bishops by death or deportation. To take charge of religious affairs in Lithuania the government appointed a "delegate"—an ordinary Lithuanian Communist who had served in the NKVD (the secret police) for several years. He appointed others as assistants in the local districts. To this "delegate" full administrative powers, properly belonging to the bishops alone, were granted. Yet, neither he nor his aides received any real jurisdiction since they merely carried out the orders and directives coming from Moscow.

Under the new administration only one seminary remained open for the entire country. Though candidates for the priesthood were not lacking, Moscow allowed only 25 to attend the seminary at one time.

Before the young men could enter the seminary, they had to obtain the approval of the "delegate" for religious affairs. Even then, the seminarians faced frequent questioning and the possibility of dismissal if the "delegate" decided that they were unsuitable. The fact that four seminary rectors were arrested between 1944 and 1954 illustrates the political stringency with which the seminary was controlled. What harmful effect this control and limitation in numbers has had on the Church can be judged from the fact that in 1967 only 9 priests were ordained while 24 died.[8]

The first bishop to become a victim of Soviet Communism was Vincentas Borisevicius, Bishop of Telsiai, who was arrested on February 3, 1946 and shot on January 3, 1947. Although even several Jews whose lives the Bishop had saved during the time of the Nazi occupation testified on his behalf, his fate was determined by the charge that he had been a "bourgeois national leader." When the judge, after announcing the sentence, boasted tauntingly, "It is we who are the victors," the Bishop calmly replied, "Your hour of victory is brief. The future is mine. Christ will be victorious."[9] His auxiliary, Bishop Pranas Ramanauskas, was also arrested and deported to Siberia at the end of 1946. About the same time Bishop Teofilius Matulionis of Kaisiadoris and Archbishop Mecislovas Reinys of Vilnius were imprisoned. Archbishop of Kaunas Juozapas Skvireckas and his auxiliary Bishop Vincentas Brizgys were deported to Germany in 1944 after they delivered to Commissar von Rental a written protest against the massacre of the Jews.[10] Antanas Karosas, Bishop of Vilkaviskis, died in 1947. By the end of this year Lithuania was left with a single bishop, Kazimieras Paltarokas, in the diocese of Panevezys. He died in Vilnius on January 3, 1958.

According to the *Chronicle,* among the Lithuanians who perished in the Siberian camps, many can be considered as "martyrs" and some as "candidates to the hosts of saints." The name of Fr. B. Andruska, S.J. is mentioned.[11] Four Lithuanian girls became known all over the world for a booklet of prayers they wrote on scraps of paper. Smuggled out of the USSR in 1959, this document attests faith and love can warm the human spirit even in concentration camps: "Jesus, have mercy on unjust judges." The theme of the Cross is frequently repeated, especially in the meditation on the Passion of Christ.[12] Crosses of different shapes made by popular artists are scattered throughout the Lithuanian countryside. The Soviets published a beautifully illustrated book on this subject. They don't share the idea that the crosses represent the "incarnation of the religious popular spirit," but rather the "creativity of old Lithuanians."[13] Even more they avoid acknowledging that many of these crosses were destroyed by the Communists. In Lithuania there is a famous hill at Meskuiciai called the Hill of the Crosses on which were erected no less than 3,000 large crosses, besides a countless number of smaller ones. The atheists desecrated the sacred place many times, tearing down the crosses and burning them. However, people always replaced the shrines on this hill. The *Chronicle* several times reported about the Hill of the Crosses, for example, in No. 8:

The Hill of the Crosses had just recovered from damage suffered during the devastation of 1961. However, at the end of April, 1973, it was once more devastated; not a sign of the crosses survived. The desolate, denuded hill seemed to be waiting for believing hands and loving hearts once more to crown its desecrated head with the symbol of the Redemption.

At midnight on May 19, 1973, an unusual procession appeared at the edge of the city of Siauliai. A small group of serious young men and women prayerfully carried a cross. They went quietly, meditatively, praying the rosary. From time to time the cross, measuring nine feet and nine inches, and weighing 99 pounds, would be transferred from shoulder to shoulder.

Lithuanian youth were carrying the cross not in quest of health, but in atonement for the desecration of the cross, and in reparation for the sins of our nation against the Redeemer.

They carried the cross also as a symbol of victory. The night of May 19, many knew of this procession with the cross and devoted an hour to prayer and the veneration of the cross. During that hour, many, with hands joined in prayer, carried the Cross of Christ in spirit.

All the cross-bearers received Holy Communion the evening before. As preparations were being made for this Way of the Cross, it was discovered that someone had informed the state security people about the project.

Security agents traveled along the proposed route throughout the night, from Siauliai to the Hill of Crosses. To the cross-bearers, the success of the procession seemed a miracle.

At 2:30 a.m. on May 20, 1973, the Hill of Crosses boasted a beautiful new cross. Around it were planted flowers, and a candle was lighted before it. Everyone knelt and prayed: "Christ our King, may your kingdom come to our country."

At 6:45, the sound of an automobile was heard. The security people rubbed their eyes. All night they had been chasing after the cross, and here it was! Angry hands tore the cross down and hauled it off. But by noon, another cross stood in its place. The more the atheists destroyed them, the more the crosses seemed to sprout from the ground.[14]

Many people used to come on foot carrying the crosses to erect them at Meskuiciai. Not a few of them had been brought from Latvia, Estonia, Byelorussia and America. Even two Russian flyers, who survived when their plane caught fire, came to erect a cross there.[15] The *Chronicle LCC* writes that the Hill of Crosses "is a real Lithuanian Golgotha." In the wake of a desecration of a cross a priest declared: "he who insults the nation's flag offends all the citizens of the country; the crucifix is the flag of the faithful, and today it has been insulted."[16]

After Stalin's death in 1953 about 35,000 of more than 300,000 deportees returned to Lithuania, among them Bishops Ramanauskas and Matulionis. But they were not allowed to minister to their dioceses or to communicate with the clergy or laity. They had to reside where directed: Bishop Ramanauskas in Sveksna, where he died on October 15, 1959, and Bishop Matulionis in Seduya, where he died on August 25, 1963. Bishop Matulionis studied at the Catholic Theological Academy in Petersburg where he became pastor of the Church of the Sacred Heart. In 1923 he was arrested and sentenced to three years of imprisonment. He was back in his parish when on February 9, 1929, Bishop Malecki secretly ordained him as Coadjutor Bishop of the Apostolic Administrator of Mohilev. But on November 24 of the same year he was again arrested and sentenced to ten years in concentration camps. He was released in October 1933 to the Lithuanian government in exchange for Soviet agents who had been caught and condemned in Lithuania. At the beginning of 1962 John XXIII named him Archbishop.[17]

During the years of the so-called "thaw" (1954-57) Moscow quietly permitted the ordination of two new bishops and the building of two new churches in the port of Klaipeda and in Svencioneliai. On September 11, 1955, Bishop Paltarokas ordained Petras Mazelis as Apostolic Administrator of Telsiai (he died in 1966), and Julijonas Steponavicius (born in 1911) as Apostolic Administrator of Vilnius. After the death of Paltarokas Bishop Steponavicius became also Administrator of Panevezys. But at the beginning of February 1961 Steponavicius was exiled to Zagare because he refused to ordain as priests three seminarians who were discovered to be communist agents. With the approval of the Pope on December 25, 1957, Bishop Matulionis ordained in his house-chapel Vincentas Sladkevicius (born in 1920) as Auxiliary bishop of Kaisiadorys. The government didn't recognize his ordination and exiled him to Naujasis Radviliskis. A Soviet pamphlet by J. Rimaitis, printed in different languages in order to propagandize "freedom of religion" in Lithuania, states:

> Candidates to bishops are chosen and their number is determined by the Vatican after consultation with the ecclesiastical hierarchy of our Republic. Naturally, the Lithuanian government, like any other self-respecting government, could not tolerate it when Pope Pius XII started consecrating bishops and appointing apostolic administrators of dioceses without the government's knowledge. Besides, he used to choose candidates from priests disloyal to the present state system. For instance, in 1956 (sic!) the Rev. V. Sladkevicius was consecrated bishop without the knowledge of the Lithuanian government, likewise the Rev. P. Silauskas was appointed apostolic administrator without any notification. There were some more similar cases. The government was compelled to react accordingly, and the newly-appointed priests were not allowed to enter upon their duties. However, they could carry on their pastoral work unimpeded. By the way, lately the Vatican has refrained from actions that might give rise to conflict.[18]

The text quoted above summarizes the new Moscow-Vatican policy which justifies Lithuanian Catholic dissenters' assertion that the Communist government now seeks to break up the Church from within. With the pretext of "disloyalty" many priests were arrested in 1957-58 and the harassment of the Church resumed.[19] The church of Klaipeda, one of the two built by the faithful since 1945, was confiscated and turned into a concert hall and the priests who presided at its construction put on trial and sentenced.[20] The frequency of church closures increased and the clergy were forbidden to make the traditional annual visitation of parishioners.[21] A massive antireligious propaganda drive was launched and more severe sanctions were applied against the clergy and the faithful.[22]

In 1961, party secretary Barkuskas wrote that previously "the main direction antireligious activities took was the unmasking of the Church and of the servants of the cult." "Now," he continued, "we have come to criticize religious ideology and to discuss positively the assertions of a scientific *Weltanschauung,* and we firmly oppose any administrative measures."[23] In effect, the newspapers, in stories about the personal behavior of the clergy, denounced them as "drunkards, men of corrupt morals, speculators, embezzlers, and the like." The purpose of such propaganda and pressure was to discredit and to isolate the clergy because their influence disturbed the laboratory-like conditions needed for the atheistic reconditioning of the people, especially the young."[24]

While persecuting the Church at home, Khrushchev agreed to show his "good will" toward John XXIII by allowing some "loyal" Lithuanian Catholic clergymen to take part in the Second Vatican Council and to attend theology courses at the Pontifical Universities in Rome. At the closing of the Council, on December 5, 1965, Msgr. Juozas Labukas-Matulaitis (born in 1894) was ordained bishop in Rome and named Apostolic Administator of Kaunas and Vilkaviskis. On Febuary 25, 1968 Juozas Pletkus (born in 1895) was ordained bishop and appointed Apostolic Administrator of Telsiai and Klaipeda's Prelacy. Two more bishops were ordained on December 21, 1969: Liudas Povilonis (born in 1910) Coadjutor of Kaunas and Vilkaviskis cum iure successionis in both dioceses, and Romualdas Kriksciunas (born in 1930) Apostolic Administrator of Panevezys. The Annuario Pontificio (the official Vatican's yearbook with the names of all Catholic residential and titular bishops and monsignors) for 1974 lists Bishop Steponavicius as "Apostolic Administrator of Vilnius ad nutum S. Sedis (impedito)" and Bishop Sladkevicius as "Auxiliary of Kaisiadoris Sedi datus (impedito)." The remark "impedito" means that the two bishops are not permitted by the Soviet authorities to exercise their duties. Msgr. Ceslovas Krivaitis, who introduces himself always as Administrator Apostolicus of Vilnius, is only Capitular Vicar of that archdiocese. In the Annuario Pontifico his name is not even listed among the monsignors. But this doesn't signify that he is not recognized at the Vatican where he is regularly received. This fact confuses foreign reporters. When in February 1975 Krivaitis visited the United States with a delegation of 19 Soviet churchmen, Catholic newspapers referred to him as Apostolic Administrator of Vilnius and reported his declaration that "nothing hinders us from serving in the two churches, and we try to accomplish our activity in the framework of Soviet law."[25]

The appointment of new bishops and administrators was possible only because the Vatican accepted the condition of the Soviet government that they should depend on the Lithuanian SSR's Deputy for Religious Affairs. The powers of this Deputy are practically unlimited and represent an evident interference in the internal affairs of the Church. Juozas Rugienis, Deputy for many years, was known as the "bishop of bishops." When in February 1973, in the wake of violent protests, he was replaced by Kazimieras Tumenas, the *Chronicle LCC* wrote: "Rugienis, a veteran of the MGB, in the course of performing his duties as Deputy, often acted in a Chekist manner: chiding, scolding, and threatening priests, etc. Kazimieras Tumenas is a Party worker, and holder of a graduate degree in history. In 1964 he graduated from the Academy of Social Sciences in Moscow and afterwards worked as leader of the lecturers' group in the Central Committee of the Communist Party of Lithuania. The change bodes no good for the Church in Lithuania. Tumenas, it appears, will be more tactful, but like Rugienis he will carry on the job of wrecking the Church."[26]

With a hierarchy "loyally" submitting to atheistic authority, a serious problem of conscience arose first among the clergy and then among the faithful. In 1967 a Lithuanian priest sent a letter out of the Soviet Union in which he bitterly complained of the policy of dialogue being pursued by the Vatican. He claimed that the visible improvement in East-West religious relations, which the Vatican was taking care not to disrupt by any of its pronouncements, was in fact being used as a cover for the continuing efforts of the Soviet authorities to root out completely Lithuanian Catholicism by the use of physical force. The editor of Elta-Press in Rome who received the letter thought it more prudent to publish it omitting some of the more incendiary passages. Nevertheless the part published includes the following:

> We would be happy if we could have as much liberty as the negroes in America. Kennedy and the Cardinals intervened for the Jews, but for us, no one...Our Communists are very shrewd, active and dedicated to their cause. They are different from those of Italy or France. We are, however, persuaded that these latter have friends even in the Vatican, or at least those who listen to their deceptive suggestions. Who induced Radio Vatican to abolish the 49-metre band when on this frequency reception was better than on any other?[27]

On January 8, 1968, 63 priests of the Telsiai diocese protested to Premier Kosygin against the arbitrary government restrictions on the training of the clergy.[28] On August 7 of the same year Fr. V. Sliavas addressed another petition to Kosygin "on behalf of all clergymen and believers." Father Alfonsas Pridotkas imitated him. On October 7, 1968, the two priests were called by Rigienis, angrily reprimanded, threatened, and transferred from their parishes. *Chronicle LCC,* after re-printing Sliavas' petition, writes: "When the first declarations of priests to the Soviet government regarding the oppression of the believers in Lithuania appeared, priests and faithful of all the diocese agreed that it is necessary to fight for the faith. Many regretted having waited and been so inactive for so long."[29]

Between 1968 and mid 1972 at least fifteen more protest documents were addressed to the Soviet authorities by the Lithuanian Catholic clergy. Considering the vulnerability of the "servants of cult" to administrative reprisals, the support they gave to this action was unprecedented in any religious group in the USSR: in five dioceses, 362 or nearly 47 per cent of all 770 priests have signed at least one of the petitions, and in the dioceses of Panevezys and Vilkaviskis the share of protesters reached 83 and almost 56 per cent respectively.

Generally the priests refrained from criticizing the hierarchy and the Vatican and addressed themselves to the civil authorities. But when in 1970 Fr. Antanas Seskevicius, S.J., was condemned to a year of imprisonment and the bishops started to blame the clergymen for disrupting the unity of the Church, ordering their clergy to stop gathering signatures in support of the priests' protests, 109 priests accused the bishops of being liars and accomplices of those Communists who terrorize the clergy. It was the first time that such strong criticism of the "loyal" attitude of the bishops approved by the Vatican was collectively expressed by the Lithuanian clergy. Their letter was addressed to the President of the Conference of Bishops of Lithuania, to the Bishops and Administrators of the Lithuanian dioceses and "for information" to Bishops J. Steponavicius and V. Sladkevicius, both exiled from their dioceses, respectively since 1961 and 1957.[30] The following are the main criticisms raised by the priests:

1. The seminary. The best candidates are excluded by an arbitrary selection of the Soviet for religious affairs. The fact that some of the teachers are allowed to complete their theological training in Rome does not imply that they are the most suited for that office. There was a petition for the removal of the rector of the seminary, Dr. V. Butkus. The bishops "reacted in its regard as well as to other requests concerning the actual problems of the church in the same manner as that of the civil government—absolute silence."

2. False declarations. Bishop J. Labukas and J. Pletkus, Msgr. C. Krivaitis (administrator of the archdiocese of Vilnius), Msgr. Barauskas (chancellor of the diocese of Telsiai) and Rev. V. Butkus (rector of the seminary) lied when they told foreign correspondents that "in Lithuania the conditions for religious work are assured" and that "the government does not interfere in the religious activities of the administrators." Other priests go frequently abroad and take part in different "peace conferences." "We want to ask whether the Holy See approves of their activity. Do they defend the interests of the Church at those conferences? In 1969 the chanceries gave thousands of rubles to the Peace Fund: "why did the clergy not know anything about this?"

3. Who is dividing and destroying the Church? We are told that the dissenters, persecuted by the government, "are destroying the unity of the Church in Lithuania. Until now we recognized only one fundament of unity: Christ and his Church. Let us ask you: what new fundament has been discovered for the unity of the clergy in Lithuania? Can this fundament be constructed on lies, fear and a spirit of subservience...? Everything is

hidden from the priests as if they were not collaborators, but enemies of the bishops." When you went to Rome you promised to make an effort for the reintegration in the offices of bishops Steponavicius and Sladkevicius. In March 1970 we presented you a petition to this effect, but none of you wanted to sign it. On the contrary "the chancery of the archdiocese of Kaunas even invited the administrators of Telsiai to show solidarity by not signing the petition. How is it possible that this kind of 'solidarity' serves the cause of God and his Church?" Our exiled bishops are completely ignored: they were not even notified of the consecration of the new bishops Pletkus, Kriksciunas and Pavilonis. The chanceries consider our petitions as an act of hostility, started to classify the priests as "faithful" and "unfaithful" and punish those who gather signatures. They ask the priests to sign declarations like this: "I didn't sign against the bishops. If somewhere a signature of mine appears it should be considered falsified." Isn't this conduct, wonder the priests, a kind of "terrorism?"

As *Chronicle LCC* writes, the priests "are pushed around like billiard balls, according to the tune Rugienis calls."[31] If the people ask why a priest is being transferred, Rugienis refers them to the bishop, seeing the bishops so pressured by government officials sometimes appealed to Canon Law, to which even a bishop should abide. For this reason Bishop Labukas, on November 10, 1970, obtained from the Holy See a dispensation from Canons regulating the assignment of priests. "This dispensation," comments *Chronicle LCC,* "subjected the Bishop still more to Rugienis' manipulations. Before, the bishop could always object to Rugienis, 'I cannot transfer a good pastor to a small parish, because Canon Law does not allow me to do so.' Now, however, the representative of the government can reply to the bishop's objections, 'You have the Pope's dispensation, so transfer this priest from this parish'."[32]

In order to cover up the government's interference in Church affairs, on March 30, 1971, the bishops issued a letter in which they limited the priests' faculties to hear confessions and preach, and outlined new "procedures" for the appointment of the clergy. "The restrictions evoked protests from the priests. In time of persecutions, the faculties of priests should be expanded, not curtailed. All these restrictions had to be made by the bishops on their own name, while the chief perpetrator, the Soviet Deputy for Religious Affairs, Rugienis, remained in the shadows." Regarding the new "procedures," the bishops wrote:

> The ordinaries, desiring to improve the quality of ministry to the spiritual needs of the faithful, have decided to change the procedure of assigning priests to parishes. It has been decided in the future to assign young, zealous, and suitable priests as pastors where there is much work, and to send older priests, unable to cope, to smaller parishes, where it will be easier for them to serve as pastors.[33]

Reading the letter, one would think that bishops in Lithuania act with complete freedom, assigning priests as they see fit. However, the practice has been, and remains, quite contrary. Immediately after publication of the letter, the young and energetic Fr. P. Dumbliauskas was transferred from Garliava to the little parish of Sunskai, while the pastor of this village, Fr. I. Pilypaitis, born in 1903, was assigned to the parish of Aleksotas, in the Archdiocese of Kaunas.

The damage and confusion created by the "loyal" bishops is even greater due to the lies told by them to foreign correspondents. According to *Chronicle LCC,* "the Soviet leadership, wishing to hide from the world its treatment of the Catholic Church in Lithuania, and nurturing hopes of deceiving the Vatican in order to get concessions from it, has more than once forced some Lithuanian bishops and administrators of dioceses to disseminate false information abroad. Examples are the interview of Bishop J. Labukas with *L'Humanité;* the interview of Msgr. Krivaitis with editor Kokubkas, and his 1972 interview with 'Elta' (Tr. note: Elta in Lithuania is the official Communist news agency; a completely distinct news agency is maintained under the same name by Lithuanians in Rome as a continuation of the pre-Communist original); Bishop Pletkus' radio broadcast to Lithuanians abroad, etc. In these interviews it has been stated that the condition of the Catholic Church in Lithuania is normal, and that the faithful are not persecuted by the government."[34]

In November 1973, Ruggero Orfei, an Italian journalist, published an article on "Religion in the Soviet Union."[35] Among other cities he also visited Vilnius, spoke with some Communist professors, attended Mass in two churches and had an interview with Msgr. Ceslovas Krivaitis. The Catholic prelate told him that he does not believe in the "Church of silence" and that the Vatican is sufficiently informed on the situation of the Church in Lithuania. The relations with Rome are so good that some priests are permitted to continue their studies at the Roman Ecclesiastical Universities. Orfei learned from the Monsignor that there is no program for building new churches because those existing are sufficient; there are no religious associations; there are new liturgical books in preparation because "the Church can publish everything it wants in the matter of religious books." Then Orfei put to Msgr. Krivaitis two questions: the relationship with the poor and with atheism and socialism. The journalist confesses his astonishment at hearing from the priest that there are no poor: "the state provides for the needs of everybody." For Orfei it's difficult to understand "the sense of a Christian life where the possibility of 'doing good' appears to be precluded ... Every attempt aiming at the re-emergence of the Christian community as ... presence of the Church in society might bear risks not immediately imaginable in juridical terms."

Regarding atheism and socialism Msgr. Krivaitis' position is quite different from that hoped for by the Vatican, expressed by Archbishop

Casaroli in his interview with Castro. According to Msgr. Krivaitis not only an "ideological encounter" with Communists is impossible, but also "a direct engagement of a Catholic in Communist political activity" is impossible. "The statute of the Communist Party of the Soviet Union requires the adherence to the principles of materialism... Peaceful co-existence is to be carried taking into account this fact." In other words Msgr. Krivaitis affirms that, despite his "loyalty" toward the regime, the maximum that a Catholic can expect in the Soviet Union is to be tolerated as a second class citizen. Orfei writes that the "professors" of the Academy of Sciences in Vilnius are more "articulate" than those in Leningrad. Nevertheless also for them "Christianity is reduced to clericalism, without nuances" or degrees of differences. He claims that in the statutes of the Communist parties of other Eastern European countries the "clause" of adherence to materialism is not expressed and therefore a "pluralism" is possible in these countries. For the moment, he concludes, a movement of "Christians for Socialism," to which he is very sympathetic, is impossible in the USSR, but if Catholics continue to change their attitude, especially through dialogues similar to those which took place in Zagorsk during the summer of 1973 between Orthodox and Catholic theologians, things will be better.

Before returning to Italy Orfei was interviewed by the Soviet agency Novosti and by *Tiesa,* the daily of the Lithuanian Communist Party. The *Chronicle LCC,* responding to those interviews, suggested that the journalist "become acquainted with all past issues of *The Chronicle of the Catholic Church in Lithaunia."* And added:

> Orfei, after visiting just two churches in Vilnius, was able to get an "objective" view of the situation of the Catholic Church in Lithuania. It is too bad that he did not notice how that architectural masterpiece of Stuoka Gucevičius, the Cathedral of Vilnius, has been converted into a picture gallery, while the artistic churches of St. Catherine, the Trinitarian Church, All Saints, and other churches have been turned into concert halls, and warehouses, while St. Casimir's Church has been transformed into a museum of atheism.
>
> One would wish that the small group of Lithuanian priests which has for many years been granting interviews to various journalists from abroad, would check their "objective" facts against the latest facts of Lithuanian Catholic life. To them this issue of the *Chronicle LCC* is dedicated.[36]

Regarding the statement that "the Church can publish everything it wants in the way of religious books," a few months previously 16,498 Catholic Lithuanians in a letter addressed to the Deputy of the Council for Religious Affairs, K. Tumenas, had already contradicted a similar declaration by Bishop Romualdas Kriksciunas:

A STATEMENT OF THE BELIEVERS OF LITHUANIA

In the March 1, 1973 edition of *Gimtasis Kraštas* we read a statement of Bishop Kriksciunas:

> The Catholics of Lithuania publish books that are needed. Recently we published *The Ritual of Roman Catholics for the Diocese of Lithuania, The Prayer Book, The Resolutions of the Second Vatican Council* and other books. The odor of printer's ink is still present on the very significant publication *The New Testament*.

We, believers, wanted to buy *The New Testament*. Regretfully, the local priests explained to us that they received only a few copies of *The New Testament*— approximately one copy for 300 believers...

If the Lithuanian Catholics publish their own religious books, why is it that in the post-war years the most important book of all, namely the Catechism, has not been published? Why were only 10,000 copies of the Bible published? Why did we not see *The Resolutions of the Second Vatican Council*, why could we not get *The Prayer Book*, even though every Catholic is supposed to have it? It is not enough that we are unable to secure the Bible for ourselves, we now hear that someone is sending thousands of copies to Lithuanians abroad? Is it possible we will have to ask our relatives abroad to send us the Bible which was published in Lithuania?

Since it is clear to us that religious books are published in very limited quantities and not by Catholics, but at the request of the bishops and you, the Representative, by the Soviet government, we are therefore requesting the reprinting of the Bible and the *Prayer Book* in sufficient quantities so that every Catholic family could have at least one copy of each. In addition, we are asking for a permit to publish an extensive catechism. If we are not granted these requests, it will be difficult to believe in any statement about the publication of the most needed Catholic books in Soviet Lithuania.

March 1973[37]

Other inaccuracies in Orfei's interviews, including his quoted article in the Italian weekly, were answered by Elta Press in Rome. Regarding the main accusation leveled by Orfei against the Lithuanian clergy of being too "nationalistic" and "clerical" and of having flirted with the "powers" before 1939 and with the Nazis during the German occupation. Elta Press reminds the Italian journalist of the shameful alliance between the Soviets and the Nazis and concludes that "evidently the meaning of the terms 'patriot' and 'faithful' (to God and to his Church) are unknown to Orfei." What Orfei missed mostly in his article is to grasp the essence of Soviet civil and religious dissenters, their fight for that pluralism and for those human rights which he seems to welcome in a future Soviet society. At any rate Orfei's interview with Msgr. Krivaitis once more evidences the failure of the Vatican's Ostpolitik. The priority given to the problems of peace, the acknowledgement of certain "values" in Socialism, the subservience of the bishops to the regime are not going to persuade the Soviets that religion is innocuous, least of all to say good.[38]

The Struggle for the Souls of the Children

Ruggero Orfei had some words of appreciation for the humanity professors he met at Vilnius' Academy of Sciences. Their ideology is less monolithic and more articulate than that of their colleagues in Leningrad. But he lamented that also for them Christianity, even "progressive" Christianity, is "clericalism." Probably Orfei ignores the fact that, despite their effort for orthodoxy, the friends of Vilnius are in trouble too. The example of J. Minkevicius, a Soviet Lithuanian philosopher, is quite interesting. In order to help the occupants to build up a Communist Lithuania, he distinguishes a "clerico-nationalistic" view of Lithuania from a "Marxist-Leninist" one and suggests that to "overcome this centuries-old relationship between nation and religion, we must further develop the nation itself, its economy and culture" and, of course, "its socialist and international relations."[39] But in doing so he falls into the heresy of "bourgeois Nationalism" and therefore does not save the principles of Marxism-Leninism. In the case of Lithuania this is even more true because, after almost 35 years of Communist rule, the continuing identification of Catholicism with Lithuanianism cannot be related to economic or political power. That's why the Soviets, while not avoiding the traps of dialogues and diplomatic encounters, in order to achieve their goals of denationalization and dechristianization, especially among the youth, hit particularly hard the teachers and the clergymen, keeping the country in a state of violence.

In six months in 1970, six of the best professors of the University of Vilnius mysteriously "died"; on May 9 Elzbieta Mikalauskaite, a teacher of the Lithuanian language; on July 12, Jurgis Lebedys, professor of history of Lithuanian literature; on October 8 Jonas Kazlauskas, dean of the philology department and professor of Lithuanian language; on October 28, Juozas Senkus, philolog and dialectolog; and in November Kazys Umbrasas, professor of history of Lithuanian and foreign literature and Stasys Budrys, professor of the history of Lithuanian art. All of them were in their forties and belonged to the Communist party, but were suspected for their nationalistic feelings. Professor Kazlauskas, of international repute, had been invited to the University of Pennsylvania. Moscow answered directly to his friends in the United States that the professor was too busy and it was impossible for him to go abroad in the near future. When Kazlauskas protested, he was picked up by secret agents on his way home and brought to a psychiatric clinic near Moscow. Later, his body was found in the river Neris.[40]

The rights of academic freedom and scientific objectivity are not allowed to Lithuanian scholars and teachers. They have to follow the party line and orders like these: "In history lessons about the Lithuanian S.S.R., we must resolutely abolish whatever gives expression to an idealization of the reactionary phenomena of the past ... "[41]; "Every ethnologist, in every phase of his work, should follow Marxist-Leninist methodology and class criteria ... It is essential to resist occasional tendencies to idealize antiquity ... and manifestations of nationalism."[42]

In the past several years, numerous ethnographic clubs became a focus of cultural activities. These clubs were interested in the past of their nation and their homeland. A crackdown on such activities as conducive to nationalism was ordered in 1973. The head of the party's Agitation and Propaganda Section, J. Kuolelis, pointed out that "in recent years not only great achievements of ethnographic enthusiasts, but also essential errors and shortcomings became evident in the work of ethnographical associations."[43] Party and youth organizations were directed to shift attention of such groups to the study of the Soviet period. In connection with this antinationalistic campaign many persons, especially young students, were investigated and put on trial.[44] In an effort to control the illegal press, the executive committees of a number of *raions* and cities demanded that all offices, farms, and organizations, as well as religious communities, register their typewriters. The homes of suspected persons were searched, typewriters and books confiscated.[45]

At his trial for attempting to defect from a Soviet ship to a U.S. Coast Guard cutter off Massachusetts, Simas Kudirka courageously denounced the oppression of Lithuania and declared his will to leave his country in order to save the future of his children:

> I do not consider myself guilty since I did not betray my homeland, Lithuania. I do not consider Russia, called the Soviet Union today, as my homeland.
>
> An independent Lithuania, in my opinion, has a sovereign government and is not occupied by any army. The government has a national administration, its own legal system, and a free democratic system of elections. The laws of other countries are not binding on this government, as the laws of Russia are here today. An independent Lithuania wouldn't be dominated by the Russian language as it is today. I would like there to be no more trials such as mine in Lithuania.
>
> The bravest and most resolute patriots of Lithuania were physically annihilated. But a new young generation has grown up which intends to go the road of their fathers. When I refused to fulfill the wish of the state security organs, they threatened me with the death sentence. I believe that this promise will be fulfilled.
>
> I am a devout Catholic. Therefore, if the supreme court sentences me to death, I would request it to invite a priest to give me the last rites of the Catholic church.[46]

The school is expressly conceived as the main instrument for the colonization and russification of the country and for the education of the youth in the so-called spirit of "patriotism" and "internationalism." The teachers are instructed that "a very important tool in teaching students the spirit of friendship is the teaching of the Russian language. All nations and ethnic groups of the USSR consider the Russian language a second native tongue. The teaching of Russian fosters the student's love and respect for this language, and develops sentiments of friendship among nations, Soviet patriotism, and internationalism. Hence the task of constantly improving the teaching of Russian."[47] The teachers' journal praised the principal of Kalesninkai intermediate school, S. Lokit, and Russian language teachers L. Supron and V. Voitkun, who try, by all the means at their disposal, to instill in their students a love for the Russian tongue. For this purpose, concerts of revolutionary songs are held at the school in Russian, Russian writings are declaimed, etc. In all schools, military training has been introduced so that "military leaders in the schools are instilling with great devotion feelings of patriotism in the youth."[48]

Another important goal of the school in Soviet Lithuania is the propagation of atheism. The teachers are instructed to work on an individual basis with every believing student, to convince the parents not to interfere with the atheistic education of the youth. A response to the continued atheistic proselytizing of students and their forced ethnic aculturation, was the following "declaration" of believing Lithuanian parents and children, addressed to the Ministry of Education of the Lithuanian S.S.R.:

> We, pupils and parents, understanding well the purposes of school and its duty to the younger generation, are often disappointed, since the students are not receiving what is really needed.
>
> The hand-book "Public Education" states: "Patriotism is one of the highest expressions of human nature... It manifests itself in love of the country in which we were born and reared, in love for its history... "
>
> How are pupils to know Lithuania's past, if J. Jurginis' *History of the Lithuanian Soviet Socialist Republic* is short (just about 100 pages) and one-sided, and A. Gaigalaite's *History of the Lithuanian Soviet Socialist Republic* (148 pages) tells only of the revolutionary movement and the post-war years? Meanwhile, *The History of the USSR* consists of four parts—650 pages in all. Hence pupils know much about Pugachev, Peter I, et al., but know next to nothing of the great past of Lithuania.
>
> The greatest evil is the atheism being instilled in students by force. It is said that religion in the Soviet Union is a private matter and that the Constitution of the U.S.S.R guarantees everyone freedom of conscience, but daily experience shows otherwise.
>
> Religious pupils are often made a laughing stock and brow-beaten for practicing their religion; their caricatures adorn school bulletin boards. Medals and crucifixes are confiscated from them. At times, teachers even yank believing children from church; e.g., during funerals.
>
> Religious pupils are forced to speak and write against their beliefs and to sketch anti-religious caricatures. Those refusing to be hypocrites are given low marks.
>
> Teachers force religious pupils to join atheistic organizations and groups; hence many are moved to act the hypocrite.
>
> Some teachers use classes for atheistic propaganda. Atheism is preached in school and out of school, even to the use of deceit; e.g., demonstrating "miracles," making fun of the Catholic Faith and purposely distorting it.
>
> Sometimes deportment marks are reduced to the minimum just for going to church. The beliefs of religious students are noted in their school records, and thus their pursuit of higher studies is obstructed.

Pupils must often respond in questionnaires to inquiries dealing with their religious beliefs. We cannot understand why there is such interference by force in matters of conscience? Some students, unwilling to reveal their beliefs, answer those questions hypocritically. What good is this?

We have mentioned but a few instances of interference with the consciences of school children, but even these force one to the conclusion that the Soviet school is concerned most not with education or development, but with the instilling of atheism. Such "education" ruins the authority of the school, and causes irreparable harm to the pupils.

We are tired of forced atheism, and this causes a reaction: a turning away from ideas instilled by force. Why do they act this way in the schools, when the Constitution of the U.S.S.R. proclaims freedom of conscience?

Hence we request the Ministry of Education to prevent these harmful manifestations in schools, so that no one might interfere with freedom of conscience.

March, 1973. 14,284 signatures.
N.B.: About 25% of these were school children.[49]

Soon after the first occupation of Lithuania, on June 28, 1940, the Soviets issued orders forbidding the teaching of religion and the recitation of prayers in schools.[50] Crucifixes and other religious objects were removed from the classrooms. Moscow emissary Pozdniakov explained to Bishop Vincentas Brizgys personally that the Catholic clergy "must understand the situation and become loyal in a truly positive sense to the new regime."[51] When the priests persisted in holding classes in religion in their churches, sacristies, and private homes, some of them received the following document for their signature:

I, the undersigned, a religious servant, residing at _____ village, _____ district and _____ county, testify by my signature, that on April ____, 1941, I recieved a formal announcement forbidding the giving of religious instruction to school children and those of pre-school age, at school, at their homes or at my quarters—in a word, anywhere. Similarly, I have no right to discuss religious questions with them. I also understand that, failing to observe this order, I shall be liable to legal action.[52]

Under Khrushchev the rules forbidding the religious instruction of children were more strongly enforced upon all religious denominations. In 1961 the bishops were called by the authorities and told that the minors could not even take part in religious ceremonies. On May 31 of that same year Dr. J. Stankevicius, acting administrator of the diocese of Kaunas and Vilkaviskis, instructed the clergy that, "according to the directive of the Deputy for Religious Cults, Rugienis, young men and women who have reached eighteen years of age, may participate publicly in liturgical services. Younger children may not serve Mass, may not sing in the choir, may not carry banners, or scatter flowers in processions. Children are to take part in liturgical-religious events only in the company of their parents."[53] After this decree some priests felt relieved. They were already refusing, according to the orders, to give religious instruction to minors. Now the head of their diocese was ordering them to keep the children away from the altar. Holding themselves strictly "within the legal framework of the Soviet Union," they not only were no more reprimanded by their bishops, but even had more chances to be promoted in their ecclesiastical career. Thus, "for example", writes *Chronicle LCC,* "in the parish of Ausros Vartai (The Gates of Dawn) in Vilnius, children approached first communion for a time without even learning their prayers properly. They would come in droves from Belorussia, where there are no priests. Their parents do not know how to prepare them, since the printing of catechisms or other religious literature is forbidden. Since the priests refuse to teach the children, *the faithful conclude that if the priest is afraid of the authorities, then the parents have even more to fear.*"[54]

Although the administration of the sacraments is purely an internal matter of the Church, the Communist officials determine where and how often the sacrament of Confirmation can be conferred. On July 8, 1973, Msgr. Krivaitis arrived from Vilnius to give Confirmation at the Ratnyciai church. From early morning checkpoints had been set up on all roads to the parish, with automobile inspectors halting cars, checking documents and questioning the people where and why they were traveling. The sellers of religious articles were seized, the rosaries, crucifixes and holy pictures torn or kicked around. The *Chronicle LCC* relates:

> That day in his sermon, Father Kunevičius publicly condemned such dishonorable conduct. The preacher said that the faithful are oppressed enough as it is: They are not allowed to have a religious press: newspapers, magazines, or books; they are not allowed to use radio or other modern means to learn more about their faith. As if that were not enough, they are not allowed even to obtain rosaries, prayer books or crucifixes.
>
> In spite of the obstacles, about 7000 persons gathered at Ratnyciai. Approximately 2700 children and youth received the sacrament of Confirmation. In church, long lines waited at the confessionals. There were very many from White Russia, since they have few priests there.
>
> The government was unhappy about the ceremonies surrounding the conferral of the sacrament. The pastor of Ratnyciai was summoned to the Varenas district, where Vice Chairman Visockis of the Executive Committee complained about the sermon by the pastor of Gerdašiai, Fr. Kunevičius. The minister of the sacrament himself was berated by Deputy Tumenas, for choosing preachers poorly at Ratnyciai. The ecclesiastical dean of Gardinas also received a going-over for sending his people to another republic. He was required to tell how many Confirmation cards had been handed out in his deanery.
>
> There is much talk today about the liquidation of the "cold war," détente and mutually useful cooperation, even with capitalistic countries. The faithful, however, experience no renunciation of cold war methods by the Soviet government against the believing public, or the loosening of the bonds of discrimination.[55]

The majority of the priests realize that now their duty is to disobey both the civil *and* ecclesiastical authorities if they want to keep the commandment of Christ of preaching the Gospel and administering the sacraments. It is impossible to give here a list of the priests harassed because of faithfulness to their ministry. We will consider the case of three priests: Antanas Seskevicius, Jvozas Zdebskis and Prosperas Bubnys, who in 1970-71 were arrested and sentenced to one year of imprisonment for having taught religion to children. Especially in the case of Fr. Zdebskis thousands of faithful were involved. Here we reproduce in the words of the *Chronicle LCC* the impressive account of this fearless struggle of the Lithuanian people for the souls of their children.

The Trial of Fr. Zdebskis[56]

Every summer thousands of Lithuanian mothers prepare their children for First Confession and Communion. This is a difficult responsibility, requiring of parents and priests a great deal of dedication.

Soviet law forbids priests to instruct children, so that the atheists might more easily sow their ideas. Some priests, having been through the terror of the Stalin era, want no trouble with the government and content themselves with quizzing the children. Others dare to obey God rather than man, and risking freedom, teach children the fundamentals of the Faith.

In the large parish of Prienai, about three hundred children annually prepare for Communion. So it was on July 16, 1971, the children, together with their mothers, gathered in the church of Prienai for catechization. As Father Zdebskis was teaching and questioning the children, a group of government officials forced their way into the church. They photographed the children, demanded their names, and began drawing up a complaint. An uproar erupted in the church. Angered by the arbitrariness of the Soviet officials, the parents of Prienai appealed to the Control Committee of the Central Committee of the U.S.S.R.:

> On July 16 of this year, we, the undersigned, brought our children to church for the priest to examine them for First Communion.
>
> Suddenly a group of men and women burst into the church. It was the Chairman of the Executive Committee, the Secretary of the Communist Youth League, teachers, militia, and others. The uninvited guests took over, began photographing the children, and asking their names. One little girl fainted from fear.
>
> The mothers could not help taking up for their children. It was a sorry spectacle. Requested not to interfere, the uninvited guests replied,
>
> "It's not we who are causing the uproar; it's the women!"
>
> Such behavior on the part of government representatives brings no honor to Soviet law. We request that the persecution of believers be terminated.

The appeal was signed by 89 parents and sent to Moscow. However, Moscow failed to reply.

APPEAL OF THE FAITHFUL OF PRIENAI PARISH

On August 26 of this year, our parish priest, J. Zdebskis, was arrested.

As a priest, he conscientiously fulfilled his duties. He did no harm to anyone. We are convinced that the arrest of our priest is some kind of misunderstanding and therefore request that you check the reasons for the arrest and order his release.

Father Zdebskis is accused of preparing children for First Confession. If he committed an offense fulfilling his priestly duties, then why does the Constitution of the U.S.S.R guarantee freedom of conscience and worship? We believe that by this arrest the laws of the Soviet government have been impudently broken.

We parents have no opportunity to prepare our children for First Confession. We do not have time, since we work in factories and on communal farms. Secondly, we do not have catechisms or religious books. In post-World War II times, our government has not allowed us to publish a single catechism.

In view of the sorry plight the faithful of Lithuania are in, what can we parents do? We take our children to the priests and ask them, "Help us to prepare our children, so that they might have at least a minimal knowledge of the Faith." A priest cannot refuse to prepare a child for First Confession.

The Soviet government requires that the priest not teach children, but merely query them, one by one. But can a priest in the space of two months examine 300-400 children who come knowing almost nothing about the Faith or Confession? Besides, our priests have many other ecclesiastical duties, since the parish of Prienai is large: about 8,000 Catholics.

Our priest has been arrested on account of our requests and demands, and therefore we are very surprised, disturbed, and scandalized. Why break up the rhythm of work, incite the faithful, and artificially incite disturbances among the people of the region?

We think that our annoyance and this protest have a basis, and that they will produce results, and that in the future there will be no recurrence of such events.

August 29, 1971

The petition was signed by about 350 persons. Citizens of Prienai personally took the request and presented it at the office of the Prosecutor for the U.S.S.R. They were promised that the matter would be investigated. The faithful also went to the Prosecutor for the Republic of Lithuania and to Deputy Commissar Rugienis of the Committee for Religious Affairs. The latter angrily retorted, "I know the priest Zdebskis!"

The parishioners replied, "We know him as well!"

On August 30, Father Zdebskis was taken to Vilnius. Beginning early in the morning, a crowd of people stood outside militia headquarters waiting for the priest to be brought out. Security agents were photographing people and trying to disperse them,

"What are you standing here for? Do you want to see a miracle?"

"More than a miracle!" the people retorted.

At 4 P.M. Father Zdebskis was put into a car and driven off, while the people wept.

On September 3, Father Zdebskis' quarters were once again searched. Someone spread the rumor that Father Zdebskis was arrested not for teaching children, but that a radio transmitter had been found in his possession, etc. Since it was government officials who spoke thus, it therefore seems that a special effort was made to compromise the arrested priest, so that the faithful would not dare defend him.

In the latter part of September, the faithful of Prienai took to Moscow another protest, which was heard around the world:

To: The Central Committee of the Communist Party of the U.S.S.R.
The Supreme Soviet of the U.S.S.R.
The Committee of Ministers of the U.S.S.R.

A DECLARATION BY THE FAITHFUL OF THE PARISH OF PRIENAI

The newspapers and radio keep telling us that we have religious freedom in the Lithuanian Soviet Republic. However, in reality it is not so.

We are "allowed" to publish religious books—We have never seen any. We do not even have basic catechisms. The last printing was in 1940.

Often we have no opportunity to hear Mass, being forced to work on Sundays, even though this is forbidden by church law.

We lack priests. About 20 priests die annually, but just about 10 candidates are allowed to enter the seminary every year. Moreover, we know what difficulties those entering the seminary endure from government officials.

Our priests are arrested for preparing children for First Confession. On August 26, our priest, J. Zdebskis, was arrested for teaching catechism, and his trial is now pending.

All this compromises the Soviet Constitution and Soviet law, to our ways of thinking.

We therefore request the leadership of the Soviet Union: Give us true freedom of religion; give our priests freedom, so that they might fulfill their duties without interference or fear; see to it that our priest, J. Zdebskis, be released from jail.

Prienai, September 12, 1971

This petition was signed by 2010 of the faithful. It was a bold protest on the part of the people against the persecution of religion. The government did not realize that the believing public was a smoldering volcano. We cannot foretell further developments. One thing is clear: *The faithful of Lithuania will fight for their rights!*

How energetically people reacted to the arrest of Father Zdebskis can be surmised from certain facts. At Siluva, a popular Marian shrine, on September 8th—the Feast of Mary's Birth, about 200 people made offerings for Masses for Father Zdebskis.

The parish of Santaika, deprived of its pastor, appealed to the General Secretary of the Communist Party of the Soviet Union to release Father Zdebskis, since the bishop has no one to appoint as pastor of the parish:

We, the undersigned Catholics, appeal to the Central Committee, requesting that it give heed to the difficult position of the faithful in Lithuania.

Government officials do not allow all those who wish to enroll in the seminary, and therefore the number of priests is quickly decreasing. As it is, the bishop does not have enough priests to take care of all the parishes. We have heard that this year the parish of Lankeliskis lost its pastor, and this month we too have been left without a permanent pastor. No one coming in from the outside can suitably take care of our spiritual needs. This pains us very much and arouses mistrust of the line taken by the Government.

Father Seskevicius, who had been sentenced for performing priestly duties, had barely been released when Father Zdebskis was taken into custody at Prienai. Father Zdebskis, as we have heard, was preparing children brought by their parents for First Confession. If this is an offense, then what are we to make of freedom of conscience and of belief?

We Catholics have no prayer books, and we make use of tattered copies. A few years ago, we received a few prayer books issued by the Government, as though it were a joke. It should be seen to, that every Catholic be able to obtain a good prayer-book. We have no Sacred Scriptures to read.

We regret very much that the rights of Catholics, like those of the Blacks, are impudently denied, and we request the Central Committee to see that government officials would restrain from interfering in the work of the seminary, that they allow our spiritual leaders annually to publish enough prayer-books, and that they release Father Zdebskis from jail. The bishop will then be able to assign him or some other priest as our pastor.

Santaika, September 26, 1973

The petition was signed by 1190 Catholics of Santaika.

Weeks and months went by, while Father Zdebskis' trial date was postponed and purposely kept secret. On the eve of November 11, the news spread like lightning through the parish at Prienai: "Tomorrow in Kaunas Father Juozas Zdebskis goes on trial!"

Beginning early in the morning, people lined three flights of the courthouse stairway and the yard. In many hands flowers could be seen. Everyone waited for Father Zdebskis to be brought. Hovering about were the militia. As the hour for the trial approached, the militia began to shout, "bring about order"—pushing people outside by force. One woman was wounded in the pushing and shoving.

The Catholics were ejected, and their places in the hall were taken by a large group of security agents. Beside them in the courtroom were the witnesses: children, parents, and various office workers brought in from Prienai. It was necessary to act as though this were a public trial, even though security agents admitted only atheists. Obviously, the government had no desire to advertise this trial.

On the stairs arrests of the faithful began. One youth was arrested for asking the militiamen why they allowed only atheists inside, and no believers. The young man was given fifteen days in jail. In the corridor of the court-house, the priest who had accompanied Father Zdebskis' mother was apprehended and taken off to security headquarters for interrogation.

Outside the courtroom the crowd continued to grow. The militia began to apprehend people in whose hands they saw flowers, and to force them into cars. This led to great confusion and shouting. The militia were ordered to disperse the crowd, which now consisted of 500-600 people. After rudely driving the crowd off, they began to arrest individuals. A priest who happened by was apprehended and accused of organizing the demonstration. Throughout the day, militiamen stood guard on Ožeskiene Street to prevent people from gathering.

"Why are you standing here like pigs!" officials of the militia greeted people. People were driven even from the stores nearby.

"Get the churchmice out of here!" shouted two militiamen, running into one store. Most of those arrested were released by nightfall. One was taken to the psychiatric hospital, and then sentenced to 15 days in jail.

That day the people demonstrated beautifully their solidarity with the priest on trial, while the security agents and militia showed how the Soviet government regards the rights of believers.

The Syrian king, Antiochus, to keep the Jewish nation cowed, used to execute monthly those whom he considered as remaining faithful to the commandments of God. However, many preferred to die rather than betray their faith (1 Mac. 1).

The support given by Lithuanian Catholics to their priests didn't limit itself to written protests and public demonstrations. On January 13, 1972, the People's Court of Naujoi Akmene considered the case of the seventy-year-old Kleopa Bicucaite, who gathered sticks for a living. She was accused of breaking the Soviet law by preparing children for First Communion. Since Miss Bicucaite herself admitted that in July 1971 for six days she had taught children prayers, the witnesses were not even necessary. Nevertheless 27 witnesses were called, mostly seven- to fourteen-year-old children. Seeing that some of the children contradicted what others said, the judge began to check their political awareness, asking how many of them belonged to the Pioneers' organization. Only four said they did. Miss Bicucaite, in her final remarks, explained that she taught the children at the request of their parents, and that those parents who are unable to teach their own children must have teaching assistance. Moreover, she had taught the children good things: not to steal, not to lie, to obey their parents. The Court sentenced Miss Bicucaite to one year's imprisonment. Upon announcement of the verdict, writes the Chronicle, "militiamen immediately grabbed the little old lady and drove her off to headquarters, so that she would no longer teach the people's children as the people wish them to be taught."[57]

On June 17, 1975, Nijole Sadunaite, born in 1938, was sentenced to 3 years in labor camps and 3 in exile for her participation in the publication and distribution of the *Chronicle of the Catholic Church in Lithuania.* The noble story of this young woman, who for several years nursed a sick priest, is narrated in a pamphlet entitled "No Greater Love." Nijole is an example of how the highest spirituality can inspire and be combined with an heroic social activism and concern for human rights.

We Must Hearken to God More Than to Man

The trial against the three priests followed a common pattern. They were accused of violating the laws of the state, the statutes and rules regulating religious activities and even the ecclesiastical laws and the instructions of the bishops. In their defence speeches the priests denied such accusations and concluded by declaring that in any case they had to follow their conscience and obey God rather than man.

Did We Violate the Constitution or the Laws of the State?

Father Antonas Seskevicius, a Jesuit priest previously deported to Siberia from 1949 to 1956 and again sentenced to prison terms in 1961 and 1963, showed a good knowledge of Soviet legislation. He told the judges that his priestly rights were guaranteed by the Constitution. He didn't break the laws because he had never organized "systematical" courses of religion for children. Regarding the "statutes" and "rules" mentioned in the indictment, he argued that he had no knowledge of them for the simple reason that they were never promulgated in the Lithuanian Republic.

> The Constitution of the Soviet Socialist Republic of Lithuania, in its basic statute, Article 96, guarantees: "The freedom for all citizens to fulfill their religious cult."
>
> For the Catholic Church, the essence of religious cult resides in the preaching of Christ's teachings, offering the Holy Sacrifice of the Mass and in the administration of the Sacraments. In a word, the Constitution grants freedom to practice these three religious functions. Therefore, the priest, in accordance with his conscience, has the full right to preach Christ's teachings to adults as well as children, while, at the same time, both adults and children have the full right to develop religious knowledge and receive the Sacraments, as this is essential to the fulfillment of their religious cult. For example, how can a priest permit a child to approach the Sacraments, for which he is desirous, but, of which he has no knowledge? It is the duty of the priest to instruct this child. According to the Constitution, the priest has the right to prepare to receive the Sacraments and it is he, and not the parents or others, who is responsible for the administration of the Sacraments as well as teaching the specially prepared truths of faith necessary for the worthy reception of the Sacraments. Certainly, parents and others can and should assist the priest in this regard, but the final word is that of the priest.
>
> Therefore, I, as a priest, according to the Constitution, have the right to fulfill this duty in conscience—and to ascertain the religious knowledge of the children and to instruct them in the truths of faith, which instruction could not and would not have been obtained from other sources. It is for this reason that the faithful support the priest with their contributions—that he might render them service in matters of religion, including the instruction of their children.
>
> Even though the Constitution guarantees freedom in the practice of religious cult, nevertheless, for doing this, I am today placed on trial; having employed this freedom of cult, I am considered guilty and in jeopardy of imprisonment according to the Penal Code, Article 143, Section 1, which states that there is a separation of Church and State and School and Church....

The law states: "The systematic implementation of religious instruction." In no manner did I ever institute systematic instructions. This is done in schools; each day, according to prescript, there is the regular taking of attendance, an ascertainment of progress in knowledge, reports are made and instruction and homework are given according to a syllabus. In no wise did I do this; here, all transpired on chance occurrence; there were no reports; no examinations; no systematic instructions; no homework; no syllabus; the children did not even have catechism books.

Therefore, to instruct systematically would be an impossibility. I am further accused of instructing the children on five different occasions. Even these occasions were not on a daily basis, but on happenstance occurrences. At most, the ascertainment of the children's knowledge would last for about a half hour. In this short period of time, it is next to impossible to establish a judgment, much less to talk about systematic instruction. . . .

There is one more condition in order for the statute to be violated: "That the instructions are in transgression of the statute's established rules." In other words, the organization of children for religious instruction and the systematic implementation of this is forbidden if there is a violation of the statute's established rules. If there is no violation of rules, then there is no ban. If so, then non-systematic instructions would be permissable. Now just what is the preparation of children for first Holy Communion?

I did not violate any rules, as there are none to violate. Having been away from Lithuania for the past 20 years, I have not been in the practice of preparing children for first Holy Communion. This first instance, due to the shortness of time, having initiated the examination of their knowledge, I could have made mistakes and I would have been grateful to anyone who would have made this known to me, or warned me. No one did so, and then, later, asking some of my confreres about these rules, not one was aware of them and, therefore, could not tell me anything about them. How can anyone violate rules, when no one knows of them and, which were never promulgated? Even now, while I stand here in judgment, I would wish you, Sirs, the official representatives of the government, to make known what these rules are and when they were promulgated, in order that the citizenry may uphold them.

Logically, in accordance with the stated clarification, one must conclude that there are several established statutes, for mention is made of "statutes" and not "statute," and, as a consequence, there must be several rules, not just one; for, "rules" are mentioned. They must be rules *(pravila),* and not instructions. In establishing this case against me, I was read an instruction in the Russian language regarding the institution of the statutes for religious cults, given on 3/16/61, (Instruktsiia po primeneniiu Zakonodatelstva o kultakh ot 16 marta 1961 g.) which instruction has no statutory validity in the Republic of Lithuania as it was not promulgated by the Supreme Council. How can citizens uphold these instructions if they are not aware of them? Every Republic has its own Constitution, with specifically affixed articles and its own penal code, and for this reason, all statutes which are to be validly binding must be promulgated by the President of the Supreme Council of the Republic of Lithuania, for the 23rd Article of the Constitution states: "The Supreme Council of Lithuania is the sole organ for the promulgation of the statutes for the Soviet Socialist Republic of Lithuania."

Had I known these rules, I would have taken note of them. But there were no rules. And any instructions or rules, which are secluded in the confines of one's pocket or kept in a desk drawer, have no legal binding force, as is evident to anyone.

Therefore, I did not undertake to organize religious instructions, did not systematically instruct the children and did not violate any promulgated rules regarding the statutes. For these reasons, I am not guilty of violating Article 143, Section 1. This is evident also from the testimony of the witnesses.[58]

Father Juozas Zdebskis (born in 1929), a curate in the South-Central Lithuanian town of Prienai, not only pleaded innocent, but told the judges that the atheists are breaking the law and the believers are discriminated against. He didn't use any coercion with the children, a reason that in a previous trial against him was sufficient for his acquittal.

"The laws of the USSR solve the problem of freedom of conscience by separating the Church from the state. However, thanks to certain atheists, the Church does not feel itself separated from the state, but on the contrary *subjected to the interests of the atheists*, quite often through *deceit and injustice.*"

> For those very reasons the faithful feel themselves "beyond the pale," and *experience inequality before the law*.
> The facts, which are widely known to the public, cannot be unknown to the Offices of the Attorney General. Why are they silent?
> Let us recall one or two facts rather closely related to my case.
> In the first place, the inequality of the faithful before the law is demonstrated by the fact that the atheists have their own press and schools, while the faithful are allowed nothing of the sort.
> If priests are to be punished for preparing children for First Confession, one would like to ask whether a single case has been brought against the atheists for abridging the rights of believers, based on the 1966 appendix to paragraph 143 of the Criminal Code. For there have been such abridgements. For example, last year a teacher at the middle school in Vilkaviškis was dismissed from her post for being a believer....
> Finally, the very paragraph on which the case against me is based, appears *to be without clear contours*. For example, we can recall a similar case in 1964, in which I was also given a year in prison for teaching children.
> A few months later, an order came from the government to release me and abolish my sentence. The decree of innocence contained the reason: "It was found that there was no coercion of the children."
> Now the court knew this, even as it sentenced me to jail. The court did not even mention coercion of children. Paragraph 143 was explained in the brief as follows: It is forbidden to organize and to teach classes of religion in school, not in church.
> Even though I was not accused of this, the court found me guilty. How can one understand this? And if I was later acquitted, why am I now brought to trial on the same paragraph? After all, the court knows well that there was no coercion of the children. This is borne out by the parents' appeal of the case to the government of the U.S.S.R.: The children were taught in church, and not in school; they were instructed according to the will of the parents.
> After all, all things being equal, the law cannot be understood one way one time, and another way the next.
> We have failed to show where the "regulations envisioned by the law" have been promulgated. Neither the prosecutor, nor the Legal Aid in Vilnius have answered this question.[59]

Father Prosperas Bubnys, residing in the parish of Girkalnis, Region of Raseiniai, spoke briefly and in a very spiritual manner. He regretted not having done enough for the children. It's ridiculous to accuse him of imparting religious instruction when he had at his disposal only 10 minutes per child. He also didn't purposely break any law.

In view of this, my conscience forces me to fear not some "offense" because I taught children the truths of faith, but rather my neglect of such serious duties, since if we add together all the time estimated by the accusers, for ascertaining just the knowledge of the most essential truths for First Communion, it did not come to 10 minutes a child. Can one call this teaching?

My one defense is that the time preceding the bishop's visit was too short. I can neither claim credit before God, nor can I be blamed before the law.

I respect the right of parents to judge for themselves whether their children are to practice religion or not. They themselves brought their children to me for examination in religious matters. There was no day appointed for anyone to bring his or her child.

To save working people's time, we accommodated ourselves to the schedule of the single bus line running through Girkalnis. I did not try purposely to ignore the officials and their demands.[60]

The priests reminded the judges that the Soviet Union accepted the UN Declaration on Human Rights. Therefore the duty of the Soviet government is to protect freedom of religion and not to limit or suppress it. Father Seskevicius dwelt more thoroughly on this matter:

The United Nations accepted the Declaration on the Rights of Man on 12/10/48 to which the Soviet Union also subscribed by becoming a cosigner. The 18th Article of the Declaration states: "Each man has a right to freedom of thought, conscience and religion: this right guarantees ... the individual ... freedom to profess his faith singly or collectively, freely to study his religion's teachings, to hold services and to perform his religious obligations."

Our government, in accepting the Declaration accepted this also: "The right for one to study his religion's teachings," but, why is this not put into practice? According to the subscribed Declaration, it is permissable not only to catechize, but, to instruct in matters of faith, for every person has a right to learn of his faith. And I am on trial because I tested the religious knowledge of several children and professed a few words of explanation to those in need.

According to this, not only should there be no case against me, but, there should be a freedom for all to be instructed in their faith outside the limits of the school classroom.

In the United Nations' Convention in Paris on 12/14-15/1960, there was written and drawn up "an Agreement for War against Discrimination in Education." This was ratified by the President of the Supreme Soviet of the U.S.S.R. on July 2, 1962, and received legal status on November 1, 1962. It was published in the *Vedomosti Verkhovnogo Soveta SSSR* in 1962, no. 44, and also in the *Vyriausybes Zinios.*

The First Article of that Agreement on p. 2, states: "In this Agreement, the word 'Education' encompasses all degrees and inclinations of education."

The Fifth Article on p. 1 states: "Governments, participating in this Agreement, hold that: b) parents and legal guardians ... may seek their children's religious and moral training according to their faith ... "

The Third Article stresses: "In order that discrimination be liquidated and abolished, as discussed in this Agreement, all participating Governments are committed: a) to abrogate all legal decisions and administrative practices, and to set aside discriminatory attitudes in the field of education."

In the light of this Agreement, how can parents insure for their children a religious and moral training, when the priest is forbidden to employ even a few words of explanation in matters not clear at the time either to the parents or the children? For this, the priest is brought to trial by that Government which ratified that Agreement. Should not that be upheld which has been accepted as legal? In view of this Agreement, my case should be set aside at once."[61]

Did We Violate the Law of the Church?

Paradoxically at their trial the three clergymen were accused also of violation of the laws of the Church. It was not difficult for them to reject this accusation. But it was clear that what the prosecutor had in mind were the oral orders and instructions accepted by the "loyal" members of the hierarchy with the approval of Rome. Fr. Zdebskis deplored the fact that the Chancery of his diocese did not release any statement in his favor, and accused the officials of the Council for Religious Affairs of usurping the powers of the bishops. He then explained to the Westerners the meaning of "peaceful cooperation" with atheists and explicitly mentioned the Vatican regarding the appointment of the bishops. In a clear warning to both the civil and ecclesiastical authorities the three priests concluded their defence-speeches with the remark that God and his judgment is to be preferred to man and human compromises.

Fr. Seskevicius:

It has been pointed out to me that I failed to observe the law of the Church and, for this reason is a case made against me, and again, because of this, we cry out accusations of persecution . . . when in actuality we ourselves are guilty of not complying with the law of the Church.

I answer: For us, the Church's regulations, contained in Canon Law, are very clear: "The essential and most important duty of the priest is to teach children the catechism." Now, would that very Church instruct the priest to sit in the confessional and call in one child at a time to whisper in his ear so others would not hear what is said? The Church's law is to teach all openly, and not in quaking stealth. That there is the practice of going beyond the Curia's regulations, in that explanations are made to individuals while seated in the confessional is an expediency for adjusting to circumstances, because, in practice, it is forbidden for priests to fulfill their essential and strict obligation—to teach children their religion. Even though the Constitution, the decrees of the Soviet Union and international commitments and Agreements guarantee freedom of conscience and religion, however, in practice, religious freedom, especially in the field of teaching children, is relegated into obscurity and is fettered in such a way as to permit a little of the proverbial nose to protrude for breathing purposes . . . Such procedures demean the law and give outsiders reason to censure our Government.

That I did not sit in the confessional, but having placed a chair in the place where, in times of devotional services, confessions are heard, and having stationed myself at this point, is a matter of so little consequence, the Curia advised me it was of no importance. It brings to mind Krylov's story of the quartet: a donkey, a goat and two other animals began to make music, but with no success. They discovered the reason for their lack of success: they must exchange places. This they did. And again the same . . . however, a nightingale, bemused in watching them, advised them: The place is not important; it's the voice that's necessary . . . hence, to adjust to conditions, to the regulations in force...the place is not important, but rather, was there an organized, systematic instruction going on "in violation of the regulations laid down by the law?"

Is it for this reason—that a priest was standing and not sitting, that he was not in the confessional, but at the Lord's Table, where confessions usually are heard during times of solemn devotions—is it for this reason, a case is being made? To sit or to stand—these are but the Curia's rubrics and are adjustable when circumstances so warrant. Certainly I am being prosecuted not for violation of the Church's rubrics, but for a violation of the laws of the Council (for Religious Affairs, n.t.)...

To be found guilty of fulfilling my priestly duties is, for me, not the least shameful; rather, I am honored. I walk in the steps of Eternal Truth, which Truth says: "Happy those who are prosecuted in the cause of right; theirs is the Kingdom of Heaven. Happy are you when people abuse you and persecute you and speak all kinds of calumny against you on my account. Rejoice and be glad for your reward will be great in Heaven" (Matt. 5, 10-11). St. Peter: "to suffer for thievery is no honor; to suffer for truth, let us not be ashamed. We must hearken to God more than to man."[62]

Fr.Zdebskis:

It seems then that I am being tried for performing my direct duties.

A look at the pages of the indictment reveals that comments from my former places of employment blame me for *doing my duty*. It is regrettable that I was unable to find there any remarks from the Chancery—would it, too, have faulted me for doing my duty?

Let us examine the matter further. In a number of cases *the atheists' conduct reeks of obvious deceit and bad faith* regarding matters of conscience. Why is none of this punished? On more than one count, the conduct of the atheists with regard to the faithful is similar to Shakespeare's portrayal of the conduct of the fifteenth century Duke of Gloucester, who in his quest for the throne of England secretly murdered all competitors, while managing to appear in public with prayer-book in hand.

1. Is it not an abridgement of freedom of conscience when the atheists try ... in a land whose Constitution guarantees freedom of conscience, to wreck the Church from within by acting as if bishops occupied their Sees, as if directives came from Chanceries, even though the assignment of priests and many other directives are dictated by atheists, in an attempt to bring the Catholic Church in Lithuania to the level of the Orthodox Church?

2. Does the effort to compromise certain priests and even bishops in the eyes of the faithful and even of the Vatican not reek of bad faith? E.g., is it the wish of the faithful that the energetic and healthy Bishop V. Sladkevicius be listed in the Vatican list of bishops throughout the world as "sedi datus" ("assigned to the see")...

What conclusion is to be drawn from all this? Although humanly speaking, in the short run, one is always tempted in such situations to repeat the words of Jesus, "Father ... let this cup pass me by"; nevertheless in reality we priests ought to *thank you* for this and similar litigations. These events force us to speak our conscience, not to fall asleep, to choose between two alternatives.

One alternative is the so-called *"path of peaceful cooperation with the atheists"*: to try to serve two masters, to placate the demands of the atheists, by driving youth out of church ourselves, not allowing them to take part in religious festivals, processions, or to serve at Holy Mass, being satisfied, in preparing children for First Communion, with the fact that they know their prayers, with no insight into the mystery of the Mass—the center of the Christian life, and for priests not to think about the condition of the country in 10-20 years! This means that priests should perform their direct duties, and that they be prepared for conflict with their conscience, being concerned only with what they are to have for lunch.

It means that the priest must try to forget that children are going to hear about God, about one who does not exist. I myself do not believe in the kind of God described by our press and radio . . .

You have shown me thousands of young people out there. Not one of them is cognizant of the kind of God one must love, a God who loves us. No one has spoken to them about such a God, no one has ever taught them to find happiness in doing good to all, even to one's enemies. I know well that if we priests do not speak out, the stones will begin to cry out, and God will demand an accounting of us.

This is what cooperation with atheism means in our circumstances; this is something the faithful living in other countries can never understand.

The other alternative is to be a priest according to the mind of Christ, determined to carry out the duties demanded by Christ and Ecclesiastical Law, and to take out what Divine Providence allows one to suffer, as we see in the present case: to choose barred windows. In the words of the interrogator: "You would not accept roast duck, so you will now eat prison fare."

However, if the courts do not try us priests today, then our nation will later! In the end will come the hour of judgment by the Almighty. May God help us priests to fear this more than your judgment.

I recall again those thousands of young people outside the Church. They do not know enough to obey their parents . . . To me the country along the banks of the Nemunas River is dear. I know well that it will not remain there long, if its children are unable to obey their parents. I spoke about this to them. I told them of God's command.

If your conscience considers all this an offense—call me a fanatic and sentence me, but at the same time judge yourselves!

I request the court to consider all aforementioned psychological factors, and not to forget that the judgment of the court can make the community of the faithful think that some paragraphs of the Constitution are mere propaganda. Can there be any respect for the requirement to go against one's conscience? Can there be respect for a law which punishes one for doing one's duty?

It remains only to repeat the words of the first apostles at their trial: "We must obey God rather than men."[63]

Fr. Bubnys:

Besides the duties to the state, I am a priest and pastor with duties to my religion and Church, which oblige me in conscience.

The essential duty of the priest, imposed by Christ himself, is to proclaim the Gospel, to teach all nations, and to distribute God's grace by conferring the sacraments.

Since the Soviet government has not yet completely closed the seminary where students study matters of faith, then it agrees that that information be used for teaching the faith.

At ordination, each priest obliges himself before God and receives a mandate from the bishop to teach and sanctify the people of God.

Therefore, if he is conscientious, he cannot refrain from disseminating and teaching religion, as the Apostle says, "I should be punished if I did not preach it" (1 Cor. 9:16).

If human law does not conform with divinely promulgated natural law, then it is not nature which is in error, but human understanding; for this people suffer, and will continue to suffer, until they ask themselves where they made their mistake, turning from God.

At this great moment appointed to me, an insignificant particle of dust, I cannot deny the Jesus who loves us, as he urges us not to keep the little ones'from approaching him. I wish to say, "Praise be to Jesus Christ."[64]

The uncompromising "one must hearken to God rather than to man" has become the answer of every good priest. These words were repeated by Fr. Ionas Survila on May 14, 1974, when he was fined 50 rubles for having permitted the children to serve Mass.[65] When priests are forbidden to gather for a spiritual retreat or to help out in parish feasts they answer in the same manner. On one of these occasions, Fr. Vitautas Uzkuraitis declared from the pulpit: "The Deputy forbade me to take part in the feast of your Patron and to preach... But I have to obey the order of Christ who says: go and preach the Gospel to all creatures... To those who forbade me to preach I recall the words of the Apostles Peter and John to the Sanhedrim: Judge by yourself if it is right to listen to you more than God."[66]

The arrest and trial of Fr. Zdebskis marked the beginning of an increasing involvement of laymen in the Catholic protest movement. We already quoted the reactions and protests of various groups and parishes. But in December 1971 and in January 1972, 17,059 signatures were collected throughout Lithuania under a "Memorandum of the Roman Catholics of Lithuania" addressed to Brezhnev; along with the imprisonment of Zdebskis and Bubnys, this document enumerated the main grievances of the believers:

> We therefore ask the Soviet Government [concluded the Memorandum] to grant us the freedom of conscience, which has been guaranteed by the Constitution of the USSR but which has not been put into practice heretofore. What we want is not pretty words in the press and on the radio but serious governmental efforts that would help us, Catholics, to feel like citizens of the Soviet Union with equal rights.[67]

An addendum to the Memorandum signed "Representatives of Lithuanian Catholics," noted that only "an insignificant portion of religious believers in Lithuania," were able to sign the memorandum "since the organs of the Militia and the KGB have used all kinds of means to interrupt the collection of signatures," including arrests of those collecting them.[68]

This massive protest document was sent the following month to the Secretary General of the United Nations for transmission to Brezhnev. In their appeal to Kurt Waldheim "Representatives of Lithuania's Catholics" justified this course by the fact that none of the earlier protests[69] had elicited any official reply but only "increased repressions"; they also pointed to the fact "that religious believers in [Lithuania] cannot enjoy the right set out in Article 18 of the Universal Declaration of Human Rights."[70]

Faced with this heroic stand of their faithful, the bishops-administrators, on April 11, 1972, issued a "pastoral letter" that will remain as the most shameful act in the annals of the Lithuanian Catholic Church.[71] Quoting abundantly from the Scriptures and the Second Vatican Council's Constitution "Gaudium et Spes," numbers 76 and 92, it called the people to "obedience" and condemned as "irresponsible" and "falsificators" those who gathered signatures of documents which might provoke "misunder-standings" in the relations between Church and State.

Commenting on the "harm" of this "unhappy," "shameful" and "deplorable" letter, Lithuanian priests revealed that it was drafted by the bishops-administrators during a meeting in the chancery of the archdiocese of Kaunas with the direct participation of Rugienis and Orlov, a representative of the Soviet for Religious Affairs purposely sent from Moscow. Here we summarize the answers given by the priests, point by point, to the "Pastoral Letter":

1. Obedience. How can we obey the bishops when they are "silent" or, if they speak, they do so in order to stop the struggle of priests and laity for freedom of belief in Lithuania? Rightly Bishop Pletkus said that "the authority of the bishops is already destroyed" because you bishops were elected under the pressures of the representatives of the government, who refer to you as "our bishops."

2. Lies and falsifications. The signers knew what they were doing because each paper signed had the full text of the memorandum that was sent to the United Nations. You, with your false declarations, deceived the foreigners and your own people, as did Msgr. C. Krivaitis recently "in a declaration of this kind . . . to the priests of his diocese."

3. Relations with the state. "Of what relations are you speaking? Of those between the cat and mouse? How can we be satisfied by apparent 'good relations'?" Unfortunately, the pastoral letter helps the atheists destroy the Church "from within" and has been already used by them to confuse the parents of the students of Panemune's high school and to "terrorize" priests.

4. Relations with the Vatican. "The Vatican is deceived. For instance, almost all of those who lately received the title of monsignor are collaborators of the government . . . We hope that this pastoral letter will open the eyes also to Vatican diplomacy. It is now evident that we have enough with all those monsignors and bishops being placed by the government . . . We priests of Lithuania, despite the persecutions and prison camps, remain faithful to the Roman Catholic Church and to the Pontiff."[72]

The tragic situation of Lithuanian Catholics who want to remain faithful to Rome, but do not approve of its policy of détente, dramatically emerged on May 14, 1972, when Romas Kalanta, a 19-year-old youth burned himself to death in the City Square of Kaunas. His last cry was: "Freedom to religion, freedom to Lithuania, the Russians out!" For two days this cry was repeated in the streets of Lithuania by thousands of people until suffocated by the Soviet army. In the following month of June, four more persons imitated the desperate protest of Kalanta. Then "peace" was restored again.[73]

The imprisonment of priests and the "useless" sacrifice of young lives seem to confirm the worth of détente. For the sake of the supreme interest of preserving "peace" the bishops and the Vatican are ready to abandon the so-called "clerico-nationalistic" position of the dissenters for a "loyal" collaboration with an atheistic and colonialist regime. But in the meantime the Church is loosing its credibility in Lithuania. Then the question to be asked is who's going to benefit from this "peace"?

In its more recent issues the *Chronicle LCC* warned the Holy See: the atheists are preparing to destroy our Church, possibly, "with the Vatican's hands." We do not want more "manikin-bishops," but more good priests. "The Church of 'silence' will never understand a diplomacy which creates the conditions for the atheists' triumph... In order to obtain diplomatic concessions the atheistic authority is ready to make a lot of promises, to sign beautiful pacts, which are going to be as dead as the Declaration of Human Rights signed by the same... The priests and the faithful of Lithuania entreat the Holy Father: a) not to name new bishops subservient to atheists, b) to ask information about candidates to the episcopal order from the exiled bishops or from those priests recommended by them..., c) not to make diplomatic concessions to the atheists, relying on their good will. It is impossible to expect from atheists concessions through accords. The Catholics of Lithuania will have as much freedom as they conquer for themselves. This truth is confirmed by more than one example in our own times. The Catholics of Lithuania will be able to obtain something if they will be strongly supported by world public opinion and by the leaders of the Catholic Church."[74]

Vaclovas Sevruskas, an atheist and former lecturer in Marxist-Leninist philosophy, after almost a year of interrogation and then commitment to an insane asylum, was allowed to leave Lithuania. He was helped by the Jews. On his way to the United States, on November 23, 1974, he began a hunger strike in St. Peter basilica at the Vatican to protest religious persecution in Lithuania and the violation of human rights in the USSR. On January 1, 1975 Sevruskas published an open letter to Lithuanian officials and also the papal Secretary of State, Cardinal Jean Villot.[75]

Moscow and the Vatican continue to keep silent. Lithuania cannot figure prominently in the Soviet vision of détente. But what about Rome? One of its main reasons in favor of détente, the nomination of new bishops, turned out to be a complete failure because what the regime wants is not only fairness, but complicity, to be loyal to the point of dishonesty and betrayal. As a result the Vatican's credibility in Catholic Lithuania fell very low. The participation of the Holy See in the Helsinki conference didn't help her regain this loss of credibility.

The time is "ripe" for religious groups in the West to demand that the USSR "stand on trial for religious freedom," declared Shmon Grilius, a

Lithuanian Jew who served in Soviet prisons with dissident Catholics, Baptists, and other prisoners of conscience. Speaking at a Greater New York Conference on Soviet Jewry, the Jewish activist said that one of his fellow prisoners at Perm prison was a Lithuanian Catholic freedom fighter who had been in prison for 20 years, serving a 25-year sentence. His wife had served 10 years and their child was born in prison: "He has been a religious Catholic all these years . . . and has tried to observe the holidays. But when he tries to pray with other Catholic prisoners, the guards break them up and throw them back in their bunks . . . It is very important to hold an international, interreligious meeting—the equivalent of a trial for religious freedom—where members of all religious groups in the West file 'legal briefs' documenting violations of rights in the USSR."[76]

The dissenters are asking for help not only because of humanitarian reasons and justice, but also because of gratitude. When on December 12, 1975, a close collaborator of Andrei Sakharov, the 43-year-old biologist Sergei A. Kovalyov, was sentenced by a court in Vilnius to 7 years in prison and 3 years in exile, Anatoly Levitin-Krasnov appealed to the bishops, priests and Catholics of the world to show by deeds their gratitude and love for this man, a Russian Orthodox, "who suffered exclusively for his heroic defense of the Catholic Church." "We Orthodox Christians," added Levitin, "were very moved by those signs of love towards our ancient Church manifested by His Holiness Pope Paul VI on Sunday, December 14, 1975, in the Sistine Chapel in the presence of the representative of our Church Metropolitan Meliton. But the rapprochement and even more the union of the Churches will be determined not by particular accords between the hierarchs, but by the respect and love between the Christian peoples. A Russian, and an Orthodox by birth, S. Kovalyov gave an example of such love for his suffering brethren. Now is your turn to show your love: intervene in his defense. . ."[77]

6

Ukrainian Catholics and Vatican Diplomacy

The shadow of more than four million Ukrainian Catholics deprived of their religious freedom by the Soviet regime and forced into Russian Orthodoxy has hung over the politico-ecumenical dialogue between Rome and Moscow since its very beginning. Meanwhile Ukrainian dissent has reached such a point of exasperation that Moscow and the Vatican can hardly continue to ignore it.

The Soviet attack on the Ukrainian Catholic Church began in 1939 when, due to the Molotov-Ribbentrop pact, the Red Army occupied the territory of Western Ukraine. At that time one of the greatest Eastern Catholic bishops, Count Andrei Sheptytsky (born in 1865) had ruled the Metropolia of Lviv since 1900. A genial apostle of ecumenism, he had been a personal friend of the Russian philosopher Vladimir Solovyov[1] and received from Pope Pius X the powers and privileges of a "patriarch."[2] Prisoner of the Russians from 1914 to 1917,[3] he defended the Ukrainian nation under Polish rule (1921-39) and the Ukrainian Orthodox Church against Polish persecution.[4] During the Nazi occupation (1941-44) he protected and sheltered the Jews so that Rabbi Kahane said of him: "I do not believe in saints, but if there were any saints I am sure the greatest of them all is the Ukrainian Metropolitan Andrei Sheptytsky."[5] The holiness of his personal life, witnessed by Catholics and non-Catholics, prompted, on January 28, 1955, a decree by the Roman Congregation of Rites giving permission to proceed with the official introduction for his cause of beatification. Many of his ideas about ecumenism and relations with the Orthodox East have been fulfilled in recent years by the Second Vatican Council.

The First Enchained

Metropolitan Sheptytsky followed with a broken heart the physical and moral suppression of Ukraine by the Bolsheviks. On July 30, 1933, during the famine which annihilated millions of Ukrainians, in an appeal to the world he wrote: "We already see the consequences of the Communist regime: each day it becomes more frightening. The sight of these crimes horrifies human nature and makes one's blood run cold. Being unable to extend material help to our dying brothers, we implore the faithful to beseech from Heaven ... divine assistance. Furthermore we protest before the whole world against the persecution of children, the poor, the sick and the innocent. On the other hand, we summon the persecutors before the Tribunal of Almighty God. The blood of famished and enslaved laborers who till the soil of Ukraine, cries to heaven for vengeance, and the plaint of the half-starved reapers has reached God in Heaven. We implore the Christians of the world, all those who believe in God, and especially our fellow countrymen, to unite with us in protest to make known our grief even in the most remote corners of the earth. We also ask all the radio stations to broadcast our voice to the whole world; perhaps it may also reach the impoverished, desolate homes of the famine-stricken and the persecuted. Thus at least the thought that they are remembered and pitied by their brothers far away, and supported by their prayers, may be a consolation to them amidst untold sufferings and imminent death . . . Let our hopes be in the Lord."[6]

As early as 1937 Metropolitan Sheptytsky in a pastoral letter presented an uncanny analysis of the possibility of a Communist penetration into Western Ukraine. He told the seminarians: "Our Church, together with the Universal Church, needs fearless priests, ready for the greatest sacrifice as were the early Christians."[7] When, under Soviet occupation, the persecution started, the old Metropolitan sought a priest for his replacement. He chose Rev. Dr. Josyf Slipyj, rector of the Lviv Theological Academy, member of the oldest Ukrainian intellectual organization, the Shevchenko Scientific Society, a man of tremendous pedagogical and organizational skills and, above all, a saintly and fearless priest. With the approval of Rome, on December 21, 1939, Father Slipyj was secretly consecrated Coadjutor Bishop of Lviv with the right of succession.

Soon after the death of Metropolitan Andrei (November 1, 1944) the Soviet government, following the steps of the tsars, liquidated the Ukrainian Catholic Church and put its faithful and property under its control through the services of the pro-Soviet Russian Orthodox Church. At the beginning of 1945 the newly elected Patriarch of Moscow, Alexei, wrote in an appeal to the Ukrainian Catholics: "Free yourselves; break the chains that bound you to the Vatican, which with its errors leads you astray into darkness and spiritual ruin and, at the present time, wants to arm you against all freedom-loving humanity and separate you from the entire world. Hasten to return into the arms of your true mother the Russian Orthodox Church."[8] On April 8, 1945, a violent article against the Ukrainian Catholic Church was published in the paper *Vilna Ukraina*.[9] A few days later, on April 11, the Soviets arrested Metropolitan Josyf Slipyj together with all the other bishops of the Province of Halych: Gregory Khomyshyn, Ivan Latyshevsky and Gregory Lakota were also imprisoned. The trial against Metropolitan Slipyj took place in Kiev behind closed doors. Although accused only of certain "crimes" committed by his predecessor, he was condemned to ten years of forced labor. The 80-year-old Bishop Khomyshyn got ten years, the others from five to ten.

Many of the major dignitaries of the chapters and dioceses were also arrested. The students of two seminaries (Lviv and Stanyslaviv) were conscripted for military service in the Red Army. A few weeks after the arrest of the Ukrainian Catholic Bishops, a "Movement for the reunion of the Greek Catholic Church with the Orthodox Church" was established in Lviv under Soviet direction. The great majority of the Ukrainian Catholic clergy opposed the action of the "Movement" and the appeal of Rev. Gabriel Kostelnyk to join it. Over 300 courageous priests signed a protest to the Vice-President of the Ministers of the Soviet Union, V. Molotov, against the activity of this "Movement," condemning it as harmful to Church and State.[10] Only after many intimidating acts of terror, 204 priests out of almost 3,000, and 12 laymen, gathered in a pseudo-Sobor (Council) at Lviv (March 8-10, 1946) and declared the Union with Rome, signed at Brest-Litovsk in 1596, terminated. At the beginning of April a delegation of the same Sobor was received by Patriarch Alexei of Moscow, who proclaimed the *return* of the Ukrainian Catholics into the bosom of the Russian Orthodox Mother Church.

This forced "return" was politically and ecclesiastically untrue. In 1596 the Metropolitanate of Kiev was not dependent on Moscow, but on Constantinople. It was much later, with the treaty of Pereyaslav (1614) that the Moscow Tsar and Patriarch took the independent Ukrainian state under their "protection," which finally led to the annihilation of Ukrainian ecclesiastical and political independence (in 1685 and 1786) through the incorporation of the Ukrainians into the Russian Orthodox Church and the Russian Empire. Ivan Dzyuba, a dissenting literary critic, writes that

> ...the Ukraine did not "reunite," but entered into a treaty of alliance, which later was perfidiously broken by Tsardom. Compare, for instance, Herzen's words: "Khmelnytsky committed himself to the tsar not out of sympathy for Moscow, but out of antipathy for Poland. Moscow, or rather Petersburg, deceived the Ukraine and made it hate the Muscovites."
> Joining Great Russia, Little Russia [the Ukraine] reserved considerable rights for herself. Tsar Alexei swore to respect them. Peter I, on the pretext of Mazeppa's betrayal, left only a vestige of these privileges. Elizabeth and Catherine introduced serfdom there. The unfortunate country protested, but could it withstand that fateful avalanche rolling from the North to the Black Sea and covering everything... with a uniform icy shroud of slavery?[11]

With a similar procedure the Soviets in 1949, after the assassination of Theodore Romzha, bishop of Mukachevo (November 1, 1947), liquidated the Union of Uzhorod (1646) in sub-Carpathian Rus.[12] When the Russian Orthodox archbishop Makary visited that country in the same year, only one priest rallied to Orthodoxy, and the prospects for reunion "seemed almost desperate."[13] It was only through the brutality of the NKVD that this second "return" was reached, setting an example to be followed by other East European countries regarding the Byzantine-rite Catholics or, as they are also called, "Uniates." In the "Iliichev report" on religion, published under Khrushchev in January 1964, the "Uniates" are expressly listed among the religious groups forbidden by law in the Soviet Union.[14]

Only a few months after the arrest of the Ukrainian Catholic bishops, Pope Pius XII in his encyclical "Orientales Omnes" (December 24, 1945),[15] which marked the 350th anniversary of the Union of Brest, recalled the steps of Ukraine's martyrdom, beginning with the days of St. Josaphat, archbishop of Polock, martyred on November 11, 1623. Through the last two centuries thousands of Ukrainian Catholics died for their faith. Tsar Peter I won a personal title of "Butcher" of the Ukrainian Catholic Church, as on July 11, 1705, he personally killed two Basilian priests. During the period of only 25 years: 1771-1796 (under the reign of Catherine II), out of 12 million faithful, 8 million were forced into Russian Orthodoxy. The same happened to some 2 million Ukrainian Catholics under Nicholas I and Alexander III in 1839 and 1875.

Pope Pius XII, aware of the tremendous amount of sufferings, in the above-mentioned encyclical remembered "in a special manner" the priest Joseph Anchevsky, "who for 32 years was kept in hard prison in a Suzdal monastery and obtained the reward of his excellent virtue in 1878 with a most pious death." In this encyclical the Pope was recalling not only the clergy (160 priests followed the example of Anchevsky), but also the simple people. The inhabitants of the village of Pratulin, he wrote:

> When the soldiers came to occupy the church...didn't reject the force with force, but uniting tightly their bodies, opposed the assailants like a living wall. Therefore many of them were wounded, many suffered horrible cruelties, others were kept for long years in prison or deported to icy Siberia, and others hit with swords shed their blood for Christ. Of those who sealed with their blood the Catholic faith the process of beatification is already initiated in their diocese and we hope one day to venerate them among the blessed of heaven.[16]

The language used by Pope Pius XII is the language of the Apostles to the Christians of the catacombs. It is important to quote it today when the spirit of "détente" and "ecumenism" seems to consider the modern martyrs of their faith, be they Baptists, Orthodox or Catholics, as fanatics, victims of political factions or religious prejudices. In the spring of 1974 a priest, member of the Secretariat for promoting Christian Unity, discussing with another clergyman the question of the Ukrainian Catholics exclaimed: "let them go back to Orthodoxy. We should even give them 25 cents apiece and get rid of these fanatics once and for all."

The particular love of Pope Pius XII for Ukrainian Catholics was due also to the fact that they were the "first" to be enchained as a Church together with all their bishops without one single exception. That's why the Pontiff took every opportunity to speak about the Ukrainian Catholic Church and to ask prayers for its faithful left without pastors and forced to keep their faith in the illegality of the catacombs. In his encyclical "Orientales Ecclesias" of December 15, 1952 the Pope wrote:

> We sadly turn Our thoughts and affection to a people, truly dear to Us, namely, to the people of Ukraine, among whom are not a few of the faithful, who look towards Rome with immense desire and earnest love, and venerate this Apostolic See as the center of Christianity and as the infallible teacher of Christian truth by reason of the mandate of Jesus Christ. This people, nevertheless, as We have learned with overwhelming grief, are oppressed in no smaller degree with persecution and find themselves already for some time in a situation no less grave than the other peoples .... In a special way We would recall the memory of those Bishops of the Oriental Rite, who were among the first in the defense of their religion to endure hardship, affliction and outrage; who, transported to the city of Kiev, were tried there and condemned to various punishments—in the city of Kiev we say, whence once shone forth throughout all those regions the light of Christian doctrine, and whence Christian worship was propagated. Some of these have already met a glorious death, and so, as one may hope, from the abode of heavenly blessedness, which they enjoy, lovingly look down upon their sons and their companions in their unarmed struggle, and implore for them the all-powerful protection of God .... [17]

Again Pope Pius XII remembered the oppressed Ukrainians in their fatherland and encouraged those living in the diaspora in his Apostolic Letter "Novimus Vos" to the Ukrainian Hierarchy of January 20, 1956. On Christmas day of the following year, the 40th anniversary of the priesthood of the imprisoned Metropolitan Slipyj, the Pope, disregarding the fear of Vatican's officials that a public statement could harm the prelate and his faithful, released a moving letter addressed to him:

Venerable Brother, Joseph Slipyj,
Metropolitan of Halych,
Archbishop of Lviv, Bishop of Kamyanets
from

Pope Pius XII

Venerable Brother,
Greetings and Apostolic Blessings!
The fortieth anniversary of your priesthood which recently occurred gives Us the opportunity to express to You Our love and respect and Our concern to comfort You in exile in the midst of Your suffering. We know that upon the completion of eighteen years of the priesthood You accepted and zealously fulfilled Your pastoral service in the Lviv Eparchy, first as Auxiliary Coadjutor with rights of succession with the consent of the Archbishop Ordinary. Because of your fidelity to this Apostolic See You were

sentenced to imprisonment and thus forced to leave your faithful flock. Then you were imprisoned in various prisons and finally carried off to Siberia where you now are in a far-away place, Maklakovo, laboring as a servant and guard at a home for the handicapped. Therefore, We express Our heartfelt gratitude to You, Venerable Brother, for the zealous fulfillment of Your priestly and pastoral office at the cost of freedom; and because You chose "to carry disgrace for the name of Jesus," We arduously implore the Divine Infant Jesus to graciously comfort and strengthen Your soul in the midst of many discomforts and unpleasantness. Meanwhile as a sign of certain heavenly protection and Our particular affection We bestow upon You, Venerable Brother, with Our whole heart, Our Apostolic Benediction.

Given in Rome at Saint Peter's, on the 25th day of the month of December on the Nativity of Our Lord Jesus Christ, in the year 1957, during the nineteenth year of Our reign as Supreme Pontiff.[18]

Pope Pius XII

In 1952, Metropolitan Slipyj was taken to Kiev and Moscow and given a test of freedom, dignity, and indication of the honors which could be his if he would renounce his allegiance to Rome and become Orthodox Metropolitan of Western Ukraine with the possibility of eventually becoming patriarch of Moscow. He spurned the offer and earned for himself another seven-year sentence. In 1958, he was ordered not to engage in any pastoral work. He did not heed the admonition. On the 20th anniversary of his consecration as bishop he issued a pastoral letter to the faithful of the Ukrainian Catholic Church existing in the underground. In it he wrote: "Do not doubt, but revive in your hearts an unshaken faith that our Church will rise again."[19] Thereupon, the courageous prelate was given a third sentence. With the exception of Bishop Vasyl Hopko, he was going to be the only survivor of the Ukrainian Catholic bishops imprisoned by the Communists. Here is the list of these martyrs and confessors of the faith:

Josaphat Kocylowsky—Bishop of Peremyshl, Sianik and Sambir, died in prison on 21st August, 1947.

Hryhory Khomyshyn—Bishop of Stanyslaviv, died in prison on 17th January, 1947.

Nykyta Budka—Auxiliary Bishop of Lviv, died in exile in Karaganda (Siberia), 6th October, 1949.

Hryhory Lakota—Auxiliary Bishop of Peremyshl died in Vorkuta (Siberia), in 1951.

Ivan Latyshewsky—Auxiliary Bishop of Stanyslaviv, died of exhaustion and wounds after ten years of imprisonment, on 2nd December, 1957.

Nicholas Charnecky—Apostolic Visitor of Volyn, died on 2nd April, 1959, after 12 years of imprisonment in Siberia.

Msgr. Petro Verhun—Apostolic Visitor for Ukrainian Catholics in Germany and Western Europe, who resided in Berlin, was arrested in 1945, deported to Siberia, and died on 7th February, 1957.

Theodor Romza—Bishop of Mukachiv and Uzhorod in Carpatho-Ukraine, died after a "road accident" with the armoured car of Russian troops, on 1st November, 1947.

Pavlo Goydych—Bishop of Prešov, imprisoned in 1950, died in a concentration camp in Czechoslovakia, 19th July, 1960.

Vasyl Hopko—Auxiliary Bishop of Prešov. Although released from prison, after serving a 17 year term, was impeded from fulfilling his pastoral duties.

As we already mentioned, the American publisher Norman Cousins, who was instrumental in John XXIII's mediation of peace between Kennedy and Khrushchev during the Cuban crisis, a few months later was asked by Vatican officials to explore the possibility of "an amelioration of the religious situation inside the Soviet Union." In December 1962 on his way to Moscow Cousins stopped in Rome to meet with Archbishop Angelo Dell'Acqua, Deputy Secretary of State, and Cardinal Augustin Bea, president of the Secretariat for promoting Christian Unity. Cardinal Bea, writes Cousins:

> like Archbishop Dell'Acqua, believed that the smallest possibility for bettering the conditions of the Soviet people should be explored.... The central question, of course, was whether such explorations would be welcomed on the other end. Was there anything specific I might ask for in Moscow that would indicate a positive response? For many years, he said, members of the religious community had been imprisoned inside the Soviet Union. It would be a most favorable augury if at least one of them could be released. Was there any particular person he had in mind, I asked. "Yes," he said, "Archbishop Joseph Slipyj of the Ukraine, who has been imprisoned for eighteen years. He is a very fine man. The Holy Father is concerned about him. He is now seventy. There may be only a few more years left to him. The Holy Father would like the Archbishop to live out those few years in peace at some seminary, where he would be among his own. There is no intention to exploit the Archbishop's release for propaganda purposes."[20]

When Cousins raised with Khrushchev the question of Metropolitan Slipyj, he detected:

> a stiffening in the Chairman's manner. "You know," he said, "I'm rather familiar with the Slipyj case. I'm from the Ukraine, The entire matter is still fresh in my mind." Then, for

almost 20 minutes, the Chairman proceeded to describe the religious situation in the Ukraine before 1947. He spoke of the competition between the Ukraine Rite Catholic Church . . . and the Russian Orthodox Church. He spoke of the struggle for power inside both groups . . . He said that Archbishop Sheptytsky died in 1944 under circumstances that indicated "his departure from this earth may have been somewhat accelerated." In any event . . . the reason for his (Slipyj's) imprisonment, the Chairman said, had to do with collaboration with the Germans during the war. He added that those who defended Slipyj claimed that "collaboration" was too strong a word and that he had been responsible for saving many lives because of his position. Once again I said that I hadn't come to argue the original case, but it was now 18 years since the Archbishop was first imprisoned. Again the Chairman shook his head. "It is not a good idea," he said. "I would like to have improved relations with the Vatican but this is not the way to do it. In fact, it would be the worst thing we could do. It would make a terrible stink" . . . The Chairman said if the Archbishop became free there would be large headlines, proclaiming, "Bishop Reveals Red Torture" . . . .

Mr. Cousins restated that Pope John wanted Slipyj's release in good faith, not for propaganda purposes. Khrushchev replied then: "Let me think about this, it is not an easy question."

Early in January 1963, Cousins was informed in Washington by the Soviet ambassador, Dobrynin, that his request for the release of the Archbishop was granted. Before departing from Moscow the Metropolitan asked the papal representative, "Must I go, or do I have a choice?" He received the answer, "It is the will of the Holy Father."[21] The Catholic press in the United States reported that he himself wanted to return to his archdiocese in Lviv. Two days after the Archbishop's release Ambassador Dobrynin called Mr. Cousins about screaming headlines, "Bishop tells of Red Torture." The Vatican denied that Archbishop Slipyj spoke to any reporter and *L'Osservatore Romano* printed on its front page: " . . . the Holy See and Archbishop Slipyj disassociate themselves completely from these reports."

The release of Metropolitan Slipyj on February 10, 1963, didn't bring the hoped "amelioration" of the religious situation inside the Soviet Union. In the summer of 1963, the father superior of an underground monastery in Lviv, who had himself served a long term of imprisonment and now is no longer living, pulled up his trouser leg, pointed to his oozing open wounds and said to a visitor:

My suffering is nothing compared to that of the primate of our Church. If his sufferings and his example are not valued by the Holy Father and by the Congregation for Eastern Churches, let our martyr return to us in the Ukraine, even if he were to perish here. A martyr here will better serve the cause of our Church and the Catholic Church as a whole than an unrecognized hero in the seat of power of the Church which he refused to betray. A dead hero here is a more powerful stimulant for the cause of religion than a live prisoner at the Vatican.[22]

News of the persecution against the Uniates continued to flow even from the official press. On November 1963 a convent of underground sisters was discovered. They worked as nurses in a hospital and lived together in house No. 43 of Muchnaya street. The police arrested three priests, Boris, Roman and Gotra "and others condemned in the past for their anti-Soviet activities," who celebrated the Liturgy in that house.[23] In the following year two more priests, Vinnitsky and Khmelevsky, and two theology students, Skral and Palchinsky, were tried and sentenced for keeping in their rooms icons and books of theology.[24]

Meanwhile the presence of Metropolitan Slipyj in Rome became more and more embarrassing for those Vatican officials who were seeking a political rapprochement with the Soviet government and ecumenical contacts with the Moscow Patriarchate. After a short residence at the Greek monastery of Grottaferrata, not far from Rome, the prelate was transferred to a more isolated house in the Vatican where he kept silent for many years. From his lips not one word came out about the "Red torture" nor did he publish his memoirs. But he made it clear to the Pope that his commitment to his people was not finished, and that he would never retire.

The juridical position of the Metropolitan became the most controversial point at the Vatican. The Holy See didn't have another "official" bishop in the Ukraine to replace the Metropolitan. This step was taken in Hungary when Cardinal Mindszenty was deposed from his see. Perhaps the Vatican did hope that a similar dealing would be possible with the Soviet government. But this was impossible. The Ukrainian Catholic Church is officially non-existent in the USSR and there is no need for a Ukrainian Catholic bishop, even the most "loyal" to the atheistic government. Also for the Moscow Patriarchate such a question could not be raised. Every once in a while this declaration is repeated orally and in writing by the Church of Moscow: "The victory (over German Fascism) made possible the realization of the age-old dream—the ecclesio-religious reunion of the Greek Catholics of the Western regions of the Ukraine with the Russian Orthodox Mother Church."[25]

Without conferring on him any real jurisdiction, in a symbolic gesture of appreciation Pope Paul VI, on December 23, 1963, declared Metropolitan Slipyj a Major-Archbishop with "quasi-patriarchal powers" and later, on January 25, 1965, named him a Cardinal. On that occasion the Pope told a Ukrainian delegation: "We wish to say that by elevating your great Metropolitan to the dignity of Cardinal, we hoped to give you Ukrainians a high spokesman for your unity, to establish a strong center for your religious and national life . . . We wish to revive great hopes among the Ukrainian people. Continue your struggle . . . ."[26]

Metropolitan Slipyj took these words literally, even realizing that, perhaps, they were said in a diplomatic language and expressed a wish for a more distant future, not for the present time. In a period of ten years since his release, the old Cardinal instituted and built a Ukrainian Catholic University and the beautiful church of St. Sophia in Rome; restored the old church of SS. Sergius and Bacchus, making it the parish church for the Ukrainian community in the Eternal City; revived an ancient monastic order of St. Theodore Studite and established its monastery, the Studion, in Castelgandolfo; initiated the translation of liturgical books from Old Slavonic into the modern Ukrainian language; twice (in 1968-69 and in 1973) visited all Ukrainian settlements and dioceses in the free world.

While the Soviets and the Moscow Patriarchate thought the Ukrainian Catholic question closed and buried forever, Cardinal Slipyj conceived and put into action a great plan of revival for his Church centered in the establishment of a Ukrainian Catholic Patriarchate. He first publicly announced his intentions a few months after his release from Siberia at the Second Vatican Council, on October 11, 1963, when he brought to the attention of the Fathers the necessity of creating a Ukrainian Patriarchate as the only means to preserve the unity and the very existence of the Ukrainian Catholic Church. By demanding the recognition of such a Patriarchate the Cardinal was not asking for privileges, but for the implementation of the promises given by Rome to his Church at Brest, which included a "quasi-patriarchal" status for the metropolitan and a quasi-autonomous or synodal form of self-government for his Church.[27] Although the trend on the part of Rome toward greater centralization had, historically, pros and cons, at the present moment it is, as the Second Vatican Council recognizes it, harmful to ecumenism and to the Eastern Churches.

The *Decree on the Eastern Catholic Churches*[28] stipulates that:

a) The Churches of the East are "in duty bound to rule themselves, each in accordance with its own established disciplines" (#5)

b) If "they have fallen short owing to contingencies of times and persons, they should take steps to return to their ancestral traditions" (#6)

c) "The rights and privileges in question are those obtained in the time of union between East and West; though they should be adapted somewhat to modern conditions" (#9).

By regaining the lost autonomy for his Church, Cardinal Slipyj feels that he can (1) better help his faithful in Ukrainian catacombs without waiting for a most unlikely Vatican settlement with the Soviets and (2) keep the traditions and unity of his dioceses scattered around the world, which do not depend now on him, but on the Vatican's Eastern Congregation or even on Latin rite bishops. While the Ukrainian Catholic Church in the Soviet Union, without churches and a "registered" clergy, is in a worse position than the Catholic Church of Lithuania, nevertheless the fact that she doesn't have bishops and priests "loyal" to the government gives her greater credibility even among the Orthodox.

An American visitor to the Ukraine found the admiration which the Ukrainian Orthodox displayed for Metropolitan Slipyj very moving. She writes:

> Lviv is, to be sure, the center of Ukrainian Catholicism. It might well be expected that in this city the Ukrainian Orthodox would share some of the sentiments of the Catholics, some of the pride in a national hero. Yet during thirteen days in eastern Ukraine—in Kiev, Odessa, Yalta, Poltava, and Kharkiv those encountered after church services expressed similar sentiments.
>
> "You are a foreigner," they would say, "yet you understand our services."
>
> "Yes, I am from the United States, but I am of Ukrainian origin."
>
> "Then, you, too, are Orthodox?"
>
> "No, I am a Ukrainian Catholic, but our rite is the same."
>
> "Oh, you are a Uniate? Then your *vladyka* [bishop] is the heroic Joseph Slipyj. We know from radio programs from the West that he has been released and permitted to go to Rome. Tell us, did you perhaps see him? Is he well? Has the Vatican honored him as he deserves? What is he doing now? Will he be made patriarch?"
>
> The interest of the Orthodox in Ukraine in seeing Metropolitan Slipyj become patriarch is not as unnatural as at first glance it would seem. It stems from national pride. Ukrainians in their native land long for representation by an illustrious personality. They are looking for a champion who does not fear to defend their legal rights. They have no such exponent in the Russian Orthodox Church.[29]

The "Obstacle"

To the astonishment of many, both Catholic and Orthodox, Slipyj's plan for the revival of his Church found strong opposition in the Roman Curia, particularly in the Sacred Congregation for the Eastern Churches or, more simply, the Eastern Congregation, and in the Secretariat for Promoting Christian Unity. Another source of opposition in Rome is represented by the officials of the Pontifical College Russicum, who entertain close relations with the Moscow Patriarchate and with the two organs of the Roman Curia just mentioned. Fundamentally the reasons of this opposition are canonical, ecumenical and political, although they can be easily reduced to one: the troublesome existence of a Ukrainian nation.

1. The objections of the Eastern Congregation are mostly of juridical nature. This Congregation grants to Cardinal Slipyj, as a Major-Archbishop, the status of quasi-patriarch and the right to rule his Church together with his Synod, but only in his own territory.[30] Therefore, being a Cardinal in exile from his homeland, he is deprived of his jurisdiction both in the East and in the West. But, after the Second Vatican Council, which opened the path toward multi-jurisdiction, the territorial limitation of the rights of the patriarchs is rejected by many theologians as outmoded and

anti-ecumenical. The Commission for the Revision of Eastern Canon Law will probably get rid of this rule which strikes at the very vitality of the Eastern Churches by impeding their natural growth.[31] Meanwhile to insist, at the present time, on this territorial objection would amount, on the part of the Eastern Congregation, to a juridical pretext in order to cover other reasons.

Metropolitan Maksym Hermaniuk of Winnipeg (Canada), who is a member of the Commission for the Revision of Eastern Canon Law, speaking at the World Catholic Bishops Synod in Rome in 1974, declared:

> On the part of the separated Eastern Churches, it is noted that the Catholic Church of the Latin rite continues to predominate over the Eastern Catholic Churches, hindering their dialogue of union. The greatest difficulties are considered in relation to the apostolic faith and it is regretted that in the Sacred Congregation for the Eastern Churches, two-thirds of the prelates are of the Latin rite. Another difficulty is the submission of the faithful of various Eastern rites who are outside their own territory to the jurisdiction of the Latin rite.
>
> In order to resolve these difficulties it is suggested that the Synods of the Eastern Churches should have all the rights which are proper to them restored or that the members of the Sacred Congregation for the Eastern Churches should be delegates from all the Eastern Churches. It is requested moreover that the jurisdiction of all the Patriarchs and Major Archbishops over the faithful who are outside their territory be recognized. They should have the right to create, if need be, their own parishes. With "beneplacitum" of the Holy See, they should also be allowed to erect new Eparchies and to appoint bishops of the Exarchate. This should be possible since the faithful of the Latin rite live with such jurisdiction in territories of the Eastern rite.[32]

2. Catholic ecumenical activities, including the relations with the Orthodox, are entrusted to the Secretariat for Promoting Christian Unity rather than to the Eastern Congregation. In fact it is known that "the very existence of the Uniate (Eastern Catholic) Churches has always been considered by the Orthodox as one of the major obstacles to any sincere theological confrontation with the Roman Catholic Church."[33] This prejudice against the Uniates is shared also by some Catholic ecumenists. This is why when, during Dubchek's experiment of "socialism with a human face" in Czechoslovakia, the Uniates asked and obtained the re-establishment of their Church suppressed in 1950, "some Catholics" regarded that event "as a great blow for Catholic ecumenism."[34]

The Ukrainian Catholics have serious reasons to believe that the Secretariat for Christian Unity too considers their Church as an "obstacle" to its ecumenical activities. It is known that for the Church of Moscow the suppression of the Ukrainian Catholics is a conditio sine qua non for the continuation of any "ecumenical dialogue" with Rome. The Secretariat not only accepted this condition, but kept silent on various occasions when the arrogance and the gravity of the attacks of the Moscow Patriarchate against Catholic Ukrainians required a minimum of solidarity with them.

Metropolitan Nikodim of Leningrad, during a visit to Rome as a guest of the Secretariat, indignantly observed: "Demonstrations such as the dedication of the church of St. Sophia in Rome by Cardinal Slipyj (September 27 and 28, 1969) are contrary to ecumenism."[35] The silence of the officials of the Secretariat gave the impression that they were sharing Nikodim's view that Ukrainian Catholics should disappear within the Soviet Union as well as outside it.

It is known that the Russian Orthodox Church shares the idea of a Russian state where the other nationalities can only have the role of satellite. Therefore, a Ukrainian Church, be it Catholic or Orthodox, cannot be tolerated by Moscow. The question now is whether or not the Secretariat for Christian Unity is ready to reject any relationship with the Ukrainians for the sake of the Russians. If yes, the "obstacle" is removed, but ecumenism is lost in the mire of politics.

The involvement of Russian Orthodox Metropolitan Filaret of Kiev in the repression of Catholic Ukrainian underground activities was denounced by Soviet dissenters in the following account published in the *Chronicle of Current Events:*

> On October 18th, 1968, searches were carried out at the homes of ten priests of the former Lvov Greek-Catholic metropolinate, including Bishop Vasyl Velychkovsky, the priests Petro Horodetsky, Mykola Ovsyanko, [Ihnaty] Tschelsky, [Ivan] Lopadchak, [Fylymon] Kurchava, [Mykola] Deyneka, [V.] Sternyuk and others. Ritual objects (chalices, crosses, vestments, Holy Sacraments) as well as religious books, cameras, tape-recorders and money were taken away.
>
> At the same time one of them, Petro Horodetsky, was arrested and charged under articles 187-1 and 138 of the Ukrainian Criminal Code, i.e. propagation of deliberate fabrications which defame the Soviet political and social system, and violation of the laws concerning the separation of Church and State....
>
> At the end of 1968 the aged Bishop Vasyl Velychkovsky was arrested in Kolomiya....
>
> In the spring of 1969 all over the west Ukraine dozens of searches were carried out among Greek-Catholic priests, also in flats where former nuns were living. Again ritual objects, books, etc., were taken away.
>
> In 1968 in Pochayev there was a meeting of West Ukrainian Orthodox priests— mainly those priests who went over to Orthodoxy under pressure in 1946. Some priests at the meeting complained that they were being interfered with by Greek-Catholic priests who had not accepted Orthodoxy, and that these priests were carrying on their religious activities underground; Metropolitan Filaret gave the Orthodox priests instructions to spy on the Uniates and report on them. He promised to appeal to the party and government and in person to the First Secretary of the Ukrainian Communist Party, Shelest, and to request him to put an end to the activity of the Greek-Catholic priests.
>
> As the Uniates affirm, referring to information received from Orthodox priests, the court and Procuracy officials have been instructed to put a stop to the activity of the Greek Catholic Church by all possible means in the course of one year—by the centenary of the birth of V.I. Lenin [in April 1970]. It looks as if precisely this was the reason for the arrests and large-scale searches.[36]

Metropolitan Filaret's collaboration with the atheists in the destruction of Ukrainian Catholicism cannot be excused if we have in mind the aims of the official campaign and the content of the articles published at that time in the Soviet press.[37] A professor of Shevchenko University in Kiev, V. Tancher, wrote: "All Churches serve the interests of the exploiting classes. But the Uniate Church played a particularly reactionary role. Uniate believers desired opposition between the Ukrainian and Russian nations; they wanted to see the countries quarrel; they attempted to isolate these two friends from each other."[38] An even more inciting article by Taras Myhal angrily pointed out that "When in the sixteenth century this monstrous child (Uniate Church) was spawned by the Roman Catholic Church, so today the Vatican still ignores the 1946 decision by the Lviv Sobor...A large number of religious publications are produced earmarked for illegal entry into Western Ukrainian territory... Priests are ordained who will be future missionaries... New Uniate bishops are being ordained at an accelerated rate...."[39]

By joining this anti-Catholic campaign Metropolitan Filaret betrayed both his Christian faith and the Ukrainian nation. Here it's no longer the question of Ukrainians (Catholic and Orthodox) being an "obstacle" to ecumenism, but of whether or not a bishop can be an accomplice to Communist crimes. Nevertheless, when, in February 1975, Filaret came to the United States at the head of a delegation of Soviet clergymen, he was received with great honors by ecumenists and representatives of the NCC.

Bishop Vasyl Velychkovsky of Lutsk, a member of the Redemptorist Order secretly consecrated in the USSR, was one of the first victims of this incredibly combined hunt against the Catholic clergy in Ukraine. He was arrested for "illicit religious activities" when he was visiting a sick person. P. Petliakov in the article "Desperate Means," published in the atheistic journal of Kiev, wrote that Bishop Velychkovsky's plan to "force union" on the Ukrainian Church was theoretically formed in his work "History of the Miraculous Icon of the Mother of God of Perpetual Help." Petliakov states that one of the means used by the Catholic Ukrainian clergy to attain the restoration of the Uniate Church "is through widespread veneration of the 'miraculous' icons."[40] The ailing bishop, who had already spent 11 years in prison from 1946 to 1957, was released on January 26, 1972, a month short of his three year sentence, and expelled from Ukraine. Asked by an Italian journalist about the thing that he most regretted during his life in the USSR, he replied: "Without any doubt my greatest suffering under the Soviet regime was that I couldn't normally conduct my pastoral work."[41] He died in Winnipeg, Canada, on June 30, 1973 as a confessor of faith. No official in Rome ever protested against Filaret's assistance to the persecutors and torturers of Ukrainian Catholics. On the contrary, the Metropolitan was subsequently received at the Secretariat and Russicum as a guest of honor.[42]

Another even more eloquent silence was kept by Cardinal Jan Willebrands, President of the Secretariat for Promoting Christian Unity, when he represented Pope Paul at the enthronization of the new Patriarch of Moscow, Pimen, in June 1971. On that occasion Pimen called upon all present to rejoice at the liquidation of the Union of Brest and "the triumphal return into the Russian Orthodox Church" of the Uniates 25 years before.[43] The Cardinal not only didn't immediately protest against Pimen's statement while in Moscow, but also failed to do so upon his return to the Vatican. Under pressure of critics he simply declared, as reported by the Italian Catholic daily *L'Avvenire* (July 4, 1971), that he did not share the "thesis" of the Patriarch.

The motives behind Cardinal Willebrands' silence may be deduced from what the rector of Russicum, Fr. Paul Mailleux, S.J., said a few months before, in March 1971: "Ukrainian Catholics cannot expect the Holy See to risk the embarrassment of raising the question of the existence of the Ukrainian Catholic Church in the Soviet Union when there is the possibility of having a dialogue with the Russian Orthodox Church."[44] This attitude is a clear and unambiguous expression of "political ecumenism" which has nothing to do with authentic ecumenism.

3. The political aspect of the Vatican's attitude regarding the Ukrainian Catholic Church can be further clarified by the following secret "memorandum" written by Fr. Mailleux, dated "Summer 1972":

SOME CONSIDERATIONS ON THE UKRAINIAN QUESTION
(Personal notes not for publication.)

1. It is clear that as a true Catholic I condemn without reservation the suppression through violence of the Greek-Catholic Church of Ukraine, of Subcarpathia, and of Rumania. Violation of consciences is inadmissible. Respect for the human person requires that those who believe before God that their obligation is to remain in full communion with the successor of Saint Peter should be allowed to do so. I have written several times on this subject (in the journal *Etudes* as early as 1944). This point ought to be clear.

2. Question of the Ukrainian Patriarchate (be it at Kiev or elsewhere).

After Chalcedonia patriarchates were created when new *political* entities were formed (Russia, Serbia, Bulgaria, Rumania).

There has never been a Ukrainian Patriarchate but a Ukrainian political, separatist movement does exist in the USSR and abroad. The establishment of a Ukrainian Patriarchate by Rome could not fail to be considered by the Soviets (and by others) as the assumption of a stand by the Holy See in Ukrainian affairs, as moral support for the separatist politicians and therefore as hostile interference in the internal affairs of the USSR.

The enemies of the Church would rejoice at such an establishment, the Holy See would really give them a pretext to reject any modification of their attitude toward the Greek-Catholics in strictly religious matters.

The only realistic means one can envisage at this point for the improvement of the situation of millions of Catholics in the USSR are persuasion, negotiation, and pressure from abroad (articles in the press etc.). There is no doubt that the establishment of a Ukrainian Patriarchate would be considered as a provocation by the Soviets and would make any negotiation with them even much more difficult. *In present circumstances* it can be asked whether there are not *provocateurs* among the promoters of a Ukrainian Patriarchate.

3. Question of total autonomy of the Ukrainian Church in Europe, America, Australia under the Major-Archbishop.

The Second Vatican Council foresees autonomy for patriarchates *on their own territory*. Here it is a question of healthy ecclesiology which the Holy See seeks to reestablish in practice. Rome suppressed the Latin patriarchates of Constantinople, Antioch, and Alexandria. There are no more nominations of bishops "in partibus." Briefly, the local and particular Churches are respected: a bishop for a[given] territory; this is the present tendency and it is very well justified. A multiplicity of bishops and rites on the same territory is a cause of weakness of the Church in the Near-East. It is necessary to be prudent and not create the same situation in the rest of the world. In other words it is not desirable to create Eastern Patriarchates (or their equivalent) which extend over parts of the Latin Patriarchate. It seems to me that this is a question of principle.

In practice, by the same token, a good number of Ukrainians of the New World, especially the young ones, do not desire to be placed under jurisdiction of bishops who know the situation in America, Australia . . . only from a distance. It is necessary to enlighten Rome, certainly it is necessary to express just desires (désiderata), but then one must leave the final judgement and decision to those who have the responsibility for the *entire* Church. It is absolutely unjust to cast doubt on their good will. In principle, it can be presumed that generally they view the needs of the Church in a more balanced manner than those who are strongly attached to one particular Church. As to the use of harmful words in addressing the authorities, whoever they may be, even on the practical level they are "counter-productive"; they make people think that the person using them is impassioned, that he does not judge with objectivity, and therefore such people will not be heard.[45]

In haste,
P. Mailleux, S.J.

Strangely enough, Fr. Mailleux, while acknowledging that the Ukrainian Catholics are denied their freedom of conscience and human rights, fails to mention the responsibility of the Moscow Patriarchate in this crime. Furthermore he suggests that the Ukrainian Patriarchal movement is mostly the work of "nationalist-separatist politicians" and sees Communist infiltration not in the Russian Orthodox Church, but only among Ukrainian Catholics. If for the Vatican to be "realistic" means to accept the suppression of the Ukrainian nation, there is no way to "improve" even the "strictly religious" situation of millions of Orthodox and Catholic Ukrainians. As Anatoly Levitin-Krasnov wrote, religious rights cannot be separated from other fundamental human rights:

I am a believing Christian, a religious man. For me there is one thing in life which is greater than any other—the rights of man surpass all else, in my view. Any kind of doctrine of discrimination, be it racial, national or religious, is irresistibly distasteful to me. If atheists were somewhere to suffer persecution on account of their convictions, I should defend them as best I could. But now it is a call to drive believers from higher education that I hear—and I intend to enter the fray against the advocates of religious discrimination with all the means at my disposal...

Let me ask this: what would happen if...we were to bar believers from higher education? The country would be deprived of hundreds of able doctors, engineers and scientific workers. But this is not the worst. A large group of oppressed and frustrated, fanatically antagonistic people would be created, like the English Catholics in the seventeenth and eighteenth centuries or the Old Believers and sectarians of Tsarist Russia. A vast number of true chameleons would appear who concealed their real convictions behind a facade. But even this would not be the worst. Worse would be the chain reaction which would set in, not only in the realm of physics, but in that of human society. As the experience of recent years has shown, when arbitrary lawlessness sets in nobody can say where it will lead. Advocating religious discrimination is a blatant call to the violation of the Constitution and the flouting of all legal standards.[46]

October, 1959

Under the pretext of "nationalism" the Soviet regime suppressed not only the Ukrainian Orthodox and Catholic Churches, but also those Ukrainian Bolsheviks who believed that Communism should respect national traditions and values. Many eminent Ukrainian communists committed suicide: the Minister of Public Instruction Skrypnyk, the writer Khvylovy, Lubchenko, head of the government, etc.

Today's Ukrainian dissenters are arrested and tortured for the same reason. In late August and early September 1965, a week or two before the arrest of Sinyavsky and Daniel, a number of political arrests among Ukrainian intellectuals took place in different Ukrainian cities. No official statements were issued regarding them, but rumors about the arrest of "nationalists" gained ground. Ivan Dzyuba, a Ukrainian writer, convinced that those arrested were honest and sincere people concerned for the conditions of Ukrainian culture, wrote an essay entitled "Internationalism or Russification?," copies of which he sent, together with a letter, to party and government authorities. In the letter he stated: "The obviously absurd tales about an underground movement, arms, a printing press, etc., have been supplanted by a new tale about 'nationalist propaganda'... From past and recent history it may be seen that in the Ukraine it was permissible to label as 'nationalist' anyone possessing an elementary sense of national dignity, or anyone concerned with the fate of Ukrainian culture and language, and often simply anyone who in some way failed to please some Russian chauvinist, some 'Great Russian bully'... Those believing these people to have been mistaken in some way ought to have answered them in the same open and principled way in which they behaved. Instead, the response was terror, first moral, and now also physical...."[47]

Far from supporting anti-Soviet opposition, Dzyuba believes the russification policies presently adopted in the Ukraine to be contrary to nationality principles of Marxism-Leninism. His book abundantly proves how in the Ukraine Russian culture has supplanted the national one in literature, press, school, theater, etc. Soviet propaganda about the equality of nations is rejected by the author as meaningless and hypocritical:

> Even the more intelligent tsarist ministers saw that a genuinely anti-Ukrainian policy lay not in forbidding the use of the Ukrainian language (which is impossible), but in causing the people to abandon it by themselves ... If we were to understand the matter in such a Philistine way, and not politically and socially, we should have to admit that the formula of tsarist Russia as a "prison of nations" is unjust ... Tsarist ministers like to stress "internationalism" and the "friendship of peoples" ... They especially pushed fraternity ....
>
> In Ukrainian universities lectures are given in Russian, on the grounds that many Russians study there (as if it were not their elementary civic duty to learn Ukrainian in such a case) ... A citizen of Odessa, S. Karavansky, established on the basis of authentic documents that of those entering the Odessa Polytechnic Institute in 1964-65 only 43 per cent were Ukrainians ... Karavansky established that as a result of discriminatory admission procedures which make it more difficult for Ukrainian school graduates to enter establishments of higher education ... the percentage of admissions in relation to applications is higher for Russians than for Ukrainians ... Karavansky requested the Public Prosecutor of the Ukrainian SSR to bring a criminal action against the Minister of Higher and Special Secondary Education of the Ukrainian SSR, Yu. M. Dadenkov ... The consequences were not long in coming: S. Karavansky was himself arrested ....
>
> Can anyone hold with the fact that with thirty thousand schools and seven million pupils in the Republic children's books are printed in thirty thousand copies? .... And here is one mother telling another: "My son hasn't gone to school because of this Ukrainian language. He hates the Ukrainian teacher so much. He calls her 'a Banderist' (satisfied laughter of two mothers)." When in 1963 the Young Writers and Artists' Club decided to honour the memory of Ivan Franko and organized a torchlight procession to his monument you could hear Russian interjections from the crowd along Kiev's main street: "Look! Banderists! What a lot of them!' Everybody heard this and knows this, just as everybody knows about the lecturer ... Professor (!) Telnova, who desecrated the Shevchenko monument, an incredible act, unheard of in any civilized country. Naturally, Telnova not only went unpunished, but on the contrary, everything was done to neutralize the consequences ... As the events of 22 May 1964 and 27 April 1965 have shown, quite a different type of person is being rounded up at the Shevchenko monument ....[48]

The nationalities policy, under both the tsars and the Soviets, has been understood as "a certain strategic game of diplomacy"[49] in order to preserve the "unity" of the empire and the centralization of power. It seems that the Vatican, too, is willing to adapt to the "strategic game" or to delay its action in favor of the oppressed nations until their liberation will be at hand or even after it already has taken place. Father Nicholas Bock, a former secretary of the Tsarist Legation to the Holy See, who later became a Jesuit, wrote in his memoirs that when Metropolitan Andrei Sheptytsky was set free after the February Revolution and remained in Russia instead of returning to Galicia in order to organize the Russian Eastern Rite

Catholics, the Vatican was worried. "The Vatican ... feared that the Catholicism he was propagating might bear the marks of hostility to Russia. Therefore, it insisted upon Sheptytsky's return to his diocese and breathed more freely when he came back to Lviv."[50] This writer is not certain whether this was a "fear of the Vatican" or a worry of the secretary of the Imperial Russian Legation. It is clearly not true that Metropolitan Sheptytsky wanted to establish a Catholicism hostile to Russia. This is proven by his appointment as Exarch for Russia of a priest, Russian by birth and nationality, Father Leonid Feodorov. And precisely this appointment is considered greatly meritorious and a signal of service on Metropolitan Sheptytsky's part by Feodorov's biographer, Fr. Paul Mailleux, S.J.[51] It should be added that this appointment was not a matter of political expediency but reflected the constant attitude of the saintly Metropolitan. Even earlier, in 1908, Metropolitan Sheptytsky appointed Father Alexei Zerchaninov, another Russian Eastern Rite Catholic priest, as his vicar general in St. Petersburg.[52]

The mentality demonstrated by the late Fr. Bock is still prevalent among Russian "experts" at the Vatican. But they do not take into consideration the fact that in the Soviet Union mentality is changing. Today the Russian democrats respect the rights of other nationalities, and the Russian Orthodox dissenters live in a true ecumenical spirit with believers of other denominations. There is no need anymore, as the Vatican "experts" think, to become pro-Russian and pro-Orthodox in order to be accepted by the Russian people. As Anatoly Levitin-Krasnov wrote in his letter to Pope Paul:

> For several decades Orthodox Christians and sectarians suffered together in Beria camps, slept side by side in prison bunks, gulped the same prison soup out of the same rusty bowls. So now the Church and the sects practically do not compete with each other ... One can see a new spirit in relationships between Orthodoxy and the sects; the old mistrust and bitterness is entirely gone, there is rather mutual respect and sympathy. Common problems facing both the Church and the sects favour still closer relationships ... Thus in Russia there is an authentic ecumenism, in living religious practice, and this ecumenism takes place without conferences, official speeches or great banquets, as in the case of Amsterdam ecumenism, but perhaps just because of this it is authentic ecumenism ... The unjust, forcible reunion of the Uniates which took place in the early post-war years shattered the relationship between Orthodoxy and Catholicism, but only for a short time. At present interest in the Catholic Church is to be noted among Orthodox youth ... The blessed personality of Pope John XXIII has great respect among believers in Russia ... And all this does not in the least weaken loyalty to our national Church ....[53]

Andrei Amalrik, in his essay "Will the Soviet Union Survive until 1984?" predicted that "the nationalist tendencies of the non-Russian peoples of the Soviet Union will intensify sharply, first in the Baltic area, the Caucasus and the Ukraine, then in Central Asia and along the Volga."[54]

In order to meet these intensified nationalist tendencies, Alexander Solzhenitsyn suggests to the leaders of the Soviet Union to concentrate on Russia and transfer the center of the nation away from Europe and even from the South, noting that, "of course, such a shift must mean sooner or later lifting our trusteeship from Eastern Europe, the Baltic republics, Transcaucasia, Central Asia and possibly even from parts of the present Ukraine. Nor can there be any question of our forcibly keeping any peripheral nation within the borders of our country."[55] After leaving the Soviet Union, Solzhenitsyn, whose grandfather was Ukrainian and grandmother half-Ukrainian wrote a very amicable letter to the Ukrainian Free University in Munich.

It was with that pro-Russian mentality prevailing in the Roman Curia that Cardinal Slipyj was confronted when he started the implementation of his program of revival of his Church. From September 29 to October 4, 1969, he held in Rome the Fourth Archiepiscopal Synod of Ukrainian Catholic Bishops which approved a petition to the Pope to elevate the Kiev-Halych Metropolia to the status of a Patriarchate. The answer of Cardinal de Fuerstenberg, then Prefect of the Eastern Congregation, was that no one in the Ukrainian Catholic Church has the right to convoke a "legislative or elective Synod" in the first place (December 1, 1969).[56] Major-Archbishop Slipyj replied to the Cardinal that "the decisions of more than 21 bishops are law to us. Your Eminence can think as he wishes. We have clarified the position of our Church. In fact therewith, a great gap between the clergy and the people has been closed. The Church has been fortified in the face of the threat of danger from within and from without ... I must say that it is not a matter of defending my modest person, the galley-slave archbishop, but of defending the thousand-year rights of our Kiev-Halych Metropolitanate."[57]

The idea of the Ukrainian Patriarchate as the only means to keep the Ukrainian Catholic Church alive at home and abroad got the unanimous backing of all Ukrainian Catholics and of many Orthodox in the free world and in Ukraine[58] and their petitions poured into Rome only to find a deaf ear.[59] In the last days of May 1971 Vatican officials refused permission for Cardinal Slipyj to visit Canada for fear that mass meetings, rallies and demonstrations would influence the decision of the Pope.

On July 7, 1971, Pope Paul wrote to Cardinal Slipyj that "at a meeting of the heads of the Congregations of the Roman Curia ... the members of this Commission justified from every possible angle the conclusions that they arrived at ... Even though Our own mind was most inclined to accept your petitions, nevertheless, We have come with difficulty once again to the conclusion that it is impossible, at least at this time, to establish a Ukrainian Patriarchate."[60] The territorial limits of the Eastern Churches played the biggest role in this denial. A second consideration brought up by the Pope was the fear that the new Patriarchate would render more difficult the situation of those Ukrainian Catholics "who have been forced to silence thus far for fidelity to their faith in countries in which they live but which do not recognize the legitimacy of the Ukrainian Church."

It was already known that in the Soviet Union the Uniates are outside the law, and the legitimacy of their Church is not recognized. What is surprising is that the Pope seems to consider this situation, although painful, hopeless or, as Levitin-Krasnov puts it, something "which has become the norm of (Soviet) life," as if the peoples of the Soviet Union in general and of the Ukraine in particular, were opposed to the existence of a Ukrainian Catholic Church. The Pope gives this impression because he carefully selects the word "countries" while the non-recognition of the Uniates comes from the Soviet and Soviet-dominated governments and Churches.

The civil rights movement and the dissenters of the Soviet Union always insist on the necessity of making a clear distinction between the people and the party, the freedoms expressed in the Constitution and denied by the regime, the will of the believers and the subservience of the Churches. On the other hand, due to its great insistence on the territorial limits of the Eastern Churches, it is very doubtful that this papal document will enhance ecumenism and attract the Christians toward Catholic unity. The Orthodox Churches will never accept the idea that the world belongs to the Pope and therefore they have no rights on their faithful living outside of their territory.

The question of the establishment of a Ukrainian Catholic Patriarchate is not new. Not long after the Union of Brest of 1596 this question was raised several times. In 1629 four Ukrainian bishops still separated from Rome declared they were ready to join those eight already reunited if a Ukrainian Patriarchate would be erected and the union discussed at a common synod of Orthodox and Catholics. The Pope was in principle favorable to the establishment of the Patriarchate, but, at the suggestion of a Commission of Cardinals, he was contrary to the idea of a mixed synod of Orthodox and Catholics. Only the Secretary of Propaganda Fide, Monsignor Ingoli, gave in writing his favorable opinion in a document dated Rome, June 4, 1629.[61] The Catholic Church, according to Ingoli, had no need to be afraid of a direct discussion with the Orthodox and it would be improper to ask the Orthodox bishops to accept the Union of Brest before the mixed synod as the Commission of Cardinals suggested. In other words the Cardinals were afraid that once the new Patriarchate was established by the Pope, the Orthodox wouldn't comply with the promise of a "universal" union of all the Ukrainians or would take the opportunity to win back the Uniate bishops into Orthodoxy.

Rome rejected the idea of a Ukrainian Patriarchate for a third time in 1636. On June 16 of that year the same Msgr. Francesco Ingoli wrote to the papal nuncio in Poland, Philonardo, not to discuss "at this time" that question with the king for the reasons already known and also "in order to avoid a greater irritation and alienate the Greeks of the East from the union with the Holy Church of Rome."[62]

The reason brought up by Ingoli in 1636 seems to be the same which persuaded Pope Paul in 1971 and in 1975 to reject "at this time" the establishment of a Ukrainian Patriarchate. With the difference that now Rome does not want to "irritate" and "alienate" the Church of Moscow. "Not at this time" was the answer given by Rome, since 1596, to the many requests for a Ukrainian Catholic Patriarchate. For this reason, among others, a great number of Ukrainian Catholic immigrants to the United States abandoned the Catholic Church at the beginning of this century.[63]

Today, although the Ukrainian Orthodox do not have any desire for a "universal" union with Rome (something that Ingoli predicted when he warned the Pope against the suggestion of the Cardinals to wait for "better times" for the erection of a Ukrainian Patriarchate), they nevertheless have the same feelings regarding the Russian Orthodox Church which, with the help of the atheistic government suppressed both Churches in the Ukraine, Orthodox[64] and Catholic. They too are "irritated" and "alienated" from being united with Rome as we can see from a resolution adopted by the Sobor (Council) of the Ukrainian Autocephalous Orthodox Church held in London from October 13 through 17, 1972. This Sobor, under the Chairmanship of Metropolitan Mstyslav Skrypnyk expressed condolences to Ukrainian Catholics in the following resolution No. 8 which reads:

> To Ukrainian Catholics who at present are painfully enduring the contemptuous attitude of Vatican policy makers toward their efforts to preserve the traditional forms of their particular Church, our Sobor expresses deep sympathy. We sincerely hope that you will survive the troublesome era brought about by the close cooperation of the Vatican and the atheistic Kremlin—both indifferent to the needs of Ukrainian Catholics.[65]

After receiving the Pope's letter, Cardinal Slipyj called upon the Ukrainian Catholics throughout the world to accept the Pope's temporary decision but to continue to strive to implement the synodal system of administration for their Church with the ultimate goal of establishing a Patriarchate. During the month of October of that same year 1971 some events gave him the opportunity to answer the Pope publicly and to gather again a Synod of the Ukrainian Catholic hierarchy: a) the World Synod of the Catholic Bishops meeting in Rome; b) the festivities for the dedication of the renovated church of SS. Sergius and Bacchus, the Ukrainian parish in Rome, and for the 375th anniversary of the Union of Brest and the 325th anniversary of the Union of Uzhorod.

When Cardinal Slipyj, among the general silence, arose to address the World Synod of Catholic Bishops in the presence of Pope Paul (October 23), somebody thought he would speak "of something related to the

Orient, because the exotic oriental things vehemently attract the minds of the Western Fathers." Instead, he delivered the following speech which will remain in history as the most authoritative document of Catholic dissent vs. Moscow-Vatican détente:

> Some Fathers might prefer that I speak of something related to the Orient, because the exotic oriental things vehemently attract the minds of the Western Fathers. Indeed there are many singular things and worthy of attention even in the Orient in reference to justice. Nevertheless, the situation of today, as we already mentioned, is very sad.
>
> Our mind is primarily occupied with the Catholic Church of the Ukrainians, whose condition today faces the "to be or not be," as it has already been explained by other speakers....
>
> During the First World War, Ukraine regained its independence, but after a few years, with the incoming of Communism, was occupied by the Soviets. Our Church was destroyed in a bloody manner, as all the Hierarchy was thrown in prison and hundreds of priests and thousands of faithful were driven by force into Russian Orthodoxy. And such a grave injustice still triumphs. The Catholic Ukrainians, who had sacrificed mountains of bodies and shed rivers of blood for the Catholic Faith and their fidelity to the Holy See, even now are undergoing a very terrible persecution, but what is worse, they are defended by no one. From the beginning of history, I don't know of any people who have suffered as much as Ukrainians.
>
> They, who were 55 million, because of battles, raids, starvation, and religious persecution, since the beginning of the First World War lost ten million people. The Soviet regime since long ago has put an end to our activity, and all our Eparchies have been suppressed.
>
> Our Catholic faithful, prohibited from making any celebration of our Liturgy and administering the Sacraments, must descend into the catacombs. Thousands of thousands of faithful, priests and bishops have been thrown in prison and deported to the polar regions of Siberia. Now, however, because of diplomatic negotiations, the Ukrainian Catholics, who as martyrs and confessors suffered so much and so many things, are put aside like fastidious witnesses of past evils.
>
> In recent letters and communications, our faithful lament: "Why have we suffered so much? Where is justice to be found?" For the ecclesiastical diplomacy, we have been considered an impediment. "Cardinal Slipyj does not do anything for his Church." And what can he do? An intercession was made by the Vatican on behalf of the Latin Catholics, but the six million faithful Ukrainians who have suffered religious persecution have been ignored.
>
> When the Muscovite patriarch, Pimen, in an electoral synod clearly declared that the Union of Brest was annulled, not one of the Vatican delegates present protested.
>
> The creation of a Ukrainian Patriarchate, proposed during the second Vatican Council, has been denied. The delegation of the Basilian sisters from Ukraine was not admitted to the general chapter. Bishops and priests are converted to the Latin rite. It is amazing that the Soviets have raised a very high voice against colonialism while they themselves oppress their people. In the synod we also heard about the diabolic manners of exterminating the defeated nations, and about the evils that the Poles have suffered because of the same oppressors. From the bottom of our hearts we must have sympathy for them. And yet, in no way has it been conceded that in the communist and Catholic Poland half a million of Ukrainians have been deprived of their most basic rights, expelled from their domiciles and indeed they cannot even call themselves Ukrainians. "Leben und leben lassen," to live and let live, must be a supreme law.
>
> Three dioceses of ours in Poland have been without a bishop for 30 years, and not

even an auxiliary bishop has been installed; and not one Ukrainian priest has been admitted to this synod.

On the other hand, the Ukrainian Orthodox have four bishops in Poland, and are to receive three more. Therefore our people complain that they have lost everything, the rite and the discipline, while the Orthodox have kept everything.

In Czechoslovakia the diocese of Priashiv, which was Ukrainian, has been lost.

One of the most eminent Cardinals was astonished that Ukrainians who have been treated so badly and unjustly have nevertheless remained Catholic.

Behold for you, Venerable Fathers, my exotic oriental things! I now end, so that the Church of Silence may not speak too much. But may the mighty voice of this Synod, under the guidance of the Holy Father Pope Paul VI, be raised in defense of those who suffered persecution. And may our prayers give new strength to those who are struggling between life and death to persevere until the final victory. For may the world perish, but let justice be done![66]

The Ukrainian bishops had hardly arrived in Rome to take part in the announced festivities and start the Synod of their "Particular Church," when a letter, dated October 29, 1971, from the Secretary of State Cardinal Jean Villot, with a reminder that no Synod should take place, was delivered to each of them except Cardinal Slipyj. But the Ukrainian bishops stood their ground and concluded their sessions with the establishment of a permanent synod of five members to minister the needs of their faithful. They also agreed that an Archiepiscopal Constitution for their Church should be drafted and submitted to them for consideration. In the following year the permanent synod held its first session and a draft Constitution was sent to the bishops. The final text was approved in November 1973.[67]

In mid-September 1972 the Ukrainian bishops received through the papal nuncios of their respective countries of residence an intimidating letter from Cardinal Villot written by "mandate of the Holy Father." In this letter the Vatican Secretary of State protested against "the drafting as well as the forwarding" of the Archiepiscopal Constitution "without the knowledge of the Holy See," and explained that referring to the Ukrainian Catholic Church as "autonomous" was wrong and "consequently, the Holy See cannot accept such a Constitution as canonically workable." The letter closed with the remark that a "consultation" between the Ukrainian bishops would be permitted in the frame of the so-called "episcopal conferences" already taking place in different countries among the Latin rite bishops and with the warning that "in such a consultation, the problem of erecting a patriarchate of the Ukrainian rite cannot be brought into discussion because of the already known pronouncement of the Holy See upon this matter."[68] Again the Vatican took this opportunity to humiliate the head of the Ukrainian Catholics by ignoring him. Not only did he not receive a copy of Cardinal Villot's letter, but on November 4, 1972, a Vatican press release declared that "even though in the Ukrainian Church there are groups of dioceses united under a supra-than-episcopal jurisdiction in the form of a Metropolia, an ecclesiastical authority does not exist to which jurisdiction the bishops as a total entity are subjected in union with the Roman Pontiff."[69]

When the text of Cardinal Villot's letter became known, widespread indignation arose among the Ukrainian Catholics. A series of protest rallies was held in centers of the greatest concentration of Ukrainian Catholics. On November 25, 1972, a protest demonstration was held in front of the residence of the Apostolic Delegate in Washington. Some of the placards carried by the marchers read: "Ecumenism requires respect of autonomy," "Orthodox and Anglicans, beware of Vatican promises," "Credibility gaps undermine Vatican reliability," "Vatican sacrificial policy is a lasting scandal," "Don't bully our bishops," "Vatican-Moscow dialogue will lead to disaster."[70]

While the bishops refrained from a pubilc protest, the priestly Society of St. Andrew sent to Paul VI a letter in which the clergymen asked the Pope:

> How can we, the clergy, explain to our parishioners that the Vatican overlooks all the rights of our church and denies it administrative self-government? How can we justify the fact that members of the Curia with the acquiescence of Your Holiness (for in their letter they refer to the will of the Holy Father) degrade the head of the Ukrainian Catholic Church and its entire hierarchy? How can we sustain respect among our faithful toward the authority of the Universal Church when our church has obviously become the sacrificial lamb on the altar of dialogue between the Vatican and atheistic Moscow?

The priests then set forth their six-point position:

> 1. We have always been, are, and always will be loyal to the head of the *Pomisna* (Particular) Ukrainian Catholic Church, His Beatitude Major-Archbishop, rather Patriarch, Joseph Slipyj and all his purposes and plans in the implementation of the resolutions of the Fourth and Fifth Archiepiscopal Synods which were elaborated upon at the first session of the Permanent Synod.

> 2. We protest against the efforts of the Vatican Curia to abrogate the rights of the head of the Ukrainian Catholic Church, against his degradation by letters from these officials, by Vatican press bulletins; we protest against repeated refusal to permit him to travel beyond the boundaries of Italy.

> 3. We firmly defend the prestige of our bishops whose jurisdiction the Vatican Curia is reviewing from the point of view of Roman Canon Law with no appreciation or understanding of the structure or rights of the Eastern churches.

> 4. We protest against the practice of the members of the Vatican Curia of writing to the head of the Ukrainian Catholic Church and its bishops as though they were subservient to the Curia, as though they did not have any conception about the laws, traditions, responsibilities toward their Particular Church, its clergy, and its people of God. According to the laws of our church, the major-archbishop, in reality Patriarch, has the right to convene synods. He, together with his synod, has the right to draft and revise a constitution for our church and to send it to his bishops for their consideration. It is time

that the members of the Vatican Curia acquainted themselves with the rights of the Eastern churches and stopped repeating their flagrant mistakes.

5. We do not recognize the apostolic delegate as the channel of communication between the Holy Father and our hierarchy or our hierarchy and the Holy Father. Our church has a major-archbishop with all the rights of a Patriarch and according to the laws of our church he is the only channel of communication between the Holy See and our church prelates.

6. We cannot pretend before our faithful that we are unaware that seven million Ukrainian Catholics have been sacrificed in the search for a dialogue of undetermined value between the Vatican and atheistic Moscow. We cannot remain silent when the Vatican not only makes no defense of our church in Ukraine, but, upon the wishes of Moscow, inaugurates a policy toward the Ukrainian Catholic Church in the free world which can result in the total liquidation of our church and thus accomplish that which neither the Russian tsars nor the communists of Moscow were able to achieve.[71]

At the first session of the Permanent Synod (June 4-8, 1972) the Ukrainian bishops, clergy and laity were invited to participate in the 40th Eucharistic Congress to be held in Australia in the following year. The issued communique stated that the presence of the entire Ukrainian Catholic hierarchy at that Congress together with a world representation of clergy and laity would be a "manifestation of the vitality" of the Ukrainian Catholic Church and an indication that Ukrainian Catholics constitute "one Particular Church." Immediately another attempt was made by the Vatican to intimidate the Ukrainian bishops not to respond to this call. On January 31, 1973, Cardinal Villot, Vatican Secretary of State, wrote to Cardinal Slipyj that he was given permission to attend the Eucharistic Congress provided he limited his visit to strictly liturgical matters, a warning that sounds strangely similar to Soviet religious policy, which allows liturgical services, but not religious propaganda. A copy of this letter was sent to every Ukrainian Catholic bishop in the world. This strategy of "divide and conquer" was only partially successful. While only the bishops of Canada and one from Yugoslavia joined the head of their Church in Australia, the Ukrainian bishops of Canada invited him to come to their country on his return trip to Rome. Cardinal Slipyj accepted their invitation. Shortly afterwards, the Ukrainian bishops of the United States invited him to America. From reliable sources it has been learned that on April 15, in Edmonton, an emissary of the Vatican pro-nuncio in Ottawa urged Cardinal Slipyj not to visit the United States. But the Cardinal did not change his mind. What the Vatican feared was accomplished: everywhere, at the airports, at the entrances of the churches, at testimonial dinners, he was acclaimed as Patriarch Joseph First. And, what is even more important, the bishops joined the laity in addressing the Cardinal as "Your Beatitude, our Patriarch."[72]

Ukrainian Catholic dissenters, as well as other Soviet dissenters, realize that most of their troubles stem from the prolonged failure to exercise their rights. Speaking on this matter, Fr. William A. de Vries, S.J., professor at the Pontifical Oriental Institute in Rome, told a Ukrainian audience:

> The fact must be stressed that patriarchates grew from below and were not founded by any decree from above, for example, by the decree of an ecumenical council or of a pope. The origin of the patriarchates is to be sought in the prescriptive right or custom simply ratified by the council and recognized by the popes ... It is very important for Ukrainians to recognize that custom creates the right. Ukrainians must create a custom and the custom will create their right.[73]

The Holy Year gave Cardinal Slipyj and Ukrainian Catholics another opportunity to make known to the world the situation of their Church and their nation. When issuing his 1975 Easter Pastoral Letter, the Cardinal signed himself as "Patriarch," and the document was countersigned by Ukrainian Catholic bishops throughout the world. In consequence of this, Pope Paul reminded the Cardinal orally (May 5, 1975) and in writing (May 24) that he "for the moment" was not ready to recognize the existence of a Ukrainian Catholic Patriarchate. Meanwhile a pilgrimage in which over 3,000 Ukrainians took part, including 16 bishops and 120 priests, gathered in Rome from July 12 to 16. During a solemn liturgy in St. Peter's basilica Cardinal Slipyj was commemorated by the deacon, the clergy and the laity as "Patriarch Joseph First of Kiev and Galicia," while thousands of leaflets in different languages in defense of the religious and national rights of the Ukrainian people were distributed in St. Peter's Square. The news of the assassination of Fr. Mykhaylo Lutsky by KGB agents confirmed the tragic situation of the Ukrainian Catholics in the USSR.[74]

The Vatican is perfectly aware that its policy of détente suffered a complete defeat in the Ukraine, where the Soviet government and the Moscow Patriarchate are not willing to compromise. Negotiations in order to "salvage what is salvageable" of Catholicism, a main aim of Vatican détente, are simply unthinkable in the case of the Ukrainian question, even at such a high price as the removal of Cardinal Slipyj from his position at the head of the Ukrainian Catholic Church in favor of a pro-Moscow Catholic hierarch. This, perhaps, explains why the Pope did not force Cardinal Slipyj to resign. The Ukrainians have to "create their rights"; the recognition of Rome (as Cardinal Slipyj frequently publicly stated) will come later. But now they are left alone. The dissenters have further proof that nobody will help them unless they help themselves.

The Voices of the Dissenters

The fight for human rights is the common bond that unites all the Soviet dissenters. This is what is happening also in the Ukraine, where

Vyacheslav Chornovil did for his fellow Ukrainians the same thing which Ginzburg and Litvinov did for their Russian and Jewish friends. He published in the form of a "petition" to the authorities of the Ukrainian SSR, a White Book on the arrest and trial of some 20 leading Ukrainian intellectuals with letters and essays of the "criminals." The facts refer to 1965-66. The reasons for the indictment and the severity of the sentences prove the fear, almost panic, of the Soviet government regarding the problems of the nationalities. Bourgeois nationalism, separatism, anti-Soviet agitation are the most common accusations supported by "evidence" such as keeping the portraits of national heroes of the past, Khmelnitsky (d. 1657) and Mazepa (d. 1709), the works of national poets, Taras Shevchenko (d. 1861), Lesya Ukrainka (d. 1913), Ivan Franko (d. 1916) or even a speech of Pope Paul VI or President Eisenhower. Skillfully constructing his defense on Marxist-Leninist principles, Chornovil writes:

> For ten years I was educated in a Soviet school. In the last paragraph of every composition I invariably endeavored to mention the Party and Stalin ... For five years I studied Marxism-Leninism at the university. All other subjects were also invariably based on the Marxist foundation. Finally, just recently I passed the master's examination in Marxist-Leninist philosophy. Then all of a sudden, quite by accident, I laid my hands on a book in Ukrainian, published abroad, and I immediately became a "bourgeois nationalist." Some time later I read the leaflet from Peking about the "opportunism of the CPSU"—would that make me a follower of Mao Tse-Tung? Later still I listened on the radio to a speech by the Pope of Rome (by the way, it was brought up in the indictment of the teacher Ozerny)—was I then a Jesuit?
>
> Could it be that Article 62 of the Criminal Code of the Ukr. SSR was devised expressly to protect Soviet citizens against such kaleidoscopic changes in their ideological outlook? Without a doubt, Marxism-Leninism is stronger than the bourgeois ideology. But in our country anyone who reads a book published in the West is subject to prosecution, whereas *our* books and newspapers, containing all kinds of criticism of capitalism, of bourgeois nationalism, and of the current policies of capitalist powers, can be easily obtained (even by mail) in the USA, Canada, and in many other foreign countries. The newspaper *Visti z Ukrainy* [News from Ukraine] is published in Kiev especially for Ukrainian émigrés, but it is impossible to read that paper here in Ukraine, because it contains specialized truths—for export only.
>
> Is it possible that non-Marxists have absorbed better than our leaders the Marxist-Leninist thesis that revolutions and social-economic changes are not exported, that an idea can be implanted on new soil only when all the social, economic, and political prerequisites are completely ripe for it, and that to forbid the spreading of ideas is to increase their strength and attractiveness? This last reason is why those who inspire and execute arrests and trials that roll like an ominous wave across Ukraine may find *themselves* punishable under Article 62 of the Criminal Code of the Ukr. SSR?[75]

The materials collected by Chornovil, especially the writings by Svyatoslav Karavansky, Mykhaylo Horyn, Opanas Zalyvakha, Mykhaylo Osadchy, Valentyn Moroz and Ivan Dzyuba, contributed greatly not only to the knowlege of the Ukrainian question, but also to the understanding of the seriousness and multiformity of dissent. Karavansky's articles on linguistic matters and his letters to the Soviet authorities and to Wladyslaw Gomulka, protesting the Russification of the Ukraine, were answered with a second sentence to a camp to complete his 25-year term. In a petition to the Chief of the camp Korolkov and to Leonid Brezhnev his wife wrote:

> For eighteen years the camp administration has been unable to exert an influence upon prisoner S.I. Karavans'ky, and the Karavans'ky family is deprived of the opportunity to maintain the contact with him permitted by law. Therefore I, the wife of S.I. Karavans'ky, ask you to *execute him by a firing squad* to terminate his long torture and his continuous conflicts with the administration.
>
> I write this petition while sober and being fully aware of its gravity.
>
> (N. Strokataya)
> December 27, 1966[76]

Valentyn Moroz, an historian, born in 1936, wrote, among other things, "A Report from the Beria Game Reserve,"[77] a stark exposé of the physical and moral brutality prevailing in the labor camps and a profound philosophical despotism and individualism in society. Unlike other Ukrainian dissenters, Moroz doesn't build his position on the necessity to return to pure Marxism-Leninism, but rather on more universal principles, closer to a Christian conception of life. *The Chronicle of Current Events* writes that he was again arrested on June 1, 1970 and charged under article 62 of the Ukrainian Criminal Code, equivalent to article 70 of the Russian Code. Investigations were conducted under the direction of KGB Major Baranov, who in 1949 was in charge of the case of students at the Lvov Polytechnic Institute (the creation of a nationalist organization), condemned to 25 years' imprisonment and in 1965 investigated the case of artist Panas Zalyvakha, who was released in 1970 after 5 years in the camps.

> At the beginning of May 1970 V. Moroz was in the village of Kosmach (in the Carpathians, SW Ukraine). There, while he was taperecording a mass in Church, an attempt was made to apprehend him, but the local inhabitants prevented this. In connection with the arrest of Moroz, searches were carried out at the homes of the priest Romanyuk in Kosmach, of V. Chornovil in Lvov, and of five other people.[78]

In his final speech at the trial Moroz reaffirmed his disillusionment with Socialism:

> The spiritual potential of Ukraine has grown enough to fill any vacuum, to replace any activist who leaves the movement on his own or by way of prison. The 1960's gave us the beginning of the great reawakening of Ukrainian life; the 1970's will not bring its demise. That "Golden Age," when every aspect of life was set into a tight official frame, is gone forever. We now have a culture without the Ministry of Culture; a philosophy without *Problems of Philosophy (Voprosy Filosofii)*. These phenomena, born without official sanction, are here to stay, and they will grow.

I am to be tried behind closed doors. But your trial will boomerang even if no one hears me, or if I sit in silent isolation in my cell in Vladimir Prison. *Silence can sometimes be more deafening than shouting*. You could not muffle it even by killing me, which is, of course, the easiest thing to do. But have you considered the fact that the dead are often more important than the living? *They become symbols*—the building blocks of spiritual fortresses in the hearts of men.[79]

Soviet religious dissent finds strong support and expression in Moroz's "Chronicle of Resistance," dedicated to Kosmach, a town in the Carpathian Mountains, "the bastion of Ukrainian resistance," and to its inhabitants, the Hutsuls, famous for their original architecture, wood-carving, brass work, weaving, ceramics and "pysanky," the traditional Ukrainian Easter eggs decorated with multicolored geometric designs, dating back to pagan and early Christian times. In 1740 Oleksa Dovbush, leader of Ukrainian rebel groups called "opryshky" that fought against oppression and exploitation in Hutsul and neighboring regions in a Robin Hood manner, contributed a large sum of money for a new church. From that time on it was called "Dovbush's Church." In 1773, writes Moroz:

the Church was reconsecrated Uniate, but this no longer had its previous meaning. There had been a change of priorities. Halychyna became a province of Austria. Polish rule was ended. The Uniate movement grew into the living body of Ukrainian spirituality and became national in character. Struggling with it ceased to be a national matter. The same happened with the cause of defending Orthodoxy. In fact, the roles were reversed. Before long, Russia made Orthodoxy a tool of Russification of Ukrainian lands taken from Poland. The Uniate reconsecration was a formality now. The church remained Dovbush's. Then came the twentieth century. Dovbush was placed on a pedestal. Kosmach was invaded by artists and art scholars . . . [80]

The troubles started with the Soviet occupation. In 1963 representatives of Kiev's Dovzhenko cinema studio borrowed the iconostasis from Dovbush's church for the filming of *Tini Zabutykh Predkiv* (Shadows of Forgotten Ancestors). The iconostasis was never returned to the town.

The Devil has many faces. Sometimes he even dons the mask of a man of culture . . . The people of Kosmach still do not know what to think. Why, they had dealings with people of culture. They thought that these people of culture would also treasure their holy relics. Of course the people of Kosmach have become used even to those who call the whole town "Banderovshchyna" . . . But these were not the same . . . These had nice, well-trimmed beards and spoke without vulgarities . . .

The Hutsuls were too naive. They sent protests and appeals to all possibly concerned. "Writing letters did not bring results, but it did surface some interesting facts. The iconostasis was given to the museum (of Ukrainian art in Kiev) according to the directives from the regional representative dealing with religious matters for Ivano-Frankivsk, Atamanyuk!"[81] After the death of Atamanyuk, the destruction of Ukrainian treasure was continued by others: V. Lyubchyk, who burned the works of Boychuk, Arkhipenko, Narbut "as well as century-old Ukrainian art." Lituyeva, the former curator of Stanyslaviv regional museum, "destroyed everything with 'crosses'. Generally speaking, the easiest way to destroy the foundation of a nation is to do it under the pretext of fighting the Church." Here Valentyn Moroz describes the intimate connection between the Church and the Ukrainian nation:

> The Church has rooted itself in the cultural life so deeply that it is impossible to touch it without damaging the spiritual structure of a nation. It is impossible to imagine traditional cultural values without the Church. It is ultimately necessary to understand that an attack against the Church is an attack against culture. How many times has the nation been saved by the Church? This was especially important when a change in faith meant a change in nationality. There where a number of villages near Kholm were Ukrainians spoke Polish. But they remained Ukrainians as long as they adhered to the Ukrainian faith and Church. Similarly, a Polish family in a Ukrainian village in Podilya would remain Polish for generations without knowing the Polish language as long as the family remained Catholic.
>
> In Eastern Europe the Church was the only power independent of the authorities. Let us take the Ukrainian revival in Halychyna, how trivial was the role played by the teacher as compared with the priest! The teacher was a state employee afraid of losing his job. The priest did not know this fear. The majority of the people working for the Ukrainian cause came from the clergy. "The Reverend" was often justifiably criticized, but it is also important to remember that it was he who kept the Ukrainian movement alive. Halychyna did not turn Polish because of the Ukrainian Church. In this and similar cases we can equate the Church and the nation—just as we can equate the Church and spirituality, in general.[82]

The movement for the freedom of the peoples of the USSR is growing stronger because the Russians are supporting it and all are uniting their efforts. Karavansky defends the rights of the Crimean Tatars, the Volga Germans, the Jews, the Lithuanians, the Latvians and Estonians.[83] Dzyuba recalls the "shame" of Baby Yar.[84] Sakharov appeals for Moroz and Leonid Plyushch.[85] Solzhenitsyn, for the first time since Hertzen, tells the Russians to support the Ukrainians' aspirations[86] and along with three Russian writers (V. Maximov, V. Nekrasov and A. Sinyavsky) sends to Cardinal Slipyj his congratulations on the occasion of the 35th anniversary of his episcopal ordination.[87]

Probably those Western politicians and Vatican officials who believe the Ukrainian question to be of secondary importance and prefer to give their attention to détente with the Soviet government are going to be, in the future, very disappointed. The absurdity of Soviet internal colonialism is being condemned by more and more people in the West. On June 24, 1974, the vice-president of the American PEN, Henry Carlisle, sent to Podgorny a telegram in defence of Moroz. Three months later the *New York Times*, in an editorial titled "Ukrainian Injustice", wrote:

The current symbols of the Ukrainian campaign against Russian domination are a 38-year-old historian named Valentyn Moroz, reportedly held by the Soviet secret police in Vladimir prison, and 35-year-old Leonid I. Plyushch, a cybernetics specialist associated with the Ukrainian Academy of Sciences until his "psychiatric detention" in 1972. Both men were openly engaged in the civil rights struggle which has tied together many of the Soviet dissidents. Such distinguished leaders of that movement as Andrei Sakharov and Pavel Litvinov have repeatedly protested the inhumane and illegal conditions of their detention.

Moroz and Plyushch are not well known in the West, and their plight has attracted little attention outside the circles of Ukrainians in this country and Canada. Perhaps for this reason, Soviet authorities have so far turned deaf ears to pleas on their behalf from international civil libertarian groups. Moscow's policymakers should not be deluded into waiting until some specific outrage against the two Ukrainians makes the protest genuinely universal.[88]

Meanwhile Anatoly Levitin-Krasnov, just before obtaining permission to emigrate as a citizen of Jewish descent, wrote a strong statement in defense of those religious groups outlawed in the Soviet Union, among them the Uniates or Ukrainian Catholics.

> To the Committee for the Defense of Human Rights from Anatoly
> Emmanuilovich Krasnov (Levitin)
> A Statement

I, Anatoly Levitin, moved by respect for those lofty humane aims, which the Committee has taken as its own, feel it my responsibility to call upon the Committee to raise its voice in defense of those people who are living in the USSR and are suffering systematic and indescribable torture for decades at a time exclusively for their religious convictions.

We are speaking about Uniates, members of the so-called "Truly Orthodox Church," and also members of the outlawed sects: the Initsiativniki-Baptists, the Reformist Seventh-Day Adventists, the Pentecostalists, in part, the Jehovah's Witnesses, and also other small sects.

The most awful thing is that the persecution of the sectarians, Uniates, and members of the "Truly Orthodox Church," which has become the norm of our life does not evoke the slightest indignation. This unheard of savagery is blatantly committed, yet calls forth no protest.

The liberal intelligentsia, which is uninformed about religious questions, not only does not protest, but even supports these persecutions indirectly, since they believe the vile slander which is spread about the sectarians, not eschewing the insinuations spread by the Black Hundreds press about the Jews during the Beilis trial.

We will permit ourselves to provide brief information about the persecution for religious convictions, emphasizing ahead of time that this statement does not exhaust the injustices to which believers have been subjected for a thousand years.

> Persecution of the Uniate, Greek Catholic Church in Western
> Ukraine and Western Byelorussia

Let us recall briefly the history of the Uniate Church.

As is generally known, the *unia* in Ukraine began in 1596 when the Council of Brest accepted the act of unification of the Ukrainian dioceses with the Pope of Rome. According to this act, Ukrainian believers remained faithful to all the rites and regulations of the Orthodox Church (in liturgics, canon law, etc.) at the same time recognizing the primacy of the Pope over the church. At first the *unia* was implanted by force and served purely political goals.

However, in time the *unia* became an organic facet of life in the West Ukrainian territories and the majority of the population came to accept it as their own, traditional, religion and that of their forefathers.

After the first and second partitions of Poland, the Russian troops, having occupied Volynia, found there to their displeasure an almost totally Uniate population.

Under Catherine II and Alexander I certain restrictions on the Uniates existed, whereas Orthodoxy was supported by the government. However, all these measures did not change substantially relations between the Uniates and the Orthodox.

With an energy and cruelty typical of him, Nicholas I set about a total uprooting of the *unia*. After 1839 when the Uniate bishops signed an act of reunion with Orthodoxy, a wave of repressions erupted in Volynia: massive whippings, running the gauntlet, lifelong exile to Siberia—these became the norm during the reign of Nicholas I in his religious policy in Volynia.

Despite all of this, the population firmly resisted. The struggle with Uniates continued for half a century right down to the reign of Alexander III.

It is characteristic that A.I. Herzen in his *Kolokol* [The Bell] spoke out in defense of the persecuted Uniates. V.G. Korolenko in his *Vospominaniya sovremennika* [Memoirs of a Contemporary] tells with indignation about the tragic situation of the Uniates who were exiled to Siberia and whom he met there in the seventies of the 19th century.

In 1946 upon the reunification of Western Ukraine and Western Byelorus' with the USSR, the Stalin regime undertook the persecution of the *unia*, employing precisely the same methods as Nicholas I.

After the arrest in March 1946 of the head of the Uniate Church in Ukraine, Metropolitan Josyf Slipyj of Lviv together with the other six Uniate bishops, a deluge of repressions was released against the Uniates. The rector of the Church of the Transfiguration in Lviv, Archpriest Gabriel Kostelnyk, became the instrument of this repressive policy. Under his leadership a "council" was convened which lasted two days and adopted a resolution of unification of the Uniates with Orthodoxy. After this Kostelnyk formed a Committee which began to implement the resolutions of the "council." An emissary of Kostelnyk's was sent to every Uniate parish. He proposed to the local priest reunification with Orthodoxy. In the event of a priest's refusal, he was immediately arrested and according to Article 58-10 was sentenced to 10 years of imprisonment in the camps. And that, incidentally, was the easiest solution. In the event of "active opposition" a Uniate priest was sentenced to 25 years in the camps on charges of "treason to the Fatherland." No judicial inquiry was conducted: all repressions were carried out through a special committee of the KGB.

If we take into account that together with the clergy, students in the Uniate seminaries, parishioners, and the most active laypeople were also punished, then it is not surprising that the number of victims soon reached the impressive figure of 300 thousand people.

All Uniate churches were turned over to the Orthodox. Uniate Divine Services were forbidden. The most savage measures were applied to the Uniates, even including separation of children from their families on a mass scale. Such an irrational and cruel policy led to a segment of the Uniates establishing contact with the Bandera movement and embarking on a path of individual terrorism. Gabriel Kostelnyk became a victim of this terror; he was slain on a Sunday in September 1968 as he came out of church. It is said that Kostelnyk's funeral turned into a mass demonstration against religious persecution.

This persecution abated somewhat after 1956 when the majority of Uniates were released. All Uniate bishops remained imprisoned, however and died without regaining their freedom. The head of the Uniate Church, Metropolitan Josyf Slipyj remained in internment right up until 1963 when he was sent out of the USSR to Rome.

Thus the Uniate Church remained interdict. In 1966 there began a "worsening" of anti-Uniate policy. Once again the arrests of Uniate priests were undertaken and a "drive to find" underground houses of worship.

Nonetheless, the campaign to destroy the *unia* failed. In Lviv alone 80 Uniate priests function almost openly. They perform in their homes the Divine Service and, upon request, religious rites. Three Uniate bishops function in the underground. As soon as one dies or is arrested, another is immediately consecrated. The authorities are obliged to tolerate this situation since they seem to feel that they cannot risk again a policy of mass repressions and the arrest of individuals, fines, and short-term imprisonment (15 days of arrest for participation in a Uniate Divine Service) do not bring any results. All this indicates that the *unia* in Western Ukraine and Western Byelorus' is a broad national movement. Its persecution constitutes not only religious repression, but also an infringement on the national rights of Western Ukrainians. If one takes into account the juridical aspect of the question, then the persecution of Uniates is nonsense. If commemorating the Pope during the Divine Liturgy and the recognition of him as head of the Church is a crime, then it is incomprehensible why Latin Rite Catholics are not persecuted. An equally ridiculous situation, however, has its tragic impact on thousands of human souls, beaten and broken by the violation of their consciences, and by the aggravation of antagonisms between the Ukrainian and the Russian peoples.

It behooves the Committee to come to the defense of the persecuted Uniates. This is only a matter of elementary humanity.

September 9, 1974
Levitin (Krasnov)[89]

While the suppression of the Ukrainian Catholics "does not evoke the slightest indignation" even from high Vatican officials such as Cardinal Willebrands, Soviet dissenters continue to help each other. From the *Chronicle LCC* we know that Fr. Vladimir Prokopiv, a Ukrainian Catholic priest living in Vilnius, toward the end of 1973, brought to Moscow a petition signed by 2,000 Catholics of the Lviv region, asking permission to open a church in Vilnius.[90] Similar petitions in favor of the outlawed Ukrainian Catholic clergy were signed also by courageous Lithuanian Catholic clergymen.[91]

The speech of Cardinal Joseph Slipyj at the World Synod of Catholic Bishops in Rome, in October 1974, is the most qualified appeal to the Pope and the Vatican on behalf not only of Ukrainian Catholics, but of the entire Ukrainian Nation. *Kontinent,* the journal edited by V. Maximov, reprinted it with an introduction by Dominic Moravsky. This is not any longer an internal affair of Catholic Ukrainians, but, as Anatoly Levitin said, "is only a matter of elementary humanity." Following is the text of the Cardinal's speech.

Holy Father, Very Reverend Presidium and Fathers,

I speak in the name of the Ukrainian Catholic Church, as a participant and a senior member of the Şynod. From the information that we have heard about missionary work in Africa, Asia, America and Europe we see that it has not been fully successful. All those speeches that we heard do not refer to the entire Church, but only to the Latin rite. For you all must know that *there are in the world millions of Catholics of the Eastern rite,* and also millions of Orthodox. When speaking of the Church, we must not limit ourselves only to the Latin rite. We also heard in the speeches references only to those countries where there is freedom of religion and one is allowed to preach the Gospel. Nothing was mentioned of those countries where there is no freedom of religion and the Church is persecuted. *I have in mind Ukraine and Ukrainians, who are persecuted by the Bolsheviks, while the Catholic states of the world seek ties and contacts with the godless Soviet and Chinese Communists and support them.*

It is very surprising that nobody speaks up for that nation which has preserved the great ancient traditions of its religion and for which it undergoes severe persecutions. For example, a priest is sentenced to three or more years of slave labor in the camps of the Siberian taiga for saying Mass; those faithful who send written petitions to the Soviet government that priests be permitted to say the Holy Liturgy are locked up in psychiatric prisons. There the faithful, the priests, the nuns and the monks perpetually suffer persecutions. They are searched, tortured, physically abused, locked into prisons, where, after several weeks, without medical attention, they die. Faith lives on in spite of those circumstances. And no one mentions the need to freely preach the word of God! Do you not think, reverend Fathers, that you, members of this Synod, must protest against this inhuman persecution? Will you not, even by words, spiritually console those suffering and persecuted, among whom faith does not die, but grows stronger? There, many highly educated people, doctors, artists and scholars are profound believers, who heroically defend their faith with all their strength and all their means.

In Ukraine parents may not teach their children to pray and believe in God; they do this in secret. I myself, being in exile in the Siberian labor camps met three students of medicine, who were sentenced to ten years and sent to Siberia only because they believed in God. What I refer to here is not politics, but atheism and the systematic persecution of religion.

Under those difficult circumstances of religious persecutions, the faithful in Ukraine do not lose faith, although they know that the world watches and keeps silent. Their spirit is kept up by Mass and sermons that they hear over the radio. One cannot even think of establishing a hierarchy where the dispensing of the sacraments is forbidden. The religious situation is much better in Communist Poland than in Soviet Ukraine.

In this Holy Year, that was proclaimed the "year of justice" throughout the world, we must be sure that this justice, based on the teachings of the Bible, is brought to all nations of the world, and not only to a few. The speeches of the Holy Father and members of the Church hierarchy have illustrated very well the persecutions in Biafra, Bengal, Chile and Palestine.

The Ukrainian nation today is being harshly persecuted for its religion and *nationality*. This persecution not only applies to the priests, but to all the faithful. The most outstanding intellectuals who acknowledge the Christian faith in Ukraine are being persecuted the most. Among those are the noted historian Valentyn Moroz, Evhen Sverstyuk, Leonid Plyushch, Vyacheslav Chornovil, Ivan and Nadia Svitlychny, Yury Shukhevych, Svyatoslav and Nina Karavansky, Ihor and Iryna Kalynets, Vasyl Stus and many, many others.

One of them, Valentyn Moroz, was sentenced to fourteen years of imprisonment and concentration camps. At the present time he is on a hunger strike since July 1st, having stated that he will continue his strike until he dies, since he is unable to suffer the persecution in the Vladimir Prison. *This outstanding historian is being persecuted because he defended Ukrainian Christian culture and was not afraid to submit to tortures in defense of his Church. He proved in his historical research that ancient Ukrainian spiritual culture is different from the Russian one; for this he has been sentenced to a long term of imprisonment.*

But he is not the only one. There are other, numerous intellecutals who defend the religious and *national rights of the Ukrainian people;* for that they are sentenced and exiled to slave labor camps. It is in this light that we must defend the rights of the entire Church and not only of some part of it. We must condemn all injustice which threatens the freedom of religion, conscience and thought. We must demand the release from prison for all those suffering cruel treatment and outrage, for all those locked up for no reason in psychiatric wards. It is about those that we must debate and defend their freedom, *for they defend the rights and the freedom of their Church and nation.* Who should defend more vehemently the rights of the teachings of our Church, if we neglect to do it?

Let this year that is called the Year of Justice through the Appeal of the entire Church of Christ be practiced by all who carry historical responsibilities before the history of the world, bring immediate freedom to all persecuted, tortured, exiled, and locked up in psychiatric prisons.[92]

Cardinal Slipyj's speech as well as the voices of Soviet dissenters are annoying the supporters of détente, including the Vatican and the World Council of Churches, who believe that peace and rapprochement with the Soviet Union and the Communist countries should have top priority in a realistic solution of world problems. As Dr. Kissinger said, in the light of the long-range problems of the US rather than the immediate ones, there is a desire "not to overload" détente with humanitarian problems. Analyzing this policy of the US Secretary of State, Andrei Amalrik, released on May 1975 after five years' imprisonment and internal exile, but still barred from residence in Moscow, wrote:

Assessing the advantages of détente over the cold war, we don't have the right, it seems, to say that détente is the alternative to war. The cold war, being a form of sublimation of hot war, was not less effective than "détente" in averting a real war, because peace depended, and still depends, on the balance of nuclear power. Therefore, even a mutual reduction of weapons, should it ever be achieved, would not reduce and would not increase the risk of war ... The other strange feature of American policy, as with the policy of the West in general, is the treatment of the USSR like a small child who must be allowed everything and not be irritated because he might start screaming—all because, they say, when it grows up it will understand everything. This prolonged "upbringing" of the USSR by the methods of Dr. Spock is reflected not only in an endless number of minor concessions by the US but also in actions that are simply humiliating for its prestige as a big power. This was most clearly illustrated by the reluctance of President Ford to invite Alexander I. Solzhenitsyn to the White House because Mr. Kissinger feared this would infuriate Leonid I. Brezhnev. Such behavior in general is very typical for representatives of the American Government. Thus, an American diplomat with whom I have been acquainted for more than 10 years and who recently returned to Moscow declined for the same reasons to meet with me, although he did send expressions of his sympathy via an intermediary. Knowing the character of those whom the Americans are trying to play up by such behavior, I believe that even though it wins approval from their side it also arouses a degree of contempt ... The fact that two persons who were able to meet more than 10 years ago without any interference and now, in the period of "détente," are unable to meet does not speak in favor of détente's humanitarian aspects.[93]

What Amalrik is saying applies also to the Vatican. When Bishop Vasyl Velychkovsky, secretly consecrated in the Ukraine, was released from the prison and arrived in Rome, the director of the Vatican press-bureau, Prof. Alessandrini, questioned by the journalists, confirmed that indeed a "Father" Velychkovsky from the Ukraine was present in Rome. A few days later, the heroic Bishop was received by the Pope, but he was not permitted to wear his episcopal insignia and his audience was not listed, as it is usually done, in the *Osservatore Romano*.[94] For the same reason his name never appeared in the official *Annuario Pontifico*. It is true that the Pope told him to "transmit there to your people that they have in Rome not enemies, but friends!" But this behavior can hardly prevent the insurgence of a feeling of abandonment in the hearts of those who are fighting for their faith. "As I get older," sadly concludes Amalrik, "it becomes ever clearer to me that the best in the world finds expression in simple human relationships: the love of a husband for his wife and parents for their children, the comradeship of men, compassion, patience and simple decency; while any ideology and doctrine, if not used with care as a working hypothesis, may lead to the chopping off of heads or, in the best of cases, to the stuffing of money bags."

If for the sake of détente, the best of humanity has to be ignored and considered as nonexistent, there is no hope to reach peace through détente. For Vatican officialdom Bishop Velychkovsky, as "Bishop," never existed. He was "illegally" consecrated. His priests and faithful, belonging to an "illegal" Church, cannot be considered in the frame of the dialogue with Moscow because from the legal point of view, they do not exist. In July of 1971, the Sisters of St. Basil the Great gathered in Rome for a general chapter meeting. Mother Marie Dolzycka, Ph.D., of Astoria, New York, was to represent the Sisters of this Order living in the Ukraine and neighboring communist countries. She had credentials from the Sisters themselves and the approval of Cardinal Slipyj and the Mother General Claudia Feddish. But the Sacred Congregation for Eastern Churches formally questioned the validity of Mother Marie's credentials. She was barred from the conclave because in the Ukraine there are not Catholic convents "legally existing" and therefore there is no "legal basis" for their representation in a general chapter.

The stifling of the voices of the dissenters as well as the humiliation of men of integrity such as Cardinals Mindszenty and Slipyj and the election of bishops "loyal" to the regime are reaching such a level of absurdity that the Vatican may be forced to review its policy of détente with the Soviet Union. During a reception for members of the diplomatic corps who, at the beginning of 1976, came to offer New Year's greetings to the pontiff, Pope Paul reaffirmed that diplomatic relations between the Vatican and various nations are important primarily because of what the Holy See can contribute to the "solution of problems of life and international order, peaceful co-existence and cooperation among peoples." The "usefulness" of diplomatic relations, he said, did not spring basically from the need to resolve problems of Church life and activities in the respective countries but rather from the contribution that the Holy See can make to help these nations. Nevertheless the Pope seemed to be not so sure of his "doctrine" of peace because he told the diplomats that international concern over the rights of oppressed peoples does not constitute meddling in a nation's internal affairs. Referring himself to the aftermath of the Helsinki conference, Pope Paul said: "The question remains whether states will effectively observe the commitments they have undertaken ... The conference established excellent principles and norms of conduct, the effectiveness of which must, however, be verified by deeds"; and he admitted the possibility for countries, "acting in bad conscience and with the disapproval of the good conscience of all mankind," to "exploit the agreement for ends contrary to those intended."[95]

These remarks, although encouraging, are still far from meeting the "glasnost" asked by the dissenters. Only a month before the press published an appeal addressed by a Ukrainian Orthodox priest to Pope Paul. Father Vasyl Romanyuk, sentenced to ten years in Mordovia's camp no. 1, pleaded especially for the imprisoned women and expressed the hope that "the Holy See will help to establish an international commission to inquire into the facts of trampling of the human rights in the USSR."[96]

What the dissenters are asking for is not another excommunication of the communists, but to establish the facts denounced by them with the names of the victims and those of the oppressors. The Vatican has a unique possibility to meet the requests of the dissenters. Without even forming a new commission, it would be enough to convey the appeals of the dissenters to the organs already established. There already exists in Rome a Commission Pro-Russia, there is a Secretariat for Christian Unity and another Papal Commission for Justice and Peace. The pontifical bodies have at their disposal an enormous number of documents to be examined that prove the violation of human and religious rights by the Soviet regime, and a large number of qualified dissenters who were released from the Gulag Archipelago remains to be heard. The Synod of the Catholic Bishops, which in 1974 heard Dr. Phillip A. Potter, general secretary of the World Council of Churches, could now invite Alexander Solzhenitsyn. It is up to the Pope to decide.

Part III

From Paul VI to John Paul II

7

Normalization or Evangelization?

The Soviet Union hoped that for the sake of détente, world public opinion would forget the dissidents, this small group of unbalanced traitors, whose support no one would have undertaken at the risk of returning to a cold war, or worse, a hot war. But the Soviet leaders were counting above all on the "wisdom" of heads of state and men of politics, including Church leaders, and on their sensitivity to what had been obtained through summit meetings and quiet diplomacy: the doors of the frontiers were at least ajar if not open; cultural and economic exchange was increasing. Détente had allowed for the emigration of groups of Jews and of Germans of the Volga region, and had even brought about the occasional release of a particularly troublesome dissident. But all this merely allowed things to proceed at their own pace, and this is precisely what the dissidents could not accept.

The dissidents did not share the Western political and ecclesiastical opinion that the situation in the USSR was no longer what it had been under Stalin and that a process of democratization was in the works. According to them, no change could be brought about by summit talks or obtained by treaties or international agreements. Changes would require a grass roots movement. Two elements must be remembered: First, as the dissident Yuri Blinov had foreseen, Brezhnev's new constitution, approved by the Supreme Soviet on Oct. 7, 1977 and put into effect the same day, not only maintained the *status quo* but reinforced the function of "supreme guidance" of the Party and its head. Second, in five months (June-July, 1977, and January-March, 1978) the Belgrade Conference had not succeeded in overruling Soviet opposition to any reference in the final draft to civil rights. This put everything off until the conference to be held in November 1980, in Madrid. The work of the Belgrade Conference was blocked by Brezhnev's negative response to an appeal by President Tito and by French president Giscard d'Estaing for some softening of the Soviet position.

In preparation for the Belgrade Conference on the application of the Helsinki accords, the Soviet dissidents had organized, proliferated their accusation, and aroused the reactions of their Eastern European comrades. In Moscow, Kiev, Vilnius, Yerevan and Tbilisi, groups formed to support compliance with the Helsinki accords. The dissidents in satellite countries took similar steps.

While dissidence spread, repression grew, and with it a general campaign of denigration which was aimed at justifying repression and in which ex-dissidents and representatives of the Church were invited to collaborate. In general, the press did not take the bait, and for this reason several correspondents were expelled from the Soviet Union. But what should be said about certain heads of state, diplomats and prelates? They didn't seem to recognize the need for public support of these dissidents, who, by freeing the people from the fear and inertia of decades, really changed the world. Valentin Turchin's *Inertsiia strakha* (The Inertia of Fear), published in New York in 1977, treats this subject.

Dissidence Spreads

Soviet dissenters have always been against resorting to violence and terrorism, preferring rather to appeal to the law and to the constitution. But the Moscow government, in the best Stalinist fashion, began to gather "evidence" of their crimes. On January 8, 1977, a bomb exploded in a Moscow subway car. There were several dead and wounded. The Soviet journalist, Viktor Louis, who was intimate with the K.G.B., wrote for the English daily, *Evening News,* that "certain Soviet dissidents might be behind the bombing." He said he had this information from official sources. Andrei Sakharov responded immediately, stating that news presented in that way constituted "the most recent and dangerous provocation of organized Soviet repression in the last few years." During an interview with Soviet journalists, the winner of the Nobel Peace prize more explicitly accused the K. G. B. of assassinating between five and seven people in 1976, including the translator Konstantine Bogatyryov, the Baptist minister Fiblienko, magistrate Evgeny Brunev, the Lithuanian engineer Tamonetz, and also in Lithuania, Lukshaeta, a devoutly Catholic kindergarten teacher who often spoke of God to her young students.[1] On January 25th, at three in the morning, Sakharov was summoned by the assistant prosecutor, General Sergei Gusev, taken into custody and threatened. In an article, Gusev summarized his exchange with the academician, who responded in another article.[2]

At this point, an unexpected event occurred: On January 27th, the U.S. Department of State took up the defense of Sakharov and declared that "any attempt by Soviet authorities to intimidate Sakharov... was in conflict with the international norms concerning human rights." The next day the American press published a letter from Sakharov to President Carter, dated January 21st. First of all, the learned scholar deplored the impossible situation of dissent not only in the U.S.S.R., but in all East European countries; second, he drew parallels between the Moscow subway explosion, and the Reichstag fire, and the assassination of Kirov; third, he listed fifteen political prisoners whose situations needed attention: Kovalyov, Svitlychny, Romanyuk, Dzhemilev, Gluzman, Rubin, Federov, Vins, Shtern, Moroz, Sergiyenko, Makarenko, Pronyuk, Semenova, Fedorenko; fourth, he asked the president to raise his voice in defense of the Yugoslav author, Mihailo Mihailov, the Czech authors of Charter 77, and the Polish Workers' defense committee; fifth, he drew attention to the wretched condition of religion and to the persecution of believers, especially those belonging to the banned religious groups: Baptists, Uniate Catholics, Pentecostals, the True Orthodox Church; sixthly, he denounced terrorism and assassinations, for example, that of poet and translator K. Bogatyryov.

A month earlier, with Kissinger still in office as Secretary of State, this letter would probably have remained secret and not received a response. But Jimmy Carter had already—since the campaign, in fact—defined certain kinds of silence as immoral. A week before his inaugural address he stated that "As free men, we can never be indifferent to the needs of freedom anywhere in the world." Some of this advisors, for example, Professor Marshall Shulman, insisted that since détente had absolute priority, governments ought to remain *pragmatically silent* [3] even if private citizens had the right to speak out. But Carter, faithful to his conscience and to the ideals validated by his electorate, answered Sakharov on February 5th. His response was delivered to the American Embassy in Moscow and was published the following day in the world press. President Carter wrote: "Human rights are a central concern of my administration... You may rest assured that the American people and our government will continue our firm committment to promote respect for human rights not only in our own country but also abroad. We shall use our good offices to seek the release of prisoners of conscience... " Sakharov, deeply moved, dictated an immediate response in which he asked Carter to get the critically ill Kovalyov transferred to a hospital, and he asked him to come to the aid of four members of the Helsinki Watch Group, A. Ginzburg, Yu. Orlov, M. Rudenko and O. Tykhy, who had all recently been arrested.

In his letter to Carter, Sakharov deplored the fact that telephone contact with the outside world was becoming more and more difficult for him. He begged the U.S. president to take steps on his behalf at the international level. But right at this time Soviet authorities were striking against both dissidents and journalists in order to discourage and prevent any contact between them. At the instigation of the K.G.B. Alexander Petrov-Agapov, a former member of groups of dissidents, accused A. Ginzburg in *Literaturnaia Gazeta* of February 2nd, of dealing in currency and of contacting American journalist George Krimsky who, along with two of his colleagues, was said to be a C.I.A. agent. The next day Ginzburg was arrested and Krimsky was ordered to leave Russia. The same tactic was used against Soviet Jews: Anatoly Shcharansky, Vladimir Slepak, Vitaly Rubin and Alexander Lerner were accused by the Jewish dissident Sanya Lipavsky in *Izvestiia* of March 4th of being C. I. A. agents. Shcharansky was arrested on March 15th, obviously to teach the dissidents a lesson by staging a spectacular trial. On May 6th, during an interview organized by *Izvestiia* for foreign correspondents, Lipavsky reiterated his serious charges. On the 12th of June, *Los Angeles Times* correspondent Robert Toth, who had already been arrested for having received a manuscript on parapsychology from Valeri Patukhov, was interrogated about his relationship with Shcharansky and then expelled from the USSR. The Soviet Jew, Veniamin Levich, who had not been allowed to attend a symposium given at Oxford in honor of his seventieth birthday, was interrogated for eight hours by the K.G.B. about his connections with Shcharansky.

The Soviet dissidents, particularly those belonging to national minorities, fought as much for the people's self-determination as for their own personal freedom. The group of democrats from Russia, the Ukraine, and the Baltic countries wrote in their statement, "The largest colonialist empire is the Soviet Union. It supports the greatest number of people around its kernal—Russia. The USSR ought to follow the example of other colonial powers and grant political independence and cultural autonomy to all people who desire it." This explains the particular severity with which the Ukrainian, Lithuanian, Armenian and Georgian dissidents were treated. Sakharov had already referred to the assassinations perpetrated by the K.G.B. in Lithuania. Tomas Venclova of the Lithuanian group monitoring the application of the Helsinki agreement and Kestutis Jokubinas of the Democratic Movement were exiled. The Georgian group also suffered the arrest, on April 7th, of Zviad Gamsakhurdia, Merab Kostava, and Victor Rtskheladze. Gamsakhurdia, the son of a well-known writer, had been attacked several days earlier in the Tbilisi newspaper, *Zarya Vostoka,* March 23. Rtskheladze, a minor official in the Georgian Ministry of Culture, an expert in historical religious monuments, and a practicing Christian, was released but lost his job.[4] Deacon Robert Nazaryan, a member of the Armenian group, stated on October 26, 1977, that he had been attacked in the May 5th edition of *Sovetakan Ajastan* and that he, as well as Edward Arutyunyan, president of the group, had been threatened with psychiatric detention or with loss of employment.[5]

The Ukrainian dissidents formed the group most feared by the Soviet government. Legal action was quickly brought to bear against the leaders of the Ukrainian branch of the Helsinki Watch Group, Mykola Rudenko and Oleksi Tykhy. They were arrested at the beginning of the year and sentenced to seven and ten years of hard labor respectively, and each was sentenced to five years of exile. In April, two other members of the Ukrainian group, Miroslav Marynovitch and Mykola Matusevych, were also arrested. Petro Ruban, a Ukrainian craftsman who made souvenirs in the town of Priluki was sentenced to eight years in a labor camp and five years in exile for having sculpted a replica of the Statue of Liberty in honor of the American Bicentennial. This information was included in a protest letter sent on June 16th by A. Solzhenitsyn to the representatives of the state of Vermont where he lives.

For the first time the new Soviet Constitution referred to the "Soviet people" instead of the "peoples of the Soviet Union," thus establishing a Soviet citizenry, affirming equality of rights, the development "and reconciliation" of the diverse nationalities. In a letter to President Carter, the Ukrainian writer Heli Snegirev, defined all of these terms of the communist vocabulary and at the same time gave the reasons for his decision to reject his Soviet citizenship. Nevertheless, repression continued with a series of condemnations and expulsions. On January 28th, the poetess Yu. Voznesenskaya was sentenced to two years in a labor camp. On August 24th Felix Serebrov was arrested in Moscow, and Viktoras Pyatkus and Antonas Terleckas, in Vilnius. With these three, the number of activists and defenders of human rights arrested in the USSR since 1977 increased to twelve.

With the Appeal of the Christian Churches of the USSR on June 20, 1976, we see an unprecedented and spontaneous ecumenical movement emerging in a country dominated by the atheism of a police state. Addressed to the Supreme Soviet of the USSR, this document refuted the government's and patriarchy's claim that religious freedom existed in the Soviet Union.

An even more comprehensive study on the same subject written by Father Yakunin and L. Regelson was sent as an open letter to Phillip Potter, the Secretary General of the World Council of Churches. This document, entitled, "The Discriminatory Nature of Soviet Legislature in Religious Matters," undertakes a detailed analysis of Soviet laws on religions and of the politics of oppression brought to bear against the believers and the Church.

Recalling that only a small fraction of the delegates, mainly the metropolitan bishops, Yuvenaly and Nikodim, had opposed their appeal to the Nairobi Assembly, Father Yakunin and L. Regelson wrote: "The participants of the Nairobi Assembly could see and hear those who were trying to convince them that one ought not to fight evil, that one should not fight the beast with all one's strength, lest one increase the misfortunes of defenseless victims. Without a doubt we Christians must show wisdom, prudence, and lucidity in the spiritual struggle in which we are engaged. But whoever preaches cowardice and pretends that the forces of evil are harmless is advising the malice and trickery that lead to the defeat of Christ's cause on earth. These advisors do not come to help victims of violence. On the contrary, keeping abuses hidden, they encourage the perpetrators of violence to further atrocities, they condemn the innocent victims to deep moral solitude, they stifle the spiritual meaning of the glorious deeds of the martyrs and confessors ... Those who misplace their zeal seeking alliances with the Church's enemies, those who put their hopes more in the powerful of this world than in Christ, those who find support in anti-Christian movements, let those people remember the terrible words of the prophet: "Woe to the rebellious children ... that take counsel ... but not of my spirit ...' " (Isaiah, 30: 1-3, 5, 15).

Then the authors of the study unmasked the "work of discrimination" that Yuvenaly and Nikodim had presented at Nairobi in the guise of "reassuring" declarations: "No one in the Soviet Union suffers because of religion ... Moreover, criminals against common law have been condemned for having violated laws regarding the separation of Church and State." Father Yakunin and L. Regelson, in response to Yuvenaly's reference to the "supposed anti-ecumenical activity of one of them," asserted that they had never attacked either the ecumenical movement nor the World Council of Churches, but that in a 1971 appeal they had expressed "a fear that the modernist theology of the metropolitan bishop Nikodim presented by him as orthodox and faithful to tradition represented a threat to ecumenism. The activity of the World Council of Churches had not been mentioned in this appeal. In fact, only certain aspects of the activities of the Conference of Christians for Peace had come under criticism. It is surprising that Nikodim who knows this document well, did not consider it necessary to amend Yuvenaly's statement."

Toward the end of their exposé, Father Yakunin and Regelson warned Dr. Potter against another maneuver by Soviet authorities to "neutralize" the effects of their revelation to the World Council of Churches: "In anticipation of the World Council of Churches subcommittee's examination of all evidence gathered concerning violations of believers' rights in the countries subscribing to the Helsinki accord—and in accordance with the Nairobi Assembly's decisions—the Religious Affairs Council of the U.S.S.R. Council of Ministers sent its delegates out to different places with the following directive: To organize among the clergy and the faithful of diverse parishes a campaign of protest destined to neutralize our direct appeal to Nairobi and to break the World Council of Churches' attempt to promote a resolution protesting the attacks against believers' rights in the U.S.S.R. Whatever the extent of this false accusation, we are certain that its perpetrators will only achieve a result contrary to their expectations. Extorted signatures, no matter how many there are, will never be able to demonstrate the absence of religious discrimination in the U.S.S.R. The vehement insistence of state activists and ecclesiastical authorities will not be able to prove it either."[6]

The failure of the petition and the brave and generous intervention of Father Zeludkov on behalf of Yakunin and Regelson has been mentioned earlier. It is significant that in spite of his tendency to "understand" the patriarchate of Moscow, Father Zeludkov has condemned the excesses and immorality of its representatives. Regelson, inspired by the purest Christian ideals, devoted many years to the study of the Russian Church. In his book, *The Tragedy of the Russian Church, 1917-1945*, published in Russian in Paris,[7] he examines the real conflict between the exhortation to follow Christ and the ecclesiastical discipline which imposes obedience to the Patriarch. His "Meditation on the First Commandment" examines the question in the framework of its Hebraic origins. The primacy of God and Christ is indisputable. "I am the Lord thy God. Thou shalt have no other God but Me . . . It is only after having accepted Calvary in his heart . . . that man is ready for the fulfillment of the promises long awaited by the Jews."

With two articles by Boris Roschin published in April 1977, in *Literaturnaia Gazeta,* the Soviet press launched a slanderous campaign against these men of high religious ideals.[8] The first attacked Father Yakunin and Alexander Ogorodnikov, a young man of twenty-six accused of organizing a clandestine religious seminary. In a letter addressed to Dr. Potter on July 27, 1976, Ogorodnikov had exposed the unbelievable persecution to which he and his friends had been submitted. Raised in atheist families, they had come to God by way of "complex and often painful spiritual discoveries." In October of 1974, they had begun to hold philosophical religious seminars where they discussed such issues as "the Church and the contemporary industrial cosmos." They studied and discussed Bergson's, "The Two Sources of Morality and Religion," Vladimir Solovyov's, "The Idea of Divino-Humanity," Billy Graham's sermons, and other writings. Because of their religious beliefs, Ogorodnikov, his brother Boris, now a monk in the grotto of Pskov, and their friends, Sergei Chuvalov, Alexander Belyakov, Valentin Serov, and others (including a twenty-one-year-old woman) whose names cannot be revealed for fear of reprisals, were all thrown out of the university, clubbed, deprived of work, and threatened with death. On the 13th of June, Serov, a movie operator, had just returned from Leningrad where he had been photographing the funeral of Rukhin, an artist who had died in a strange fire in his studio. As Serov came out of his friend's house, he was attacked by three people, beaten to the ground, and left with a broken arm and numerous contusions. "But," wrote Ogorodnikov, "the saddest fate befell my friend Alexander Argentov, one of the members of the seminary. On July 14, he was summoned by the military command . . . and sent to a clinic for psychiatric examination. That same day he was committed to an asylum. His appeal to Patriarch Pimen, and other appeals addressed on his behalf to various important figures did no good."[9]

The second attack in *Literaturnaia Gazeta,* on April 20, 1977, was directed against Father Dmitry Dudko. He responded the following day in a *samizdat* piece which was published on May 5 by the Russian newspaper in Paris, *Russkaia Mysl.* Accused of "rabid antisovietism" and "Nazi collaboration," denounced as "being of kulak descent," this courageous priest refuted the slander and asked, "Who are they who want to judge me?" In a crescendo of emotion and disgust, Father Dudko listed the crimes of the godless against the starving people, the little children, his own father savagely trampled and left half-dead for a fistful of wheat. After recalling that a poem he had dedicated to his father had been confiscated by the KGB, he exclaimed: "What was my father . . . a kulak! And what am I . . . the son of a kulak!" He continued to list the murders committed by those who wanted to judge him: the tsar, the nobility, the peasants, the priests . . . But to those who want to deprive Russia of the last treasure that remains to her—Faith—he says with all strength: Nyet! He stays close to God's altar. "Until now they haven't deprived me; but they are threatening to do so!" He prays that the miracle of liberation will take place and that he will still have the strength to forgive God's enemies and his. But he calls all mankind to the rescue. Several weeks earlier he had asked the help of all who could help, admonishing them not to remain indifferent. "Indifference in our day means ruin, and not only for us . . . For the salvation of everyone, the ultimate and decisive war of liberation from this captivity must begin—a worldwide holy war." And he signed his appeal: "Soldier of the Russian Army, priest Dmitry Dudko."[10]

Fr. Dudko saw the storm approaching that would envelop him and the entire dissident movement. His cry for help remained unheard. Arrested and tortured, he recanted. Lev Regelson did the same. Fr. Sergei Zeludkov died peacefully on January 29, 1984. . . . But dissidence is not dead. Rather, it is spreading to Eastern Europe.

* * *

At the end of June 1976, Polish dissidence, which had remained submerged, strengthened when workers were condemned for taking part in a demonstration against rising prices. A committee for the workers' defense was formed at that time. Then in March 1977, a much wider movement was founded for the defense of human rights.[11]

Cardinal Wyszynski intervened several times on behalf of the workers and the unions. Groups of priests wrote letters of protest and some participated in hunger strikes.[12] On March 7, when Stanislas Pyjasm, a twenty-three-year-old student at the University of Krakow and a sympathizer with the K.O.R. (Workers' Defense Committee), was murdered, the protests intensified and the number of arrests increased. On May 16, the consecration by Krakow's Cardinal Karol Wojtyla of the Church of Mary Queen of Poland at Nowa Huta—where, according to the communists, a city without God and without churches was to be founded—turned into a protest demonstration. Several days later, Cardinal Wyszynski, preaching at Saint Anne's Church, lamented that humankind should be so deprived of social values and "seem to be so troubled whenever it invoked fundamental rights and sought their application with impatience. This comes from the loss, at each moment, of a little more of its freedom."

The brutal halt to the Czech experience of "humane socialism" by Brezhnev's tanks is the base of dissidence and the human rights movement in the U.S.S.R. It was natural, therefore, that the movement be revived where it began. Czechoslovakia, having approved the final resolution of the Helsinki Accord, also ratified, on March 23, 1976, two international conventions, one on political and civil rights, the other on social, cultural, and economic rights, conventions, which as we saw in the first section of this book, provided more than one loophole for all sorts of violations. But the Czech dissidents didn't see it this way, and so on January 6, 1977, in a document entitled Charter 77, they held that from that time on the "conventions" had acquired legal status. "Our fellow citizens," they proclaimed, "have the right, and our State bears the duty to uphold them strictly." This document, though, demonstrated the fault with establishing a catalogue of provisions put forth at the conventions but not applied. "Tens of thousands of citizens find themselves unable to work at their specialties simply because the opinions they express differ from the official opinion... Innumberable young people are denied an education because of their beliefs or those of their parents... Religious freedom, expressly guaranteed by Article 18 of the First Convention, is systematically limited by the whims of power which restrain as it pleases the activities of ecclesiastics who live constantly under the threat of withdrawal of the state authorization necessary to the exercise of their functions. Other measures fall heavily on those who profess their religious convictions in words or deeds, and still others repress religious education."

This document pointed out, among other things, the omnipotence of political power that proceeds by control and surveillance. Individuals and organizations, in case of conflict, have no recourse to any independent body of the Party, because none exists. So the freedom to associate, the right to participate in the direction of public affairs, equality before the law, freedom of the unions, the right to strike, etc.... are all seriously limited.[13]

Among the signers of Charter 77, whose initial number of 240 doubled in less than a month, one finds: Jiri Hajek, ex-director of the Party's school of advanced studies, Frantisek Kiegel, Zmedek Mlynar, Ludvik Vakulik, Rudolph Slanski's widow and children, economist Venek Silhan, playwright Pavel Kohout, and Professors Vaclav Havel and Jan

Patocka. These last two along with Jiri Hajek, were designated as spokesmen for the group. A campaign of insults and slander was launched against them, followed quickly by house searches, police surveillance, interruption of telephone communication, interrogations, warnings, dismissals, and arrests. Within two weeks, the situation had become so serious that on January 26, the U.S. Department of State publicly denounced the Prague government's violation of the Helsinki Accord.

Meanwhile, Brezhnev's friend, I. Kapitonov arrived from Moscow in February, followed in March by Minister of Internal Affairs Sokolov. And soon the hard line of Vasil Bilak was in effect. The first victim of the Czech Stalin, made infamous by the trials and purges following the fall of Dubcek, was Professor Jan Patocka. On March 3, after ten hours of interrogation, he suffered a heart attack, and on the 13th of March he died. A month earlier he had written to the International Committee to uphold the principles of Charter 77 in Paris, saying: "It is necessary to put up with disagreements, to risk not being understood, and even to risk physical danger... A higher authority exists which binds individuals in conscience and binds states whose representatives sign international pacts... This obligation is not the function of opportunism and does not bend to the rules of public convenience... So far, no sort of submission has changed a situation which in fact has grown much worse. The greater the fear, the greater the servility, and the greater becomes the despotism."[14]

Patocka's noble words hold true for Western countries as well as for communist countries. We are reminded by them of what Bukovsky said in America about the need for "firmness and inflexibility." Speaking before a U.S. Senate committee on security and cooperation in Europe, he stated: "Public opinion, the parliaments and governments of the West must arm themselves with patience. I find the West too impatient. When attempts haven't produced results you give in to despair. I don't hesitate to declare that the fate of the world depends on the bearing of the Western countries during this increasingly intense period of crisis. A firm, inflexible, consistent behavior will compel the Soviet Union to recognize the political reality."

In Rumania, Charter 77 was immediately signed by eight intellectuals, among them the writer Paul Goma. With the number of supporters increasing, President N. Ceaucescu, attacked the dissidents on February 17, calling them, "outcasts, traitors of their country, who denigrate their homeland... in order to gain the regard of their patrons and to receive money—as did Judas." It should be pointed out that it was the Rumanian representatives who proposed the clause to the original Helsinki document which stated that the independence of each nation and of its own constitution was to be respected—this in view of guarding against possible Soviet aggression.

In East Germany the smouldering dissent suddenly burst into flames on November 16, 1976, when the government decided to deprive singer-writer Wolf Bierman of his citizenship. At the time he was performing a concert in front of thousands of cheering young people at the Cologne stadium in Western Germany. Then in January of 1977, author Thomas Brasch was expelled. On January 13, a committee for the defense of freedom and socialism founded by East German intellectuals revealed that at least twelve dissidents were still in prison. On June 26, Manfred Krug, another famous singer, was exiled. Speaking of the fate of the East Germans, he said that "the worst for them was feeling cut off."[15]

Meanwhile, the communist government, by limiting contacts between citizens and refusing exit visas, especially to young people, was making life impossible for the dissidents, pushing them each day to request to leave. And so, many did: Sarah Kirsch, persecuted also as a Jew, Rudolf Schneider, Reiner Kunze, Bernhard Jentzsch, Gunther Kunert, Jurek Becket, and the composer Tilo Medek. Rudolf Bahro, economist and party member, not only fought for freedom of expression and for human rights, but also for a radical change in the system. And he called for the coming of "true socialism." On August 24th, two days after the appearance in *Der Spiegel* of excerpts from his book, *The Alternative* (still in print in West Germany), and after an interview on R.F.A. television, he was arrested and charged with espionage. Having foreseen this arrest, Bahro declared himself ready to disappear from circulation "for a while." "But," he added, "the police will remain powerless against my ideas."

The Vatican Remains Perplexed

Not all Western heads of state responded in the same manner to the dissidents and their supporters. Particularly inconsistent was the response to their request for *glasnost,* a request to avoid making general statements, to take a stand on concrete cases, to give names, to openly receive persecuted people. The Dutch foreign minister, Van der Stoel, visited Jan Patocka at his home. But French President Valéry Giscard d'Estaing, and West German Chancellor, Helmut Schmidt, refused to receive Andreï Amalrik, and they criticized Carter's politics, which, according to them, constituted interference in the internal affairs of the U.S.S.R. and jeopardized both the success of the Belgrade Conference and détente.

The Holy See, in spite of repeated appeals to Pope Paul VI from the dissidents and their friends, remained faithful to its political stance: "détente," dialogue, "summit meetings," negotiations, "normalization of relations with communist countries," "quiet diplomacy." Anatoly Levitin-Krasnov, again requesting Paul VI to support A. Ginzburg, reminded him that on five previous occasions he had asked the Pope's support for

Bukovsky, but in vain. In order to understand the seeming insensitivity of Paul VI, one must remember what he said on June 21, 1976, to the College of Cardinals on the subject of the Vatican's Ostpolitik:

> The phenomenon which during the last decades has so characteristically and negatively influenced the relations between Church and State, between religious and civil society throughout vast areas of Europe and Asia, has been the establishment of political forces whose ideologies, practical programs, and particularly strategic programs have been founded on what they claim to be humanity's liberation from a supposed religious alienation. During our papacy, we have followed the history of these relations ... with prayer ... and through negotiations and dialogue, as it is called, a dialogue carried on by our close and qualified associates, an active and tireless dialogue, one patient and open, a dialogue as firm in its affirmation of the principles and rights of the Church and the faithful as it is given to accept all honest and loyal attempts to comply with those principles and rights. It is not our intention today to propose evaluations that can only be made correctly by means of an historical perspective, that is, illuminated by what is called philosophy or by the theology of history. While confirming our commitment and that of the Church, founded more on hopes and divine promise and charity for all than on wisdom and human forces, we only wish to express in public the pain in our hearts when we see that a great part of the world, governed by Marxist regimes, continues not only to remain closed to agreements but even to any contact with the Holy See.[16]

No doubt the dissidents appreciated the Pontiff's public expression of sorrow, but they had also expected that he would make public their appeals that he not put too much hope on "contacts" and "normalization of relations" with communist countries. As the vice president of the U.S.S.R. Committee on Religious Affairs, Fourin, affirmed, relations between Church and State are "normal" when modernist tendencies and renovations which constitute active support for internal and external Soviet politics are introduced into parish life."[17] The Polish minister of cults, Kasimir Kakol, stated the following to journalists in a news conference held on May 5, 1976:

> Normalization has been talked about since 1971. The term lacks precision. As if there had ever been a normal situation. Why? Who decides? Who insists on it? Certainly not the Church. Everything depends on us. Normalization does not mean capitulation. We will give into nothing with the Church. She has the right to practice her faith only within the limits of the sanctuary, in the sacristy. We tolerate the processions of Corpus Domini and of the icon (...the Virgin of Czestochowa...). But we will never allow evangelizing outside the church. We will not allow the religious education of children. We will not tolerate any Church influence on cultural and social life. To extricate religion from human conscience and thought is a complicated and lengthy process... Our first objective is to isolate the episcopacy... Free Saturdays and a judicious vacation calendar will neutralize the liturgical calendar and banish the religious holidays celebrated in families....

In Germany, "normalization," that is, the creation of an autonomous episcopal conference for the R. D. A., undoubtedly established direct "contacts" between Rome and the bishops of the communist zone, but it

Normalization or Evangelization?   219

increasingly made prisoners of its inhabitants. Speaking to the Czech bishops on March 18, Pope Paul VI again revoked the tribulations of the faithful. But he failed to mention the sacrifice of Jan Patocka who had died five days earlier. Nor did he mention Charter 77, whose noble principles had been embraced by many Catholic priests. It is significant that a group of Czechs belonging to diverse orders and congregations had sent to the episcopat a memorandum denouncing discrimination in the courts and protesting the suppression of the fact that they were being threatened: "The religious people ... do not seek the restitution ... of their confiscated and nationalized property. They seek the freedom to live their religious beliefs without forgetting the progress put into motion in the new socialist society. They want lifted the prohibitions against recruiting new membership and attending university classes ... they want lifted the particular restrictions against priests whose missions call them abroad ... they want discrimination against the clergy in matters of housing, allotment, and salary to cease ... they want control imposed over other citizens to cease ... they want lifted the obstacles to free choice of confessors, spiritual leaders, and preachers of spiritual retreats."

The Roman magazine *La Civiltà Cattolica,* which published this memorandum on page 588 of the June 18, 1977 edition, failed to say that the clergy had made a mistake in the address, a reproach it did make to Solzhenitsyn when he sent his letter to the Patriarch of Moscow. For Czechoslovakia as for Russia, however, the unfortunate state of religion resulted more from government action than from that of the bishops. But everyone knows that the Czech bishops ordained by Msgr. Casaroli collaborate with the regime as do the bishops dependent on the Moscow Patriarchate. Fortunately, among the simple priests as among the faithful, courageous people are not lacking. Such is Father Stefan Javorsky, curate of the Slovak town of Muran, condemned to two years of incarceration to be purged in a "re-education" group for his religious activity among the young. But the heroism of these men was not inspired by the bishops' example nor by the choices of the Ostpolitik.

How little it took to satisfy the Vatican and to obtain its silence as well as its praises for the generosity of communist leaders! This was evident during the visit to Pope Paul VI by Janos Kadar, first Secretary of the Hungarian Communist Party. Pleased to have been able to name a bishop to every Hungarian diocese, the Pope paid hommage to his guest, ... "the principal and most authoritative promoter of normalization of relations between the Holy See and Hungary."[18] But the Pope did not name the high price of this normalization: the installment in important Church positions of "priests of peace," appointments which Cardinal Mindszenty described in his *Memoirs* as undermining the confidence of loyal priests and of the Catholic laiety in the upper levels of the hierarchy. In fact, Catholics were stunned to hear Cardinal Mindszenty's successor, Cardinal Laszlo Lekai, promise to intensify the dialogue between Catholics and Marxists, or to hear Jozsef Czerhat, Secretary of the Episcopal Conference of Hungarian Bishops, speak of a "desire" among Catholics to cooperate with authorities. This huge lie led to a serious lack of confidence among the clergy and the faithful in the episcopacy. Even Cardinal Lekai had to admit, according to the bulletin of the Kipa Agency, April 19, 1977, that "many communities, often in good conscience, are turning their backs on the bishops." Following Kadar's visit to Paul VI, the Archbishop Cardinal of Vienna, Franz Koenig, president of the secretariat of non-believers, felt it necessary to inform the public that the communist regimes of Eastern Europe considered "atheism" to be their "state religion," and that the meetings at the Vatican should not be taken as a sign of a possible alliance between Christianity and communism. This clarification seemed to be a prelate's veiled criticism of the Vatican's Ostpolitik.

Public opinion and the Catholics would not have needed such warnings and clarification if Rome had listened to the voices of the dissidents and answered their appeals. On the occasion of Sakharov's summons by the KGB in the beginning of 1977, four Soviet intellectuals, Lydia Chukovskaya, Vladimir Voinovich, Lev Kopelev, and Vladimir Kornilov, contacted not only President Carter but also Pope Paul VI. But whereas the American president reacted in the manner we've already examined, the Pope did not respond at all. Later, Carter received Bukovsky. A number of dissidents went to Rome. None were received by the Pope.

Sakharov in his letter to President Carter named several Ukrainian dissidents in prison. He listed among the most persecuted religious groups the Ukrainian Uniate Catholics. Ludmilla Alexeyeva, referring to Sakharov's statement, added that the Ukrainian Catholic Church participated in underground activities and was established in several parishes which for security reasons were unknown to each other. The dissidents confirmed the existence of several clandestine Ukrainian Catholic bishops and stated that among the seventeen Catholic Ukrainians in prison, nine were secret priests.[19] In another letter to Carter, A. Levitin called attention again to "the Eastern or Uniate Catholics who make up a large part of the Ukraine and western Byelorussia."[20] Meanwhile, Rome continued to underestimate the Ukrainian problem. Even the Russians themselves recognized the reality of the problem and its importance to the civil and religious rights of all the Soviet peoples. On December 13, 1976, Pope Paul VI reiterated to Cardinal Slipyi and to the Ukrainian Catholic bishops, concerning emigration: "Circumstances beyond the control of this Apostolic See keep us from acceding to the request so often presented ..." But these same circumstances which impeded the erection of a Ukrainian Catholic patriarchate did not prevent the sending to Moscow of more or less official representatives from the Holy See. The Ukrainian Orthodox priest Vasyl Romanyuk, who without doubt knew of these trips, had written to the Pope: "My colleagues and I hope the Holy See will bring its aid to the formation of an international commission to examine the fate of human rights in the U.S.S.R. We ask that representatives of international public opinion come here so that they may see for themselves what is happening here." But Rome's representatives had other things to do in Moscow.

Among the Pope's envoys who went often to Moscow was Cardinal J. Willebrands. In 1976, September 25 through 27, he led a papal delegation to Armenia. During this trip he was to stop off in Moscow for a courtesy visit with the officials of the Russian Orthodox Church. Several months earlier an important appeal from the Christian Churches of the Soviet Union was sent, based on an extraordinarily valuable ecumenical witnessing. It did not appear that Cardinal Willebrands, president of the Secretariat for Christian Unity, cared to visit any one of the signers of the appeal. He preferred to render hommage to the leaders of the Church which yesterday offered incense to Stalin and today exalts Brezhnev, whose "efforts will enable a peaceful sky to shine over our planet."[21] And when Levitin-Krasnov called on the Church to defend the signers of the appeal and the religious dissidents, who had been viciously slandered in the Soviet press, the Secretariat, presided over by Cardinal Willebrands, remained silent.[22]

It must also be said that those responsible for the ecumenical movement—Protestants as well as Catholics—warmed to the eventuality of a public response to the religious dissidents' appeals. For this reason, in January of 1977, a hunger strike was staged in front of the American seat of the World Council of Churches in New York.[23] The same month, at a week of prayer offered for unity among Christians, I was in a parish in Brooklyn celebrating a mass for persecuted believers in the Soviet Union. The fervent Catholic, Simas Kudirka, was the guest of honor. We had both sent a letter to Bishop Bernard Law, president of the Commission for Ecumenical and Interfaith Affairs of the Conference of American Catholic Bishops. We asked him to form a permanent commission charged with carefully following the religious situation in the U.S.S.R.[24] Msgr. Law's response was, to say the least, disappointing. On February 7th he wrote to me that the "Commission for Ecumenical and Interfaith Affairs was not qualified to cover the problem mentioned." He would forward my letter, however, to the Secretary General of the Conference of American Bishops, Archbishop Bernardin, and his colleagues. Not until May 4 did the Conference make a statement on the issue: "Human Rights in Eastern Europe: A Case of Religious Freedom." No name was mentioned, no reference made to the numerous appeals from the dissidents.

In order to justify their behavior, the Vatican and those who supported its political line, frequently put forth the opinion of bishops inside the Iron Curtain favored "quiet diplomacy." Others went so far as to counsel wariness and non-support towards the dissidents. On this subject one ought to read the unbelievable article by the Swiss Jesuit, Father Robert Hotz, which appeared in *La Civiltà Cattolica* on May 21, 1977, in which the dissidents are reproached for lack of common principles, for showing fascist-chauvinist tendencies, for annoying the communist regimes, for allowing themselves to be exploited by anti-communists, for contributing to the aggravation of East-West tension, for not even coming to the aid of Euro-communists who could not support them for fear of finding themselves allied with Carter.[25]

Meanwhile, as a group of Lithuanian priests pointed out, the politics of the Holy See in the nomination of bishops was becoming more and more a copy of that of Moscow's Patriarchate. How could such bishops not favor silence and the stifling of the dissidents' voices? Furthermore, it is foolish to worry, as does R. Hotz, about what the Soviet dissidents and their allies think. Dissidence is a phenomenon of spontaneous reaction against injustice and repression. It was not born at the instigation of the C.I.A., nor was it financed by capitalists—despite what Soviet newspapers say. Dissidents are not criminals. They haven't even broken the Soviet laws governing the separation of Church and State—despite what Metro-politan Alexis writes.[26] If Euro-communists are more preoccupied with Carter than they are with the substance of the dissidents' claims, then one must doubt the sincerity of their "communism with a human face." "When I came to Europe," Leonid Plyushch said, "I was a communist but since my contacts with the French communist party, I consider myself solely a Marxist. I had serious disagreements with Marchais which earned me the reputation of a political schemer and warmonger in the cold war." And the Soviet mathematician, clarifying his opinion of Italian communism, deplored the fact that *L'Unità,* the newspaper of the Italian Communist Party had not published Amalrik's response to Lombardo: "This for me, proceeds from Stalinism, from which it is difficult for them to free themselves, even by means of an evolutionary process. This evolution is too slow; main-tained on the outside of the struggle for human rights, it will only lead to the victory of totalitarianism." Thus it came about in the U.S.S.R. where "Marx-ism became a dead thing for having rejected all opposition... An ideology without opponents can only become a dead thing."[27]

Leonid Plyushch responded to the criticism made to the dissidents that they had no common thought: "There is great confusion at the level of words... So for me, Brezhnev is a reactionary of the extreme right, but for others he is a leftist bandit... The Solzhenitsyn case reminds me a bit of that of Dostoevsky in his relationship with the democrats of the past. Lenin correctly identified Dostoevsky as an 'arch reactionary.' Yet, Dostoevsky wrote most profoundly on the dynamics of the left. I don't esteem certain of Solzhenitsyn's political statements, but what there is of depth and truth in his books interests me . . . See *The Gulag Archipelago,* for example . . ."[28]

Yes, the dissident voices are diverse. But these diverse voices are going to change a world of injustice and lies. These are the voices of men who were raised in atheism and who are now seeking God. Such is the voice of Alexander Zinoviev, author of a novel which has appeared in Switzerland, written in Russian, and which Modesto tells us is "the most lucid, the most fierce, and the most desperate book about the Soviet Union." And what it makes us hear is the voice of the "believing atheist:"[29]

"To live without Someone who sees . . . I can no longer do it. That is why I scream until I am breathless: Father, I don't pray. I demand: Be! I murmur, I howl: Be, Father, Be! No, I don't demand, I implore you: Be!"

None of this was enough to make the Vatican overcome its perplexities, to lift its reserve and mistrust towards the dissidents.

The Election of John Paul II Revives the Dissident's Hopes

The Belgrade conference gave the Vatican the perfect opportunity to publicize (with names and facts to support it) the suppression of believers' rights. But the Holy See's representative, Msgr. Achille Silvestrini, under-secretary of the Council for the Public Affairs of the Church, wanted to adopt a more moderate stance. Without naming names, he declared:

> Appeals, evidence, requests . . . are multiplying . . . because in various regions life is far from being sufficiently free and normal. What is more serious, open wounds persist, wounds we firmly hope to see tended and healed. Such is the case for the Catholic Church in certain communities of the faithful of Eastern rite, who in other times enjoyed a religious life in the pluri-secular tradition and who, in the new post-war juridico-political bases have lost their civil status and their right to exist. This fact is all the more tragic because it strikes at the core of religious freedom . . .

A fine effort on the part of the Vatican diplomat to say and to not say! The art of euphemism employed in such a way as to not offend the powerful adversary. No question of naming Ukraine, Rumania, or Czechoslavakia where the Catholic Churches of the Eastern rite were banned and the unjust annexations of territories are euphemistically called "new juridico-political foundations." And fearing to have said too much and to have publicly offended the very respectable governments of sovereign and independent States, Msgr. Silvestrini is quick to clarify:

> Naturally, the Holy See deems its duty and propriety to continue to reserve the negotiation of concrete problems of interest to the Catholic Church to the bilateral dialogue further developed in recent years. Far from trying to make the final act of Helsinki into a polemic for an abhorrent return to cold-war tensions, our delegation

wants to renew here the expression of its confidence in the possibility... for this work of interpretation and meditation... to succeed... in welcoming these aspirations of vital and primary scope.[30]

Several months later, at the closing of the Belgrade Conference, Msgr. Silvestrini admitted:

The results were rather limited. While there were nearly a hundred proposals presented and discussed, the final document only records the decision setting the next meeting in Madrid, in November 1980, and the related decisions concerning the meeting of experts in Montreux, Bonn, and La Valette.[31]

The Vatican was aware of the poor results of its *Ostpolitik*. In the face of spreading criticism and principally of dissidence, the Holy See, far from changing its politics, persisted in dialogue and "quiet diplomacy." The mission of explaining the validity of the Vatican *Ostpolitik* to the international public was given over to Msgr. Agostino Casaroli who made two important statements about this issue, one in Austria, the 17th and 18th of Nov., 1977, and one at Georgetown University in Washington in Feb., 1978. Note that these statements were published in *l'Osservatore Romano* on the 7th and 16th of Feb., 1978, right at the time when criticism of the *Ostpolitik* had attained alarming proportions with the hearings of the Sakharov Tribunal in Rome[32] and the Biennale on Dissidence in Venice in Nov. and Dec. 1977, and with the publication of the *Chronicle of the Catholic Church in Lithuania,*[33] by the Lithuanian information service *Elta-Press.*

Msgr. Casaroli adamantly confirmed that there was no replacement for detente, that regimes could change, that it was necessary to carry on the "dialogue," to accept sacrifices and "lesser evil" solutions. Despite risks and disappointment, the Holy See's politics with regard to communist countries remained fundamentally optimistic. To those suffering and sending appeals, the Vatican answered that they should be patient and ready for cautious but "loyal collaboration."

Obviously, Msgr. Casaroli no longer accepted as valid the statement of Pope Pius XI according to which the principles and practice of communism were "intrinsically perverse." [34] He also refused to uphold the fact that the democratic evolution of communist dictatorships is impossible. It is in this framework that he sought to answer the critics, acknowledging their point of view that this *Ostpolitik* better served the Vatican than it did individual Christians.

It was noted, and rightly so, that the improved attitude in communist countries turned out to be softer toward the Holy See whose contributions to peace are recognized and appreciated, than towards the Church, specifically in what concerns the religious lives of the people... But it would be neither just nor objective to consider the problems of

Church-State relations and their solutions outside of their context or without taking into account the priorities that hold for each of them as a function of the necessary and the possible... or the consequences to be expected or desired from what is possible to do at this time, or in a more or less distant future. Thus the Holy See is often reproached for its priorities which give undue preference to essential questions, to institutional issues, and to the nomination of bishops in the country in question. It should be clear that the preoccupation of the Holy See in the order of proposed ends, to use scholastic terms, is the full and free choice of the Church and its action, as is also the freedom of religious life. On the contrary, *in the order of execution,* it would not be wise to refuse today what is today possible because, although partial and imperfect, there is not by definition any obstacle to the proposed end; whereas, *in the order of means,* one must consider what is most important to ensure precisely in order to arrive at the proposed end.

Apparently sound reasoning. But we don't see that it respects the spirit of the Gospel. Jesus Christ, who also wanted "peace," was not preoccupied with what the authorities might have said; in order to do good for mankind, the sick, the sinners, the pagans, he entrusted them to the care of spiritual pastors, not to mercenaries and worldly men. If it is true that we cannot conceive of the Church of Christ without a hierarchy, it is also true that the Church is above all the society of Christians. In earlier times, the communists sought to destroy the Church by striking at its ministers. Now they reveal themselves to be more crafty and seek to destroy it by providing it with unworthy ministers to lead it.

At the death of Paul VI, some journalists put forth the hypothesis that the Vatican *Ostpolitik* had been unilaterally conceived and carried out by Msgr. Casaroli without the knowledge of the Pope. One should read, for example, the article by Lucio Lami in *Il Giornale* of August 8, 1978, entitled "Paul VI and the Silent Church." Having recalled the vast documentation on the persecution of believers in the USSR and its satellite countries, he asks himself:

How much did the Pope Montini know? How much of the news got to his desk?... Paul VI valued prudence, but not to the point of allowing the implication of a moral complicity with the persecuters whatever their colors. It's not by chance that of all the popes, he most stood up for communities and individuals... Had he known the details of the situation he would not have kept quiet in the face of overwhelming official documentation. One thing is certain: in the East, no one believed the Pope knew. A Polish priest told me: "When Msgr. Casaroli made visits to our government, we no longer knew how to justify ourselves to the indignant faithful. Most often we got out of it by saying that these were personally initiated visits, made without the knowledge of His Holiness." I heard this same story in Rome during the hearing of the Sakharov Tribunal where, with the exception of the "mad bishop" Slipyi, no authority was present even at the session in which the persecution of believers was under discussion. What of it? Who kept the dissidents from having an audience with the Pope? Maybe such publications as *The Chronicles of the Catholic Church in Lithuania* never reached the Pope's desk? This is the mysterious page which historians will need to explain in order to complete the portrait of Paul VI. It will be a difficult task for them, one that will not fail to revive polemics.

My opinion is that Paul VI knew, if not everything, at least much, and that it was he who sketched out the guidelines of the *Ostpolitik*. No doubt, counselors and experts belonging not so much to the Secretariat as to the other Roman organizations mentioned earlier, intervened often on points of detail. In his last address to the members of the diplomatic corps accredited by the Holy See, Paul VI, after having denounced those who did not respect the rights of religion and family, then expressed his hope for an evolution, for a detente of spirits. And then, defending the politics of dialogue, he denied that it had not produced any result. We reproduce here that part of the Pope's speech, originally in French, published in *l'Osservatore Romano*, January 15, 1978. He showed disappointment and a certain impatience in light of the fact that the Ostpolitik, in spite of the concessions and of the confidence in the sincerity of the communist leaders, was not developing as had been foreseen. In particular, the Pope here alludes to an audience granted to Edward Gierek a few days earlier:

> As for us, we have always encouraged the pastors and the faithful to demonstrate patient perseverance, to be loyal to legitimate powers, to participate generously in the civic and social domains for all that serves the good of their countries. We have recently given public proof of our position on the occasion of defferential and courteous visits from high civil authorities. For a long time, except in the case of a few countries with which we have not been allowed to communicate, we have initiated open and frank dialogue which has had some result and which we hope will come to include difficult points not yet touched. We would like now, giving way to a broader perspective and speaking not only for Catholics but for all believers, to formulate a question. Here it is: Is not the time ripe from now on, is not historical evolution sufficiently advanced that certain inflexiblilties of the past can be overcome and that the pleas of millions of people can be heard, and that all—in the fairness of conditions among citizens and in the mutual cooperation of all for the civic and social good of their countries—can benefit from freedom of faith in both its personal and communal expressions? Is there not in the vicissitudes of the peoples, even after the most radical upsets, a natural maturation of events, an expansion of minds, and a progression of generations reaching toward a new and more humane stage, in which what welcomes, reunifies, and makes brothers of men is reborn and affirmed? It seems to us that justice, wisdom and realism converge to support the hope and fond wish that a moment capable of bringing happiness to so many hearts, be not postponed and avoided.

Paul VI again had the opportunity to speak of the possibility of a collaboration between Catholics and Communist regimes during an audience granted to three Cuban bishops on June 22, 1978. He expressed his desire that in Cuba "Catholics within the framework of justice, in accordance with the freedom preserved for their faith and beyond their personal and community expressions," could contribute usefully to the "civil and social good of the country." He recalled that "the Church educates the social conscience of the faithful favoring their active collaboration in the common good, teaching all to overcome egoism, reinforcing the unity of family and all the values attached to it..."

Obviously the Pope avoided any allusion to Castro's subversive activity in Africa in which Catholics could scarcely collaborate, even for the price of a little freedom to practice their religion.

The optimism of the Holy See even in regard to China was again expressed by Msgr. Casaroli on the eve of his departure for New York where he was to deliver a message from Pope Paul VI before an extraordinary session on disarmament at the U.N. The prelate spoke about signs of a "very slow thaw." He characterized the state of the relations between the Vatican and East European countries as a "state of movement, slow, but, movement." Words and facts clash, as is shown by the dissidents' situation; Stalinism is not yet dead in the USSR and its satellite counties. For any observer of Soviet current events the difficulty will always be to accept as truth what to any reasonable person seems improbable and unbelievable: that under the communist boot, nothing changes and nothing moves.

Why was Paul VI surprised to have to report at the end of his papacy that even after much effort, one did not see in the East this maturation of events, this expansion of spirit, this common path which had seemed permissible to hope for.

The election to the Papacy of Cardinal Karol Wojtyla, the Archbishop of Krakow, gave hope for a more realistic approach from the Vatican towards the communist countries. Those who struggle for civil and religious freedom are capable of promoting ecumenism and democracy even where the icy immobility of the endless winter so well described by Boris Pasternak has reigned for so long. On the day of his coronation John Paul II asked in a voice strong and heavy with emotion:

> Help the Pope... to the power of salvation, open the borders of the states, economic and political systems, the vast fields of culture, civilization, and development. Do not be afraid. Christ knows what is in man. He alone knows. Today, all too often, man does not know what is within him, in the depths of his soul, in his heart; frequent is his uncertainty about the meaning of his life on earth. Allow Christ to speak to mankind.

The dissidents want to help the Pope.

They are not afraid. They want the frontiers of their states to be opened and they look, some even without knowing it, for Christ and the saving power of His word. But until this moment, they have not had access to the Pope, their appeals have remained unanswered, their requests for audiences have remained on the desk of the head of the pontifical antichamber, Msgr. Dino Monduzzi. This happened at the time of the hearings of the Sakharov Tribunal. The Lithuanian Catholics, alluding to their bishops, wrote to the Pope: "What we await are not words to anesthetize us, but words to encourage us." The Czech priests begged Msgr. Casaroli: "Don't give us any more state bishops when we have a martyr bishop, Msgr. Joseph Korec, who, after twelve years in prison, is now a worker in a factory in Bratislava."

Father Vasyl Romanyuk, a Ukrainian orthodox priest who has been in prison for some years, wrote a letter to *l'Osservatore Romano* that was never published,[35] asking why Rome didn't establish a Ukrainian Catholic Patriarchate to save the outlawed Ukrainian Catholics. General Grigorenko, a defender of oppressed minorities in the Soviet Union, supported this request, praising the noble confessor of the faith, Cardinal Joseph Slipyi. The main representative of Soviet dissidence, the academician Sakharov, who is not a believer, sent an appeal on Nov. 28 1978, to John Paul II asking him to intervene in favor of Vladimir Shelkov, an 83-year-old member of the Pansoviet Church of Seventh Day Adventists. Shelkov, along with fourteen other people, was arrested at Tashkent for having "spread false rumors which defamed and slandered the social order and the Soviet State." According to Sakharov, Shelkov's arrest was a "punitive action in the face of a purely religious activity and of a struggle carried on for many years without compromise for freedom of conscience and faith." Perhaps the Secreteriat for the Union of Christians, not recognizing the ecumenical character of Sakharov's position, counseled John Paul II to pigeon-hole it. But events happened quickly: The Metropolitan of Leningrad, Nikodim, died in the reign of John Paul I. John Paul II was expected to change the policies of the Secretariat. Wouldn't Sakharov be a better expert than were men like Nikodim, who had on his conscience the suffering of many priests and religious people and in particular Lev Konin, committed to a psychiatric hospital in the beginning of 1978?

Many dissidents sent their wishes to John Paul II on the occasion of his election. V. Bukovsky, N. Gorbanevskaya, V. Maximov, E. Neizvestny, and V. Nekrasov wrote to him: "Now and henceforth the eyes of all who suffer on earth are turned to you." Mstislav Rostropovich and his wife Galina Vishnevskaya sent the following telegram: "Your election gives us renewed hope and strength. Our family is filled with joy and enthusiasm."

Epilogue: The Vatican's Ostpolitik under John Paul II

As soon as he was elected Pope (October 16, 1978), John Paul II became overwhelmed by the fact of being the first Slav to occupy the chair of St. Peter. Many times, especially during his first trip to Poland (June 2-10, 1979), he reflected, while addressing the crowds almost as if talking to himself, about the meaning of this fact for so many different groups of Slavs. George Huntston Williams writes about *a Papal transfiguration of Polish Messianism* operated by the Polish Pope: "... one can but wonder that he was able to be so much the Pole that he was also the more the Universal Pope. But Polish Catholicism does allow for particularity within the context of universal aims for the good of all mankind: 'We fight for our freedom and yours,' is a traditional phrase."[1] And there is no doubt that Karol Wojtyla took his election to the papacy as a particular mission inside the more universal one. Recalling the miracle of the tongues on Pentecost day, the Pope, speaking in the cathedral of Gniezno, said:

> Today, in the year of the Lord 1979, on this anniversary of the descent of the Holy Spirit, as we go back to those beginnings, we cannot fail to hear also—as well as the language of our own forefathers—other Slav languages and related languages, languages in which there then began to be heard the voice of the upper room that was opened wide to history. These languages cannot fail to be heard especially by the first Slav Pope in the history of the Church. Perhaps that is why Christ has chosen him, perhaps that is why the Holy Spirit has led him—in order that he might introduce into the communion of the Church the understanding of the words and of the languages that still sound strange to the ear accustomed to the Romance, Germanic, English and Celtic tongues. Is it not Christ's will that the Holy Spirit should make the Mother Church turn, at the end of the second millennium of Christianity, with loving understanding, with special sensitivity, to those forms of human speech that are linked together by their common origin, their common etymology, and which, in spite of the well-known differences, even in way of writing, sound close and familiar one to another?
>
> Is it not Christ's will, is it not what the Holy Spirit disposes, that this Pope, in whose heart is deeply engraved the history of his own nation from its very beginning and also the history of the brother peoples and the neighboring peoples, should in a special way manifest and confirm in our age the presence of these peoples in the Church and their specific contribution to the history of Christianity?
>
> Is it not the design of Providence that He should reveal the developments that have taken place here in this part of Europe in the rich architecture of the temple of the Holy Spirit?
>
> Is it not Christ's will, is it not what the Holy Spirit disposes, that this Polish Pope, this Slav Pope, should at this precise moment manifest the spiritual unity of Christian Europe? Although there are two great traditions, that of the West and that of the East, to which it is indebted, through both of them Christian Europe professes "one faith, one

baptism, one God and Father of us all" (Eph. 4: 5-6), the Father of our Lord Jesus Christ.... This Pope... comes here to speak before the whole Church, before Europe and the world, of those often forgotten nations and peoples. He comes here to cry "with a loud voice." He comes here to point out the paths that in one way or another lead back towards the Pentecost upper room, towards the cross and resurrection. He comes here to embrace all these peoples, together with his own nation, and to hold them close *to the heart of the Church,* to the heart of the Mother of the Church, in whom he has unlimited trust.[2]

"Spiritual unity of Christian Europe": this is another conception very dear to John Paul II, about which he wrote already before becoming Pope.[3] This is also the reason why in his Apostolic Letter *Egregiae virtutis* (December 31, 1980), he proclaimed the Apostles of the Slavs, Saints Cyril and Methodius, Patrons of Europe together with St. Benedict of Norcia.[4] But, of course, this conception is not only a pious theory nor a futile exercise in historic-cultural curiosities, but it bears very serious consequences for the "forgotten peoples" in general and the dissidents in particular. Without Christ man cannot understand himself "nor what true dignity is," man becomes victim of abuse, brutality and murder. Visiting the infamous concentration camp at Oswiecim (Auschwitz), the Pope remembered a Polish Catholic priest who gave his life to save that of a father of a family:

> In this site of the terrible slaughter that brought death to four million people of different nations, Father Maximilian voluntarily offered himself for death in the starvation bunker for a brother, and so won a spiritual victory like that of Christ Himself. This brother still lives today in the land of Poland.
> But was Father Maximilian Kolbe the only one? Certainly he won a victory that was immediately felt by his companions in captivity and is still felt today by the Church and the world. However, there is no doubt that many other similar victories were won. I am thinking, for example, of the death in the gas chamber of a concentration camp of the Carmelite Sister Benedicta of the Cross, whose name in the world was Edith Stein, who was an illustrious pupil of Husserl and became one of the glories of contemporary German philosophy, and who was a descendant of a Jewish family living in Wroclaw.
> Where the dignity of man was so horribly trampled on, victory was won through faith and love.
> Can it still be a surprise to anyone that the Pope born and brought up in this land, the Pope who came to the see of St. Peter from the diocese in whose territory is situated the camp of Oswiecim, should have begun his first Encyclical with the words "Redemptor Hominis" and should have dedicated it as a whole to the cause of man, to the dignity of man, to the threats to him, and finally to his inalienable rights that can so easily be trampled on and annihilated by his fellowmen? Is it enough to put man in a different uniform, arm him with the apparatus of violence? Is it enough to impose on him an ideology in which human rights are subjected to the demands of the system, completely subjected to them, so as in practice not to exist at all?[5]

The speeches, pronounced by John Paul II in Poland in the presence of Communist authorities and heard in person or on television by the entire nation, marked a change in the Vatican's Ostpolitik from the practice of speaking in a complicated manner, hiding the truth among a lot of words, and not naming names. In his first encyclical, *Redemptor hominis* (The Redeemer of Man), published on March 4, 1979, the Pope wrote very strongly about human rights. If somebody still didn't understand, he explained very candidly and courageously that, while speaking those truths, he had in mind Poland and its people who fell victim to totalitarian regimes. Here are some of the thoughts proclaimed in the encyclical, which were going to have such a tremendous impact in Poland in the months ahead:

> Already in the first half of this century, when various state totalitarianisms were developing, which, as is well known, led to the horrible catastrophe of war, the Church clearly outlined her position with regard to these regimes that to all appearances were acting for a higher good, namely the good of the state, while history was to show instead that the good in question was only that of a certain party, which had been identified with the state. In reality, those regimes had restricted the rights of the citizens, denying them recognition precisely of those inviolable human rights that have reached formulation on the international level in the middle of our century. While sharing the joy of all people of good will, of all people who truly love justice and peace, at this conquest, the Church, aware that the "letter" on its own can kill, while only "the spirit gives life," must continually ask, together with these people of good will, whether the Declaration of Human Rights and the acceptance of their "letter" mean everywhere also the actualization of their "spirit." Indeed, well-founded fears arise that very often we are still far from this actualization and that at times the spirit of social and public life is painfully opposed to the declared "letter" of human rights. This state of things, which is burdensome for the societies concerned, would place special responsibility towards these societies and the history of man on those contributing to its establishment.
>
> The essential sense of the state, as a political community, consists in that the society and people composing it are master and sovereign of their own destiny. This sense remains unrealized if, instead of the exercise of power with the moral participation of the society or people, what we see is the imposition of power by a certain group upon all the other members of the society. This is essential in the present age, with its enormous increase in people's social awareness and the accompanying need for the citizens to have a right share in the political life of the community, while taking account of the real conditions of each people and the necessary vigor of public authority. These therefore are questions of primary importance from the point of view of the progress of man himself and the overall development of his humanity.
>
> The Church has always taught the duty to act for the common good and, in so doing, has likewise educated good citizens for each state. Furthermore, she has always taught that the fundamental duty of power is solicitude for the common good of society; this is what gives power its fundamental rights. Precisely in the name of these premises of the objective ethical order, the rights of power can only be understood on the basis of respect for the objective and inviolable rights of man. The common good that authority in the state serves is brought to full realization only when all the citizens are sure of their rights. The lack of this leads to the dissolution of society, opposition by citizens to authority, or a situation of oppression, intimidation, violence, and terrorism, of which many examples have been provided by the totalitarianisms of this century. Thus the principle of human rights is of profound concern to the area of social justice and is the measure by which it can be tested in the life of political bodies.
>
> These rights are rightly reckoned to include the right to religious freedom together with the right to freedom of conscience. The Second Vatican Council considered especially necessary the preparation of a fairly long declaration on this subject. This is

the document called *Dignitatis Humanae,* in which is expressed not only the theological concept of the question but also the concept reached from the point of view of natural law, that is to say from the "purely human" position, on the basis of the premises given by man's own experience, his reason and his sense of human dignity. Certainly the curtailment of the religious freedom of individuals and communities is not only a painful experience but it is above all an attack on man's very dignity, independently of the religion professed or of the concept of the world which these individuals and communities have. The curtailment and violation of religious freedom are in contrast with man's dignity and his objective rights. The Council document mentioned above states clearly enough what that curtailment or violation of religious freedom is. In this case we are undoubtedly confronted with a radical injustice with regard to what is particularly deep in man, what is authentically human. Indeed, even the pheno-menon of unbelief, a-religiousness and atheism, as a human phenomenon, is understood only in relation to the phenomenon of religion and faith. It is therefore difficult, even from a "purely human" point of view, to accept a position that gives only atheism the right of citizenship in public and social life, while believers are, as though by principle, barely tolerated or are treated as second-class citizens or are even—and this has already happened—entirely deprived of the rights of citizenship . . . [6]

At the moment of his departure for Rome the Pope was invited by Cardinal Wyszynski to come back to his "motherland" in August 1982 for the sixth centennial of the icon of Jasna Gora. The Communist authorities also were at hand, happy that the trip was over and hopeful that it would serve the "normalization" and the "desired development of relations between the Apostolic See and the government of the Polish State." But there were still too many conflicts and too many violations of human rights going on in Poland, and now, after the clear call of the Polish Pope to a pacific revolution in order to restore human dignity and human rights, nobody could guarantee that there would be another trip of John Paul II to Poland. Economic and political discontent of the workers caused the downfall of Gomulka in 1970. The same was going to happen to his successor Edward Gierek one year after the visit of the Pope.

Long-simmering public discontent over the shortages of basic foodstuffs and housing, dependence on the Soviet Union, and the lack of freedom exploded, as it was to do later, over the announcement of widespread price increases. Anti-regime feeling took its most violent form in Gdansk, where shipyard workers took to the streets and burned the Party headquarters. The result was an estimated 70 workers killed by the internal security forces. Gomulka was deposed and replaced as first secretary by Edward Gierek, a member of the Politburo and the party chief in Silesia . . .

The uneasy equilibrium between the communist authorities and the opposition was upset in the mid-1970s. Heartened by the human rights provisions of the 1975 Final Act of the Conference on Security and Cooperation in Europe (CSCE, also known as the Helsinki Agreement) and by activity of dissidents in the Soviet Union in a climate of East-West détente, the adversaries of the regime were emboldened to act more openly. The retreat of the authorities on constitutional amendment issues in 1976, when faced with protest from the church and thousands of intellectuals, further served to encourage the opposition.

The violent suppression of worker demonstrations in June 1976 resulted in the establishment of the Committee for the Defense of the Workers (Komitet Obrony

Robotnikow—KOR), after September 1977 known as the Committee for Social Self-Defense-Committee for the Defense of the Workers (Komitet Samoobrony Spolecznej-Komitet Obrony Robotnikow—KSS-KOR). This group included some respected prewar socialists and wartime resistance figures. Among the most prominent of KOR activists were former student leaders who had been imprisoned after the 1968 demonstrations, including historian Adam Michnik and sociologist Jacek Kuron. Initially only 14 strong, the group expanded to 33 members and had perhaps 2,000 active supporters. KOR was formed to circulate underground reports on mistreatment of the demonstrating workers and to solicit funds for their medical and legal bills. Working openly, KOR avoided official restrictions by not adopting a formal structure, although its representatives were active in all major cities. Gradually expanding its goals but adhering to moderate tactics of dialogue with the PZPR, KOR pressed for stronger guarantees of civil rights, free trade unions, an easing of censorship, and an end to religious discrimination. KSS-KOR members were accepted as advisers to the striking workers in August 1980, reinforcing Solidarity's effectiveness through tactical and legal guidance. In spite of its moderate approach, KSS-KOR came under sustained attack from the government as counterrevolutionary and subversive. The committee dissolved itself in October 1981, announcing that it had fulfilled its function and was superfluous in view of Solidarity. The leading KSS-KOR activists were interned when martial law was declared. In early 1983 Kuron, Michnik, and three other KSS-KOR leaders were awaiting trial on charges of violation of martial law.[7]

The events of August 1980-December 1981 showed Solidarity's emergence as an alternative force to the Polish Communist Party (PZPR). July 2, 1980: Warsaw factory workers strike to protest the increase in meat prices and to demand pay increases. July 3 and 4: scattered wildcat strikes sweep large factories across the country. July 17: The army is called in to maintain essential services in the southern city of Lublin when 80,000 workers there join a general strike. August 14: Workers take over the Lenin Shipyard in Gdansk and the national radio confirms widespread work stoppages, especially in the Baltic industrial region. September 5: E. Gierek is dismissed by the Politburo and replaced by Stanislaw Kania. September 17: The new independent labor unions forge a single national labor organization at a meeting in Gdansk. October 24: for the first time in any Soviet-bloc country an independent union wins legal status. November 10: the Polish Supreme Court rules that the charter legalizing the independent union movement may stand without a reference to the "leading role" of the Communist Party. January 24, 1981: millions of Polish workers heed Solidarity's call and take a "free Saturday" to back the union's demand for a five-day workweek. February 9: Prime Minister Pinkowski is dismissed and Gen. Wojciech Jaruzelski, the Minister of Defense, is nominated to replace him. March 27: millions of Polish workers stage a four-hour nationwide strike to protest police violence in Bydgoszcz. It is the largest organized protest since Communism came to Poland. It begins and ends exacly on schedule without reports of major incidents. May 12: Court recognizes Rural Solidarity union for farmers. September 10: Solidarity calls for free elections to the Polish Parliament and local legislative bodies.

November 8: the Politburo instructs Parliament to pass a law banning strikes. December 2: Polish policemen and army units mount a helicopter assault on the academy of striking fire cadets and remove 300 without bloodshed. December 12: Solidarity leaders meeting in Gdansk propose holding a national referendum on their own on a vote of confidence in Gen. Jaruzelski and for establishing a temporary non-Communist government and holding free elections. December 13: Gen. Jaruzelski announces martial law and military rule, banning strikes and public meetings, restricting travel, and suspending union activities. More than 5,000 persons are arrested, including Lech Walesa and the Solidarity leaders who can be found.

On October 8, 1982 the Sejm approved a law sponsored by the government to abolish the existing trade unions, including Solidarity.[8] The few Solidarity leaders still at large and in hiding formed an underground commission (TKK). At this moment the Church intervened and, as Archbishop Glemp said, speaking at Taranto (Italy), a danger of bloodshed was avoided.[9] He counseled against provocative actions that would only delay reconciliation and dialogue with the government, but also suggested that it was in the interest of the authorities to establish a date for the visit of the Pope, who had made the lifting of martial law and a general amnesty a condition for his visit. The visit was tentatively scheduled for June 18, 1983. On November 11, 1982, the release of Lech Walesa was announced.

John Paul II arrived in Poland June 16. Both President Jablonski and Gen. Jaruzelski stressed the "advanced normalization that is taking place in the country." The General confirmed his will to abolish martial law, suspended since the beginning of the year, and to adopt solutions "adequate, humanitarian and legal." For his part the Pope said that he was not losing hope that the actual difficult situation could open the way to a "social renewal, the beginning of which is constituted by the social accords stipulated between State authorities and representatives of the workers ... according to the principles elaborated with such a great effort during the critical days of August 1980."[10] From the moment he kissed the soil of his "motherland" and on many other occasions the Pope mentioned those "who suffer, the prisoners ... those who taste the bitterness of disappointment and privation of liberty, ... of their human dignity trampled upon ...," and also called on Poles who could not see him "to welcome my presence in those places where my pilgrim path does not go."

Gdansk and Lublin were expressly excluded by the authorities from the itinerary of the Pope. Lech Walesa was denied a permit to go to see the Pope, so he waited hours and hours near the phone hoping to be called. Only hours before the departure of John Paul II he was taken by helicopter to the Tatra mountains where he spoke to the Pope alone. On that same day, June 23, the Pope had a non-scheduled meeting with General Jaruzelski and nobody knows exactly the content of these two secret conversations. Among the different interpretations one aroused a storm of controversy: the last commentary on the Pope's trip, published in the Vatican newspaper *L'Osservatore Romano* (June 25) by its deputy editor Rev. Virgilio Levi, was titled *Honor to the Sacrifice.* According to Levi, Lech Walesa was a good man, but now he was defeated, so it would be better for him, for the others and for the Church to step aside honorably: "Sometimes it is necessary to sacrifice uncomfortable persons so that something better might be born for the community.... By receiving him the Pope gave satisfaction to his people. By receiving him privately he avoided causing any damage to the delicate moment of national reconciliation. Not everybody will agree, and in Poland almost nobody. We are sorry for that. But there were reasons of greater importance. Let's honor the sacrifice of Walesa!" The following day Fr. Levi was fired.

Anyone who knows anything at all about *L'Osservatore Romano* knows that it operates under the closest supervision of the Pope and his aids. So it is impossible that Fr. Levi published the article without any approval. On the other hand the approval could not come from the Pope because 1) he always defends and respects human dignity, 2) he publicly, during the trip, proclaimed the validity of the principles of the Gdansk Agreement, 3) he certainly does not want the Church to assume Solidarity's functions, as he consistently declared that the proper role of the Church might be to mediate but never to participate in the political process, 4) on April 1985 he named as Cardinal the Archbishop of Wroclaw, Henryk Roman Gulbinowicz, a great friend of Walesa and Solidarity who, soon after the second trip of the Pope to Poland told the reporters in Rome when they inquired about Walesa's future; "Walesa is not finished yet!"

The approval of Fr. Levi's article came necessarily from those Vatican authorities who, as a principle of their Ostpolitik, sacrificed in the past individuals and peoples in exchange for empty Communist promises. The most illustrious victim of them was Cardinal Mindszenty. It is true that, after the visit of the Pope, martial law was abolished and the political prisoners were released, but the Sejm approved a law even worse, so that the consequences of martial law were not lifted, but made harsher[11] The persecutions against religion and dissent continued, including the beating and the murdering of the people. Adam Lopatka, Minister of Religious Affairs, sent a letter to Cardinal Glemp insisting that he restrain 69 priests; otherwise the government would act against them for what it considered their anti-socialist activities (December 1983). Polish dissidents released from jail under the amnesty decree, on August 21, 1984, met at St. Stanislaus church in Warsaw where about 10,000 cheering supporters greeted them as returning heroes. Among those who participated were Solidarity officials Seweryn Jaworski, Jacek Kuron, Adam Michnik, Zbigniew Romaszewski and others. It is this kind of moral support given to the dissidents by some priests that the bishops are supposed to forbid and punish. In February 1984 Cardinal Glemp transferred Fr. Mieczyslaw Nowak from the parish of Ursus, a town near Warsaw where the Polish tractors' factory is located, to Leki Koscielne, 100 km. from Warsaw. The reason? After the introduction of martial law he started to celebrate masses for the fatherland. The parishioners of Ursus initiated a hunger strike to have their priest back, but in vain.

The whole world heard about another priest who was transferred not by a bishop but by the secret police, not to a parish 100 km. from Warsaw, but to the other world: Fr. Jerzy Popieluszko. Strangely enough the reason of the horrible murder was the same as that given by the killers of Christ and by the followers of the old Ostpolitik: "a smaller evil was necessary to stop a larger evil." This was the reason Capt. Grzegorz Piotrowski gave at the trial for murdering Fr. Popieluszko. Piotrowski, who worked in the interior ministry department monitoring Catholic Church affairs, together with his accomplices, Lt. Waldemar Chmielewski and Lt. Leszek Pekala admitted to the kidnap and murder of the priest (October 19, 1984), whose body was found in a frozen reservoir of the Vistula River (October 30). Another officer, Col. Adam Pietruszka, their chief, according to Piotrowski, had said to them that "this is a decision of the highest level." But of course no people from the highest level showed up at the trial, and none of them was sentenced. It's interesting to note that Piotrowski, during the trial, mentioned other possible targets for kidnapping and murder, which incuded Fr. Henryk Jankowski of Gdansk and Fr. Stanislaw Malkowski of Warsaw. Fr. Jankowski is a close friend and adviser of Lech Walesa. Fr. Malkowski, an outspoken critic of communism, at the beginning of 1985, was really banned from preaching in Warsaw churches by Cardinal Glemp.[12]

* * *

The visits of John Paul II to his "motherland" were followed with enthusiasm by the Catholics of the nearby countries, who began to hope that the Pope might visit them on the occasion of important anniversaries such as the 500th anniversary of the death of St. Casimir, patron saint of Lithuania (March 1984), and the 600th anniversary of the federation of Poland and Lithuania with the subsequent introduction of Christianity in Lithuania (1987). The bishops were hopeful to obtain the agreement from the Soviet government to a visit of the Pope because, toward the end of 1982, Moscow had permitted the appointment of two new bishops in Lithuania and one in Latvia, and in February 1983 the Soviet Union got its first official resident cardinal, Julijan Vaivods, 87, bishop administrator of Riga (Latvia), who was allowed to go to Rome for the ceremony of the imposition of the red hat. On the other hand the Lithuanian bishops had already received permission to go to Rome at the beginning of April of the same year for their first visit *ad limina,* a collective report to the Pope which takes place every five years which the Lithuanian bishops were never able to take part in after the Soviets annexed Lithuania in 1940. The visiting bishops were: Liudas Pavilonis of Kaunas, Romualdas Kriksciunas of Panevezys, Vincentas Sladkevicius of Kaisiadorys, Antanas Vaicius of Telsiai and Klaipeda. They were accompanied by Canon Algis Gutauskas, who heads the Vilnius Archdiocese in Bishop Steponavicius's enforced absence. Bishop Julijonas Steponavicius has been living in banishment in a Lithuanian village since 1961. There is a rumor that he is the cardinal *in pectore* (without disclosing his name) announced by the Pope in 1979.

But the situation of religion in Lithuania deteriorated with the sentencing to seven years of Fr. Alfonsas Svarinskas (May 6, 1983), one of the founders of the Catholic Committee for the Defense of Believers' Rights (November 13, 1978). Another member of the Committee, Fr. Sigitas Tamkevicius, was arrested on the same day right in the courtroom. Immediately the faithful started to collect signatures for his liberation as they did for Fr. Svarinskas. The Catholic Committee for the Defense of Believers' Rights, on January 31, 1983, sent the following letter to Yury Andropov:

> On January 26, 1983, the Pastor of Vidukle, Father Alfonsas Svarinskas, was arrested, and at the homes of the Pastor of Valkininkai, Father Algimantas Keina and the Associate Pastor of Telšiai, Father Jonas Kauneckas, searches were carried out. Since these priests belong to the Catholic Committee for the Defense of Believers' Rights, it is a sign that a campaign has begun against the Committee.
>
> We protest against this action on the part of the USSR Prosecutor's Office, and especially against the arrest of Father Alfonsas Svarinskas, since neither in the activites of the Catholic Committee, nor in those of Father Alfonsas Svarinskas personally, was there anything anti-State or anti-Constitutional.
>
> We repeatedly emphasize that the Catholic Committee's purpose is to strive that the faithful of Lithuania have at least as many rights as do the atheists of Lithuania, supported by the state and fighting against the Church. Can this activity be considered anti-Constitutional, when the Constitution of the USSR guarantees all citizens equal rights regardless of nationality, race or religion? (Par. 34)
>
> Father Alfonsas Svarinskas' arrest evoked the greatest outrage among the faithful. The faithful constituting a majority in the Lithuanian SSR, are asking: What does the arrest of the most zealous priests mean? Is it perhaps a declaration of open warfare against the Church?
>
> In 1874, Friedrich Engels called open war against religion madness, and stated that this was the best way of reviving interest in religion. His ideas were praised by Lenin (*Writings of Lenin,* Vol. 17, pp. 415-426). The juridical persecution of Father Svarinskas will confirm the idea of Engels and Lenin, as it was confirmed eleven years earlier by the trials of three Priests: Juozas Zdebskis, Prosperas Bubnys and Antanas Šeškevičius. From that time, the Catholic Church in Lithuania has experienced a renaissance.
>
> Members of the Catholic Committee for the Defense of Believers' Rights:
>
> Docent Vytautas Skuodis (in labor camp)

Fathers:
Alfonsas Svarinskas (in prison)
Leonas Kalinauskas
Algimantas Keina
Vaclovas Stakenas
Sigitas Tamkevicius
Vincas Velavicius
Kazimieras Zilys[13]

The imprisonment of Fathers Svarinskas and Tamkevicius (sentenced to 6 years in camp) was proof that Yury Andropov was not that gentleman that many thought, especially in the West. The *Chronicle LCC* already warned in the preceding issue (no. 56) that "pressure from Moscow mounts." Notwithstanding some gestures apparently indicating good will, like the reinstatement and return of Bishop Sladkevicius to his diocese, and the nomination of a Latvian Cardinal, the Council for Religious Affairs was increasing its campaign to have priests implement the Regulations for Religious Associations, manipulate their elections, and for failing to do so, priests and bishops were warned, reprimanded, called "extremists" or even fined:

At the beginning of December 1982, the official of the Council for Religious Affairs assigned to Catholic Matters came from Moscow to Lithuania. He visited the seminary, the bishops and even some of the deans, trying to convince them that it would be better for the priests if Church affairs were run not by priests, but by parish "executive organs."

In order that the will among Lithuanian priests to resist the Regulations for Religious Associations might be dissipated, Father Alfonsas Svarinskas, Pastor of Vidukle, and a member of the Catholic Committee for the Defense of Believers' Rights, was arrested. The most important reasons for the arrest were the following:

The courageous stance of priests in Lithuania is arousing the greatest concern on the part of the Soviet government. The arrest of one of the boldest priests was supposed to instill fear in the rest and to force them to heed the Regulations for Religious Associations.

Functionaries of the Council for Religious Affairs blame the Catholic Committee for the Defense of Believers' Rights more than anything for "religious extremism"; that is for obeying Canon Law instead of the Regulations for Religious Associations. The KGB considered Father Alfonsas Svarinskas as the soul of this Committee, so his arrest was bound to contribute to the paralyzing of the Committee's work.

The Soviet government in Lithuania has always reacted paranoically to any events which disturbed it; e.g., processions to Siluva, youth groups, etc. The arrest of Father Svarinskas shows clearly that the Soviet government feels very weak, and sees a mortal enemy in the Catholic Church in Lithuania and in every active clergyman.

With the approach of the Jubilee of Saint Casimir and the 600th Anniversary of the introduction of Christianity into Lithuania, a spiritual revival can be felt in the nation. The Soviet government, wishing to paralyze this revival, put all means of propaganda to work and when these did not help, they called on the KGB to help stifle the most zealous priests in Lithuania. Nevertheless, the enemies of the Church always make a serious mistake: Guillotines, scaffold and labor camps always rouse the Church to new life.

Vilnius

On May 22-23, 1984, ballots were being counted in the election of representatives to the Priest's Council of the Archdiocese of Vilnius. When Religious Affairs Commissioner Petras Anilionis was informed of the results of the voting, he severely reprimanded the administrator of the archdiocese, Father Algirdas Gutauskas, for conforming with the directive of Bishop Julijonas Steponavičius to conduct the elections by secret ballot, and for not interfering with the election to the Priests' Council of Fathers Algimantas Keina, Jonas Lauriunas and Donatas Valiukonis.

Anilionis told Administrator Gutauskas whom he was supposed to appoint to the Priests' Council, and who should constitute the board of consultors. Of those elected to membership in the council, only one priest is suitable for the board of consultors in the opinion of Anilionis. Eight priests were elected to the Priests' Council, but Anilionis is allowing only six; he refuses to acknowledge two of the priests elected, Kazimieras Vasiliauskas and Jordanas Šlenys. If the aforesaid priests join the Priests' Council in spite of the interdict, Anilionis said, he would immediately move Father Vasiliauskas out of Vilnius, and release compromising pictures of Father Šlenys in the press.

Anilionis threatened the Apostolic Administrator of the Archdiocese of Vilnius, Bishop Julijonas Steponavičius, that for interfering in what was not his business (i.e., the makeup of the Archdiocesan Priests' Council and Board of Consultors—Ed. Note), he would be exiled from Žagare to a place where no one would be able to reach him. The commissioner was annoyed because priests of the archdiocese visit their bishop and associate with him.

Similarly, Anilionis pressured Panevėžys Diocesan Adminstrator, Kazimieras Dulksnys, directing him how to put together a Priests' Council and Board of Consultors acceptable to atheists.

Kaunas

In May, 1984, the Deans of the Archdiocese of Kaunas and the Diocese of Vilkaviškis were summoned to a meeting with Religious Affairs Commissioner, Petras Anilionis. The Commissioner devoted his lecture to justifying the conviction of Alfonsas Svarinskas and Sigitas Tamkevičius. He argued that even in "bourgeois" Lithuania, priests were put on trial.

Anilionis urged the deans to acknowledge the convicted priests, Alfonsas Svarinskas and Sigitas Tamkevičius, as state criminals, and in return, he promised to consider the possibility of increasing the number of students admitted to the seminary.

In his talk, Anilionis expressed dissatisfaction with the behavior of the deans of the Archdiocese of Kaunas and the Diocese of Vilkaviškis: It seems that what he had said to them a year ago had all been transmitted to the Vatican, "and you can't call that anything but swinish behavior!" Anilionis angrily ended his lecture.[14]

The propaganda of the representatives of the Department for Religious Affairs among the parish committees (dvatzatka) and the Priests' Councils continued in the following months (see *Chronicle* no. 58), so that now more people had changed their mind about the "new course" of Brezhnev's successor. But some were still having doubts about the way the "extremists" were fighting.

The plight of the Church in Lithuania has significantly deteriorated since Yuri Andropov assumed power. The best priests are being blackmailed, threatened with imprisonment, and the like. People collecting signatures to protests are being rounded up and penalized, and the faithful—children as well as adults—are being investigated. Atheistic propaganda and anti-clerical libel are widespread. The press and television explain that children under eighteen may not serve Mass, participate in processions or sing in choirs. People are being interrogated and penalized for organizing Christmas celebrations (in Simnas, Prienai and Kybartai) and All Souls' Day processions.

Teachers and in some places even militia lurk about the churches to see whether children are not being prepared for First Communion. Sometimes, children are stopped in the street on the suspicion that they are on their way to catechism class. The more government atheists persecute the Faith within the country, the more they try afterwards to convince public opinion abroad of the complete freedom of religion in Lithuania. They let bishops out of Lithuania for *ad limina* visits to Rome and put priests in jail.

Peace delegations of priests travel about to various congresses, while in Lithuania there is the greatest pressure to comply with the so-called Regulations for Religious Associations, which are intended for the complete destruction of the Church.

Efforts of the Church in Lithuania to regain its constitutional rights appear, humanly speaking, to be hopeless; the government is not responding to any protests, nor is it replying to petitions signed by scores of thousands; the faithful are discriminated against; the ranks of the clergy are thinning, and the number of parishes which have no priest is increasing.

At this critical moment, Lithuania is losing two of its most zealous priests, Father Alfonsas Svarinskas and Sigitas Tamkevičius.

Keeping in mind all of the above, the question arises in the mind of more than one person: Was it necessary? Was it not possible to get along without this sacrifice?

Of course, these two Lithuania priests could have avoided arrest and imprisonment if they had been blind to the injustices perpetrated against the faithful, if they had remained deaf to the voices of those calling for help, and, in the words of the old Lithuanian expression, rested quietly under the broom, keeping their own comfortable spot, as more than one is doing today. But is that everything? As true shepherds, they could not act otherwise.

Some consider them imprudent for such boldness....

To Father Alfonsas Svarinskas and Father Sigitas Tamkevičius, currently in prison, Harnack's words apply, "There is something greater than freedom; it is truth." Yes, they could not put up with lying, of which there is so much among us today, and they struggled for the truth, thereby losing their freedom.

Everone is probably acquainted with the statement by the world-renowned Jewish scientist, Albert Einstein, "I was never interested in the Church, but now I feel a great respect and sympathy for it, because only the Church has the courage and tenacity to defend the truth and human freedom. As a lover of freedom, I thought that when Hitler seized power in Germany, at least the universities would defend freedom, since they are, after all, the disseminators of truth. But the universities were silent. Then I thought that freedom would be defended by newspaper editors, who used to write powerful articles on behalf of freedom. But after a few weeks, they too fell silent. Only the Church stood in Hitler's way the whole time, when he wanted to crush truth and destroy freedom." It is like this in Lithuania today. It is mostly the priests who are struggling against the lies being spread by every means.[15]

Unless a priest accepts becoming a collaborator and/or an informer, disobedience to the rules, written and non-written, of militant atheistic regimes is unavoidable. One of the most important services of religious dissent is to reveal and denounce this multifaceted and hidden action of the

Communists, who prefer to destroy the Church from within. During the festivities in honor of St. Casimir very few major pilgrimages were organized, due to the "prudent" suggestions of some clergymen not to provoke the police. For the same reason some pastors were reluctant to invite outside preachers, and if somebody dared on his own, at the most important moments the lights and the microphones didn't work.

Everyone knows that the pastor is the authority in his own church, and that no one can act without his permission. However, under special conditions, zealous priests in Lithuania without wishing to hurt the pastors or cause them unpleasantness, speak from the pulpit without permission from the pastor. If you ask the pastor for permission, it will be embarassing for him not to allow it; if the pastor allows it, then a great share of the responsibility for the sermon delivered will fall on his shoulders. A good priest would rather assume the risk himself, unwilling to have another blamed for his actions. . . .

During the closing ceremonies of the Saint Casimir Jubilee, August 30, after the evening Mass, the pastor of Pociuneliai, Father Antanas Jokubauskas, ascended the pulpit. The preacher had hardly begun to speak when from the sacristy emerged the pastor, Docent Pranciškus Vaičekonis, an instructor at the Kaunas seminary, shouting and gesticulating for the organ to play, and for the people to disperse. The congregation, however, would not budge, and the organ remained silent. The preacher continued to speak calmly. Losing control, the pastor rushed to the microphone in the sanctuary, telling him not to interfere with the sermon.

Seeing that the people were not dispersing and that the priest continued preaching, Dr. Vaičekonis began excoriating Father Jokubauskas, "People, do not recognize him! The church is no place for rallies! . . . "

Suddenly, the lights began to go out one after another and the church grew dark. When Father Jokubauskas began speaking about the imprisoned priests, the pastor sent two men in surplices to escort the preacher from the pulpit. The men in surplices had hardly begun ascending the pulpit when someone from the crowd suddenly jumped up, restraining one of the functionaries. However, the first had already reached the preacher, and touched him. Father Jokubauskas, making the Sign of the Cross, turned to descend. At that moment, the pastor charged into the crowd, trying to push his way to the pulpit. The faithful at first made way, but suddenly the crowd pushed forward and forced the excited pastor into the sanctuary.

As Father Jokubauskas left the pulpit, the congregation began to applaud. In Lithuania, it is not the custom to applaud in church, however, because there was no other way of showing agreement with the preacher, the faithful, regardless of tradition, applauded so thunderously that one could not hear the pastor loudly scolding the crowd and the preacher. As soon as the applause died down, the pastor reprimanded the faithful and the preacher even louder. To drown out the pastor, the people resumed their applause. And so it went, back and forth. Seeing that the pastor would not stop scolding, the crowd began singing the hymn, *Marija, Marija.* It was a sad and frightening experience. It would have been better to see a militiaman or some government official pushing a priest around, or striking him.

Why did the pastor silence Fr. Jokubauskas? What did he say? He affirmed that the faithful are not allowed to fear sacrifice, even death, if fidelity to the Church and God requires it. Indeed, what is an idea worth if one is unwilling to sacrifice and die for it? He mentioned those who are already walking the way of sacrifice: the priest-prisoners Alfonsas Svarinskas and Sigitas Tamkevičius.

(Here the rest of the lights were extinquished, and the preacher was escorted out.)

Is it possible to attach a political meaning to these words? Yes, it is politics, but it is the politics of Christ, the Church, God and only God! The preparation of priests is the exclusive responsibility of the ecclesiastical hierarchy, and not of the civil government! The atheists, by the most refined trickery and deceit, are overtly wrecking the Church in our hearts. Only the cowardly and the naive can fail to see this! To detest the work of the devil—sin—is the Catholic's calling, the theme of St. Casimir's life! Unity with those suffering is a duty of neighborly love. (Our Holy Father acted no differently by remembering Lithuania so sensitively these days.) To visit the prisoner is a good work. We visit prisoners by constant prayer and frequent remembrance of their honorable sacrifice. We have no other means...

And here Father Kazimieras Vaičionis, speaking during evening services, August 24, declared that the fact that Lithuania was incorporated in the Soviet Union is a blessing from God! Is this not politics?

So we are in a tragic situation. We are urged to pray for unity, but under what flag: that of Christ's Truth or atheistic politics? We want our lives to be lived only under the banner of Christ, to that end we are doing everything, often at great risk.

Postscript: On June 29, in the Church of SS. Peter and Paul, during a religious festival, Father Vaičionis tried to say in a sermon that there is no need for petitions or collecting of signatures—that this only hurts the Catholic Church. So this time, we merely state the above-mentioned painful fact (We cannot remain silent, we hear the voice of conscience, we believe that by keeping silent we would do wrong), without collecting signatures, even though we could.[16]

The above mentioned "painful fact" brings up the question of the pro-Communist priests, which in Lithuania, due to the vigilance of not only the dissidents, but also of the majority of the clergy and the faithful, is less serious than in other Communist countries, as for instance Czecho-slovakia, and now also in Latin America and Asia. In the past years I heard priests put the blame on the Holy See for its silence on this question, for not giving clear guidance to the bishops, and for occasionally dealing directly with these pro-Communist priestly associations. Now Pope John Paul II, introducing another change in his Ostpolitik, has clarified this question. On March 8-9, 1982, the Vatican newspaper *L'Osservatore Romano* published a Declaration of the Sacred Congregation for the Clergy, in which was stressed the inopportunity for members of the clergy to participate in political movements or trade union organizations alien to the nature of their ministry. Ten days later, on March 18, the same congregation answered to Cardinal Frantisek Tomasek of Prague that the Czechoslovakian associa-tion "Pacem in terris" was to be included among those described in the Declaration. Due to the furious attacks of the Czechoslovakian press against the Holy Father and the inhuman treatment of the dissidents and believers,[17] Pope John Paul II instructed the Secretary of State, Cardinal Agostino Casaroli, to write more extensively to Cardinal Tomasek on the question of peace. Consistently with his two first encyclicals, wrote Cardinal Casaroli, the Pope wants true peace, the one which is based on truth and the respect for human rights[18].

In 1985 the Czechoslovakian Church marked the 1100th anniversary of the death of St. Methodius whose relics are kept in Moravia. After receiving many petitions from the faithful, Cardinal Tomasek, in a letter of April 11, 1984, informed the government that he invited the Pope to visit Czechoslovakia. The same month the Cardinal criticized *Tribuna,* the weekly of the Central Committee of the Czech Communist Party, for calling the Pope "one of the most reactionary pontiffs of the century." In a letter to *Tribuna* the Cardinal wrote: "Your atheism doesn't give you the right to calumniate and offend people with other ideological views." In this climate of tensions and persecutions the visit of the Pope didn't take place. But in a message, made public by the Vatican April 10, 1985, John Paul II encouraged the Czechoslovakian clergy to minister to their fellow countrymen even during "difficult and sometimes bitter" historical times: "It is necessary to continue fearlessly along the way of evangelization and witness . . . Your nation, Europe and the whole world are in need of the truth and salvation, and they turn to the Catholic Church, to the priests and Religious." The "Religious" mentioned by the Pope are monks or members of Orders and Congregations, all suppressed by law in Czechoslovakia.

* * *

We saw how the dissidents, especially in Poland and the Soviet Union, help each other in a powerful manifestation of solidarity. The *Chronicle of the Catholic Church in Lithuania,* for instance, always remembers among "our prisoners" Sergei Kovalyov, a Russian who got a very harsh sentence only because he helped the *Chronicle* to continue its publication. Under the title "The Church in the Soviet Republics" the *Chronicle* publishes valuable information about Eastern Rite Catholics in Ukraine and Byelorussia, where they are completely suppressed. Here is what the *Chronicle* writes about Ukrainian Catholics in the region of Lvov:

> On September 27, 1981, in the Uniate Catholic church of Dobrianych, the patronal feast of the church was in progress. (Nowhere in Ukraine are Uniate Catholic churches licensed by the government.) KGB agents and militia surrounded the church, and waited for the arrival of the Uniate Catholic priest. When he did not arrive, they broke into the church and began to look for the priest there. The chekists' attention was drawn by the people who were more actively praying, especially the servers. Later they were all given fines.
>
> In 1982, before Easter, the Uniate Catholic church of Morshyn was burglarized. Pupils of the vocational school, herded into church, gathered up all the liturgical vessels, vestments and icons, piled them into automobiles and drove off with them.
>
> In the spring of 1982, in the Village of Berezhany, a meeting of the residents took place. Participating in the meeting were about thirty KGB agents who threatened the people in various ways to stop gathering in the Uniate Catholic church to pray, or at

least to convert to the orthodox religion. "Otherwise, your church shall be closed," threatened the KGB agents. Upon leaving, the chekists sealed up all the liturgical vessels in the church.

Before Easter, 1982, KGB agents attacked the Uniate Catholic church of Brikunai. Part of the liturgical vestments and icons they destroyed on the spot, the others they took away. The church was robbed at a time when most of the faithful were working. Women who tried to defend the church were badly beaten by the burglars—some of them had to be hospitalized.[19]

Fr. Alfonsas Svarinskas was filled with great joy by a letter from Joseph Cardinal Slipyj, proclaimed by his people Patriarch of the Ukrainian Catholic Church, living in exile in Rome. Fr. Svarinskas was 21 when he received his first sentence to the camps on December 31, 1946. He was still in the *Gulag,* Abeze, on October 4, 1954, when he was ordained secretly to the priesthood by bishop Ramanauskas. In 1958 he got another sentence for six years. At one time the camp administration decided to lock him up in a small area intended for especially dangerous individuals who could have a "negative influence" on other prisoners. It was there that Fr. Svarinskas met a number of zealous priests, among them Archbishop Joseph Slipyj. When the old Cardinal heard in Rome about the new arrest of his friend, he wrote to the priests and faithful of Vidukle the following letter:

> The circumstances and reasons for the arrest of Father Alfonsas Svarinskas are not known, but one thing is certain: This dedicated priest, loyal to the Church of Christ and the gospel of Christ, has committed no crime, neither against the state nor against the law. The only offense which can be ascribed to him by those who are prejudiced is love of God and people, service of neighbor, and the carrying out of Christ's command to preach the gospel throughout the world. What is Father Svarinskas being punished for?
>
> Twenty years ago, we used to meet often with Father Svarinskas. We were both bearing the harness of prisoners in the "katorga" (penal labor—trans. note) when we were arrested and sentenced to a strict regime camp; we both bore the same cross of suffering, humiliation and terror. Fr. Svarinskas was very patient and loyal like Titus to whom the Apostle Paul wrote. From him I experienced much comfort, strength and sustinence. Father Svarinskas is the pride and glory of the Catholic Church in Lithuania and of the Lithuanian nation.
>
> The news of his arrest and his impending sentence is very painful, but it reminds us of Christ's apostles. When the apostles were arrested and scourged, they left the council, rejoicing that in Jesus's name they had earned opprobrium. For this arrest we express our deepest sympathy to Father Svarinskas and to the Lithuanian nation which is losing a zealous priest, but at the same time, praise be to God that He has granted this courageous Confessor of the Faith the grace of witnessing Jesus Christ the Redeemer in the chains of oppression. The voice of confessors bound by the chains of oppression is very powerful, when they proclaim freedom and truth in Jesus Christ.... May the merciful Lord lead Father Svarinskas along his way of suffering. May our prayer obtain from him strength and comfort. I wish you the blessings of the Lord.[20]

The Lithuanian dissident priests suffered when they were accused by Rome of being "extremists"and elements of "division." Cardinal Slipyj, too, suffered when Rome wanted to sacrifice him and his people in exchange for Soviet empty promises. But things began to change. Soon after the election of John Paul II, Cardinal Slipyj issued a declaration in which he recalled what Cardinal Wojtyla had said just a year before: "It is impossible to take away from a man his rights to the truth." And added: "From these words we may conclude that he (the Pope) will be a courageous defender of the divine truth and of the human rights in the world. Among those who are most in need of these rights is our Church and our Ukrainian people, who for years have tried to obtain these rights, unfortunately without due help and understanding. We hope now to have this help; it is especially awaited by our Ukrainian Church. The burdensome and thorny way of the Polish Catholic Church during the last decades gave him a great experience, which people don't and didn't have in the West. . . . It is true that the Polish hierarchy, to which, in Poland, our Ukrainian Catholic Church is subordinate, so far has not expressed signs of understanding for us, but now, in the world's eye, Pope Wojtyla . . . will certainly look at the meaning of our Church and the other Eastern Churches in that uneven struggle with atheism, in the efforts for a true and sincere ecumenism and for the rights of the peoples and the individuals" (October 17, 1978).

The answer of the Pope came in his Apostolic letter of March 19, 1979, which announced the celebration in 1988 of the millennium of Christianity in Ukraine. After interesting historical reflections, John Paul II touched the important question of the "juridical unification" of the Ukrainian Church, which he thought could be obtained "gradually, taking into account all the canonical, historical and other circumstances," until it would be possible to achieve "a more complete solution."

Meanwhile the Pope summoned the Ukrainian Catholic bishops to an extraordinary synod, which met March 24, 1980, in the Vatican and over which he presided. The main purpose of this gathering was the election of a coadjutor with the right of succession to His Beatitude Cardinal Slipyj. "With the decision to call for such an election, the Pope has also granted the Ukrainian Catholic Church recognition of the long-desired *Pomisnist* or self-government in the manner of a particular Eastern Church, as the Major Archiepiscopate of Lviv of the Ukrainians."[21] From among the three candidates presented to him by the bishops, the Supreme Pontiff appointed the Most Rev. Myroslav Ivan Lubachivsky, Metropolitan of Philadelphia (USA), since he had received the highest number of votes. On the question of "why the appointment of a coadjutor" Archimandrite Victor J. Pospishil writes:

> We can surmise that possible repercussions in Ukraine of a vacancy in the post of the Major Archbishop of Lviv could have suggested the appointment of a coadjutor with the right to automatically succeed His Beatitude Josyf.

It had been speculatively mentioned that a "Greek-Catholic" or "Ukrainian Catholic" church could be recognized in Galicia by the Soviet government, which could limit such a "Church" in the number of faithful as well as activity and then demand from the Holy See the appointment as Archbishop of Lviv of any priest residing there, knowing full well that he would be under the government's control. The Pope could not easily refuse such a request. However, once such a major archbishop would begin to assert his primatial jurisdiction or authority over all Ukrainian Catholics in the world, pressured into it by the Soviet government, he would cause a split in the Ukrainian community around the globe, as has happened with the Serbian Orthodox Patriarchate of Yugoslavia and its faithful in the Free World, and as was the fate of the Romanian Orthodox Church in the United States, Canada, Australia, etc. Separate hierarchies or sets of bishops have been established for the warring factions, and in nearly every parish have been formed two groups of these churches which battle each other in civil courts with great loss of money and spiritual harm to the members and the churches.

It can be conjectured that this dreadful possibility motivated the Pope to prevent any further split by making certain that there would be no vacancy in the post of Major Archbishop of Lviv and head of the Ukrainian Catholic Church.[22]

Taking advantage of the new juridical situation, the Ukrainian bishops asked and obtained permission to have a synod to discuss the preparation of the millennium of Christianity in Ukraine, the ecumenical collaboration with the Ukrainian Orthodox Church in the diaspora, the printing of liturgical books, etc. The synod, presided over by Cardinal Slipyj, took place in Rome from November 25 to December 2, 1980. On the last day the 15 bishops present in view of the coming Christmas' festivities wrote a pastoral letter to the Ukrainian Catholics at home and all over the world and signed a declaration in which they reaffirmed the invalidity of the so-called *Synod of Lviv* of 1946 which, according to the Russian Orthodox Church, broke the unity with Rome. With no Catholic bishops present at that *Synod* (they were all imprisoned) and the majority of the faithful opposed, the unity of the Ukrainian Catholic Church with Rome was never broken and the return of this Church into the bosom of the "Mother Church of Moscow" never took place.[23]

As soon as the news of the declaration reached Moscow, Patriarch Pimen wrote to Rome, asking John Paul II (December 22) to "take steps in order not to validate this Declaration . . . ," dangerous to the good relations between the Churches of Rome and Moscow. The Pope answered saying that the declaration was still not submitted to his approval, that the Vatican advised its *Nunziature* of the fact that the text published was not official and its circulation should be avoided, although the Holy See was still "firm on the positions always maintained regarding the rights of the Ukrainian Catholics" (January 24, 1981). This letter is very interesting: it still shows the duplicity and quibbles of the old Ostpolitik, and at the same time the forthright and honest style of John Paul II. On his part Patriarch Josyf Slipyj expressed his satisfaction and assured that he would do anything "to favor a sincere and honest ecumenical dialogue, which presupposes the acknowledgement and full respect of our rights and of the truth."

The synodal declaration of December 2, 1980, marks a turning point in Vatican Ostpolitik and consequently in the history of the Ukrainian Catholic Church too. From now on (namely after the proclamation by John Paul II of *truth* and *human rights* as the guiding principles also in the relations with the Communist regimes) no more silence about oppression and persecution under the pretext of not harming Christians living in the catacombs. No more inferiority complex on the part of Rome and the Churches in union with her, before the Church of Moscow, supported—as Solzhenitsyn pointed out in his letter to Pimen—by an atheistic super-power, and "preserved . . . with the lie . . . certainly not for Christ." No more fears that the long-suffering Ukrainian Catholic Church could seriously constitute an obstacle to a sincere ecumenical dialogue between members of truly free Christian Churches. No more feelings of isolation and abandonment among the Ukrainian Catholics in Poland, where they don't have a bishop (while the Orthodox have several) and are not sufficiently supported by the Latin rite bishops.

After World War II the East European Communist countries, following the example of Stalin, suppressed the Eastern Rite Catholic Churches. Accepting this situation, the Vatican Ostpolitik, till recently, was directed, at least openly, only toward the betterment of the lot of the Latin rite Catholics. Now John Paul II, in his love for *truth* and *human rights* everywhere, has turned his attention to the Eastern Rite Churches united with Rome, whose bishops were murdered or exiled. This is also true in Poland, as Cardinal Slipyj reminded the newly elected Pope, who did not forget the frank lament of the old Patriarch. From June 21 to July 7, 1984, by order of John Paul II, the Ukrainian Archbishop Myroslav Marusyn, Secretary of the Congregation for the Eastern Churches, visited the Ukrainian communities in Poland and ordained five new priests. Reading his report,[24] I was very much impressed by the great number of Polish bishops he visited and by the very warm reception he received: they knew who was sending this Ukrainian Archbishop. . . . At the beginning of August of the same year, a big group of 130 young Ukrainians from Poland chose freedom while on a pilgrimage to Rome. In interviews, published by the Austrian and German press, they complained that in Poland the Ukrainian Catholics are still considered second-class Catholics, there are no Ukrainian schools, people are still deported to the Soviet Union or murdered.[25]

On September 7, 1984, Patriarch Josyf Slipyj died at the age of 92. He will be remembered as a great leader of the Ukrainian people. He was admired and respected especially by the Soviet dissidents of every nationality, as I personally witnessed when he spoke at Sakharov's hearings in Rome. In his testament he remembers his fellow prisoners with these words:

"Sitting on the sleigh..." my thoughts extend to all my brothers and sisters in Ukraine and the vast expanses of the whole Soviet Union, to those who suffer in freedom and to those who languish in jails, prisons, hard labour camps or death camps... In their midst I can see new ranks of fighters, scientists, writers, artists, farm workers and labourers. I can see among them those who search for truth and those who defend justice. I can hear their voices raised in defence of the basic human rights of the individual and nations. I watch them with wonder and see how they defend our native Ukrainian word, how they enrich our native Ukrainian culture, and how with the full power of their minds and hearts they save the Ukrainian soul. And I suffer alongside them, for they are persecuted for this as common criminals.

I pray for you, my Brothers, and ask God to grant you strength to carry on defending the natural and Divine rights of every individual human being and of the whole society. I extend my blessings to you as the Head of the Ukrainian Church, as a Son of the Ukrainian nation, as your brother, your fellow prisoner and your co-sufferer![26]

When Cardinal Slipyj was writing this testament in Ukraine, a young man, Josyf Terelya, was gathering an initiative group for the defense of the rights of the believers and the Church. The members of this group, among them some priests, in January 1984 began to publish a "Chronicle of the Catholic Church in Ukraine." Terelya was again arrested, and again a Russian young Orthodox woman, Yelena Sannikova, wrote to the Pope a beautiful letter, asking help for this "magnificent man" and his persecuted Church. She admired this friend because he was "ready to give his life for his Church and for his friends,"[27] but she must also be a determined, strong young lady: on October 10, at the age of 25, she received one year of hard work in the camp and 4 years of exile. George Zarycky writes in *The Christian Science Monitor* (March 6, 1985) that the *Chronicle* "could prove to be a source of considerable embarrassment to the Kremlin. Ironically, it could also be a nettlesome factor in the Vatican's strategy regarding the Soviet Union and Eastern Europe":

The appearance of the Chronicle, eight issues of which have been smuggled out of the USSR, offers disquieting proof to the Soviets that four decades of vigorous persecution, coupled with the efforts of an elaborate atheist propaganda apparatus, have failed to quash the church or dampen the faith of its followers. The tales of arrests, trials, and acts of civil disobedience outlined in the journal strongly suggest a marked resurgence of the church, particularly in the rural and rugged Transcarpathian region bordering Czechoslovakia, Hungary, and Poland.

Paradoxically, the widespread renaissance of the church, which signed a union with Rome in 1596, may prove somewhat awkward for Pope John Paul II. He is an avowed champion of Roman Catholicism in the Eastern bloc and the man most responsible for emboldening Ukrainian Catholics and other persecuted Christians in Eastern Europe to profess their faith openly.

For decades the Vatican has had to play a delicate balancing act with Moscow, virtually writing off the Uniate Church in the Ukraine in order to secure safeguards for Latin-rite Catholics in Lithuania and Poland...

The appearance of the Chronicle, and the resilience of the Ukrainian Catholic Church it represents, might force the Vatican to reevaluate this strategy.

The journal itself consists primarily of reports documenting repression against Uniate activists in western Ukraine. First published in January 1984, it was set up in 1982 by former political prisoner Yosyp Terelia to work for the legalization of the Ukrainian Catholic Church and to publicise the plight of its members.

The monthly issues have also included details on the persecution of Baptists, Jehovah's Witnesses, Pentecostals, and other Protestant denominations, as well as reports on activities by the KGB (the Soviet secret police), incidents of armed resistance and sabotage, the number of men from Transcarpathia killed in Afghanistan, and the arrest of several Ukrainian Red Army officers for allegedly ploting to assassinate the late Soviet defense minister, Dmitry Ustinov.

Perhaps the most poignant accounts are those describing individual cases of persecution and suffering. There is the case of a man in the village of Dolgoye who was arrested in January 1984, severely beaten, and sentenced to two years in a labor camp for taking part in a traditional Christmas play. In another incident, young carolers in the small village of Lisichevo were attacked and beaten by militiamen.

The Chronicle details worsening conditions in psychiatric hospitals and labor camps, where men and women sentenced for religious activities are regularly placed in solitary confinement or tortured to get them to renounce their faith.

One labor camp, VL 315/30 in Lvov, is reportedly located on the site of a former Nazi concentration camp where 70,000 Jews and 42,000 Ukrainians, Russians, Frenchmen, Belgians, and Gypsies were murdered. Today the camp houses 300 Catholics, 29 Baptists, two Pentecostals, 15 Jehovah's Witnesses, five Seventh Day Adventists, and 39 Orthodox believers, according to the Chronicle.

The Chronicle also reports that some 900 Ukrainian Catholics either burned or surrendered their internal passports to protest the persecution of Christianity by the Soviet government. Mr. Terelia is quoted as saying that he expected some 3,000 others to follow suit. In another action, 59 men from Transcarpathia, 18 of them Jehovah's Witnesses, were recently convicted for refusing, on religious grounds, to serve in the military.

Despite a concerted effort by Soviet authorities to eradicate the Uniates, the Chronicle provides evidence of continued vitality. It notes that from early 1981 to the beginning of last year, some 81 priests were secretly ordained in the Transcarpathian region alone, and that young children in the area receive a Christian education at an underground monastery.

The Chronicle appears at a time when the human-rights movement that gained momentum in the 1970s has been all but muted by arrests, deportations, and the exiling of dissidents to the far reaches of the country.

Moreover, the apparent revitalization of the Uniate Church in western Ukraine, historically a region of strong Ukrainian nationalism and deep-rooted anti-Soviet sentiment, must be disconcerting to the Soviets, because of the area's proximity to Poland. The Chronicle contains a letter from Terelia to Lech Walesa, leader of the banned Polish trade union Solidarity, in which he says that the struggle of the Polish nation for freedom "is the hope which gives us strength for the resistance." The Ukrainian Catholic Church is legal in Poland, where there is a large Ukrainian minority. Any links between Ukrainian activists and their counterparts in Poland would surely make the Kremlin uneasy.

According to Keston College in London, which monitors religious activity in the communist world, some 50 percent of the members of unregistered Protestant churches in the Soviet Union live in the Ukraine, where they have been active despite official harassment.

Moscow has been trying to improve its image in the West, particularly as arms negotiations get under way. An underground journal depicting the brutal persecution of Christians will do little to enhance the nation's human-rights record. It seems likely that

information provided by the Chronicle will be cited by the United States and its NATO
allies at a meeting on human rights scheduled for this May in Ottawa.[28]

When, after years of cold relations, a meeting between the American
and Soviet Foreign Ministers was announced (Geneva, Jan. 7-8, 1985),
John Paul II welcomed it as "a glimmer of hope on the world's horizon."
But he also warned that no negotiations would be fruitful unless based on
"[a] few simple axioms," among them the "abandonment of egotistic or
ideological interests."[29] So far "peaceful coexistence" has not worked
because it doesn't extend to ideology; ideologically Moscow is still at war.
The dissidents are the first victims of this continued war. Who can save
them? Can we do something for Andrei Sakharov, for Anatoly Shcharansky, for Fr. Alfonsas Svariskas, for Josyf Terelya? Many say yes. Among
them my good friend Anatoly Levitin-Krasnov, who continues to send
letters to Pope John Paul, the Ecumenical Patriarch, Cardinal Casaroli
and even to the General Superior of the Jesuits.[30] He wants them to help to
get his nephew Fr. Gleb Yakunin, and his disciples Vladimir Poresh and
Alexander Ogorodnikov, out from the Gulag. He takes this opportunity to
remind Cardinal Casaroli of his past mistakes, and to complain with Fr.
General Peter-Hans Kolvenbach that "some members of your Order flirt
with the Moscow Patriarchate and the K. G. B. which stands behind it." Fr.
Kolvenbach was the only one who answered Levitin-Krasnov.[31]

Pope John Paul II met for almost two hours, on February 26, 1985,
with Soviet Foreign Minister Andrei A. Gromyko for the first time in more
than six years. In a private conversation where there are not long speeches
and crowds who are listening, it is difficult to imagine that Gromyko spent
too many words on convincing the Pope that President Reagan's "Star
Wars" plan is bad. Gromyko was probably more interested in speaking and
hearing about Poland, while the Pope was more interested in hearing about
his non-trip to Lithuania and in summarizing the pile of petitions and
letters he received in six years from the Soviet Union. The conversation
could have gone on without end. At a certain moment when finally they
realized that what they were doing was not a dialogue, but a monologue
between two "deaf" men, they got up, smiled and exchanged their
"mementos."

Notes

Chapter 1

1. M.S. Agurski, "In difesa di Sakharov e Solzhenitsyn contro i fratelli Medvedev," in *Russia Cristiana* (Milano), 1974, No. 133, pp. 64-65. The author expressed the same ideas in his review of R. Medvedev's book on Stalinism: ibid., No. 131, p. 63.
2. A. Sakharov, *Sakharov Speaks,* pp. 116, 121, 134.
3. Z. Medvedev was put in a mental hospital for his works on "Biology and the Cult of Personality" and "Fruitful Meetings Between Scientists of the World" published abroad: see *The Medvedev Papers.* An account of Zhores' experience of the inhuman use of medicine for political purposes was published by the two brothers: Z. and R. Medvedev, *A Question of Madness.*
4. R. Medvedev, *Let History Judge.*
5. *The New York Times,* March 22, 1975.
6. A. Sakharov, op. cit., pp. 204, 213.
7. Ibid., p. 167.
8. *Russia Cristiana,* 1974, No. 133, p. 73.
9. A. Solzhenitsyn, *Nobel Lecture,* pp. 22-24.
10. *Russia Cristiana,* 1974, No. 133, pp. 75-76.
11. A. Sakharov, op. cit., p. 171.
12. *La Civiltà Cattolica* (Rome), March 1, 1930, pp. 388-391.
13. N. Struve, *Christians in Contemporary Russia,* pp. 379-390.
14. On Pius XI's work for Russia see C. Korolevskij, *Metropolite Andre Szeptyckyj,* pp. 248-259.
15. Connected with Russicum or inspired by Pope Pius XI's activity for Russia are the following Catholic research centers: 1) Belgium—The "Foyer Chrétien" of Bruxelles which published in the Russian language (Izdatel'stvo Zhizn' s Bogom) valuable works. Among them the writings of Vladimir Solovyov (16 volumes) and Vyacheslav Ivanov, and the *Slovar' Bibleiskogo Bogosloviya* (1974). The Benedictine Monks of Chevetogne publish the journal *Irenikon,* which follows closely the current religious life in the USSR. 2) France—The "Centre Dominicain des Etudes Russes" of Paris publishes the journal *Istina* of the highest intellectual and theological standard. 3) Italy—The "Centro Studi Russia Cristiana" of Milano publishes the journal *Russia Cristiana* which represents the best Catholic contribution to the research on civil and religious dissent in the USSR. Among the books edited by Russia Cristiana should be mentioned the translation of *Vekhi* and *Iz Glubiny* and the volume *"Samizdat. Cronaca di una vita nuova nell 'URSS."* 4) Germany—The Benedictine Ecumenical Institute of Niederalteich, founded by the Russian-born Fr. J. Chrysostomus, author of *Kirchengeschichte Russlands der neuesten Zeit* (3 vols.).
16. V. Ivanov, *Sobranie sochinenii,* pp. 197-198. The Russian poet taught Church Slavonic language at Russicum and at the Pontifical Oriental Institute in Rome.
17. *La Civiltà Cattolica,* March 1, 1930, pp. 385-387.
18. E.A. Walsh, "Why Pope Pius XI Asked Prayers for Russia on March 19, 1930," p. 26.
19. A. Rhodes, *The Vatican in the Age of the Dictators,* p. 139.
20. M. Sheinman, *Vatikan mezhdu dvumia voinami,* p. 40.

21. M. Sheinman, *Ot Piia IX do Ioanna XXIII*, pp. 107-113.
22. E. Vinter, *Papstvo i Tsarizm*, pp. 510-511.
23. See the protest of Dmitry Merezhkovsky in R. Graham, *Vatican Diplomacy*, p. 361.
24. A. Solzhenitsyn, *Gulag Archipelago*, p. 342.
25. R. Graham, *Vatican Diplomacy*, p. 362, and H. Stehle, *Die Ostpolitik des Vatikan*, pp. 28-29. About Stehle see K. Rudnytsky's article in *America*, Sept. 3, 1985.
26. A. Solzhenitsyn, *Gulag Archipelago*, p. 343.
27. Ibid., p. 347. For the 1932-33 famine in Ukraine see pp. 159-60.
28. *Russia Cristiana*, 1972, No. 121, pp. 71-76.
29. R. Graham, op. cit., p. 362.
30. A. Solzhenitsyn, op. cit., p. 344.
31. M. D'Herbigny, "L'aide pontifical aux enfants affamés de Russie," in *Orientalia Christiana* (Rome), 1924, No. 4. About Msgr. D'Herbigny's "mission" to Russia see R. Graham, op. cit., p. 368, and note 50.
32. A. Solzhenitsyn, op. cit., p. 37. On Mrs. Abrikosova, founder of a community of Dominican sisters in Moscow, her husband Father Vladimir, and their relations with Nikolai A. Berdiaev and other members of Russian intelligentsia see P. Mailleux, *Entre Rome et Moscou. L'exarque Leonid Feodoroff*, pp. 97-100.
33. On this trial see L. Gallagher, *Edmund Walsh, S.J., a Biography*, pp. 31-61.
34. P. Mailleux, op. cit.
35. J. Ledit, S.J., Archbishop John Cieplak.
36. Pius XI at the Concistory of May 23, 1923, in R. Graham, op. cit., p. 365.
37. R. Graham, op. cit., p. 358.
38. Ibid., p. 359.
39. G. Zizola, *L'Utopia di Papa Giovanni*, p. 176.
40. A. Rhodes, op. cit., p. 133.
41. A. Solzhenitsyn, *Gulag Archipelago*, p. 348.
42. Ibid., p. 344.
43. L: Gallagher, op. cit., p. 92.
44. Ibid., p. 93.
45. A. Sakharov, op. cit., 212-215.
46. L. Gallagher, op. cit., p. 63.
47. Ibid., p. 64.
48. Ibid., pp. 65-69.
49. A. Rhodes, op. cit., pp. 135-139.
50. H. Stehle, op. cit., pp. 100-204, 291-315.
51. R. Graham, op. cit., p. 351.
52. A. Aradi, Pius XI, pp. 159-160.
53. An attempt to demonstrate that Pius XI's knowledge of Marxism was insufficient and based on Stalin's deviations was made by Arturo Gaete in *Mensaje* (Santiago, Chile), June 1972. Gaete's article was translated into English by LADOC (Washington), January 1974, pp. 19-37.
54. Pius XI, *Divini Redemptoris*, Nos. 59 and 72. For the English translations of papal encyclicals we use the texts published by St. Paul Editions (Boston).
55. Samizdat. *Cronaca di una vita nuova nell'URSS*, p. 9, and Solzhenitsyn's speech to the AFL-CIO, in *The Wanderer* (St. Paul, Minn.), July 17, 1975.
56. Dmitri Nelidov, "La coscienza ideocratica e la persona," in *Russia Cristiana*, 1974, No. 135, p. 56.
57. Abram Terts, *Mysli vrasplokh*, p. 88.
58. Samizdat. *Cronaca di una vita nuova nell'URSS*, p. 13.
59. M. Bulgakov, *The Master and Margarita*, pp. 11-15 and 136. An interesting essay on Bulgakov's novel was written by Soviet religious dissenter A. Krasnov, "Khristos i Master," in *Grani* (Frankfurt, M.), Nos. 71-72, pp. 162-196 and 150-193.

60. Pius XII's broadcast to the World, August 24, 1939, in M. Chinigo, *The Pope Speaks,* pp. 324-325.

61. C.M. Cianfarra, *The Vatican and the War,* pp. 197-199.

62. *America* (New York), July 12, 1941, p. 367.

63. Ibid., pp. 373-374.

64. Pius XI, *Divini Redemptoris,* No. 58. For a new interpretation of this text see A. Gaete's article (note 53). The Pope's thought can be easily understood from what he affirms in No. 24:

> In making these observations it is no part of Our intention to condemn *en masse* the peoples of the Soviet Union. For them We cherish the warmest paternal affection. We are well aware that not a few of them groan beneath the yoke imposed on them by men who in very large part are strangers to the real interests of the country. We recognize that many others were deceived by fallacious hopes. We blame only the system, with its authors and abettors who considered Russia the best-prepared fields for experimenting with a plan elaborated decades ago, and who from there continue to spread it from one end of the world to the other.

65. *America,* September 6, 1941.

66. Ibid., September 20, 1941, pp. 649-650.

67. *Actes et Documents du Saint Siege,* vol. V, pp. 163-178. Msgr. Michael Ready of Cleveland, who accompanied Archbishop Mooney on his visit to Welles, wrote: "If guarantees of the freedoms that are dear to us can be obtained from Russia as a condition for our continued aid, not only would the dangers of the present position be obviated but its providential character would stand revealed," ibid., p. 174.

68. Ibid., p. 180.

69. Ibid., p. 183 ff. Another story was spread, in and outside the Soviet Union, that Pius XII and Hitler agreed that the Nazi invasion of the USSR would be a Holy War against Communism and, in return for moral support, the Catholic Church would be allowed to evangelize Russia (M. Sheinman, *Ot Piia IX do Ioanna XXIII,* pp. 106-115). Documents recently published prove just the opposite. Hitler and two of his top aids, Martin Borman and Arthur Rosenberg, were convinced that the Holy See was plotting to "gain, or re-gain, religious influence in Russia." The Nazis took a "countermeasure," approved by Hitler July 16, 1941, that no civilian priests or military chaplains would be allowed to minister to the people of the occupied territories: see R.A. Graham, S.J., "Come e perché Hitler bloccó il Vaticano in Russia," in *La Civiltà Cattolica,* Nov. 4 and Dec. 2, 1972, pp. 241-252 and 435-442.

70. M. Chinigo, op. cit., p. 343.

71. M. Sheinman, *Ot Piia IX do Ioanna XXIII,* pp. 115-116.

72. Ibid.

73. *Broadcast to the World,* December 23, 1956, in M. Chinigo, op. cit. pp. 325-326.

74. Ibid.

75. Ibid., pp. 344-345.

76. *Russia Cristiana,* May-June 1974, pp. 5-6.

77. A. Solzhenitsyn, *The First Circle,* pp. 148-149: "It was two days before the birthday of the Mother of God, and a long litany was sung in praise for her. The litany was infinitely eloquent, the attributes and praises of the Virgin Mary rolled forth in a torrent, and for the first time Yakonov understood the ecstasy and poetry of the prayer. No soulless church pedant had written that litany, but some great unknown poet, some prisoner in a monastery; and he had been moved not by passing lust for a woman's body but by that higher rapture a woman can draw from us."

78. A. Solzhenitsyn, *Nobel Lecture,* p. 23.

79. V. Maksimov, *Karantin,* pp. 85-87.

80. A. Galich, *Pokolenie obrechennykh,* pp. 286-287.

81. John XXIII, *Ad Petri Cathedram,* p. 43.

82. D.L. Pokhilevich, *Sovremennyi katolitsizm,* penultimate chapter, entitled "New Pope—Old Course."

83. A. Hatch, *His Name was John,* pp. 117-118.

84. G. Zizola, op. cit., pp. 297-301.

85. A. Hatch, op. cit., pp. 156-157.

86. The Soviet newspaper *Sovetskaia Rossiia* on August 26, 1959, reported an alleged declaration on the existence of freedom of religion in the USSR released by La Pira, who strongly denied it; see *Testimonianze* (Firenze) 1959, No. 17.

87. N. Cousins, *The Improbable Triumvirate,* p. 10 ff.

88. Ibid., p. 48.

89. John XXIII, *Mater et Magistra,* No. 239.

90. John XXIII, *Pacem in Terris,* Nos. 159-160.

91. N. Habegger, *Camilo Torres Prete e Guerrigliero,* p. 71. See also A. U. Floridi, "O Radicalismo Catolico Brasileiro," pp. 307-330 and document n. 3.

92. *La Civiltà Cattolica,* 1968, I, p. 435.

93. Paul VI, *Populorum Progressio,* No. 81.

94. Paul VI, *Octogesima Adveniens,* Nos. 31-34.

95. *L'Osservatore Romano* (Vatican City), June 19, 1971 and B. Sorge, *Capitalismo, scelta di classe, socialismo,* pp. 129-148.

96. Some of the dissenters are Marxists, others Christians, but all of them passed through the Soviet experience and their "dialogue" can be very helpful for the Western world. Solzhenitsyn reopened this dialogue in *Iz-pod glyb (From Under Ruins),* a volume of eleven essays to which contributed Igor Shafarevich, a world-famous algebraist, Mikhail Agurski, art historian Yevgeni Barabanov and historian Vadim Borisov. One of the two articles signed by Shafarevich is about socialism. Specifically, the book reaches back to a famous collection of articles called *Vekhi (Landmarks)* published in 1909. Among the contributors to *Vekhi* were Christian philosopher Nikolai Berdyayev, liberal politician Pyotr Struve and religious philosopher Semyon L. Frank. An article by Frank (1877-1950) on "The Problematic of a 'Christian Socialism,'" published in 1939, is still very much pertinent to today's situation. Frank's ideas are still inspiring Soviet Christian dissenters (see S.L. Frank, "La problematicita del 'socialismo cristiano'," in *Russia Cristiana,* 1973, No. 130, pp. 3-17.

97. *Moskovskaia Pravda,* September 30, 1973.

Chapter 2

1. *America* (N.Y.), December 1, 1973, p. 424 and Francis X. Murphy, *Vatican Politics: Structure and Function, in World Politics,* July 1974, pp. 542-559.

2. *The Month* (London), March 1973 and *National Catholic Register* (Fort Worth, Te.), June 24, 1973.

3. *America,* December 1, 1973, pp. 423-424.

4. *Vestnik Russkogo Studencheskogo Khristianskogo Dvizheniia* (Paris), No. 108-110 (1973), pp. 272-274.

5. *La Civiltà Cattolica* (Rome), July 21, 1973, pp. 171-172.

6. Robert A. Graham, S.J., "A Vatican Dilemma: Can Religion and Politics be Kept Separate?", in *Columbia* (New Haven, Conn.), October 1971, p. 8, and "Vatican State: A Stumbling Block to Ecumenism?", ibid., August 1975, p. 23.

7. Archbishop Benelli on the "Validity of Pontifical Diplomacy," in *L'Osservatore Romano* (English edition), March 23, 1972.

8. *The Pilot* (Boston), January 18, 1974.

9. *L'Osservatore Romano,* February 26, 1971.

10. Archbishop Casaroli was accompanied by Msgr. Achille Silvestrini, an official of the Vatican Secretariat of State, and Dr. John Kwaku Nimo, of the Council of the Laity.

11. *The Pilot,* February 27, 1971.
12. Archbishop Poggi's contacts with Communist governments are mainly related to the betterment of local Church-State relations. In January 1975 he went to Romania where the Eastern Rite Catholics are completely suppressed. On February 24 he started a month-long visit to Poland trying to persuade Cardinal Wyszinski to agree on the establishment of diplomatic relations between the Vatican and Poland's Communist regime. In July he went to Hungary.
13. Peter Hebblethwaite, "The Kissinger of the Vatican," in *The Critic* (Chicago), May-June 1974, pp. 26-34.
14. This and the following quotations are taken from different sources, mainly from *La Civiltà Cattolica,* March 20, 1971, pp. 593-602.
15. *National Catholic Register* (Huntington, Ind.), March 10, 1974.
16. *The Pilot,* February 2, 1973.
17. On the Vatican's new secrecy regulations see *New York Times,* March 15 and *The Pilot,* March 22, 1974. Three books in German on Vatican's Ostpolitik by W. Daim, R. Raffalt and H. Stehle were differently received by the public. The first is a shameless slander of the Roman Pontiffs and victims of Communism (see G. Codevilla's review in *L'Est* (Milano), 1973, No. 4, pp. 164-166). The second was criticized as a "fruit of fantasy" by *L'Osservatore Romano,* March 5, 1975. The third, more favorable to Vatican's policies, fails to recognize the value of underground Christians, the Church of silence and martyrdom (see P. Modesto's review in *Religiia i ateizm v SSSR,* Konigstein, April 1975, pp. 1-3).
18. *La Civiltà Cattolica,* March 20, 1971, pp. 593-602.
19. *The New York Times,* July 11 and October 22, 1975.
20. A. Amalrik, *Will the Soviet Union Survive until 1984?,* pp. 5-6, 55-58.
21. Ibid., p. 65.
22. *The Pope's Journey to the United States,* p. 109.
23. *The New York Times,* December 5, 1970.
24. *Catholic Standard* (Washington), July 26, 1973. When a pro-Maoist priest, Fr. Louis Wei Tsing-sing, published in Paris a book on the Holy See and China and expressed his views in a press-conference in Rome (November 1971) the Vatican qualified them as "personal opinions" (*Est & Quest,* Paris, 1975, n. 546).
25. *Fides* (Rome), March 31, 1973. See also the articles of V. Lapomarda (*S.J. News,* Boston, February 1974) and H. Dargan (*National Catholic Reporter,* Kansas City, June 20, 1975). The views of the *Fides* article were repeated and amplified at Louvain (Belgium) during an ecumenical colloquium on "Christian Faith and the Chinese Experience" (*The Pilot,* October 18, 1974).
26. *The New York Times,* April 19, 1973.
27. *The Pilot,* May 18, 1973.
28. *Twin Circle* (Fort Worth, Tx.), June 8, 1973. Fr. Raymond de Jaegher, director of the Public Relations' office of the archdiocese of Taipei in New York said that Cardinal Yupin attempted several times to convince Pope Paul VI to condemn Chinese communism, but never succeeded.
29. A. Solzhenitsyn, *Nobel Lecture,* pp. 24-25, 34.
30. *The Pilot,* May 30, 1975.
31. *La Civiltà Cattolica,* August 4 and 18, 1973, pp. 286-298.
32. *Relazioni Internazionali* (Milano), February 12, 1972, pp. 161-165.
33. *The Tablet* (London), November 10, 1973, pp. 1075-6.
34. L. Capodistria, "Il caso Mihajlov," in *Russia Cristiana,* May-June 1975, pp. 67-70.
35. *The Pilot,* May 20, 1972. For the text of the Protocol see H. Stehle, op. cit., pp. 422-424.
36. *Il Giornale d'Italia* (Rome), October 1-2, 1974.
37. *Vecernje Novosti* (Belgrad), November 8, 1974.
38. *The Pilot,* April 12, 1974.

39. A.U. Floridi and A.E. Stiefbold, *The Uncertain Alliance,* pp. 28-32, 98-101.
40. Bartolemeo Sorge, "Il Movimento dei Cristiani per il Socialismo," in *La Civiltà Cattolica,* 1974, vol. II, pp. 111-130; vol. III, pp. 456-474. About the so-called "Theology of Liberation" see Leonardo Boff *Chiesa, carisma e potere,* p. 220ff. Rome condemned these "theologies" in a document of the Congregation of the Faith (August 6, 1984) published in *L'Osservatore Romano,* Sept. 3-4, 1984. An example of how these "theologies" and "theologians" work can be seen in Nicaragua where four Catholic priests are members of the marxist government and hundreds of activists (turbas) disturbed the Mass of John Paul II during his visit in February 1983.
41. "Letter to the Synod Bishops"—A Message signed by a Group of Catholic Lay Leaders and brought to the Synod by the Archbishop of Havana," in *LADOC* (Washington), March 1975, pp. 34-37. A new Pronuncio to Cuba was appointed by the Vatican in July 1975.
42. Fr. Frederick McGuire, director of the USCC's Division for Latin America, who very often denounced violations of human rights in Latin American countries, kept silent about these same violations in Cuba: "we cannot speak without facts," he said, "we've tried to get the Cuban facts but we haven't been able to": see *National Catholic Register,* July 9 and September 3, 1972 and *The Pilot,* July 22 and August 26, 1972 and February 22, 1974. On May 5, 1974, the Committee to Denounce Cruelties to Cuban Political Prisoners (Miami, Fla.) answered Fr. McGuire with a documentation which was sent also to the Vatican and to all US Catholic bishops. Dr. Jose Lasaga, one-time president of the Catholic Organizations in Cuba and Bishop Masvidal warned, respectively, US congressional leaders and theologians on Cuba's "freedoms" and a pro-Socialist "theology of liberation" (see *The Pilot,* July 25 and September 19, 1975).
43. A. Sakharov, *Sakharov Speaks,* pp. 204, 213.
44. *Literarni Listy,* March 14, 1968. On the activities of the Priestly Peace Movement, today called "Pacem in Terris," see C. Slovak and J. Inovecky, *Eroi o traditori?,* pp. 27-35, 363-365.
45. *Nova Mysl,* January 1972 and Giovanni Rulli, S.J. "On Atheistic Education in Czechoslovakia," in *La Civiltà Cattolica,* July 20, 1094, pp. 190-200 and August 3-17, 1974, pp. 284-294.
46. *L'Eco dell'Amore* (Rome), July-August 1974.
47. Robert A. Graham, S.J., "How the Holy See Avoids Entanglement in Border Disputes," in *Columbia,* September 1972, p. 34.
48. *New York Times,* May 8, 1973.
49. *New York Times,* April 15, 1974. In the article "Priests in Poland Troubled by Vatican Détente," M.W. Browne writes: "Many Roman Catholic priests in Poland feel that a growing friendship of the Vatican toward Communist governments has undermined the priests' position in this country . . . Catholic leaders say at least 500 new churches are needed in Poland," but this year the government issued only one permit for a new church: ibid., October 5, 1975.
50. *L'Osservatore Romano,* February 8, 1974.
51. *Il Giornale d'Italia* (Rome), February 5-6, 1974 and *The New York Times,* April 15, 1974.
52. V.C. Chrypinski, "Polish Catholicism," a mimeo paper prepared for the International Symposium on Religion and Atheism in Communist Societies at Carleton University, Ottawa (Ontario), March 31-April 4, 1971, pp. 11, 19-20.
53. *The New York Times,* July 7, 1974.
54. Synodus Episcoporum. Assemblea Generale 1974. Comitato per l'Informazione. Bulletin No. 4, October 1, 1974, p. 1.
55. *L'Osservatore Romano,* October 12, 1974.
56. *Diakonia* (New York), 1972, No. 2, p. 103.
57. *Boston Globe,* December 2, 1974.

58. Jozsef Cardinal Mindszenty, *Memoirs*, pp. 222-223.
59. Ibid., p. 226.
60. Ibid., p. 242.
61. Ibid., pp. 246-247.
62. *The Pilot* (Boston), January 17, 1975.
63. Ibid.
64. *Kontinent* (in Russian) 1974, No. 1, p. 5.
65. *Diakonia* 1972, No. 2, p. 105.
66. Samizdat. *Cronaca di una vita nuova nell'URSS*, pp. 149-177.
67. Ibid., pp. 183-206. See also the chapter on Lithuania in the second part of this book.
68. *L'Osservatore Romano*, November 11-12 and December 29, 1974.
69. Ibid. The same thoughts were expressed by Archbishop Casaroli during his visit to the Democratic German Republic (June 9-14, 1975). Outlining again what he called Pope Paul's "philosophy of peace" at a dinner given in his honor by Foreign Minister Oskar Fischer, the Archbishop stressed the necessity for the Church of keeping its religious "credibility" among the "world of believers and non-believers" in dealing with Communist states (see *Civiltà Cattolica*, July 5, 1975, p. 90). This signifies that the Holy See is aware of the dilemma of its Ostpolitik: too many concessions to the Communists will result in a loss of credibility among the believers, while a clear opposition will compromise the hopes for more concessions. See also the already quoted speeches of Paul VI to the diplomatic corps on Jan. 12, 1974 and Jan. 11, 1975.

Chapter 3

1. A. Sakharov, *Progress Coexistence and International Freedom*, p. 29.
2. *Pravda*, June 22, 1960 and A.U. Floridi, *Il dilemma dell'Unione Sovietica*, pp. 124-137.
3. S. Talbot, *Khrushchev Remembers*, p. 512.
4. *The New York Times*, January 21, 1975.
5. Christmas message of 1954 and O. Halecki and J.F. Murray, *Eugenio Pacelli: Pope of Peace*, pp. 238-239.
6. Ibid., p. 314.
7. M. Chinigo, *The Pope Speaks*, p. 360.
8. *Pravda*, November 16, 1969.
9. Z. Brzezinski, "The Deceptive Structure of Peace," in *Foreign Policy*, No. 14, 1974, pp. 40-43.
10. "A. Sakharov v borbe za mir," pp. 106-121 and A. Solzhenitsyn, "Pis'mo vozhdiam Sovetskogo Soiuza," pp. 14-16, 36-37.
11. A. Sakharov, *Sakharov Speaks*, pp. 87-88.
12. A. Brumberg, *In Quest of Justice*, p. 299.
13. A. Marchenko, *Moi pokazaniia*, p. 7.
14. *The New York Times*, September 21, 1973.
15. *Pravda*, October 13, 1969.
16. *The New York Times*, October 9, 1969 and L. Goure (and others), *Convergence of Communism and Capitalism*, p. 17.
17. Dokumenty Komiteta Prav Cheloveka, pp. 5-6.
18. A. Sakharov, *Sakharov Speaks*, pp. 153-155.
19. Programma Demokraticheskogo Dvizheniya Sovetskogo Soyuza, p. 75.
20. Ibid., pp. 21-22.
21. Ibid., pp. 9-12.
22. Ibid., p. 63.
23. *The New York Times*, July 5, 1973 and A. Sakharov, *Sakharov Speaks*, p. 166 ff.
24. A. Sakharov, op. cit., pp. 204-205.
25. See articles against Sakharov in *L'Humanité* (Paris), August 23, 1973 and in

Information Bulletin (issued by the World Marxist Review in Toronto), December 7, 1973 and Sakharov's reply to Samuel Pisar in *New York Times,* October 8, 1973.

26. *Time,* May 6, 1974.
27. *The New York Times,* October 10, 1975. For Sakharov's recommendation to the Oslo Committee by the Soviet dissenters see *Khronika Zashchity Prav v SSSR* (N.Y.), September-October 1973, p. 44.
28. *The New York Times,* September 11, 1973.
29. Ibid., September, 5 and 8, 1973 and *Khronika Tekushchikh Sobytii* (N.Y.) No. 28-31, p. 106. In December 1973 Sakharov received the award of the International League for the Rights of Man: A. Sakharov, *Sakharov Speaks,* pp. 228-229.
30. The letter, written on September 5, 1973, was published only after Solzhenitsyn's expulsion from the USSR with few corrections made by the author: see *The New York Times,* March 3 and 5, 1974.
31. A. Solzhenitsyn, *Pis'mo vozhdiam Sovetskogo Soiuza,* p. 19.
32. Ibid., pp. 19-21. About Sakharov's "convergence" see Solzhenitsyn's article "Na vozvrate dykhaniia i soznaniia," in the anthology *Iz-pod glyb* [From under the Rubble], pp. 7-28.
33. See Solzhenitsyn's answer to Sakharov's criticisms in *Kontinent* (München) 1975, No. 2, p. 351 and the anthology *Iz-pod glyb,* pp. 115-150.
34. *The New York Times,* April 15, 1974 and A. Sakharov, "O Pis'me A. Solzhenitsyna vozhdiam Sovetskogo Soiuza," pp. 10-12.
35. See Solzhenitsyn's speech to the AFL-CIO (June 30) in *The Wanderer* (St. Paul, Minn.), July 17, 1975. Nine days later, speaking in New York to the same organizations, Solzhenitsyn denied that he was advocating cold war and calling upon the US to liberate the Russian people. The cold war, he said, "is still going on, but from the other side . . . I have always told my countrymen that they must save themselves, and not look to outsiders." but, he added, "when they bury us alive, please do not send them shovels and the most up-to-date earth-moving equipment" (*The New York Times,* July 10, 1975).
36. From Herzen's *My Past and Thoughts,* quoted in M. Malia, *Aleksander Herzen and the Birth of Russian Socialism,* p. 312.
37. A. Sakharov, *My Country and the World,* as quoted in *The New York Times,* July 30, and *Time,* August 4, 1975.
38. *The New York Times,* July 22, 1975.
39. Ibid., August 1, 1975.
40. *The New York Times,* December 17, 1973 and *Khronika Zashchity Prav v SSSR,* No. 5-6, p. 10.
41. V. Chalidze, *Prava cheloveka i Sovetskii Soiuz,* p. 51.
42. A. Sakharov, *Sakharov Speaks,* pp. 212-213.
43. *Pravda,* September 20, 1973.
44. *The New York Times,* March 28, 1973.
45. See Chalidze's letter to the General Secretary of UNESCO in *Khronika Zashchity Prav v SSSR,* No. 2, pp. 66-69.
46. *The New York Times,* September 28, 1973.
47. Ibid., September 22, 1973.
48. Ibid., December 29, 1973.
49. Ibid., December 31, 1973.
50. Ibid., September 21, 1973 and May 8, 1974.
51. *Pravda,* September 26, 1973.
52. See Volpin's report of January 14, 1971 in *Dokumenty Komiteta Prav Cheloveka,* pp. 67-122.
53. *The New York Times,* September 29, 1973.
54. *Pravda,* September 28, 1973.

55. Quoted from *The Violations of Human Rights in Soviet Occupied Lithuania,* pp. 16-17.
56. A. Solzhenitsyn, *Nobel Lecture,* pp. 25-26.
57. *The Pilot* (Boston), December 14, 1973 and *La Civiltà Cattolica* (Rome), December 15, 1973, pp. 590-597.
58. *The Pilot,* November 16, 1973.
59. Ibid., August 8, 1975.
60. See the text of the declaration in N. Struve, *Christians in Contemporary Russia,* pp. 362-366.
61. G. Rar, *Plenennaia tserkov',* pp. 26-37.
62. The "Catacomb Church" still exists in the USSR although its numerical strength is not known. To this Church belong "in spirit" all the Russian Orthodox who do not agree with the policies of the Moscow Patriarchate. "Russia and the Church Today" is the first document of the Catacomb Church published in samizdat: see *Russia Cristiana* (Milano), July-August 1972. See also about this subject the opinions of other dissenters: V. Maksimov, ibid., May-June, 1974; D.M. Panin, in *Religiia i Ateizm* (München), October 1973 and June 1974; A. Levitin, etc. A. Solzhenitsyn in a letter addressed to the bishops of the Russian Orthodox Church in exile wrote that he does not believe there is in the USSR a Catacomb Church numerically relevant, although his attitude is inspired by the martyrs of that Church (for the text and a summary of the letter see *Novoe Russkoe Slovo,* September 27, 1974 and *Diakonia,* 1975, No. 2, pp. 153-154).
63. The concessions to the Russian Orthodox Church in the Soviet Union were never put in the form of law, nor were the restrictive provisions of the 1929 religious legislation abrogated: see V. Gsovski, *Church and State behind the Iron Curtain,* pp. XXV-XXVI and R. Conquest, *Religion in the USSR,* p. 34.
64. *Izvestiia,* February 10, 1945 and (II) *Cristianesi mo nell'Unione Sovietica,* pp. 294-295.
65. W. Stroyen, *Communist Russia and the Russian Orthodox Church,* pp. 55-56.
66. N. Struve, op. cit., pp. 155-157 and 315. See also the book by W.C. Fletcher, *Nikolai.*
67. W.C. Fletcher, *Religion and Soviet Foreign Policy,* chapter 5.
68. A.U. Floridi, op. cit., pp. 460 and 519.
69. N. Struve, op. cit., p. 103.
70. *Zhurnal Moskovskoi Patriarkhii,* 1958, No. 9, pp. 29-36 and N. Struve, op. cit., p. 111.
71. *Istina* (Paris) 1955, No. 1, pp. 51-106.
72. N. Struve, op. cit., 114.
73. A.U. Floridi, *Dr. Hromadka and the Christian Peace Conference,* pp. 33-34.
74. Ibid., pp. 117-119.
75. Ibid., pp. 61, 120-121.
76. *The Journal of the Moscow Patriarchate* (in English), 1974, No. 6, p. 38.
77. *The New York Times,* September 18, 1973.
78. *Izvestiia,* February 10, 1945 and R. Conquest, op. cit., p. 37; N. Struve, op. cit., p. 97.
79. N. Struve, op. cit., p. 102.
80. L.N. Velikovich, *Krizis sovremennogo katolitsizma,* pp. 21-42. See also *Voprosy Nauchnogo Ateizma,* No. 6, 1966: this issue is completely dedicated to Vatican Council II with contributions by many Soviet atheist writers.
81. *La Civiltà Cattolica,* January 28, 1961, pp. 238-252.
82. *Zhurnal Moskovskoi Patriarkhii,* 1961, No. 6, pp. 76-80.
83. Ibid., 1961, No. 5, p. 73.
84. *And on Earth Peace,* pp. 63-67. For similar attacks see also *Zhurnal Moskovskoi Patriarkhii,* 1959, No. 7, p. 10 and 1961, No. 11, p. 16.
85. *Izvestiia,* September 21, 1961.
86. *La Croix* (Paris), October 21, 1961.
87. *Informations Catholiques Internationales* (Paris), January 1, 1962.

88. *Christ und Welt,* October 19, 1962. See also R. P. Moroziuk, *Politicized Ecumenism,* p. 2ff.
89. *America* (N.Y.), November 11, 1962, p. 1080.
90. R. B. Kaiser, *Pope, Council and World,* p. 100.
91. X. Rynne, *Letters from Vatican City,* p. 80.
92. *La Civiltà Cattolica,* 1964, vol. IV, pp. 461-462.
93. M. M. Sheinman, *Sovremennyi klerikalizm,* p. 80.
94. G.F. Svidercoschi, *Storia del Concilio,* pp. 601-607 and A.U. Floridi, *Humanismo Sovietico,* pp. 288-289.
95. *Diakonia* (N.Y.), 1968, No. 1, pp. 41-42, 74-75.
96. *Informations Catholiques Internationales,* No. 269-270, August 1966.
97. E. Duff, S.J., *Chiesa e Società.* Conferenza del Consiglio Mondiale delle Chiese, in *Civiltà Cattolica,* 1966, vol. IV, pp. 40-47. See also World Conference on Church and Society, pp. 101-119.
98. *Zhurnal Moskovskoi Patriarkhii,* 1967, No. 9, pp. 34-40.
99. N. Theodorowitsch, *Religion und Atheismus in der USSR,* pp. 202-207 and *Testi Letterari e poesie da riviste clandestine dell'Unione Sovietica,* pp. 159-168.
100. M. Hayward and W. Fletcher, *Religion and the Soviet State,* p. 62.
101. Ibid., p. 68.
102. See the following chapter.
103. *Diakonia,* 1971, No. 1, pp. 74-75.
104. W.C. Fletcher, *Religion and Soviet Foreign Policy* and *Russia Cristiana,* July-August 1971, p. 62.
105. *The New York Times,* April 9, 1972.
106. *Diakonia,* 1974, No. 1, pp. 97-104.
107. *The Journal of the Moscow Patriarchate,* 1973, No. 7, p. 53.
108. Ibid., p. 51.
109. Ibid., p. 52.
110. *Russia Cristiana,* May-June 1974, pp. 25-56 and *Khronika Tekushchikh Sobytii,* No. 28-31, pp. 105-106.
111. E. Barabanov, "Raskol tserkvi i mira," in *Iz-pod glyb,* pp. 184-185, 196.
112. Ibid., p. 197.
113. E. Barabanov, "La premessa morale dell'unità cristiana," in *Russia Cristiana,* January-February 1974, pp. 3-15.
114. *Russia Cristiana,* July-August 1974, p. 28.
115. Ibid., May-June 1974, pp. 5-9.
116. A. Brumberg, op. cit., pp. 232-240.
117. *The Tablet* (Brooklyn, N.Y.), July 10 and 17, 1975.
118. *Diakonia,* 1967, No. 2, pp. 201-202.
119. Ibid., 1970, No. 1, p. 74. An explanation on the Holy Synod's decision was offered by Metropolitan Nikodim on the following May (see *Diakonia,* 1970, No. 4, p. 408). See also Card. Willebrands' article in *Avvenire* (Milano), July 4, 1971.
120. See the chapter on the Ukraine.
121. A. Galich, *Pokolenie obrechennykh,* p. 13.
122. *Novoe russkoe slovo,* Dec. 10, 1975. A letter from the Russian Orthodox deacon Vladimir Rusak, dated Moscow, July 1983, addressed to the VI Assembly of the World Council of Churches gathered in Vancouver (Canada, July 24-Aug. 10, 1983) was not even presented to the delegates by the Council's general secretary Philip Potter: see *Russia Cristiana,* 1983, n. 5, pp. 15-19 and n. 6, pp. 3-11. Mr. Rusak uses a staff member of the *Zhurnal Moskovskoi Patriarkhii.* Another letter from the Christian Committee for the Defense of the Believers in the USSR was not taken into the Assembly: see *The New York Times,* August 9, 1983.

Chapter 4

1. *Relazioni Internazionali* (Italy), February 12, 1972, pp. 161-165.
2. A. (Levitin) Krasnov, *Stromaty*, p. 150.
3. A.D. Sakharov, *Sakharov Speaks*, p. 213.
4. V. Chalidze, *Prava cheloveka i Sovetskii Soiuz*, p. 62.
5. See a letter of B. Pasternak to Sinyavsky (June 29, 1957) in A. Ghinsburg, *Libro Bianco sul caso Sinjavskij-Daniel*, pp. 132-133.
6. A. Brumberg, *In Quest of Justice*, p. 29.
7. P. Reddaway, *Uncensored Russia*, p. 18. See also K. Bosley, *Russia's Underground Poets*, pp. xv-xxvi.
8. A. Brumberg, op. cit., pp. 35-38.
9. N. Cousins, *The Improbable Triumvirate*, p. 23.
10. Ibid., p. 57.
11. M. Hayward, *On Trial*, p. 44.
12. Ibid., p. 98.
13. A. Ghinsburg, op. cit., pp. 177-78.
14. A. Terts, *Mysli vrasplokh*, pp. 88, 110, 137, 141.
15. M. Hayward, op. cit., pp. 47, 83-84.
16. A. Brumberg, op. cit., pp. 93-99.
17. P. Litvinov, *The Demonstration in Pushkin Square*, pp. 14-15.
18. P. Litvinov, op. cit., pp. 13-14 and P. Reddaway, op. cit., p. 11.
19. P. Litvinov, op. cit. and K. Van Het Reve, *Letters and Telegrams to P.M. Litvinov*, pp. 2-17.
20. P. Litvinov, op. cit., p. 102.
21. Ibid., pp. 106-108.
22. Ibid., pp. 116-117.
23. Ibid., p. 110.
24. Ibid., p. 115.
25. A. Brumberg, op. cit., p. 247 and *Politicheskii dnevnik*, pp. 264-278.
26. A. Belinkov, "What is the Soviet Censorship?" in *Studies on the Soviet Union* (Munich) 1971, No. 2, p. 5.
27. *The New York Times*, January 10, 1974 and samizdat, *Cronaca di una vita nuova nell'USSR*, p. 79.
28. In the US the documents of samizdat are gathered by the Arkhiv Samizdata—Sobranie Dokumentov Samizdata. Material reproduced by the Center for Slavic and East European Studies (The Ohio State University, Columbus, Ohio) from master copies on file in the Arkhiv Samizdata which is maintained by Radio Liberty in Munich, Germany.
29. K. Van Het Reve, op. cit., pp. 45-46.
30. *The New York Times*, September 6, 1973. Before his arrest Yakir told *London Times* correspondent D. Bonavia: "If they beat me, I will say anything. I know that from my former experience in the camps. But you will know it will not be the real me speaking. Another thing, I shall never in any circumstances commit suicide. So you will know that if they say I have done away with myself, someone else will have done me in" (*Time*, July 3, 1973, p. 21).
31. *The New York Times*, August 1, 1973.
32. *A Chronicle of Human Rights in the USSR* (N.Y.), No. 9, May-June 1974, p. 5.
33. S. Talbot, *Khrushchev Remembers*, p. 596.
34. See how later Khrushchev explained the annexation of the Baltic countries; ibid., p. 148.
35. G.V. Stalin, *Opere Complete* (in Italian), vol. I, Roma 1949, p. 71.
36. Ibid., vol. IV, Roma 1951, pp. 417-418.

37. G.A. Wetter, *Dialectical Materialism,* pp. 196-201.
38. Quoted in *Voprosy Istorii KPSS* 1971, No. 7, p. 27. See also B.D. Wolfe, *Khrushchev and Stalin's Ghost,* pp. 270-279.
39. A. Brumberg, op. cit., pp. 208-213.
40. "Programma Demokraticheskogo Dvizheniia Sovetskogo Soiuza," p. 22.
41. A. Amalrik, *Will the Soviet Union Survive until 1984?,* p. 64.
42. *The New York Times,* December 28, 1974.
43. I. Dzyuba, *Internationalism or Russification?,* p. 77.
44. Baby Yar Address by I. Dzyuba, in A. Brumberg, op. cit., p. 202.
45. Brumberg, op. cit., p. 304.
46. L. Leneman, *La tragedie des Juifs.*
47. A.U. Floridi, "The USSR against the Jews," in *Atlas* (N.Y.) 1961, pp. 432-438.
48. Ibid., p. 435.
49. Ibid., p. 436.
50. S.J. Roth, "Problems of National Religious Duality" (a mimeographed paper presented at the International Symposium on Religion and Atheism in Communist Societies, Carleton University, Ottawa, 31 March-4 April, 1971.
51. V. Polonskii, "Kriticheskie zametki o Babele," in *Novy Mir,* 1927, No. 1, p. 286.
52. A. Dagan, *Moscow and Jerusalem,* pp. 38-39.
53. L. Leneman, op. cit., p. 79 ff.
54. *Il Paese* (Roma), January 28, 1961.
55. *Journal of International Commission of Jurists* (The Hague), vol. V, Summer 1964.
56. *The New York Times,* December 27, 1974; January 9, 10 and April 24, 1975.
57. S. Ettinger, "Russian Society and the Jews," in *Bulletin on Soviet and East European Jewish Affairs* (London), May 1970 and E. Oberlander, "La Campagna antisionista nell'URSS," in *Russia Cristiana* (Milano), November-December 1971, pp. 43-63.
58. A. Dagan, op. cit., p. 163.
59. *A Chronicle of Current Events* (London), No. 18, June 1971, p. 121.
60. *The New York Times,* December 21, 1974 and notes 64 and 70.
61. *Pravda,* December 22, 1974.
62. *Literaturnaia Gazeta,* December 25, 1974.
63. *The New York Times,* December 23, 1974.
64. *The New York Times,* June 30 and July 7, 1975.
65. *The New York Times,* December 22, 1974.
66. *The New York Times,* December 23, 1974.
67. *Russian Literature Triquarterly* (Ann Arbor, Mich.), No. 5, Winter 1973, p. 27. See also Korzhavin's article "Opyt poeticheskoi biografii," in *Kontinent* (Munich), No. 2, 1975, pp. 199-279.
68. A. Anatoly (Kuznetsov), *Baby Yar,* p. 7.
69. A. Kuznetsov, "The Soviet Self-Censorship," in *Studies on the Soviet Union* (Munich) 1971, No. 2, pp. 30-36. These remarks prompted a polemic exchange of letters between the author and A. Amalrik: see A. Amalrik, op. cit., pp. 95-124. Kuznetsov now wishes to be known as A. Anatoly in order to show that he has broken with his past as a Soviet writer.
70. *The Boston Globe,* September 13, 1975. See also Fr. Drinan's proposals to break the impasse on the emigration of Soviet Jews in *Congressional Record*—House, September 22, 1975, pp. H8955-H8958. Under Ronald Reagan's presidency Jewish emigration has been effectively choked off and now only several dozen Jews leave each month. Valery Senderov and Boris Kanevsky got seven and five years respectively in prison-camps for proving the discrimination against Jewish students in the Soviet universities (*Russia Cristiana,* 1984, n. 2, pp. 78-80 and n. 5, pp. 65-66).
71. I. Braznik, F.I. Dolgikh, *O religii,* pp. 517-522.
72. *Pravda,* November 11, 1954.

73. *Pravda,* August 21, 1959.
74. *Kommunist,* 1964, No. 1, pp. 23-46.
75. G. Codevilla, *Stato e Chiesa nell'Unione Sovietica,* pp. 271-281.
76. M. Bourdeaux, *Religious Ferment in Russia,* pp. 53-65.
77. Samizdat, *Cronaca di una vita nuova nell'URSS,* p. 177.
78. Ibid., p. 149. On January 31, 1975, G.P. Vins was condemned to five years in prison camp and five in exile: *Religiia i ateizm v USSR,* April 1975, p. 7. Now he is living in the United States.
79. A. Solzhenitsyn, *One Day in the Life of Ivan Denisovich,* pp. 153-155.
80. *Eastern Churches Review,* vol. V, Spring 1973, pp. 40-41. The letter is dated Sunday of the Veneration of the Cross which in 1972 fell on April 12.
81. Ibid., pp. 41-44.
82. *Russkaia Mysl'* (Paris), June 26, 1969.
83. K. Van Het Reve, op. cit., pp. 155-163.
84. *Eastern Churches Review,* op. cit., p. 44.
85. Ibid., pp. 44-52.
86. W. B. Stroyen, *Communist Russia and the Russian Orthodox Church,* pp. 136-140.
87. *Zhurnal Moskovskoi Patriarkhii* 1961, No. 8, pp. 15-17.
88. *URSS: Dibattito nella Comunista Cristiana,* pp. 93-102.
89. M. Bourdeaux, *Patriarch and Prophets,* p. 189 ff.
90. *Russkaia Mysl',* August 25, 1966. On April 19, 1975 Fr. Yakunin wrote a protest against the government's decision to declare Easter Sunday a working day: *Religiia i Ateizm v USSR,* April 1975.
91. M. Bourdeaux, *Patriarch and Prophets,* p. 238 ff.
92. Ibid., p. 304 ff.
93. *Vestnik RSKhD* (Russkogo Studencheskogo Khristianskogo Dvizheniia), Paris, 1972, No. 106, p. 245.
94. *The Journal of the Moscow Patriarchate* (in English), 1974, No. 5, pp. 9-10.
95. *Religiia i ateizm v USSR* (Munich) 1974, n. 8, p. 10 and *Vestnik RSKhD,* 1974, No. 111, p. 133.
96. *The Journal of the Moscow Patriarchate* (in English), 1974, No. 5, reprinted Metropolitan Serafim's attack (p. 7) along with another condemnation by Metropolitan Aleksei of Tallin (pp. 7-8) and a declaration by Metropolitan Yuvenaly of Tula against Archbishop Vasily of Bruxelles (p. 9), who had criticized Serafim.
97. *Veche,* No. 2 and *Russia Cristiana,* September-October 1971, pp. 75-76. The first number of *Veche* appeared on January 1, 1971. On March 1, 1971, V.N. Osipov, editor of *Veche,* denied that his journal was illegal, chauvinist or reactionary. But three years later, in March 1974, due to internal dissentions, Osipov announced the suspension of the publication.
98. *The New York Times,* May 9, 16, 20, 1974. For the text of Fr. Dudko's declaration see D. Dudko, *O nashem upovanii,* pp. 191-194, 253-257.
99. *Khronika Zashchity Prav v SSSR* (New York), 1974, No. 9, pp. 27-28.
100. *Russia Cristiana,* March-April 1972, pp. 60-65.
101. V. Chalidze, *Prava cheloveka i Sovetskii Soiuz,* pp. 126-182.
102. Ibid., pp. 213-247. For a comment on the juridical aspect of the case, see *Russia Cristiana,* January-February 1972, pp. 53-58.
103. V. Chalidze, op. cit., pp. 223-224.
104. I.R. Shafarevich, *Zakonodatel'stvo o religii v Sovetskom Soiuze.*
105. *Russkaia Mysl',* May 7, 1966.
106. M. Bourdeaux, *Religious Ferment in Russia,* p. 188.
107. *Possev* (Frankfurt/M), September 23 and October 1, 1966.
108. See Levitin's article on Troitse-Sergieva Lavra in Ioann San-Frantsissky, *Dialog s tserkovnoi Rossiei,* pp. 35-41.

109. N. Struve, op. cit., pp. 303-310 and Ioann San-Frantsissky, *Zashchita very v SSSR*, p. 63 ff.
110. A. Brumberg, op. cit., p. 244.
111. *Possev*, September 23 and October 1, 1966.
112. *Vestnik RSKhD*, 1966, No. 4, p. 5 and M. Bourdeaux, op. cit., p. 331.
113. M. Bourdeaux, op. cit., p. 143. About the *dvadtsatka* see G. Codevilla, *Stato e Chiesa nell'Unione Sovietica*, p. 99ff.
114. Ibid.
115. Ibid., p. 138.
116. Ibid., pp. 335, 339.
117. P. Reddaway, op. cit., pp. 325 and 472, notes 31-33.
118. M. Bourdeaux, op. cit., pp. 331-332.
119. G. Simon, *Church State and Opposition in the USSR*, pp. 198-199. The letter was written shortly after Pope Paul's seventieth birthday in 1967, but was made public only toward the end of 1969.
120. *A Chronicle of Current Events*, No. 17, April 1971, p. 63.
121. E. Kuznetsov, *Dnevniki*, p. 321.
122. *The National Catholic Register* (Kansas City) February 4, 1973.
123. T.E. Bird and E. Piddubcheshen, *Archiepiscopal and Patriarchal Autonomy*, p. 64.
124. *Vestnik RSKhD*, No. 108-110, 1973, p. 274.
125. R.A. Graham, S.J. "How Should the Vatican Deal with Warring States?" in *Columbia* (New Haven), January 1974, p. 8.
126. *Boston Globe*, January 19, 1974.
127. Ibid.
128. *The Pilot*, February 22, 1974.
129. Ibid., January 26, 1974 and *Religious News Service* (N.Y.), January 28, 1974, pp. 21-22.
130. *The Pilot*, March 1, 1974.
131. *Boston Globe*, January 26, 1974.
132. *Boston Globe*, August 16, 1970.
133. *Survey* (London), No. 77, 1970, pp. 139-145.
134. A. Artemova, L. Rar, M. Slavinsky, *Kaznimye sumasshestviem*, pp. 470-471.
135. *A Chronicle of Current Events*, Nos. 19-23 and *Russia Cristiana*, May-June 1972, pp. 72-73.
136. *The New York Times*, April 15, 1974.
137. *Russia Cristiana*, September-October 1974, pp. 17-18.
138. G.P. Fedotov, *The Russian Religious Mind*, pp. 316-343.
139. Ibid., pp. 339-340.
140. See the letters of V.I. Levin and of an "old friend" in A. Ghinsburg, *Libro Bianco . . .*, pp. 95-96. Pyotr A. Chaadaev (1793-1856) in his famous philosophical letter criticized Russian reality as stagnant and barbaric because it was outside the main stream of history as represented by Western Europe and Catholicism. He was declared insane by the tsarist regime and his works banned.
141. Z. and R. Medvedev, *A Question of Madness*, pp. 168-169.
142. *The New York Times*, December 22, 1974.
143. Peter Alagiagian, S.J., *My Prisons in Soviet Paradise*, pp. 146-149 and Pietro Leoni, S.J., *Spia del Vaticano*, pp. 105-115, 425-444.
144. A. Solzhenitsyn, *The First Circle*, p. 146. Father R. Hotz, S.J., in an article against Solzhenitsyn in *La Civiltà Cattolica* (June 17, 1972, pp. 598-608) repeats almost literally the words of Metropolitan Cyril: Patriarch Pimen "did just what he should have done." According to Fr. Hotz, Solzhenitsyn in his Open Letter to the Patriarch of Moscow "is talking to the wrong man." He should have addressed his letter to the Communists who are persecuting the Church.
145. Samizdat. *Cronaca di una vita nuova nell'URSS*, pp. 59-61.

146. I Cor., 3: 18.
147. G. Lauter "Come può e deve porgere aiuto l'Occidente?," in *Russia Cristiana*, 1972, No. 125, pp. 49-50.

Chapter 5

1. *Lietuvos Kataliku Baznycios Kronika—Chronicle of the Catholic Church in Lithuania* (hereafter *Chronicle LCC*), illegally published in the USSR in Lithuanian and in Russian *(Kronika Katolicheskoi Tserkvi v Litve)*. Since 1972 it has appeared approximately quarterly in typewritten form of about 30 typed pages each issue. In later issues the *Chronicle LCC* began to include some materials not directly related to religion. It has reported on the suppression of human rights in general and particularly on the suppression of national rights. The Lithuanian Roman Catholic Priests' League of America translated it into English in separate pamphlets under the titles: *From the Catacombs* (No. 4), *Christ behind Wire* (No. 5), *Out of the Depths* (No. 6), *Desecrated Shrines* (No. 7), *The Church Suffering* (No. 8), *Freedom to Die* (No. 9), *Struggle for Survival* (No. 10), *We Will Not* (No. 11).
2. "The True State of the Catholic Church in Lithuania," in *From the Catacombs*, pp. 1-12 (in this issue the pages are not numerated).
3. J. Savasis, *The War against God in Lithuania*, p. 22 and V.S. Vardys, "The Partisan Movement in Postwar Lithuania," in *Slavic Review*, September 1963, pp. 499-522.
4. V.S. Vardys, *Lithuania under the Soviets*, especially chapters 8-10.
5. *Chronicle LCC* (in Russian) No. 10, p. 9 and V.S. Vardys, *Lithuania under the Soviets*, pp. 104-106.
6. *Chronicle LCC* (in Russian) No. 9, pp. 14-15 and Nos. 12 and 13.
7. *Chronicle LCC* (in Russian) No. 10, pp. 40-45. Bishop P. Bucys was Superior General of the Marian Fathers, a priestly Order which he, together with Archbishop George Matulaitis helped to reform. Archbishop G. Matulaitis is listed by the *Chronicle LCC* (in Russian) No. 10, p. 10, among the greatest bishops of modern Lithuania (see also A.U. Floridi, "Il servo di Dio G. Matulaitis e la conversione della Russia," in *La Civiltà Cattolica* 1957, vol. II, pp. 491-503 and vol. III, pp. 60-71). Father Bucys was ordained bishop in Rome in the byzantine rite in 1930 (see C. Korolevskij, Metropolite Andre Szeptyckyj, pp. 255-256). Since 1926, when he was named Superior General Bishop, Bucys resided in Rome at the headquarters of his congregation where he died in 1951.
8. V. Brizgyz, *Religious Conditions in Lithuania under Soviet Russian Occupation*, pp. 17-18 and *The Baltic Review*, (New York) 1971, No. 38, pp. 54-64.
9. J. Savasis, op. cit., p. 16.
10. F.I. Milani, *La repressione culturale in Lituania*, p. 33.
11. *Chronicle LCC* (in Russian), No. 11, p. 2.
12. *Mary, Save Us*, pp. 25-37.
13. Lietuviu Liandies Menas, Mazoji Architektura, pp. xvi-xvii.
14. *The Church Suffering*, pp. 27-28.
15. *From the Catacombs*, p. 30.
16. Ibid., pp. 30-32.
17. V. Maculis, "Das Religiose und Kirchliche Leben in Litauen," in *Acta Baltica* (Konigstein in Taunus), vol VIII, 1969, pp. 19-20. For a biography of other Lithuanian bishops see this article and *Encyclopedia Lituanica*. Boston: J. Kabocius. Until 1974 only 3 volumes were published out of 6 planned.
18. J. Rimaitis, *Religion in Lithuania*, p. 22.
19. Some names of the priests arrested are mentioned in the *Chronicle LCC* (in Russian), No. 10, p. 2.
20. V.S. Vardys, *Lithuania under the Soviets*, pp. 224, 230, 233.
21. V. Maculis, op. cit., pp. 27-29 and J. Savasis, op. cit., pp. 82-85.

22. V.S. Vardys, *Catholicism in Lithuania,* in R.H. Marshall Jr., *Aspects of Religion in the Soviet Union,* pp. 388-393.
23. *Komunistas,* 1961, No. 11, p. 7.
24. V.S. Vardys, *Catholicism in Lithuania,* p. 391.
25. *The Pilot* (Boston), February 28, 1975.
26. *Out of the Depths,* p. 24.
27. *Elta-Press* (Rome), September-October 1967, pp. 21-22.
28. Arkhiv Samizdata (Radio Liberty) No. 1247. See the reference to this protest in the January 1, 1969 petition signed by over 30 priests of the Vilkaviskis diocese, in K. Krasauskas and K. Gulbinas, "Die Lage der Katolischen Kirche in Litauen," in *Acta Baltica* (Konigstein in Taunus), vol. XII, 1973, p. 47.
29. *Chronicle LCC* (in Russian), No. 9, pp. 42-44.
30. F.I. Milani, op. cit., pp. 131-140.
31. *From the Catacombs,* p. 5.
32. Ibid., pp. 5-6.
33. Ibid., p. 6.
34. Ibid, pp. 3-4; *Christ Behind Wire,* pp. 44-46; *Out of the Depths,* pp. 40-44.
35. *Sette Giorni* (Italy), November 18, 1973.
36. *The Church Suffering,* pp. 5-6.
37. *Lituanus* (Chicago), 1974, No. 4, pp. 64-65.
38. *Elta-Press* (Rome), January 1974, p. 3.
39. V.S. Vardys, "The Roman Catholics in Lithuania," a mimeographed paper presented at the International Symposium on Religion and Atheism in Communist Societies, Carleton University, Ottawa (Canada), 31 March-4 April, 1971.
40. F.I. Milani, op. cit., pp. 89-91.
41. *Tarybine Mokykla,* 1971, No. 3.
42. *Tiesa,* March 27, 1973. See also "Soviet Cultural Policies in Lithuania," in *Lituanus,* 1973, No. 2, pp. 67-72.
43. *Komunistas,* 1973, No. 3, p. 12.
44. *Out of the Depths* pp. 25-29, and *Chronicle LCC* (in Russian), No. 10, pp. 16-28.
45. "A Storm of Searches," in *The Church Suffering,* pp. 6-16.
46. *Boston Globe,* August 7, 1971 and *Lituanus,* 1972, No. 3, pp. 7-12.
47. *Tarybine Mokykla,* 1973, No. 3.
48. *Tarybinis Mokytojas,* March 21, 1973.
49. *Out of the Depths,* pp. 7-9.
50. *Chronicle LCC* (in Russian), No. 11, pp. 1-8.
51. J. Savasis, op. cit., p. 19.
52. J. Savasis, op. cit., pp. 17-18.
53. *From the Catacombs,* p. 8.
54. Ibid., p. 7.
55. *Desecrated Shrines,* pp. 20-23.
56. *Chronicle CCL,* No. 1. English translation by Rev. Casimir Pugevicius, director of Lithuanian-American Catholic Services (Baltimore).
57. Ibid. A long list of names of children, parents and teachers persecuted for participating in religious services in 1974-75 is reported in the *Chronicle LCC,* No. 14. In 1974 17,844 people were confirmed (ibid., No. 12).
58. F.I. Milani, op. cit., pp. 112-127. At the time of his trial Fr. Seskevicius was 56 and pastor of Dubingiai parish. His defence speech was translated into English by Rev. Francis A. Ruggies of St. Matthias parish, Ridgewood, N.Y.
59. See note 56.
60. Ibid.
61. See note 58.
62. Ibid.

63. See note 56.
64. Ibid.
65. *Chronicle LCC,* No. 11, 1974 (in Russian), p. 24.
66. Ibid., pp. 24-25. See also the declaration of Fr. B. Laurinavicius (April 30, 1974) at pp. 14-17 and 29-30.
67. F.I. Milani, op. cit., pp. 165-166 and B.R. Bociurkiw, "Religious Dissent in the USSR: Lithuanian Catholics" (a paper presented at the International Slavic Conference, Alberta, Canada, on September 5, 1974), p. 9. An Italian translation of this paper was published by *Russia Cristiana,* No. 142, July-August 1975, pp. 31-57.
68. Ibid., pp. 166-167.
69. Ibid. The appeal to Waldheim also pointedly noted that "Lithuania does not have its own representative at the United Nations."
70. Ibid.
71. F.I. Milani, op. cit., pp. 168-171.
72. Ibid.
73. Ibid., pp. 180-190. For details see *Lituanus,* 1972, n. 4, pp. 58-69. About the present "calm situation" in the Catholic Church of Lithuania see *Christ Behind Wires,* p. 1 ff., and *The Violations of Human Rights in Soviet Occupied Lithuania,* pp. 41-94.
74. *Chronicle LCC,* 1974, No. 10 (in Russian), pp. 2-12.
75. Fr. Casimir Pugevicius, "Physicist Sakharov Reveals. Underground Journal Focuses USSR Pressure on Lithuania," in *The Pilot,* February 28, 1975. The hunger strike of Marxist V. Sevrukas in protest against mistreatment of believers in the USSR was praised in a letter to the *Chronicle LCC* (No. 15). The writer also 1) expresses sympathy for Sergei Kovalyov, arrested in connection with the dissemination of the *Chronicle LCC,* 2) expresses respect for A. Sakharov, chairman of the Moscow Committee on Human Rights, 3) voices gratitude to the church hierarchy of Australia and to the opposition party of Australia, and the government of Canada, for refusing to recognize the Soviet take-over of the Baltic states, 4) thanks Cardinals Slipyj, Wyszynski and Benghsh in Rome, 5) thanks *Kontinent* for remembering the plight of Lithuania.... Meanwhile the United States, following its policy of détente, was diluting a 35-year-old stand of refusing to recognize the incorporation of the Baltic nations into the Soviet Union. The American consul in Leningrad was de facto becoming the US ambassador to the three republics, making direct contacts with party and government officials of these Soviet occupied lands (*New York Times,* May 18, 1975).
76. *Eastern Catholic Life* (Passaic, N.J.), November 16, 1975.
77. *Novoe Russkoe Slovo* (New York), December 25, 1975.

Chapter 6

1. G. Prokoptschuk, *Der Metropolit,* p. 64.
2. C. Korolevskij, *Metropolite Andre Szeptyckyj,* pp. 197-202.
3. W.H. Chamberlain, *The Ukraine,* p. 35.
4. H. Luznyckyj, *Ukrainska Tserkva mizh Skhodom i Zakhodom,* p. 536.
5. C. Korolevskij, op. cit., pp. 376-381.
6. *First Victims of Communism,* pp. 15-16. The appeal was signed also by all the Ukrainian Catholic Bishops of the Ecclesiastical Province of Galicia. See also M. Dolot, *Execution by Hunger: The Hidden Holocaust.*
7. C. Korolevskij, pp. cit.
8. *First Victims of Communism,* p. 39.
9. Ibid., p. 33.
10. Ibid., pp. 39-40.
11. I. Dzyuba, *Internationalism or Russification?,* p. 74.
12. V. Markus, *L'incorporation de l'Ukraine Subcarpatique à l'Ukraine Soviétique,* p. 41

ff. Zinkewych, Osyp and Rev. Lonchyna, Taras, eds. *Martyrology of the Ukrainian Churches in Four Volumes—Vol. 11, The Ukrainian Catholic Church* (in Ukrainian), pp. 237ff.

13. *Zhurnal Moskovskoi Patriarkhii*, 1949, No. 10, p. 5.
14. *Kommunist* (Moscow), 1964, No. 1, pp. 23-46.
15. *First Victims of Communism*, pp. 59-60.
16. A.G. Velykyj, *Documenta Pontificum Romanorum Historiam Ukrainae Illustrantia*, vol. II, pp. 574-592.
17. *First Victims of Communism*, pp. 74-83.
18. *Welcome to Pittsburgh*, p. 7.
19. E. Piddubcheshen, *And Bless Thine Inheritance*, p. 7.
20. N. Cousins, *The Improbable Triumvirate*, p. 29 ff.
21. E. Piddubcheshen, op. cit., p. 10.
22. Ibid.
23. *Ogonek* (USSR), 1963, No. 46.
24. *Molod Ukrainy* (USSR), September 11, 1964.
25. Vitaliy Politylo, "Protopresbyter Gavriil Kostelnik (25th anniversary of his martyrdom)," in *The Journal of the Moscow Patriarchate* (in English), 1974, No. 1, p. 12.
26. E. Piddubcheshen, *In One Decade: From Prisoner to Patriarch*, p. 4.
27. J. Madey, *Le Patriarcat Ukrainien vers la perfection de l'état juridique actuel*, pp. 80-81.
28. W.M. Abbot, *The Documents of Vatican II*, pp. 372-386.
29. E. Piddubcheshen, *And Bless Thine Inheritance*, pp. 10-11.
30. Mario Rizzi, "S.E.R. Mons. Slipyj Arcivescovo Maggiore," in *SICO* (Servizio Informazioni Chiesa Orientale), January 31, 1964, pp. 1-5. Rizzi's article was reprinted in *L'Osservatore Romano*, February 6, 1964.
31. *SICO*, January-February, 1974.
32. Synodus Episcoporum. Bulletin No. 4, October 1, 1974, p. 15.
33. Fr. Aleksandr Schmeman in his "Response to the Decree on Eastern Catholic Churches," in W.M. Abbot, op. cit., p. 387.
34. M. Lacko, S.J., "The Re-establishment of the Eastern Catholic Church in Czechoslovakia," in *Diakonia* (New York), 1969, No. 2, p. 150.
35. E. Piddubcheshen, *And Bless Thine Inheritance*, pp. 48-49.
36. P. Reddaway, *Uncensored Russia*, pp. 332-333 and *Ukrainski Visnik* (samizdat), 1974, No. 7-8.
37. *Russia Cristiana* (Milano), 1966, Nos. 73-74.
38. *Pravda Ukrainy*, 1968, No. 28.
39. *Kultura i Zhittia*, January 3, 1969.
40. Eastern Rite Information Service (Chicago), September 1971, p. 5.
41. *Tserkovnyi Visnyk* (Chicago), 1973, No. 14, pp. 3-5.
42. *Diakonia* 1973, No. 2, p. 102.
43. *Zhurnal Moskovskoi Patriarkhii*, 1971, No. 6, p. 4.
44. T.E. Bird and E. Piddubcheshen, *Archiepiscopal and Patriarchal Autonomy*, p. 66.
45. First made public by Dr. Maria Klachko of New York City at meetings of the Ukrainian Catholic laity and offered as an appendix in the April 18, 1973 letter to Pope Paul VI written by the Society for a Patriarchal System in the Ukrainian Catholic Church: *Diakonia*, 1974, No. 3, pp. 294-300 and *Za Patriarkhat* (Philadelphia, Pa.), July-August 1973, p. 25.
46. A. Levitin-Krasnov, "On Two Humorous Articles and One Very Serious Matter," in Ioann San-Frantsissky, *Dialog s Tserkovnoy Rossiei*, pp. 26, 28.
47. I. Dzuyba, op. cit., pp. 5-6.
48. Ibid., pp. 100-105. "Banderist" is another term for "Ukrainian Nationalist" derived from Stepan Bandera (1909-1959), leader of a faction of the Organization of Ukrainian

Nationalists (OUN). Bandera was killed in Munich by a Soviet agent.
49. Ibid., p. 38.
50. N. Bock, S.J., *Russia and the Vatican on the Eve of the Revolution*, pp. 33-34.
51. P. Mailleux, *Entre Rome et Moscou. L'Exarque Leonid Feodoroff*. See also the 833-page volume (in Russian) on Fedorov by deacon Vasilij OSB, *Leonid Fedorov*, pp. 321-322.
52. C. Korolevskij, op. cit., pp. 187-259.
53. A. Levitin-Krasnov, "Letter to Pope Paul VI," in G. Simon, *Church, State and Opposition in the USSR*, pp. 195-196.
54. A. Amalrik, *Will the Soviet Union Survive until 1984?*, pp. 62-63.
55. A. Solzhenitsyn, "Letter to the Leaders of the Soviet Union," in *The Ukrainian Quarterly* (New York), 1974, No. 2, pp. 117-124.
56. E. Piddubcheshen, *And Bless Thine Inheritance*, p. iv.
57. E. Piddubcheshen, "The Ukrainian Catholic Controversy," in *Idoc-North America* (New York), January-February 1973, p. 47.
58. E. Piddubcheshen, *And Bless Thine Inheritance*, pp. 11, 29, 37, 59.
59. L. Rudnytsky, "The Voice of the Christian Conscience: A Note on the Popularity of His Beatitude Major Archbishop Joseph Card. Slipyj," in *Looking East* (Fatima, Portugal) 1973, No. 13, pp. 17-19.
60. *Blagovisnik. Litterae Nuntiae Archiepiscopi Maioris Ritus Byzantino-Ucraini* (Castelgandolfo, Rome) 1971, vol. 1-4, pp. 51-53.
61. *Monumenta Ukrainae Historica* (Rome), vol. II, 1965, pp. 92-95.
62. Ibid., vol. XI, 1974, pp. 612-613.
63. Yu. Bachynskyj, *Ukrainska immigratsiya v Zedynenykh Derzhavakh Ameryky*, pp. 256-309.
64. *First Victims of Communism*, pp. 19-22; H. Kostiuk, *Stalinist Rule in the Ukraine*, pp. 62-65; W. Mykula, *The Gun and the Faith*, p. 16 ff.
65. *Ukrainian Orthodox World* (So. Bound Brook, N.J.), December 1972, p. 4.
66. *Blagovisnik*, op. cit., pp. 46-48.
67. *Patriarkhalny Ustav. De Constitutione Patriarcali Particularis Ecclesiae Catholicae Ucraninorum* (Ruthenorum), in *Blagovisnik*, 1974, No. 3.
68. E. Piddubcheshen, *The Ukrainian Catholic Controversy*, op. cit., pp. 48-49.
69. Ibid.
70. *Za Patriarkhat* (Philadelphia), October 1972, p. 37.
71. E. Piddubcheshen, *The Ukrainian Catholic Controversy*, op. cit., p. 50.
72. E. Piddubcheshen, *In One Decade . . .*, op. cit., 10-12.
73. W. de Vries, S.J., "The Origin of the Eastern Patriarchates and Their Relationship to the Power of the Pope," in T.E. Bird and E. Piddubcheshen, op. cit., pp. 15 and 26.
74. *Schlach Peremohy* (Munich), August 10, 1975 and *Religious News Service* (New York), October 29, 1975.
75. V. Chornovil, *The Chornovil Papers*, pp. 12-13.
76. Ibid., p. 221.
77. V. Moroz, *Boomerang*, pp. 7-61.
78. *A Chronicle of Current Events* (London), No. 17, April 1971, pp. 41-43.
79. V. Moroz, op. cit., pp. 3-4. *Voprosy Filosofii* is a monthly journal published in Moscow by the Philosophy Institute of the Soviet Academy of Sciences.
80. Ibid., pp. 91-95.
81. Ibid., pp. 95-96.
82. Ibid., p. 103.
83. V. Chornovil, op. cit., pp. 191-207.
84. Ibid., pp. 222-226 and S. Stetsko, *Revolutionary Voices*, pp. 142-143.
85. *The New York Times*, February 20, 1974 and *A Chronicle of Human Rights in the USSR*, No. 9, p. 36.

86. See note 55.
87. *Tserkovnyi Visnik* (Chicago), March 30, 1975, pp. 4-5.
88. *The New York Times,* September 12, 1974.
89. *Looking East,* 1975, No. 16, pp. 51-54. Translated from Russian by E. Piddubcheshen.
90. *Chronicle LCC,* No. 9 (in Russian), pp. 31-32.
91. *From the Catacombs,* p. 16. Fr. B. Laurinavicius, replying in writing to several accusations made against him and other Lithuanian priests by Soviet Deputy for Religious Affairs J. Rugienis, writes: "We requested that the Ukrainian priests be allowed to go back to work, because the faithful of the Ukraine give us no peace,, asking us to work among them. We asked that their priests be put back to work, since they have never been sentenced by the court."
92. *ABN Correspondence* (Munich), January-February 1975, pp. 1-2. See also *Kontinent,* 1975, No. 3, pp. 187-196.
93. *The New York Times,* October 22, 1975.
94. V. Markus, "Vladyka Vasyl Velychkovskyj Ispovidnik Viri," in *Kalendar Golosu Spasitelya* [Redeemer's Voice Almanac] 1976 (Yorkton, Canada), pp. 36-46.
95. *Our Sunday Visitor* (Huntington, Ind.), January 25, 1976.
96. *Russkaia Mysl',* December 4, 1975.

Chapter 7

Il Tempo, January 30, 1977.
2. *The New York Times,* February 23, and March 29, 1977.
3. *The New York Times,* January 21, 1977.
4. *The New York Times,* May 28, 1977.
5. *Russia Cristiana,* 1978, no. 4.
6. *Russia Cristiana,* 1976, numbers 5 and 6.
7. *YMCA Press,* 1977.
8. *Literaturnaia Gazeta,* 1977, numbers 15 and 16.
9. *Russia Cristiana,* 1976, numbers 5 and 6.
10. *Russkaia Mysl',* May 5, 1977.
11. *The New York Times,* April 16, 1977.
12. *The New York Times,* June 10, 1977.
13. *The New York Times,* January 27, 1977.
14. *Le Monde,* February 10.
15. *The New York Times,* June 27, 1977.
16. *La Civiltà Cattolica,* January 1, 1977.
17. *Kronika,* no. 41, August 3, 1976.
18. *Il Tempo,* June 10, 1977.
19. *Schlach Peremohy,* June 5, 1977.
20. *Novoe Russkoe Slovo,* July 7.
21. *Zhurnal Moskovskoi Patriarkhi,* 1977, no. 2, p. 3; See Patriarch Pimen's telegram to Brezhnev on his seventieth birthday.
22. *Novoe Russkoe Slovo,* February 27 and April 28, 1977.
23. *Novoe Russkoe Slovo,* January 26.
24. *Religious News Service,* January 28, and *Catholic News,* February 3.
25. *La Civiltà Cattolica,* May 21, 1977, pp. 339-350.
26. *Zhurnal Moskovskoi Patriarkhi,* 1977, no. 5, pp. 7-9.
27. *Il Tempo,* May 31, 1977.
28. *Russia Cristiana,* 1977, no. 3, p. 2.
29. *Ziiaiushchie vysoty,* Lausanne, L'Age d'Homme, 1976.

30. *L' Osservatore Romano,* October 8, 1977.
31. *L' Osservatore Romano,* March 11, 1978.
32. O. Zinkewych and Rev. T. Lonchya, op. cit., pp. 752-754.
33. See chap. 2, part 2: "The Credibility of the Church in Lithuania."
34. The encyclical *Divini Redemptoris.* Cf. Part 1, chaps. 1 and 2.
35. For Fr. Romanyuk's letter to *L'Osservatore Romano,* see O. Zinkewych and Rev. T. Lonchyna, op. cit., pp. 619-623. Soviet sources reported in April 1983 that Fr. Romanyuk made a "declaration" in which he condemned his past activities and pledged loyalty to the Soviet state: see *America* (Philadelphia, May 31, 1983)—Serge Schmemann writes in the *New York Times* (May 27, 1984:

> The human rights movement that sprouted in the 1960's and blossomed as the Helsinki agreements were being signed in 1975 has been routed and splintered. But many elements that fed it remain alive: Lithuanian Catholics, Jews denied emigration, banished Crimean Tartars, ethnic Germans, Ukrainian and Estonian nationalists, fundamentalist Christians, Russian Orthodox activists and advocates of human and political rights.
>
> An underground chronicle known as Bulletin B circulates with extraordinary regularity. Hardly a week passes without news of an arrest or conviction. The names may lack the international resonance of earlier activists such as Yuri Orlov, Anatoly Shcharansky or Dr. Sakharov, but the arrests, exiles or imprisonments of Yelena Sannikova, Tatiana Trusova, Valery Senderov, the Rev. Alfonsas Svarinskas, Yosif Begun, Yuri Tarnopolsky, Sergei Khodorovich, Vladimir Albrekht and many others testify that the K. G. B. did not eliminate the dissident movement's roots. The authorities evidently fear that if they let down their guard for even a minute, it could all coalesce again into a political challenge....
>
> Another telling development in the last year was the passage of amendments to laws that made it dangerous to receive material support from abroad in any form and illegal to divulge ill-defined workplace secrets, and gave penal authorities the right to extend prison or labor camp terms for any infringement of regulations. The last measure essentially gives the state a tool for keeping political prisoners in camps indefinitely.

Epilogue

1. George Huntston Williams, *The Mind of John Paul II. Origins of His Thought and Action.* New York: The Seabury Press, 1981, p. 313.
2. *Pilgrim to Poland, John Paul II.* Boston: St. Paul Editions, 1979, pp. 89-40.
3. K. Wojtyla, "Una frontiera per l'Europa: quale?," in *Vita e Pensiero,* 1978, quoted by Giovanni Rulli, S. J., "Le radici cristiane dell'Europa," in *La Civiltà Cattolica,* 2 giugno 1984, pp. 460-471.
4. The father of Cyril and Methodius was a state official in Thessaloniki in Greece. Historians are not sure about their nationality. Some say that their father was a Slav and their mother a Greek; others say that both parents were Slavs; still others say that both were Greek. St. Methodius, the elder brother, was born in 815, his brother in (approximately) 827. Both brothers received a good education. There were many Slavs in Thessaloniki, so that it is possible that they spoke Slavonic as well as Greek.

   The great prince of Moravia, today's Czechoslovakia, Rostyslav, asked the patriarch of Constantinople to send some missionaries. The Patriarch sent the brothers Cyril and Methodius. They came to Moravia in 863.

Their desire was to make the Slavic people understand the language of the Holy Liturgy and the other services. For this reason Cyril created a Slavonic alphabet on the basis of the Greek and began to translate the Holy Scriptures and the Liturgy into Slavonic. Thus they laid the foundation for, and created, the Slavonic rite.

But in those times, German missionaries were also spreading the Christian faith in Moravia—in the Latin rite. They denounced Cyril and Methodius to the Apostolic See for the alleged introduction of ritual novelties. Pope Adrian II called the two brothers to Rome, examined the situation and approved the Slavonic rite. Cyril entered a monastery in Rome and died there on February 14, 869. Methodius was consecrated by the Pope to be a Moravian bishop. After his return to Moravia, the Latin bishops persecuted him and even imprisoned him for a time. They set him free at the request of Pope John VIII. St. Methodius died on April 6, 885. After his death, the Germans banished the disciples of Cyril and Methodius from Moravia. They were received by the Bulgarian King Simeon. There they translated the Greek Liturgy into the Slavonic tongue. The Slavonic alphabet received the name "Cyrillic" in honor of Cyril.

The disciples of SS. Cyril and Methodius, expelled from Moravia, brought the Slavonic rite to Bulgaria. The Bulgars took their liturgical service-books from the Moravians and adapted them to their own Bulgarian tongue. And from the Bulgars, they were taken by Rus-Ukraine. And thus, the old Bulgarian language became the Church-Slavonic language. See I. Ševčenko, *Byzantine Roots of Ukrainian Christianity,* pp. 9, 13 and the encyclical *Slavorum Apostoli* (6.2.85).

5.   *Pilgrim to Poland,* op cit., pp. 208-209.
6.   *The Redeemer of Man,* Encyclical Letter of His Holiness Pope John Paul II. Boston: St. Paul Editions, 1979, pp. 37-39.
7.   *Poland,* A Country Study Area handbook Series. Washington, D.C.: The American University, 1984, pp. 30, 256-263. For the text of the "Gdansk Agreement" see pp. 419-427.
8.   *The New York Times,* December 14, 1981, and *Poland,* op. cit., p. 257ff.
9.   G. Rulli, "Normalizzazione in Polonia," in *La Civiltà Cattolica,* Feb. 5, 1983, p. 295.
10. G Caprile, *La seconda visita del Papa in Polonia,* in *La Civiltà Cattolica,* July 16, 1983, pp. 162-165.
11. *The New York Times,* July 29, 1983.
12. *The Tablet,* January 19, 1985.
13. *Chronicle of the Catholic Church in Lithuania,* no. 57, April 3, 1983, pp. 9-10. The number and the date are those of the original *samizdat.* The pages and the English translation (Rev. Casimir Pugevicius) refer to the booklets published by Franciscan Fathers Press, 341 Hiland Blvd. Brooklyn, N. Y. 11207.
14. *Chronicle . . . ,* no. 56, February 14, 1983 and no. 63, July 1, 1984, pp. 38-39.
15. *Chronicle . . . ,* no. 59, August 15, 1983, pp. 4-9.
16. *Chronicle . . . ,* no. 64, October 7, 1984, p. 10.
17. *La Civiltà Cattolica,* July 2, 1983 and *L'Altra Europa,* 1985, no. 1, pp. 133-152. From the beginning of 1985 *Russia Cristiana* is published under the new title *L'Altra Europa.*
18. *L'Osservatore Romano,* March 4, 1983.
19. *Chronicle . . . ,* no. 57, April 3, 1983, pp. 66.
20. *Chronicle . . . ,* no. 56, February 14, 1983, pp. 13-14.
21. Victor J. Pospishil, "Pomisnist achieved. Ukrainian Catholic Church receives equality with Eastern Catholic Patriarchates," in *Ukrainian Vatican Synod 1980.* St. Basil Seminary, Stamford, Ct., pp. 8-17.
22. Ibid., p. 10.
23. G. Caprile, "Sollecitudini del Papa per le Chiese dell'Europa Orientale," in *La Civiltà Cattolica* 1982, II, pp. 578-79.
24. *The Way,* Aug. 27 and Sept. 30, 1984.
25. *America,* Aug. 27 and Sept. 19, 1984.

26. *America*, Jan.-Feb. 1985.

27. I. Hvat, *The Catacomb Ukrainian Catholic Church and Pope John Paul II*, pp. 293-294. For the Ukrainian text of the *Chronicle*, see *Visti z Rymu*, Jan. 1985 and ff.

28. This major international conference on human rights ended on June 17 with the 35 participating nations failing to agree on a final report after six weeks of closed meetings: see the article of Christopher S. Wren in *The New York Times*, June 18, 1985.

29. *L'Osservatore Romano*, Jan. 2-3, 1985.

30. Copies of the letters, dated Luzern, July 16, 1984, can be obtained from Centro Russia Ecumenica, Rome, Italy.

31. The following is the text of Fr. Kolvenbach's letter:

Rome, 8 August 1984.

Dear Mr Levitin-Krasnov,

The letter which you recently sent to me about your nephew and other Christians imprisoned for their faith touches me very much. I am grateful for your confidence in our Society and would willingly do anything in my power to help these men who are suffering so heroically.

The present situation is, as you are well aware, a most difficult one. Contact with the Russians can so easily be interpreted as collaboration with them, but without contact there is no hope of gaining freedom for those in prison. It has been the policy of the Society for some years now, in the time of Father Arrupe's generalate, to try to maintain a dialogue with the Orthodox Church in Russia. This has seemed the way that offers most hope of helping Christians in Russia, all of them, Orthodox or Catholic, hierarchy or "dissidents," are living under constant restraint and pressure.

In keeping with this policy of bringing relief and showing support for all those who are suffering, I assure you that our Society will take every opportunity of defending the cause of the priests who are in prison, and, in particular, your own nephew P. Gleb Jakunin. I keep this intention in my prayers.

Yours sincerely in Christ
(signature)
Peter-Hans Kolvenbach
The Superior General
of the Society of Jesus

Bibliography

This bibliography includes only those books cited in the notes. Titles are given in the language of the edition consulted by the author.

Abbot, Walter M., S.J., ed. *The Documents of Vatican II.* New York: America Press, 1966.

Acts et Documents du Saint Siege Relatifs a la Seconde Guerre Mondiale. Vol. 5 (Le Saint Siege et la Guerre Mondiale, Juillett 1941-Octobre 1942). Citta del Vaticano: Libreria Ed. Vaticana, 1969.

Alagiagian, Peter, S.J. *My Prisons in the Soviet Paradise.* Gardenvale, P.Q.: Harpell's Press, 1969.

Amalrik, Andrei. *Will the Soviet Union Survive until 1984?* New York: Harper & Row, 1970.

Anatoly A. (Kuznetsov). *Babyi Yar.* Frankfurt, M.: Possev-Verlag, 1970

And On Earth Peace. Documents of the First All-Christian Peace Assembly. Prague: CPC, 1961.

Arkhiv Samizdata. Sobranie Dokumentov Samizdata. Material reproduced by the Center for Slavic and East European Studies (The Ohio State Univ., Columbus, Ohio) from master copies on file in the Arkhiv Samizdata which is maintained by Radio Liberty in Munich, Germany.

Artemova, Rar and L. Slavinsky, eds. *Kaznimye sumasshestviem.* Frankfurt, M.: Possev-Verlag, 1971.

Bachynskyj, Yulijan. *Ukrainska immigratsiya v zedynenykh derzhavakh Ameryky.* Lviv: Nakladom Yu. Balitskogo i O. Garasevicha, 1914.

Bird, Thomas E. and Eva Piddubcheshen, eds. *Archiepiscopal and Patriarchal Autonomy.* New York: Fordham University, 1972.

Bock, Nicholas, S.J. *Russia and the Vatican on the Eve of the Revolution.* New York: Fordham University, s.a.

Boff, Leonardo. *Chiesa: carisma e potere.* Roma: Edizioni Borla, 1984.

Bosley, Keith, ed. *Russia's Underground Poets,* New York: Praeger, 1969.

Bourdeaux, Michael. *Religious Ferment in Russia: Protestant Opposition to Soviet Religious Policy.* New York: St. Martin's Press, 1968.

_____. *Patriarch and Prophets: Persecution of the Russian Orthodox Church Today.* New York: Praeger, 1970.

Braznik, I. and F.I. Dolgikh, eds. *O religii* (Khrestomatiya). Moscow: Nauka, 1963.

Brizgyz, Vincent, *Exiled Auxiliary Bishop of Kaunas. Religious Conditions in Lithuania under Soviet Russian Occupation.* Chicago: Lithuanian Catholic Press, 1968.

Brumberg, Abraham, ed. *In Quest of Justice. Protest and Dissent in the Soviet Union Today.* New York: Praeger, 1970.

Bulgakov, Mikhail. *The Master and Margarita.* New York: The New American Library, 1967.

Chalidze, Valery. *Prava cheloveka i Sovetskii Soiuz.* New York: Khronika Press, 1974.

Chamberlain, William H. *The Ukraine. A Submerged Nation.* New York: Macmillan, 1944.

Chinigo, Michael, ed. *The Pope Speaks. The Teachings of Pope Pius XII.* New York: Pantheon Books, 1957.

Chornovil, Vyacheslav, ed. *The Chornovil Papers.* New York: McGraw-Hill, 1968.

Church Suffering (The), Chronicle of the Lithuanian Catholic Church, No. 8. Maspeth, N.Y.: The Lithuanian Roman Catholic Priests' League of America, 1974.

Cianfarra, Camille M. *The Vatican and the War.* New York: E.P. Dutton, 1944.

Codevilla, Giovanni. *Stato e Chiesa nell'Unione Sovietica.* Milano: Jaca Book, 1972.

Conquest, Robert, ed. *Religion in the USSR.* New York: Praeger, 1968.

Cousins, Norman. *The Improbable Triumvirate. John F. Kennedy, Pope John, Nikita Khrushchev. History of a Hopeful Year, 1962-1963.* New York: W.W. Norton, 1972.

Christ Behind Wire. Chronicle of the Lithuanian Catholic Church, No. 5. Maspeth, N.Y.: The Lith.R.C. Priests' League of America, 1974.

Cristianesimo (Il) nell'Unione Sovietica. Roma: Ediz. La Civiltà Cattolica, 1948.

Dagan, Avigdor. *Moscow and Jerusalem.* London-N.Y.: Abelard-Schuman, 1970.

Daim, Wilfried. *Der Vatikan und der Osten.* Vienna: Europa Verlag 1967.

Desecrated Shrines. Chronicle of the Catholic Church in Lithuania, No. 7. Maspeth, N.Y.: The Lith.R.C.Priests' League of America, 1974.

Dokumenty Komiteta Prav Cheloveka. New York: The International League for the Rights of Man, 1972.

Dolot, Miron. *Execution by Hunger: The Hidden Holocaust.* New York: W. W. Norton & Co., 1984.

Dudko, Dmitrii, sv. *O nashem upovanii.* Paris: YMCA-Press, 1975.

Dzyuba, Ivan. *Internationalism or Russification? A Study in the Soviet Nationalities Problem.* London: Weidenfeld & Nicolson, 1970.

Fedotov, G.P. *The Russian Religious Mind.* Vol. 2. Cambridge, Mass.: Harvard University Press, 1966.

First Victims of Communism. White Book on the Religious Persecution in Ukraine. Rome: Analecta OSBM, 1953.

Fletcher, William C. *Religion and Soviet Foreign Policy, 1945-1970.* London: Oxford Univ. Press, 1973.

Fletcher, Nikolai. *Portrait of a Dilemma.* N.Y.-London: Macmillan, 1968.

Floridi, Alexis U. *Il dilemma dell'Unione Sovietica. Mito e realta di un umanesimo.* Roma: Ed. La Civiltà Cattolica, 1966.

_____. *Humanismo Sovietico.* Rio de Janeiro: Agir, 1968.

_____. *Dr. Hromadka and the Christian Peace Conference. Failure of an Experiment in East-West Dialogue.* Boston: Spaulding Co., 1970.

_____, and Annette E. Stiefbold. *The Uncertain Alliance: The Catholic Church and Labor in Latin America.* Miami: CAIS, Univ. of Miami, 1973.

_____. *O Radicalismo Catolico Brasileiro.* Sao Paolo: Hora Presente, 1973.

From the Catacombs. Chronicle of the Catholic Church in Lithuania. No. 4. Maspeth, N.Y.: The Lith.R.C. Priests' League of America, 1972.

Galich, Aleksandr. *Pokolenie obrechennykh.* Frankfurt, M.: Possev-Verlag, 1974.

Gallagher, Louis, S.J. *Edmund Walsh, S.J., A Biography.* New York: Benzinger Br. Inc., 1962.

Ghinsburg, Aleksandr. *Libro Bianco sul caso Sinjavskij-Daniel.* Milano: Jaca Book, 1967.

Goure, Leon and others. *Convergence of Communism and Capitalism. The Soviet View.* Miami: CAIS, University of Miami, 1973.

Graham, Robert A., S.J. *Vatican Diplomacy. A Study of Church and State on the International Plane.* Princeton: Princeton Univ. Press, 1959.

Gsovski, Vladimir, ed. *Church and State behind the Iron Curtin.* New York: Praeger, 1955.

Habegger, Norberto. *Camilo Torres Prete e Guerrigliero.* Firenze: Cultura Ed., 1968.

Halecki, Oscar and James F. Murray Jr. *Eugenio Pacelli: Pope of Peace.* N.Y.-Toronto: Farrar, Straus & Young, 1951.

Hatch, Alden. *His Name was John.* London: George G. Harrap, 1963.

_____, and William C. Fletcher. *Religion and the Soviet State: A Dilemma of Power.* New York: Praeger, 1969.

Hvat, Ivan. *The Catacomb Ukrainian Catholic Church and Pope John Paul II.* Cambridge, Ma.: Ukrainian Studies Fund, Harvard University, 1984.

Ioann San-Frantsissky, Arkhiepiskop, ed., *Zashchita very v SSSR.* Paris: Ikhtys, 1966.

_____. *Dialog s tserkovnoi Rossiei.* Paris: Ikhtys, 1967.

Ivanov, Vyacheslav. *Sobranie sochinenii.* Vol. 1. Bruxelles: Foyer Oriental Chretien, 1971.

Iz-pod glyb. Sbornik Statei. Paris: YMCA Press, 1974.

Kaiser, Robert B. *Pope, Council and World. The Story of Vatican II.* New York, London: Macmillan, 1963.

Korolevskij, Cyrille. *Metropolite Andre Szeptyckyj (1865-1944).* Rome: Opera Theologicae Societatis Scientificae Ucrainorum, 1964.

Kostiuk, Hryhory. *Stalinist Rule in the Ukraine. A Study of the Decade of Mass Terror (1929-1939).* New York: Praeger, 1960.

Krasnov, (Levitin) Anatoly. *Stromaty.* Frankfurt, M.: Verlag Possev, 1972.

Kuznetsov, Eduard. *Dnevniki.* Paris: Les Editeurs Reunis, 1973.

Ledit, J., S.J. *Archbishop John Cieplak.* Montreal: Palm Publishers, 1963.

Leneman, Leon. *La tragedie des Juifs en URSS.* Paris: Desclee & Bronwer, 1959.

Leoni, Pietro, S.J. *Spia del Vaticano.* Roma: Ediz. Cinque Lune, 1959.

Lietuviu Liandes Menas. *Mazoji Architektura.* Vilnius: Vaga, vol. I, 1970.

Litvinov, Pavel. *The Demonstration in Pushkin Square. The Trial Records with a Commentary and an Open Letter.* Boston: Gambit, 1969.

Luznyckyj, Hrihoryj. *Ukrainska Tserkva mizh Skhodom i Zakhodom.* Philadelphia: Providence Assoc., 1954.

Madey, Jean. *Le Patriarcat Ukrainien vers la perfection de l'état juridique actuel.* Roma: Ed. Opera Theologicae Societatis Scientificae Ucrainorum, 1971.

Mailleux, Paul. *Entre Rome et Moscou.* L'Exarque Leonide Feodoroff. Bruxelles: Desclee de Bronwer, 1966.

Maksimov, Vladimir E. *Karantin.* Frankfurt. M.: Possev-Verlag, 1973.

Malia, Martin. *Aleksander Hertzen and the Birth of Russian Socialism.* New York: Grosset & Dunlop, 1965.

Marchenko, Anatoly. *Moi pokazaniia.* Frankfurt, M.: Possev-Verlag, 1969.

Markus, Vasyl. *L'incorporation de l'Ukraine Subcarpatique à l'Union Sovietique (1944- 1945).* Louvain: Centro Ukrainien d'Etudes en Belgique, 1956.

Marshall Jr., Richard II. et al. *Aspects of Religion in the Soviet Union (1917-1967).* Chicago: The Univ. of Chicago Press, 1971.

Medvedev, Roy A. *Let History Judge. The Origins and Consequences of Stalinism.* New York: Random House, 1973.

Medvedev Papers, The. New York: Macmillan, 1971.

Medvedev, Zhores A. and Roy A. *A Question of Madness.* New York: Random House, 1972.

Milani, Felix I., ed. *La repressione culturale in Lituania.* Milano: Jaca Book, 1972.

Mindszenty, Jozsef, Cardinal. *Memoirs.* New York: Macmillan, 1974.

Monumenta Ukrainae Historica. Roma: Editiones Universitatis Catholicae Ucrainorm, vol. II (1965) and XI 1974).

Moroz, Valentyn. *Boomerang. The Works of V. Moroz.* Baltimore-Paris-Toronto: Smoloskyp Publishers, 1974.

Moroziuk, Russel P. *Politicized Ecumenism: Rome, Moscow and the Ukrainian Catholic Church.* Montreal: Concordia University Printing Services, 1984.

Mykula, W. *The Gun and the Faith.* London: Ukrainian Information Service, 1969.

Out of the Depths. Chronicle of the Catholic Church in Lithuania. No. 6. Maspeth, N.Y.: The Lith.R.C. Priests' League of America, 1974.

Piddubcheshen, Eva. *And Bless Thine Inheritance.* Schenectady, N.Y.: Eric Hugo Printing Co., 1970.

_____, ed. *In One Decade. From Prisoner to Patriarch.* New York: National Office and N.Y. Branch of Society for a Patriarchal System in the Ukrainian Catholic Church, 1973.

Pokhilevich, D.L., *Sovremennyi katolitsizm.* Moscow: Nauka, 1960.

Politichesky Dnevnik (1964-1970). Amsterdam: The A. Herzen Foundation, 1972.

Pope's Journey to the United States, The. New York: Bantam Books, 1965.

Programma Demokraticheskogo Dvizheniia Sovetskogo Soiuza. Amsterdam: The A. Herzen Foundation, 1970.

Prokoptschuk, Gregor. *Der Metropolit. Leben und Wirken des Grossen Forderers der Kirchenunion Graf Andreas Scheptytzkyj.* Munich: Verlag Ukraine, 1955.

Raffalt, Reinhard. *Wohin steuert der Vatikan? Papst zwischen Religion und Politik.* Munich: Piper, 1973.

Rar, Gleb (A. Vetrov). *Plenennaia tserkov'.* Frankfurt, M.: Verlag Possev, 1954.

Reddaway, Peter, ed. *Uncensored Russia. The Human Rights Movement in the Soviet Union. The Annotated Text of the Unofficial Moscow Journal A Chronicle of Current Events* (Nos. 1-11). London: Jonathan Cape, 1972.

Repressione culturale in Lituania, La. Milano: Jaca Books, 1972.

Rhodes, Anthony. *The Vatican in the Age of the Dictators (1922-1945).* New York-London: Holt, Rinehart & Winston, 1973.

Rimaitis, J. *Religion in Lithuania.* Kaunas: Karolis Pozela Press, 1971.

Rynne, Xavier. *Vatican Council II (First Session).* New York: Farrar, Straus & Co., 1963.

Sakharov, Andrei, *Progress, Coexistence and International Freedom.* New York: W.W. Norton, 1968.

––––––. *My Country and the World.* New York: A. Knopf, 1975.

––––––. *Sakharov Speaks.* New York: Random House, 1974.

––––––. *O Pis'me A. Solzhenitsyna vozhdiam Sovetskogo Soiuza.* New York: Khronika, 1974.

––––––. *V borbe za mir.* Frankfurt, M.: Verlag-Possev, 1973.

Samizdat. *Cronaca di una vita nuova nell'URSS.* Milano: Ed. Russia Cristiana, 1974.

Savasis, J. *The War Against God in Lithuania.* New York: Manyland Books, 1966.

Ševčenko, Ihor. *Byzantine Roots of Ukrainian Christianity.* Cambridge, Ma.: Ukrainian Studies Fund, Harvard University, 1984.

Shafarevich, Igor R. *Zakonodatel'stvo o religii v Sovetskom Soiuze. Doklad Moskovskomu Komitetu prav cheloveka.* Paris: YMCA Press, 1973.

Sheinman, Mikhail M. *Vatikan mezhdu dvumia mirovymi voinami.* Moscow: Izd. Akad. Nauk SSR, 1948.

––––––. *Sovremennyi klerikalizm.* Moscow: Nauka, 1964.

––––––. *Ot Piya IX do Ioanna XXIII.* Moscow: Nauka, 1966.

Simon, Gerhard. *Church, State and Opposition in the USSR.* London: C. Hurst & Co., 1974.

Slovak, Cyril and Inovecky, Jozef. *Eroi o traditori?* Roma: Citta Nuova-Pro Fratribus, 1974.

Solzhenitsyn, Aleksandr. *One Day in the Life of Ivan Denisovich.* New York: The New American Library Inc., 1963.

––––––. *The First Circle.* New York: Bantam Books, 1969.

––––––. *Nobel Lecture.* New York: Farrar Straus & Giroux, 1974.

––––––. *The Gulag Archipelago 1918-1956* (I-II), New York: Harper & Row, 1974.

––––––. *Pis'mo vozhdiam Sovetskogo Soiuza.* Paris: YMCA Press, 1974.

Sorge, Bartolomeo. *Capitalismo, scelta di classe, socialismo.* Roma: Coines, 1973.

Stalin, G.V. *Opere complete.* Roma: Ed. Rinascita, vol. I (1949), vol. IV (1951).

Stehle, Hansjakob. *Die Ostpolitik des Vatikans.* Munich-Zurich: Piper Verlag, 1975.

Stetsko, Slava, ed. *Revolutionary Voices, Ukrainian Political Prisoners Condemn Russian Colonialism.* Munich: ABN Press (2nd ed.), 1971.

Stroyen, William B. *Communist Russia and the Russian Orthodox Church (1943-1962).* Washington: The Catholic Univ. of America Press, 1967.

Struve, Nikita. *Christians in Contemporary Russia.* New York: C. Scribner, 1967.

Svidercoschi, Gian Franco. *Storia del Concilio.* Milano: Ed. Ancora, 1967.

Talbot, Strobe, ed. and trans. *Khrushchev Remembers.* Boston-Toronto: Little Brown, 1970.

Terts, Abram. *Mysli vrasplokh* [Thoughts Unaware]. New York: Rausen, 1966.

Testi letterari e poesie da riviste clandestine dell'Unione Sovietica. Milano: Jaca Book, 1966.

Theodorowitsch, Nadeshda. *Religion un Atheismus in der USSR.* Munich: Claudius Verlag, 1970.

URSS. Dibattito nella Comunita Cristiana. Milano: Jaca Book, 1968.

Van Het Reve, Karel, ed. *Letters and Telegrams to Pavel M. Litvinov (December 1967-May 1968)*. Dordrecht: D. Reidel, 1969.

Vardys, V. Stanley, ed. *Lithuania under the Soviets. Portrait of a Nation (1940-1965)*. New York: Praeger, 1965.

Vasilij, Dyakon, Ch.S.V. Leonid Fedorov, *Zhizn' i deiatelnost'*. Rome: Nauchnyi i literaturnyi publikatsii 'Studion' Studitskikh Monastiriv, ch. III-V, 1966.

Vekhi. La Svolta—L'intelligencija russa tra il 1905 e il 1917. Traduzione di A.U. Floridi. Milano: Jaca Book, 1970.

Velikovich, L.N. *Krizis sovremennogo kapitalizma*. Moscow: Nauka, 1967.

Velykyj, Athanasius G., OSB, ed. *Documenta Pontificum Romanorum Historiam Ukrainae Illustrantia*. Roma: Analecta OSBM, vol. II, 1954.

Vinter, E. *Papstvo i tsarizm*. Moscow: Progress, 1964.

Violations of Human Rights in Soviet Occupied Lithuania. A Report for 1973. Glenside, Pa.: Lith.-American Community Inc., 1974.

Walsh, Edmund A., S.J. "Why Pope Pius XI Asked Prayers for Russia on March 19, 1930. A review of the facts in the case together with proofs of the International Program of the Soviet Government." New York: The Catholic Near East Association, 1930.

Welcome to Pittsburgh. A Memento of a Visit of H. B. Archbishop Major Joseph VII Cardinal Slipyj (May 17-19, 1973). Pittsburgh: Regional Reception Committee, 1973.

Wetter, Gustav A. *Dialectical Materialism*. London: Routledge & Kegan Paul, 1958.

Whitney, Thomas P., ed. *Khrushchev Speaks. Selected Speeches, Articles and Press Conferences* (1949-1961). Ann Arbor: The University of Michigan Press, 1963.

Wolfe, Bertram D. *Khrushchev and Stalin's Ghost*. London: Atlantic Press, 1957.

World Conference on Church and Society (Geneva, July 12-26, 1966). Geneva: WCC, 1967.

Zinkewych, Osyp and Rev. Lonchyna, Taras, eds. *Martyrology of the Ukrainian Churches* in Four Volumes. Vol. II: *The Ukrainian Catholic Church. Documents, Materials, Christian Samvydav from Ukraine* (in Ukrainian). Toronto-Baltimore: V. Symonenko Smoloskyp Publishers, 1985.

Zizola, Giancarlo. *L'utopia di Papa Giovanni*. Assisi: Cittadella Editrice, 1973.